CULTURAL WAYS

A Concise Edition of
Introduction to Cultural Anthropology

Third Edition

ROBERT B. TAYLOR
Kansas State University

ALLYN and
BACON, INC.
Boston   Sydney
London   Toronto

Dedicated

to

FLORIS

Interior and Cover Designer — *Armen Kojoyian*
Preparation Buyer — *Linda Card*

Portions of this material also appeared in *Cultural Ways: A Compact Introduction to Cultural Anthropology*, Copyright © 1969 by Allyn and Bacon, Inc., in *Introduction to Cultural Anthropology*, Copyright © 1973 by Allyn and Bacon, Inc., and in *Cultural Ways: A Concise Edition of Introduction to Cultural Anthropology, Second Edition*, Copyright © 1976 by Allyn and Bacon, Inc.

Library of Congress Cataloging in Publication Data
Taylor, Robert Bartley, 1926–
   Cultural ways.

   Bibliography: p.
   Includes index.
   1. Ethnology.   I.   Title.
GN316.T38   1980   306   79-25383
ISBN 0-205-06963-0

Printed in the United States of America.

Credits

The author and the publisher deeply appreciate the assistance of those who supplied photographs for this text.

CONTENTS

PREFACE

Many anthropology instructors have concluded that beginning students absorb cultural concepts most effectively by exposure to ethnographic description. *Cultural Ways: A Concise Edition of Introduction to Cultural Anthropology, Third Edition,* was written to provide a balanced introduction brief enough to be used in conjunction with ethnographies, books of readings, or other primary sources.

This edition is somewhat shorter than the second edition. Also, the treatment of concepts has been revised for greater clarity and currency, and most of the examples have been drawn from nine cultures in an attempt to reduce the fragmentation that results from referring to many cultures. The book can be used alone effectively if the instructor so desires. Those who wish to use it in combination with several ethnographies should consult the teacher's manual for ways of integrating *Cultural Ways* with ethnographies.

Cultural Ways reflects my conviction that the main task at the introductory level is to provide a foundation of knowledge of the field and an appreciation of the range and variety of human responses to living. This goal can be realized most effectively by combining explicit explication of concepts with integrated ethnographic descriptions. Since too much attention to the changing fashions of anthropology easily distracts from the important task of providing a balanced picture of cultural diversity, I have taken care to limit treatment of the latest theoretical controversies to manageable dimensions.

It is impossible in a work on fundamental concepts to give credit for the origins of all my ideas. Instructors learn not only from teachers of anthropology and anthropological writings but from students who sharpen our understandings by questioning our ideas and prompting us to explore them more carefully. The same people, both students and colleagues, who influenced the first edition must be given credit for the present version. Paul G. Hiebert, James O. Morgan, and Patricia J. O'Brien evaluated portions of the first edition manuscript that are retained with only moderate modifications.

In addition, Professors Hiebert, Harriet Ottenheimer, and Martin Ottenheimer have positively affected the present work by commenting on *Cultural Ways* as they used it in teaching cultural anthropology. I also owe much to the several anthropologists who reviewed the manuscripts of each edition for my publisher, for their criticisms significantly affected the final results.

R.B.T.

1

THE NATURE
OF
ANTHROPOLOGY

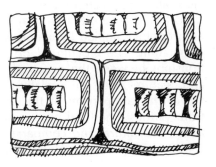

Anyone with a wide range of interests should enjoy studying anthropology. Many anthropologists, in fact, confess that they were attracted to their field partly because it covers such a wide variety of phenomena. But the essence of anthropology is not its diversity, since this is only a byproduct of an ideal. The most important characteristic of anthropology is its *holistic ideal:* the commitment to understanding human nature by drawing together and interrelating data about every facet of the human condition from every possible kind of human group, wherever it is found and from all times.

This holistic orientation leads anthropologists to probe any area that shows promise of helping them answer their questions. The mechanisms of blood type inheritance, the techniques of disciplining children, the evolutionary significance of the opening in the base of the skull, and the sociopsychological functions of witchcraft are among the multitude of topics anthropologists have studied. And they have collected and continue to collect data—biological and social—about groups as diverse as the African man-apes, the Cro-Magnon people of prehistoric France, the aborigines of Australia, reindeer herders of Siberia, Grecian peasants, Navajos in Los Angeles, mid-twentieth century corn producers in Indian Mexico, school children in American public schools, and tramps in Seattle, Washington.

It is difficult to maintain the unity of so diverse a field, but anthropology remains a single discipline embracing a rather impressive variety of specialties. These specialties are kept under one tent because so many anthropologists believe in the holistic ideal—that the most adequate understanding of human nature results from maintaining an integrated view and approach to the study of humanity. They wish to avoid the distortion that results from fragmentation. Consequently, they try to keep anthropology unified by maintaining both a biocultural and a comparative orientation. The *biocultural orientation* requires exploration of the relationships between the genetically inherited features of humanity's nature and features that are socially learned; the *comparative orientation* involves the comparison of the greatest possible variety of human groups from various times and places. Accordingly, *anthropology may be defined as the biocultural and comparative study of human nature.*

One way anthropologists try to keep the field from fragmenting,

Figure 1–1 *Cro-Magnon Man (restoration by J. H. McGregor). Anthropologists collect data—biological and social—about groups as diverse as the African man-apes, the Cro-Magnon people of prehistoric France, the aborigines of Australia, and tramps in Seattle, Washington.*

especially in the United States, is to require all anthropologists to develop basic competence in all major subdivisions of the discipline, whether they are preparing to be cultural anthropologists, linguistic anthropologists, prehistoric archaeologists, or biological anthropologists. Second, several of the major journals publish articles from all major areas of anthropology. Finally, the fact that anthropologists regularly discuss the threat of disintegration and how to avoid it helps keep the field intact.

THE UNIQUENESS OF ANTHROPOLOGY

Anthropology differs from other disciplines concerned with human nature. Its uniqueness consists of its biocultural and comparative emphases and the great variety of interrelated research problems that derive from them. The biocultural approach is the study of people based on the awareness that human nature is made up of both genetically transmitted and socially learned elements intertwined with one another. Anthropologists wish to avoid exclusively biological or cultural explanations for human behavior, for they realize that both must be considered. Many Europeans and Americans erroneously assume that aggression, sexuality, and numerous other traits are closely governed by genetic factors. One manifestation of this belief is the supposition that children must look and act like their parents, and some people have embarrassed themselves by commenting on resemblances of a child to an adult they mistakenly assumed to be the parent. Another long-standing assumption is that blacks are inherently more rhythmic and more athletic than whites, which fails to take into account how such capacities are affected by individual and social experiences. Anthropologists refuse to assume without further investigation that these or other traits are essential elements of the inherited nature of humanity in general or of particular categories of people.

Currently, some American scholars tend to overlook cultural influences and attempt to explain too much biologically. Among the unwarranted assertions made by zoologist Desmond Morris in his book *The Naked Ape* is that it is natural and inevitable for young people to reject their parental home as a breeding base and to establish their own home. The tendency to suppose that the way things usually are in one's own society is inborn to human nature is a common error. Actually, in many of the world's cultures one spouse or the other remains in the parental home after marriage, bringing the husband or wife under the parental roof.

Human biology seems much less variable from society to society than culture, so it would seem that the social scientist is not so likely to make mistakes by ignoring biological differences as the human biologist is by overlooking cultural factors. This very assumption, however, may cause a misleading sense of security. Genetic differences may be related to cultural differences in ways that could be obscured by an anthropologist's commitment to racial equality. The assertion has been made that the athletic excellence of many blacks developed entirely as a form of compensation for cultural deprivation in other areas of life, but evidence from physical anthropology suggests that certain foot and limb proportions give many blacks an advantage in sprinting.

Their comparative orientation prompts anthropologists to be more careful than some to avoid the notion that American and European traits are universal or natural patterns. It was with this orientation that Bronislaw Malinowski once challenged the Freudian doctrine that a boy is naturally and inevitably jealous and hostile because of his father's sexual access to his mother (1937:80). Similarly, Margaret Mead questioned the idea that it is natural for teenagers to be awkward, rebellious, and insecure (1928:197). Comparing the Trobriand Islanders with Americans and others, Malinowski claimed that Trobriand boys were not hostile toward their fathers; and Mead reported that Samoan young people failed to experience the emotional upheavals and rebellion of American teenagers. The challenges of Malinowski and Mead stimulated controversy and valuable reconsideration of these two issues, and comparisons by other anthropologists have had similar effects.

The concern with biocultural matters is reflected in anthropology's division into two main areas—*physical anthropology and cultural anthropology*. Physical anthropologists are concerned mainly with traits that are either genetically inherited or heavily influenced by genetic factors, while cultural anthropologists concern themselves with traits that people acquire from social experience. In accord with the comparative approach both physical and cultural anthropologists use data not just from urban and industrial societies of historic times but, also, from human groups in every corner of the earth from the present back through prehistoric times. Physical anthropologists make special efforts to avoid basing conclusions about human biological nature on studies of Euroamerican biological types only, and cultural anthropologists base their conclusions on the study of both literate and nonliterate groups and include prehistoric cultures along with those of the present and historic past. The subdivisions and specialties of physical and cultural anthropology described below reflect anthropology's biocultural and comparative emphases.

Physical Anthropology

During the decades before anthropology came to be regarded as a single discipline (perhaps around 1860), people from a number of professions were pursuing several lines of investigation which eventually became parts of anthropology. One was biological evolution, an idea suggested in part by the similarities of humans to apes and other primates; another was the physical appearance of non-European groups, whose differing facial features and skin colors stimulated scholars to try to classify humanity into races and explain their origins. Both of these interests are concerned mainly with inherited biological features, and they became major concerns of twentieth-century physical anthropologists.

Human palaeontology, the study of the fossil remains of prehistoric humans and near-humans for what can be learned about human origins and evolution, continues to be a major branch of physical anthropology. Neanderthal man, Java man, the African "man-apes," and Zinjanthropus are among the many noted fossil forms studied. *Comparative human biology* is the study of the genetically inherited differences apparent among the world's peoples—anatomical, physiological, and, if any exist, psychological. There is so much overlapping of characteristics among human groups that anthropologists have largely given up trying to divide people into racial categories, and a number have abandoned the race concept. Though certain biological traits appear much more frequently in some parts of the world than in others and some are absent in places, it remains impossible to place most of the peoples of the world into categories according to combinations of traits. Some define races as populations sufficiently isolated from others that there is little or no exchange of genes among them. Such populations can be found, but great numbers of people around the world are members of no such isolated group. A growing number of physical anthropologists prefer to study human biological variation by investigating the frequencies of individual traits throughout the world.

In recent decades physical anthropologists have been less interested than before in trying to classify people according to external biological features and more interested in the conditions and processes of change for the genetic makeup of humanity. A major result of this change is the establishment of a branch of *human genetics* within anthropology. Now the study of both human fossils and living people is pursued in the light of what physical anthropologists have learned about the genetic makeup and change processes in human populations. Physical anthropologists are also concerned more than ever with understanding human biology within the context of socially acquired behavior, a concern which is well in accord with anthropology's traditional emphasis on relating the biological and the cultural to one another.

Some physical anthropologists are concerned mainly with *comparative primatology,* the study of the similarities and differences among the primates, namely, tree shrews, lemurs and lorises, tarsiers, monkeys, apes, and humans. They hope to learn more about human nature and development through these comparisons. Such studies include attention to the social behavior of nonhuman primates as well. It is not assumed that their social behavior is just like that of earliest humans, but scholars hope that such studies may reveal clues to the origins of human behavior, and behavioral comparisons among forms biologically similar to people help stimulate attention to certain human behaviors. In addition to human palaeontology, comparative human biology, human genetics, and comparative primatology, physical anthropologists have been interested in *human growth* and *body types.*

Cultural Anthropology

In cultural anthropology the comparative orientation takes the form of the *cross-cultural approach,* the comparison of cultures from various times and places as the basis for understanding human life. This orientation was present before anthropology became a single field. During the early part of the nineteenth century (and earlier), amateur archaeologists had become greatly intrigued with the evidence supporting the existence of prehistoric culture. This evidence was in the form of crudely worked stone tools associated with the bones of extinct species of mammals. Other scholars investigated and discussed the "manner and customs" of the so-called primitives or savages, which greatly interested Europeans and astounded many. These two interests, much revised, are the basis for the two main branches of modern cultural anthropology, namely, *prehistoric archaeology* and *ethnology.* Both belong under cultural anthropology because they concentrate on the study of socially learned human traits rather than biological features. Since the things people make are often found close to their bones, field archaeologists may dig up both bones and artifacts, but the study of the bones themselves is a biological problem which, consequently, pertains to physical anthropology. The archaeologist, being basically a cultural anthropologist, is interested mainly in reconstructing socially learned traits of extinct groups.

Prehistoric archaelogy extends the sample of human behavior beyond the bounds of historic time, while ethnology, which is the description of the world's living cultures and the building of generalizations about human nature by comparing those cultures, provides us with a more representative sample by including the lifeways of groups in every part of the globe. Both cultural anthropology and physical anthropology became identified with the study of prehistoric and so-called primitive races and cultures because the other human sciences had largely ignored the great variety of human groups. Others were already studying literate civilizations of the past, so anthropologists concentrated on prehistoric cultures. Cultures such as ancient Rome or ancient Egypt are studied mostly by classical archaeologists, although a number of anthropologists study literate civilizations. And in line with the cross-cultural emphasis, anthropologists use the conclusions of classical archaeologists in making their generalizations. Also, many ethnologists have taken up the study of literate communities in modern Euroamerican and other complex societies. Since anthropology is cross-cultural it seems quite proper to include the anthropologist's own culture and others like it.

Since this is a book on ethnology, a closer look at its subject matter is in order. Ethnology can be divided into specialties in different ways. First, it may be subdivided according to aspects of culture which given ethnologists choose to specialize in, such as economic organization, technology, kinship, political life, law, art, music, folklore, medicine, or religion, making it possible to partition ethnology into specialties such as economic anthropology, political anthropology, social organization, medical anthropology, ethnomusicology, educational anthropology, and so on. The term *social anthropology* has been given several meanings, but it is frequently applied to the study of aspects of culture that extensively involve social interaction, such as family life, kinship, law, or political and economic matters. So understood, social anthropology tends to be somewhat less concerned with technology, the arts, language, and cultural history than ethnology in general. By this definition social anthropology falls within ethnology.

A second way of subdividing ethnology is according to particular problems or sets of problems concerning the nature of cultures. Among the several ethnological specialties of this kind are cultural dynamics, psychological anthropology, cultural ecology, semiotic anthropology, and cognitive anthropology. *Cultural dynamics* is the study of the conditions and processes by which customs change or persist. The question of change is so basic that cultural dynamics is often set apart as a major specialty in anthropology, and its concern with process and the large number of anthropologists who specialize in change study justify its recognition as an important area within ethnology.

   Psychological anthropology is the investigation of the relationships between culture and the human mind. Many specialists in this area, known for some time as students of *culture and personality,* have studied how a child's personality is shaped to preexisting customs, especially through childrearing practices. Many anthropologists turned away from such studies, since a number of the attempts to correlate adult cultural and personality traits with specific childrearing customs—such as the cor-relation of infant swaddling with adult political submissiveness—proved unsound (see page 260). But some persisted, and this type of study continues as part of a revitalized and broadened endeavor under the title of *psychological anthropology.* Earlier errors have been confronted and at least partially corrected, and anthropologists realize that there is much of value to learn about how people acquire their lifeways, what determines how people perceive things, how cultural changes affect people psychologically, what the relationships are between cultures and mental illness, and many other issues concerning culture and individual psychology.

   Cultural ecology is a specialty which concentrates on studying the relationships between subsistence (food) technology and the natural habitat and how those relationships affect and are affected by social patterns, religion, and other aspects of culture. Cultural ecological studies have taken anthropologists in many directions, since the web of relation-ships between the natural habitat and human behavior is complex. They also draw anthropologists into interdisciplinary endeavors, since geo-graphy, biology, sociology, and other fields are concerned extensively with ecological issues.

   Semiotic anthropology (also known as *symbolic anthropology*) is the investigation of the relationships between the symbols that are part of every group's culture and the people's behavior. Semiotic studies are yielding a variety of interesting and significant information on how symbols in various cultures affect what people do. For instance, Manuel Hidalgo's use of the banner with the image of Our Lady of Guadalupe on it gathered widespread support for the Mexican revolution because it had symbolic value for both the Indians and the mestizos (Turner 1974:108). And the king of the Nyoro of Africa is the symbol of the Nyoro state itself, which requires that he maintain good health and his sicknesses be kept secret from the people (Beattie 1959:137).

   Cognitive anthropology overlaps some with semiotic anthropology and psychological anthropology. It is the study of how particular societies perceive (cognize) and organize things, events, behavior, and emotions. It stresses the categories and organizing criteria used by the people under study, avoiding those that come from the outsider's thought system. More will be said about cognitive anthropology under other topics.

Linguistic anthropology could be considered as the investigation of one of the aspects of culture or as a problem area within ethnology. Commonly, however, it is granted separate status and is here considered as a third subdivision of cultural anthropology along with archaeology and ethnology. This is because language is usually thought of as occupying a special place among the aspects of cultures and because linguists have been able to develop highly specialized techniques of analysis. In studying language, anthropologists have occupied themselves with both cross-cultural study of grammatical structures and the relationships of language to social organization, religion, values, and other aspects of life.

To this point I have described anthropology in terms of its subject matter—composed of two major divisions (physical anthropology and cultural anthropology) and their respective subdivisions. It may also be divided according to four major divisions in which anthropologists may specialize, namely, physical anthropology, archaeology, ethnology, and linguistics. In most graduate level anthropology departments students must decide in which of these four areas they will achieve special competence, and anthropologists often identify themselves to one another by this scheme. One is a *physical anthropologist, ethnologist* (sometimes called a *cultural anthropologist* or *social anthropologist*) *archaeologist,* or *linguistic anthropologist.* Though archaeology is technically an aspect of cultural anthropology, it has become common to use cultural anthropology as a synonym for ethnology. The subtitle of this book indicates that it is an introduction to cultural anthropology, but it deals almost entirely with ethnology.

Whatever the area of specialization, the ideal of the anthropologist is to remain aware of the relationships of the biological and cultural in human nature and the importance of comparing data from various times and places. The physical anthropologist must remember the importance of cultural influences, and archaeologists, ethnologists, and linguistic anthropologists must seek the relevance of biological findings to their studies. Both physical anthropologists and cultural anthropologists gather their data from groups everywhere in time and space and try to make sure to base their conclusions on a representative sample of the total universe of human life.

Some Newer Anthropological Specialties

Partly because of its biocultural and comparative emphases, anthropology is a growing, changing discipline. Currently, the growth is not so much in numbers as in the diversity of specific human issues under investigation and the variety of occupations in which anthropology is being applied to practical affairs. Though most professional anthropologists teach or do research at colleges and universities, the shrinking academic market of the 1970s has forced more to make their way into applied and other nonacademic work. Many people still think of anthropologists as adventurers and diggers of cities and bones (Kiefer 1978:15), but even this brief review of anthropology demonstrates that its subject mattter is poorly represented by such views. A look at some of the developing research areas with more obvious relevance to practical matters will further illustrate this.

Medical anthropology, one of the most rapidly growing areas, is the study of standardized responses to disease as an aspect of culture, how cultural factors affect health and disease, and the relationship of disease to human biological and genetic characteristics and the various habitats that groups occupy. Definitions of health and disease in different cultures, how people classify diseases, what they believe about the nature and causes of diseases, and the ways people avoid and cure diseases have been major research concerns of anthropologists. They also have investigated how people's value systems, religious beliefs, kinship relations, family life, technological activities, and other nonmedical aspects of cultures affect the amount and kinds of disease that occur and the possibility of avoiding and curing diseases. Such research has many practical implications for health, which is one of the reasons for the current popularity of medical anthropology. Anthropologists have studied problem drinking,

Figure 1–2 *San healing dance. Definitions of health and disease in different cultures and the ways people avoid and cure diseases have been major research concerns of anthropologists.*

drug addiction and treatment of drug dependency, homicide and suicide, physical and psychological well-being of the aged, various cultural devices for delivering health care to the ill, and programs for the reduction and eradication of diseases.

To a significant degree this research is affected by the biocultural and comparative ideals of anthropology. Disease is not just a biological phenomenon to anthropologists. It is affected and, in turn, affects cultural factors; and the most effective treatment and prevention must take both factors into account. Doctors working at a clinic in Indian Guatemala were puzzled by the frequent refusal of Mayan patients to take prescribed medications or to eat certain foods they were served. A medical anthropologist noted that the doctors were failing to realize that disease is a cultural as well as biological phenomenon. The Indian patients classified diseases, foods, and medications as "hot," "cold," or "neutral," and firmly believed that, for example, "hot" medications should not be used to treat "hot" diseases and "hot" or "neutral" foods should be eaten with a "cold" disease (Logan 1973:391). (Hotness and coldness have to do more with the effect on one's system than the temperature of the disease, food, or medication.)

Medical anthropology falls under both physical and cultural anthropology; and, in line with the comparative approach, anthropologists seek a more adequate understanding of disease by studying it in many societies. An increasing number of universities have medical anthropologists on their faculties and are granting degrees in medical anthropology. The use of medical anthropology in the training of physicians, nurses, and other health science specialists is also increasing.

Nutritional anthropology overlaps extensively with medical anthropology, but it appears to have become an area of research and application of its own. In harmony with the biocultural emphasis, nutritional anthropologists are concerned with biological influences on and reactions to food habits and nutritional states and, also, with the interdependence of food and nutritional practices with values, religion, social organization and other aspects of the total cultural situation. Bolton, for example, has suggested that among the Qolla Aymará Indians of Bolivia, there are ties among weather unpredictability, depleted soil, poor diet, low blood sugar, physical aggression, legal conflict, infrequency of communal agricultural work, and population size (1973:251). The study of nutrition is a multidisciplinary enterprise, but the comparative orientation of nutritional anthropology emerges in the variety of cultures drawn on. One relatively short reader reports on nutritional aspects of life in prehistoric Greece, modern North America, Mestizo and Indian Mexico, Jamaica, highland New Guinea, West Africa, and South Asia (Fitzgerald 1976:vii).

Another multidisciplinary area is the study of urban life. It might seem that anthropology, so often erroneously defined as the study of primitives, has little reason to study urban life, but *urban anthropology* has become a major specialty. Anthropologists had built a tradition of studying either small, remote, nonliterate communities or tribes or trying to reconstruct nonliterate cultures by probing the memories of elderly survivors of once-viable societies. As the world changed, anthropologists added the study of small rural communities integrated with and dependent to some degree upon the modern and developing nations within which they were located until, during the 1950s and 1960s, half or more of American anthropological field investigations were being done in such communities (Foster and Kemper 1974:5). Then, many of these so-called peasant societies abandoned their traditional cultures for modern technology and lifeways, and many peasants moved to urban locations. The study of these changes and the resulting new lifeways brought into being the field of urban anthropology.

In large part anthropologists were studying what happened to strongly traditional cultures as they became urbanized. Urban anthropology has continued to develop from this base, and now, many urban anthropologists are proposing and attempting holistic studies of modern cities. In accord with the holistic approach, anthropologists study traditional cultures as wholes, including technology, economics, social and political life, religion, art, world view, etc., and how they interrelate with one another to form a functioning lifeway. In cities anthropologists have tended to limit themselves to relatively small subcommunities of traditional orientation (former nonliterates or peasants) or of economically underprivileged status. Now, in spite of the great internal diversity, anthropologists want to study cities using the holistic approach of their field (Friedl and Chrisman 1975:20). Obviously, what anthropologists learn by comparing city cultures from many parts of the world can be applied to the solution of urban social problems, and urban anthropology often manifests a practical orientation.

Educational anthropology is older, perhaps, and expanding less rapidly than fields such as medical and urban studies. Specialists in this sub-area have studied educational processes in many cultures and have applied the resulting knowledge and viewpoints to understanding and evaluating classroom and other education environments in Euroamerican nations. They also have been concerned with the development of more adequate educational goals and methods in non-Western nations. There is a fairly extensive literature on anthropology and educational processes and problems, and anthropologically trained people use their knowledge in education positions. A number, for example, are involved in bilingual education.

Medical, nutritional, urban, and educational anthropologists are concerned with a number of issues studied in disciplines other than anthropology. This stems from the nature of the field. Anthropologists look for answers to many of the same questions as other human sciences, but they bring different emphases and methods—especially the explicit, comprehensive integration of the biological with the cultural and the broader, less culture-bound perspectives gained from comparing many kinds of human groups. Consequently, anthropology has become of practical relevance to many areas of human endeavor and distress. The four fields mentioned above are only some of the areas where anthropology has practical applications. There also are anthropologists who study reactions to disasters, economic development, migration phenomena, death in contemporary society, industrial organization, sex roles, ethnic group identity, the ecology of primate behavior, extraterrestrial community design, and so on. *Anthropology is unique for the way its biocultural and comparative emphases lead to the holistic study of every kind of human problem.*

ANTHROPOLOGY IN THE CHANGING OCCUPATIONAL SCENE

The shrinking demand for people with a Ph.D. is affecting anthropology as surely as other fields, and it has stimulated a wide-ranging discussion among anthropologists as to their place in society. During the 1960s newly trained anthropologists could expect to step into a teaching position with little difficulty, usually before they completed their dissertations and were awarded doctoral degrees. During the 1970s, though the number of openings continued to increase, the supply of anthropologists increased at a faster rate, and there were no longer enough academic jobs to go around. Moreover, there have been few openings for anthropologists outside of colleges and universities, since the nonanthropological world generally lacks knowledge as to how anthropologists can contribute to human enterprises.

Anthropology as a profession is assuming increasing responsibility for informing society of anthropology's practical value and developing professional openings in nonacademic areas. Much of this results from efforts by unemployed anthropologists to find work, and each such successful venture helps demonstrate the relevance of anthropology to human affairs. The *Anthropology Newsletter,* published by the American Anthropological Association, has presented the stories of several successes. Margaret M. Kiefer found that by the time she received her doctorate in 1974, there were few academic openings for people with her type of preparation. Without a job, she spent a year of research on her own studying the consequences of the 1976 earthquake in Guatemala. She began teaching part-time at a university in Guatemala, where she made contact with Intertect, a Texas-based organization of disaster consultants. Her function as a professional anthropologist on the Intertect staff is to provide information on the existing cultural mechanisms used by groups to cope with disasters. More specifically, she evaluates programs, develops culturally appropriate methods for putting them into effect, trains people to plan and evaluate disaster relief programs, and promotes greater awareness of cultural factors in aid programs among public and private groups (Kiefer 1978:15).

Though Noel-David Burleson received his Ph.D. in 1964, the changed job market also affected his career. Following work at Harvard, he held a teaching position on the Faculty of Medicine at the University of El Salvador, where he also worked on the development of population and family planning programs. Subsequently, he worked on population and education projects for several institutions, but as funding practices and the job market changed, he found himself with several international consultancies but no specific job. At that time he accepted the position of Programme Specialist at the Population Education Section of UNESCO in Paris (Burleson 1978:17).

James E. Fitting also received his Ph.D. in 1964 and taught at the University of Michigan and chaired the Department of Anthropology at Case Western Reserve University. He became dissatisfied with some aspects of academic life and resigned in 1972 to become State Archaeologist for Michigan. In 1975 he was invited to join the firm of Gilbert/Commonwealth, where he eventually became manager of the Human Resources Planning Department of the Environmental Systems Division. Dr. Fitting has had to add training in business management, business law, and managerial accounting and must keep current with a wide variety of fields, but he reports thoroughly enjoying the challenge of applying the full range of anthropological and business skills to a constantly changing series of projects (Fitting 1978:24).

It would be wrong to take these examples as evidence that there are many openings for these kinds of anthropologists. But they certainly illustrate (1) some of the directions professional anthropology may take as academic jobs become relatively scarcer, (2) the possibilities that may be worked out by anthropologists of high competence, adequate training and experience, and sufficient initiative, and (3) the relevance of anthropology to legitimate human concerns.

Professional anthropology positions are available mainly to those with doctoral degrees, but biocultural and comparative perspectives and anthropological knowledge are of considerable value to those in other professions. A B.A. in anthropology is not a professional certificate, but it can be combined with other types of training to prepare for a variety of kinds of positions (Bernard and Sibley 1975). Many employers have little appreciation of the advantages of anthropological training, so an undergraduate degree in anthropology does little or nothing to help one find jobs in other fields. But anthropologically trained people in jobs having to do with human behavior will inevitably find their background relevant to their work, and they may perform more effectively than without it. The use of anthropological training to prepare for nonanthropological occupations is a valuable option for those who enjoy anthropology and are interested in applying its perspectives in their lives and work.

Anthropology is fascinating to many. It is interesting to learn that Aymará women of Bolivia may kick one another's clay stoves apart during quarrels; that some human groups eat spiders; or that some pygmy groups have infantile body shapes while others have relatively "athletic" builds. But anthropology is not just an interesting subject taught to students who in turn become anthropologists to teach anthropology to more students. Most anthropologists believe that, properly applied, the perspectives of their field can contribute much to human fulfillment and to the solution of practical problems. Some people who are only briefly exposed to anthropology gain a few useful viewpoints, and many who enjoy prolonged exposure acquire more. In this way anthropological understandings become part of the useful intellectual equipment of people in many walks of life. In addition, generalizations based on anthropological research find their way to the layperson through widely read books and magazines, public lectures, and interpersonal contacts. Without question anthropological study is relevant to daily life. How extensively its perspectives are applied and whether they are to be used for good or for ill remains to be seen.

045660

2

CULTURAL
VARIABILITY

The main concern of cultural anthropologists is the investigation of what they call *cultures*. In popular terms a culture may be thought of as the way of life of a community or other group. An anthropologist learns about a culture by living among the people and observing what they do. The late Robert Lowie, prominent ethnologist at the University of Calfornia, lived among the Crow Indians of the western plains of the United States and published several volumes describing their culture. Margaret Mead investigated the culture of the Samoans of Manu'a and published volumes on their social organization and the roles and experiences of Samoan adolescent females. In fact, nearly all professional anthropologists have studied at least one culture other than their own.

Cultural variability refers to the differences among the lifeways of human groups. Cultural anthropologists learn about these differences by studying cultures in every possible place and time level. They insist that a representative sample of this variability is the only adequate foundation for generalizing about human nature. Whether it is how to get enough to eat, how to explain the existence of the universe, how to behave toward one's relatives, how to dispose of the dead, or any other of the vast number of such problems of existence, the anthropologist wants to know the range and variety of ways people handle them. Anthropologists feel that this approach yields a superior view of the potentialities and limitations with which humans are born, and this is why the cross-cultural approach is one of the most distinctive emphases of anthropology. Many anthropologists believe that they should not publish the results of their first field research until they have studied a second alien culture, on the grounds that field experience in at least two cultures is prerequisite to the cross-cultural perspective recommended for the best description and analysis of any culture. Cultural variability is important to anthropologists, and this chapter explores some of the relevant concepts and problems.

NINE CULTURES

The more anthropologists know about every culture that exists or ever has existed, the better prepared they are to understand any particular culture or to formulate a generalization about human nature. They still make mistakes from time to time as the result of failures to draw on the total range of cultural differences, but they constantly seek to expand their grasp of human diversity and correct their mistakes in the light of additional knowledge.

The difficultly of handling cultural diversity is even greater for beginning students of anthropology. In an introductory course so few of the world's cultures can be examined in any depth that the student is apt to acquire a distorted view of cultural variability. This introduction attempts to provide some balance by drawing mainly from nine different cultures. They are:

1. The !Kung San, a nomadic hunting and gathering tribe of southern Africa.
2. The Basseri of southern Iran, nomadic herders of sheep and goats.
3. The nineteenth-century Crow Indians of the northern plains of the United States, nomadic horsemen and hunters of bison.
4. The Dugum Dani, sweet potato horticulturalists and pig raisers of the interior of western New Guinea.

Figure 2–1 *Twentieth-century Miskito Indians. Of the village of Asang in Nicaragua, subsistence and cash crop farmers of Christian persuasion.*

5. The twentieth-century Miskito Indians of the village of Asang in Nicaragua, subsistence and cash crop farmers of Christian persuasion.
6. The Nuer, cattle herders and horticulturalists of the Sudan region of eastern Africa.
7. The Nyoro, politically complex farmers of western Uganda.
8. The Samoans of the island of Manu'a, twentieth-century Christian-pagan horticulturalists.
9. North Americans of the United States of America.

Though several types of cultures are represented in this list, it is by no means a fully representative sample of human cultures. It is not even possible to find examples in these cultures of all of the major features of cultural variability that should be presented in an introductory text, and it has been necessary several times to refer to cultures other than these nine. Also, it is well to remember that every culture anthropologists have studied has been found to be very complex, which means that you will learn about only a miniscule fraction of the customs of the nine groups. The diversity and complexity of human custom are vast, and all who fail to take them into account in their attempts to understand human behavior are doomed to serious error and gross misunderstanding.

CULTURAL DIFFERENCES

When anthropologists say that cultures differ from one another, how do they distinguish one culture from another? In many instances, of course, easily identifiable groups manifest enough differences in their customs that we readily regard them as living by distinct cultures. The Crow Indians of the late nineteenth century, who were nomadic buffalo hunters living in tipis, were easily distinguished from their neighbors who dwelled in large earth lodges and farmed. Neither do we have trouble distinguishing culturally between geographically removed groups, such as the Nuer of the African Sudan region and the Basseri of Iran. But in many other cases it is difficult to say where one culture leaves off and another begins. Within the Grand Valley of the interior of western New Guinea, and even beyond the valley, it is impossible to separate the Dani-speaking people who live there into culturally distinguishable societies. There are about a dozen military alliances in the valley, but they break apart and regroup from time to time and cannot be distinguished along cultural lines. There is cultural diversity within the valley. Those in the southern portion avoid killing or eating bats because they regard them as ghosts, while the Dugum Dani do not believe this and hunt and eat them. The Dani of the southern Valley eat dogs, while dog flesh is taboo to the Dugum Dani (Heider 1970:57). These and a fair number of other differences have been exposed by anthropologists working in different parts of the valley, but they are irregularly distributed, constitute only a small fraction of any community's culture, and, therefore, provide no basis for identifying separate cultures. It is this way in many areas of the world.

Within a society there will also be cultural differences that mark off subgroups and subcategories from one another. In all societies the customs of women are significantly different in many ways from those of men. There are some societies, in fact, where men and women speak slightly different languages, the Koasati Indians of southwestern Louisiana being an example (Haas 1964). There are always cultural differences between men and women in the types of labor they do, in the degree of their political participation, and a number of other ways. If economic special-ization beyond sexual division exists, specialists of a given kind differ culturally from the rest of the society, and there may be differences associated with club membership, religious participation, and other sub-group distinctions. Within culturally diverse nations subcultural variability is extensive. Throughout the United States, although neopentecostal charismatics are indistinguishable in many basic ways from other Ameri-cans, they live daily lives notably different from noncharismatics. Families also differ from one another in their customs, both in modern nations and in nonliterate societies, so it is proper to speak of family subcultures.

It is clear that the cultures distinguished by anthropologists and others often overlap extensively, that some cultures differ from others only in a small portion of their customs, and that there are cultural differences within cultures. For the sake of study, anthropologists select groups or categories of people distinguishable from others in some proportion of their customs and refer to all their customs as their culture. Heider, for example, could discern no sharp cultural boundaries among the Dani of the Grand Valley, but he located a cluster of hamlets where the people seemed to interact daily with one another more than they did with people in other hamlets, and he studied the customs of the Dani living in that neighborhood (1970:8).

Anthropology turns out to be in large part the comparison of cultural differences for the purpose of understanding humankind better. Perhaps the foregoing discussion points to the universality of cultural differences. A few have suggested that, as "primitive" cultures disappear and a kind of world culture develops, the subject matter of cultural anthropology will disappear. But what we are finding is that cultural differences con-tinue, since the capacity of human groups to go in different directions culturally remains very much alive. Nonliterate cultures and many features that distinguish them may disappear, but the cultures of the future seem destined to develop diverse cultural characteristics unknown to peoples of the past and present.

DIMENSIONS OF CULTURAL VARIABILITY

As Europeans initially explored other parts of the world and its peoples, they described a great variety of customs and cultures. Many of the newly contacted societies lacked writing and were seen as having relatively simple cultures. In the minds of both anthropologists and lay people, the groups without writing systems made up a category apart from the literate cultures of Europe, North Africa, and Asia. Actually, the cultures of non-literate groups vary so much from one another that some anthropologists object to treating them as a distinct category. But we cannot ignore the fact that they constitute a type of culture in the minds of many and that our society has formed a set of notions, many of them erroneous, about their characteristics. To communicate the diversity and complexity of nonliterate cultures to nonspecialists, we are forced to talk about them as a category, whether we label them primitive, nonliterate, folk, traditional, or otherwise.

The cultural characteristic which comes closest to distinguishing nonliterate cultures from others is that they communicate their customs and interact with one another without the benefit of systems of writing. Messages, knowledge, belief, and behavior can be communicated only by direct interpersonal contact or by observing artifacts which, since they carry no writing, communicate a minimum of information. There is no possibility of communicating large volumes of detailed information to those in remote times and places, which limits the volume of knowledge and belief that can be built up and transmitted to future generations.

Apparently some nonliterate societies have made up in part for the lack of writing by developing the ability to retain orally transmitted information. This seems to have made it possible for Alexander Haley to locate the West African community of his ancestors (1976:719). An ancestor of Haley's, six generations removed, had been captured by slave raiders and brought to the United States. He instilled in his daughter the tradition of his origins and personal history, and at least one descendent in each generation kept parts of the story alive. When Haley went to Africa with the few clues remaining from this story, he discovered that he was able to match them with information orally maintained through the generations by men who specialize in preserving and telling the histories of clans, families, and villages—including the story of Haley''s ancestor's capture by the raiders. This emphasis on oral traditions is not inevitable in societies without writing, however. The Dani, for example, have little interest in preserving oral traditions. They are uninterested in genealogy, and a grown man rarely can remember his relatives more than one generation beyond those he knew as a child (Heider 1970:70). The Dani have developed conversational art and story telling, but their stories are not the myths and legends about the past so important in some nonliterate groups but dramatic retellings of recent events and experiences (Heider 1970:190).

Since the time of first contact with Europeans, many nonliterate groups have become literate. In many cases they have learned to read and write the languages of colonizing Western nations, and in other cases missionaries or linguists have developed writing systems for previously unwritten languages. Today, when anthropologists refer to primitive or nonliterate groups, they mean those who were nonliterate at the time of European contact. In many places most of the people are still unable to read or write, and they manifest many of the cultural features they had at the time of contact.

It is important to stress the magnitude of the cultural differences among nonliterate peoples. Within that category are hunting and gathering groups such as the !Kung and the Crow, livestock herders such as the Nuer, and horticulturalists such as the Dani. Lewis points out (1951:434), as others have, that treating nonliterate peoples as a uniform cultural type means riding roughshod over fundamental cultural differences. With this stricture in mind, it may be useful to indicate four characteristics that are commonly, though not universally, found in nonliterate and other strongly traditional societies and that are probably different from those of the native cultures of most American readers of this book.

Often members of a nonliterate society are more like one another in their customs than are members of urbanized societies. This *homo-geneity* may apply in all major areas of life, including techno-economic matters. Basic differences always exist in the tasks of men and women, but beyond this, many nonliterate communities show little division of labor. Even the pre-European cities of the Yoruba of West Africa, some of which approached or exceeded 100,000 in population, consisted mostly of farmers (Bascom 1955:446, 448). They fell far short of the degree of diversity and general complexity of industrial cities. Homogeneity also applies to stratification, since prestige levels which differ from one another in lifestyle are much more common in literate cultures than in more traditional societies.

A second characteristic common in nonliterate societies is *economic production for largely local use*. To the extent that intercommunity trade occurs, and it is important in many places, it usually is on a much smaller scale than that between literate societies. Nonliterate groups have tended to produce mostly for themselves, free of the economic controls of a large society (Wolf 1966:3).

Societies without writing systems are often *kinship oriented*. Activity and interaction are often governed much more by family, clan, and other such relationships than they are in most literate societies, though kinship is more important in many modern cities and other literate communities than some investigators have realized. In spite of this, and in spite of the fact that kinship is much more significant in some nonliterate com-munities than in others, the comparison has general validity. In these kinship-oriented societies, administrative, economic, and other decisions and activities tend to be carried out as part of the obligations relatives have to one another rather than by organizations which specialize in governing political or economic matters.

Some anthropologists have suggested that societies without writing are more *traditional* than literate cultures; that is, they accept their values and behaviors as given rather than reflecting upon or questioning them. This, again, is valid only in a general sense, for there is more critical reflection in some traditional societies than in others. Interest in questioning and evaluating one's customs is often stimulated by learning about the customs of culturally alien societies, and many nonliterate societies seldom contact culturally very different groups. Still, reflective persons are sometimes found in such isolated societies. Kạobawä, a respected headman among the Yạnomamö, a rather isolated society in southern Venezuelan and northern Brazilian jungles, questions and privately pokes fun at some of the Yạnomamö ideals, beliefs, and explanatory myths (Chagnon 1977:17).

Many anthropologists avoid the word *primitive* in referring to cultures without writing systems. Cultures were originally called primitive because they were thought to be survivals of humankind's primitive (primeval) past. Early scholars thought of these cultures as "living fossils" from the earliest stages of culture and believed that by examining their customs they could learn what prehistoric cultures were like and reconstruct the stages of cultural evolution. They placed cultures that impressed them as the simplest and most unlike European cultures at the bottom of the evolutionary scale, while others were placed at various levels along the scale closer to Europeans, depending on their complexity and degree of similarity to European culture. Basically, this approach is wrong, because all non-Western cultures actually are different in many ways from whatever they were originally. They have to be, because, as anthropologists have established, no culture stops changing completely. Consequently, we cannot reconstruct cultural evolution in detail by examining the customs of "our primitive contemporaries." We may learn some basic things about hunting and gathering cultures of the past by studying today's hunters and gatherers, but this does not justify the conclusion that today's hunter-gatherers are identical to those of the past or that it is possible to determine the exact course of cultural evolution by arranging today's cultures in series from the most simple to the most complex.

Because people tend to repeat the errors of early evolutionary scholars and so many think of "primitives" as inferior or somewhat less than fully human in various ways, my position is that it is better to avoid referring to any group as primitive. But some anthropologists think that since the public refuses to give up the word "primitive," it is better to use it and try to purge it of its undesirable connotations. Though rejecting the faulty evolutionary constructions of early scholars, they regard *primitive* as a legitimate term for cultures which, in general ways, are indicative of the nature of early human culture. Whatever our usage, there is no adequate basis for the notion that nonliterate cultures are necessarily inferior, and this book avoids the use of the word *primitive* for them.

PEASANT AND PURCHASE SOCIETIES

In some respects cultural variability has increased as a result of worldwide culture contact. New customs are developed by the combination of pre-existing ideas, so the more people know about from contact with culturally different groups the greater the likelihood that they will invent new ideas that may become a part of their culture. As nations controlling relatively large stretches of territory have developed, both in modern times and before the age of exploration, they have brought under their influence and control societies that were formerly nonliterate. The result is that there have been and continue to be a vast number of rural, relatively homogeneous, tradition-oriented groups which are part of and subject to some larger, urban-oriented population. They manifest many of the same characteristics discussed previously for nonliterate groups, but they are parts of larger societies and are heavily influenced by them economically, politically, and perhaps in other ways. If part of a literate society, they may be largely or entirely *illiterate,* that is, unable to read or write the language of the larger society of which they are a part. There are also many rural, tradition-oriented, relatively homogeneous societies that have been literate for as far back as it is possible to trace their past.

Many anthropologists refer to communities of the kind just described as *peasant societies,* while others reject the term because of the connotations of inferiority it sometimes carries. Whatever they are called, they are significant, partly because, as Foster estimates, half or more of all people who have existed since human origins have lived a peasant life. The study of such cultures has been a major endeavor of cultural anthropology for many years and will continue to be for some time to come. These cultures are found in all parts of the world—in Indian Mexico, black Africa, on Pacific islands, in rural Southeast Asia, China, and India, for example—and anthropologists are studying them in many places. Again, however, it is well to remember that peasantry is no more a uniform cultural type than nonliterate culture. Variability is the rule.

Even those anthropologists concerned with studying peasantry have failed to agree on a definition. Some limit it to small-scale farming societies; others would include fishing communities and herding societies. There also are small-scale rural communities not under the economic and political control of a larger society, though they have been influenced by national cultures to a significant degree. Such is the twentieth-century culture of the Miskito Indians. Though they live within the borders of a modern nation and their culture is a blend of traits from Indian, African, British, and other cultural sources, the Miskito have remained free of national political and economic control. Accordingly, anthropologist Mary Helms proposes to call them a *purchase society* rather than a peasant society. She suggests that Miskito and many other societies have become what they are by contact with the wider world through trade and wage labor without sacrificing their political and social independence. The Miskito of Nicaragua and Honduras have not engaged in trade and commerce with representatives of those nations; they have paid little in the way of taxes and have not been drafted for labor or armed service. Instead, over a period of three hundred years they have interacted economically with representatives of England and the United States (Helms 1971:5, 6).

LEVELS OF SOCIOCULTURAL INTEGRATION

It should be apparent that world cultural variability is difficult to classify. There is great diversity among the cultures of civilized nations and among cultures which lack writing, and as the result of contact between nonliterate and literate cultures, a vast variety of other cultures have been emerging. A different scheme of classification anchored to the notion of evolutionary scale has been used by some to group these cultures.

Though the abuses of the nineteenth-century evolutionary anthropologists were rejected, the idea that nonliterate peoples somehow exhibit something of the nature of early human lifeways never quite died out. Archaeologists continued to refer to the pre-agricultural period as Paleolithic or Old Stone Age; and from time to time one still heard the comment that Paleolithic and Neolithic peoples of ancient times must have lived lives somewhat like those of contemporary nonliterate groups. Some anthropologists, notably Leslie White of the University of Michigan, began to seek aggressively to restore the evolutionary approach to ethnology. While discussion and even controversy continue, it may be said that during the last two to three decades the concept has been restored to respectability in the eyes of most anthropologists. They no longer avoid using the word *evolution;* there has been some revival of the word *primitive;* and some now use the classification and comparison of cultures by evolutionary levels as a device for dealing with cultural variability and for explicating cultural processes.

Julian Steward, a leading change theorist, has introduced the concept of *levels of sociocultural integration* (1955). Following Steward's lead, Sahlins and Service (1960), have suggested that the world's cultures may be divided into two basic levels, each containing sublevels.

1. At the *primitive level* the needs of the society are met and its activities are planned and carried out largely as a by-product of kinship relationships and groups.
    a. The least developed primitive level is the *band* type of integration, based ordinarily on hunting and gathering techniques and having, therefore, little more control of energy than what is provided by human muscle power. There is relatively little subgroup specialization or the effective means of integration that it requires, and the ability to adapt to different natural habitats is slight. Economic, military, and other administrative matters in these societies are handled basically at the personal and family levels without impersonal, formal leadership. Such leaders as do arise are neither powerful nor permanent, their influence and its duration depending mainly on their personal qualities. The !Kung San of southern Africa fall into this category.

b. *Tribal integration* is based on agricultural and/or pastoral technology. This permits greater subgroup differentiation, manifested mainly by division into clans and other kinds of kinship groups. Basically integration is accomplished by the operation of what Service calls *pantribal associations:* groups such as clans, age associations, secret societies, military groups, and other groups and associations which contain members of different

Figure 2–2 *Medicine-Crow, a leader of the Crow Indians. Tribal societies lack anything significant in the way of specialists, political leadership, or prestige ranks, and the Crow Indians fall in this category. Though among the most influential Crow, Medicine-Crow was not a full time political leader.*

families and other residential units (1978:5). This cross-cutting of residential groups provides integration of the society's activities not available to band level peoples. Tribal societies have more parts and more integration than band societies, but they still lack anything significant in the way of specialists, political leadership, or prestige ranks. The Dani of New Guinea, the Nuer of East Africa and the Crow Indians fall in this category.

   c. The *chiefdom level* of integration is the most advanced grade of the primitive stage. At this level people have achieved a technology that provides a food surplus which permits specialization in non-food producing activities, making it possible for a number of adjacent local groups to combine under the leadership of a specialist in the integration and administration of sub-groups—that is, a chief. Since there is specialization of labor beyond simple division by sex, the society consists of diverse parts, including a governmental component. With specialization integrated by centralized leadership, the society can accomplish more and exercise greater control over its social and natural environment. The aboriginal Samoans may be placed at this level.

2. *Civilization,* in this scheme, is separated from primitive culture by existence of a *state*. The mark of a state is the explicit and fully legalized use of force or threat of force by a centralized government as the ultimate means of social integration and administration. While the chiefdom level of primitive culture provides permanent and centralized leadership, the chief and his associates govern by the support granted them because of the effectiveness with which they perform their responsibilities. A chief does not enjoy the legalized monopoly on power over the people within a fixed territory that characterizes state government (Krader 1968:9). As a mode of integration, the state system obviously makes possible a greater variety of accomplishments than less organized means.

   a. Under civilization, Sahlins and Service recognize an *archaic* form that lacks the industrial technology necessary to the highest degree of integration of groups and their affairs. The Nyoro, a nonliterate society of Uganda, fall under this rubric.

   b. The *nation-state* level is made possible by industrial technology. It is more highly developed and more territorially integrated than the archaic type.

Peasant societies, purchase societies, and other such cultures are without a slot in this classification. Service now classifies them in a level of integration which he places just above archaic civilization, which he now refers to as the *primitive-state* level (1978:9). They are treated as rural communities under the heading of civilization. Among the societies most often used for examples in this book, the Basseri of Iran, the Miskito Indians of Nicaragua and Honduras, and the modern Samoans of Fitiuta probably fit best in this class.

THE SOURCES OF CULTURAL VARIABILITY

All cultures are composed of the same general categories of phenomena. All of them have customs that can be classified as technological, economic, social, political, legal, religious, aesthetic, recreational, or educational. It has been said that, in this sense, there is a *universal pattern* for cultures (Wissler 1923:73).

The obvious reason that cultures everywhere manifest customs of these kinds is that all people are born with similar biological characteristics and into similar natural habitats. Habitat and biology, however, differ some from one place and from one group to another, which partially accounts for cultural variability. Other factors also play a part, such as demographic, distributional, and cultural-historical factors.

Each of the world's cultures is usefully viewed as a component of an *ecosystem*. A *system* is a set of functionally interdependent parts, rather than a collection of unrelated elements. So, to say that a culture is part of an ecosystem is to declare that the customs that it is composed of are influenced by and influence elements of the total environment in which they occur. An ecosystem, then, is a configuration of interrelated animals, plants, humans, and physical objects, arrangements, and substances. The components of a given culture's ecosystem may be listed as (1) culturally alien humans and their customs; (2) biological features of the bodies of the society's members; (3) domesticated and undomesticated plants, animals, and other nonhuman organisms; (4) artificial objects and other physical arrangements; (5) natural objects, topographical features, weather conditions and other inorganic elements of the natural habitat; and (6) the people and customs of the society in question. The fullest understanding of the cultures of the Basseri, Dani, Miskito, or any other of the thousands of known cultures requires knowledge of how they are affected by, and, in turn, affect the noncultural context within which they exist and function.

In considering the relationships between a culture and the rest of the ecosystem, it is useful to think of the culture as existing within a milieu or context of surrounding, *external* elements, *specifically;* the group's biological characteristics, characteristics of the natural habitat, population, and other cultures. In exploring these relationships anthropologists have found, first, that *external factors limit a culture*. Due to the size of ostrich eggshells, it is impossible for the !Kung to use them for dwellings, and it is impossible for Eskimos to do without clothing. Of course, people may find ways of overcoming some limitations. It once seemed that there was no possibility of flying, but this is now a cultural reality.

Second, the *external elements of the ecosystem allow a variety of possibilities* for a culture. No biological or habitat factor determines precisely how food will be transported to the mouth. Fingers, leaves, tortillas, chopsticks, and metal implements have been employed. Some habitats provide the possibility of bark cloth, woven fabrics, or animal skin for clothing, though only one or none may be used. Psychologically it is possible to believe in one god, a hundred, or none.

Third, *external factors make some things more likely* in a given culture or in all cultures than others. A few societies are said to be ignorant of the male role in conception, but the tendency seems otherwise. Human respiration is such that most people remain under water for only short periods, though the biological possibility of staying under water for up to three minutes has been exploited. The biologically based tendency is to use flat-soled footwear, if any, but some people wear shoes with long supports beneath the heels, which hold the foot in a basically uncomfortable position and make walking difficult.

Fourth, *in building their cultures people select among the possibilities and tendencies* provided by the ecosystem. There is a variety of ways of meeting many of the demands of living. Moreover, the variety is so great that no single society can use all of them. Every society, in effect, has selected a relatively small proportion of the customs possible in the particular ecological niche that they occupy. Some have selected the habit of eating two meals a day, while others eat three times daily or have only one main meal each day. Some associate each person with the mother's kin, some with the father's, and still others with both. Some societies have separate terms for green and blue, while others combine them. Discerning why some groups have arrived at one possibility rather than another is one of the major problems of anthropology. Answers to such questions are profoundly relevant to helping people make choices concerning the goals of their societies.

Finally, *external elements of the ecosytem may be changed by cultural means.* The face of the earth has been radically altered in many modern nations; for example, former desert areas have been turned into fertile crop lands. Some groups bind their infants' heads to make them unnaturally elongated, and modern medical research has produced artificial organs. Most significant of all, perhaps, is the possibility of scientifically manipulating the genetic code to produce people with certain desired characteristics, whatever those may prove to be.

Some people suppose that only urban industrial societies have altered the habitat significantly, but this is not so. For example, nonindustrial peoples have deforested large areas by slash-and-burn agriculture, which has resulted in severe erosion in some parts of the world.

Culturally altered ecosystems, in turn, provide new limitations, possibilities, and tendencies to which groups must react. Some think that Euroamerican emphasis on humanity's ability to conquer and control nature has caused them to overlook this fact. Some alterations may be so severe as to make human life unpleasant or even impossible. If humans agree that it is desirable to preserve the world's ecosystems and to direct their changing internal relationships along satisfying lines, it becomes important to acquire the best possible understanding of the links that bind together the cultural and noncultural elements of the ecosystem.

Human Biology and Cultural Differences

Some people argue that differences between cultures are the result in large part of biological differences among human groups. It must be granted that some minor cultural differences are the consequence of physical differences. The lack of tatooing among blacks, for example, is partly related to the fact that foreign matter introduced beneath the skin would not contrast well with dark pigmentation. Also, scarification is probably more extensive among blacks than others because their skin tends to be more responsive to the scarring technique. It also has been proposed that archers and spearmen tend to have different body types (Brues 1959).

There seem to be few significant differences of this kind, however, and people of all races or biological types are closely similar anatomically, physiologically, and in their psychological potential. Most supposed differences, such as the greater visual acuity of some hunters and gatherers, turn out to be due to learned powers of observation not appreciated by an outsider. Marshall comments on what appears to us to be the extraordinary ability of the !Kung to detect a thread-thin fragment of vine among grass stems, thereby ascertaining the presence of an edible root (1976:97). She also describes how such visual impressions are informally planted in the minds of !Kung infants and children as they constantly participate in and observe their mothers' gathering activities. As with other human skills, constant practice makes the difference.

Many people, including some scholars, assume that some cultures or subcultures are inferior to others and that this is because some races are naturally inferior to others. But it is important to remember that nearly all who take this position are talking about large categories, such as white, black, Amerindian, and Mongoloid, which have little or no scientific validity. These large categories are derived from the popular thought of the Western world, not from the careful scientific work of the physical anthropologist or the population geneticist. They are so large that there is great diversity within each category, and this diversity—combined with the fact that it is impossible to discover sharp boundaries between the categories—renders them useless for comparing inherited intelligence differences. Since most people cannot be classifid with certainty in one or another of these large biological categories, the boundaries of the category to be sampled for purposes of comparing races are not known. It is therefore impossible to know whether or not the samples we use are adequately representative of blacks, whites, American Indians, or other such large, ill-defined units.

Because of their experiences living in and studying various nonliterate groups, anthropologists are qualified to deal with the question of whether black Africans, Australian aborigines, Pacific islanders, Indians of the South American jungles, and other such groups are inferior mentally to Europeans and North American whites. Although their experiences provide no quantitative measures of intelligence, anthropologists have found that groups of all biological types manifest the same kind and degree of ingenuity and intelligence in meeting the demands of life. They, therefore, reject the notion that inherited psychological differences account for the differences between literate, urban cultures and traditional, technologically simple cultures.

Why sub-Saharan Africans apparently did not develop writing in premodern times is not known, but the absence of writing does not demonstrate mental inferiority. It may be that only one or two societies in all human history invented writing from scratch, (that is, without learning the basic idea from another society). This means that nearly all white groups failed to invent systems of writing on their own, but no one uses this fact to argue that they are mentally inferior to groups who did. Neither, then, is anyone justified in using the lack of writing systems in sub-Saharan Africa as evidence of inherent mental inferiority of blacks. It may be significant that black Africa was very sparsely settled, for elaborate cultural developments are most apt to occur in areas of high population density and intense cultural contact. In the Old World such cultural developments occurred around the eastern end of the Mediterranean Sea, and in the New World in and between the margins of North and South America. In spite of the apparent absence of writing in pre-European black Africa, many groups there were socio-politically and technologically accomplished. The sub-Saharan Africans had a flair for creating complex governmental machinery, and they developed vaccination techniques and processes for producing carbon steel. In fact, there are old men among the Haya of Tanzania who remember how to make steel, and archaeological evidence indicates that smelting furnaces capable of producing the high temperatures and other states necessary to make carbon steel date back 1,500 to 2,000 years (Schmidt and Avery 1978:1186).

It is very reasonable to assume approximately equal mental and cultural potential among human groups in light of the nature of the human experience. The key element of cultural significance in intelligence is adaptability, and none of the popular racial categories is associated with cultures that put a higher premium on ability to adapt than others. South African San, Pacific Island Samoans, New Guinea Highlanders, and

Central American Miskito must be intelligent to have adapted as they have. Or, as one anthropologist remarked, tribal living often requires a great deal more intelligence than going to college. Ashley Montagu has suggested that, in virtually all societies, those most likely to survive and pass their genes on to the next generation are those who show wisdom, maturity of judgment, and ability to get along well with others (1963:79). Such traits characterize the plastic (flexible) personality, and groups in all parts of the globe place a high premium on plasticity. With relatively weak inherited predispositions, but highly developed ability to learn and to symbolize, human cultural potentialities are manifold. There are enough nonbiological explanations for cultural differences that we are not stuck with biological explanations alone.

Currently, the assumption that racial categories are approximately equal in inherited capacity to originate and participate in complex civilization is under attack by a few nonanthropologists. Since some of these people are accomplished scholars who utilize sophisticated approaches, lay people unacquainted with the issues and the relevant data may be troubled by their arguments. It should be remembered that the racial samples they compare are from the traditional, popularly developed racial categories rather than from scientifically delineated races. In view of this weakness—as well as the possibility that the race concept is fallacious—the results of their comparisons are questionable (see page 31). It may prove helpful to indicate some of the fallacies in two major lines of attack on the assumption of equality.

One approach cites the ten to fifteen point difference between the intelligence test scores of whites and blacks in North American countries. The issue is complex, but it has become quite evident that current methods of intelligence testing provide an inadequate basis for comparing the native intellectual capacities of blacks and whites. It has been shown that intelligence tests call for responses that people other than middle and upper class white Americans have not been prepared by experience and training to respond to favorably. Culturally different groups, including minority groups within the United States, are unfamiliar in varying degrees with the nature and content of the test questions. This point has been widely published, and there is no need to belabor it here.

But there are other major difficulties with intelligence testing, one being the ways tests are administered to people who may not be trained to respond well to formal testing situations. Arthur Jensen, an educational psychologist known for his belief that there may be significant differences among human populations in native intelligence, found that tests given to disadvantaged children without establishing proper relationships between the tester and the children usually yield scores from eight to ten points less than average (1969:100). He rectifies the difficulty by gaining the children's confidence through play and craft sessions, then retesting them. Yet virtually all intelligence test comparisons between blacks and whites use scores from tests that were given without establishing such relationships. This accounts for much of the average difference between blacks and whites. When inferior educational background, poor motivation for success, and other factors are added, intelligence test differences make sense from a cultural viewpoint and do not require genetic explanations.

A second line of attack is to cite studies of brain samples which indicate inferiority in size, weight, and anatomy of the brains of blacks. Frequently mentioned is a study of the brains of black Kenyans which reported (among other things) that the supragranular layer, the relative thickness of which is alleged to affect ability to think abstractly, is about 14 percent less in the brains of Kenyan blacks than in whites. Actually, because of unresolved and unreported difficulties in measuring the thickness of the supragranular layer, comparisons of the two brain samples on this point are completely meaningless. It has been shown that measurements of the layer's thickness can vary by as much as 100 percent because of difficulties in deciding where and how to divide it from adjoining layers and because of varying techniques of measurement (Tobias 1970:21). The author of the Kenya study does not report where and how he determined the thickness of the supragranular layer, and the investigator of the white sample fails to specify his techniques. Tobias has pointed out that existing studies of brain anatomy fail to allow for a variety of factors affecting brain characteristics, such as age, nutrition, illness, the nature of the person's death, and where the brain was severed from the spinal cord (3).

Intelligence testing and brain comparisons are only two of the areas to consider. Anthropologists add the powerful evidence gotten from participating in the cultures of hundreds of groups, which indicates highly intelligent people are found in approximately equal proportions in all societies. They feel fully justified in proceeding with the study of cultural differences on the assumption that all major racial categories have about the same range of inherited intelligence potential.

Natural Habitat and Cultural Differences

Anthropologists have long rejected the notion that a culture's content is determined mostly by its natural environment. This is because they have found culturally different groups in closely similar habitats and very different cultures at different times in the same location. !Kung hunter-gatherers and Bantu-speaking farmers are both found in arid southern Africa, and modern American towns and cities now dot the areas where the Crow and other plains tribes once hunted the bison. Obviously, factors in addition to habitat must be granted major significance.

While the habitat does not determine precisely what a culture is like, there is no denying that many cultural differences are due to habitat variability. Marshall notes the simple fact that the use of mangetti nuts is an important part of the culture of some !Kung communities, whereas in other !Kung communities it is of no importance. Without question this cultural difference is related to the fact that the mangetti is found in some !Kung areas and not in others (1976:93). In terms of the kinds of relationships between a culture and the rest of the ecosystem that were mentioned earlier (see page 29): (1) a culture is limited by its habitat; (2) the habitat allows a variety of possibilities for the culture; (3) the habitat makes some things more likely for the culture than others; (4) the society has made only some of the possibilities afforded by the habitat a part of its culture; and (5) the habitat is changed by the culture. For example, before the whites introduced fish into their rivers, fishing was not a cultural possibility for the Dugum Dani (Heider 1970:58). At one time, at least, both gardening and hunting and gathering were possibilities as the main food source for the inhabitants of the Grand Valley where the Dani now live, since climatic and soil conditions made cultivation feasible and the forests contained game. The current habitat, however, makes hunting less likely than gardening, since game is now scarce. This is a consequence of cultural alteration of the habitat, since the game has been hunted out and good hunting can be found only by long trips to areas where game is still plentiful.

It was indicated earlier that *cultural ecology*, the study of the relationship between a culture and its habitat, has become a major specialty within anthropology. Cultural ecologists have discovered that culture-habitat relationships are many and complex. Other examples will be provided in later chapters, but one major aspect of the culture-habitat relationship is that technological-economic factors are much more directly influenced by the habitat than most social, ideological, and religious components of a culture. Accordingly, a major concern of cultural ecologists is how techno-economic and habitat factors affect one another. They have also noted that some cultures are much less restricted by the natural environment than others, since they have the ideological concepts, economic organization, and technological devices necessary to exploit the environment effectively. This is one reason technologically elaborate cultures commonly dominate others.

Anthropologists have also been increasingly interested in how contact between cultures affects how a society responds to the habitat, for alien customs are also part of the ecosystem. A society may be stimulated to react to its habitat in ways it would not if it were not in competition or conflict with another group. Hopi and other Pueblo Indians of the American Southwest located their villages on mesa tops to provide security from Apache and Navajo raiding. There is abundant evidence that habitat factors are involved in accounting for cultural variability in a variety of complex ways.

Demographic Factors and Cultural Differences

Large population size has been found to be positively associated with cultural heterogeneity and a high rate of innovation. The relationship seems to be circular. Population cannot increase beyond the ability of technology to support it, but once the population has grown sufficiently, it is possible to develop more complex technology and social organization. This again provides a basis for more population growth.

This is by no means all there is to the relationship. For one thing, a large population does not guarantee cultural complexity. Some societies, in fact, have reacted by dividing into several small societies rather than becoming more complex culturally. Nor is population size all that has cultural consequences; demographers also concern themselves with population density and distribution. Additional implications would be suggested by reviewing the previously outlined relationships between a culture and the rest of its ecosystem. The intention here is simply to indicate that population is related to cultural diversity.

Isolation and Contact as Sources of Cultural Variability

Spatial isolation of one society from others permits a culture to evolve along its own course without interruption. Accordingly, it differs increasingly from other cultures—unless other noncultural influences are so similar that they tend to follow parallel paths. And when cultures are in contact with one another, they may become similar to one another by mutual borrowing. At the same time, they become increasingly different from those cultures with which they are not in contact.

Cultural contact is usually studied under the heading of *cultural dynamics* (see page 9), and the change that occurs in a group's customs as the result of contact is usually known as *acculturation*. It is important to remember that the customs of alien cultures are part of the extracultural environment of a culture being studied just as surely as purely noncultural features.

Cultural History and Variability

Anthropology students often ask how cultures that they are studying about came to have the customs which they often find so fascinating. If anthropologists had been present when given customs became part of a culture, and if they could have observed the relevant occurrences, they probably could point to the biological, habitat, population, and other influences that brought the customs or complexes of customs into being. Apparently, however, most cultural differences emerged from specific events and conditions in a culture's history that are probably unrecoverable. Many such specifics fall in the category of accidents, a word used to indicate unexpected events for which we know no explanations. A man just happens to shake with emotion during a religious ceremony, and shaking becomes a standardized expression of spiritual possession. A starving man eats a tomato, and tomatoes become a regular food. A canoe builder experiments with different keel shapes to see which provides the greatest stability, and others adopt his solution. Such specific factors have been observed to be the stuff of cultural change during historical times, and we must assume that they have given rise to many cultural differences in all times and places. The specific motivations and conditions that result in such changes are reviewed in the final chapter.

PERCEIVING AND UNDERSTANDING CULTURAL DIFFERENCES

No issue is more important to the adequacy of cultural anthropology or to international understanding than whether we perceive and understand alien customs in terms of our own cultural background or within the context of the culture in which they exist and function. All who have had no contact with a culturally different group have no choice, when they first learn about alien customs, but to experience those customs in terms of their (the observers') native personal and cultural frames of reference. As we observe the actions and utterances of cultural aliens, what we see and hear and what we fail to see and hear are affected to a significant degree by the concepts and percepts that we have learned from and share with other members of our society—that is, our culture. The result is that our perceptions of what the customs of other cultures are like are always distorted. To put it another way, our perceptions, being distorted by our native frames of reference, never match what is actually there. This distortion can be reduced significantly by the alternative of relating customs to their own cultural contexts as we try to understand them.

Anthropologists nearly always define *ethnocentrism* as judging alien customs and cultures to be inferior to one's own, but many of them go beyond the definition as they use the word. Actual usage, then, seems to justify defining ethnocentrism as perceiving, interpreting, or judging the customs of other cultures from the viewpoint of one's native cultural background. The alternative of relating customs to the cultural contexts in which they function in order to understand and evaluate them has sometimes been called *cultural relativism*. Ethnocentrism and cultural relativism, then, may be viewed as alternative modes of reacting to alien customs and cultures. Ethnocentrism leads to misunderstanding, since the observer views the alien ways from the wrong frame of reference, while cultural relativism, so to speak, leaves the alien customs in their natural context.

Ethnocentrism is well illustrated by the American perception of how the Hopi, a Pueblo tribe of northern Arizona, use the three-dimensional images of supernatural beings known as *kachinas.* The Hopi give these carved figures to their children at the time of the ceremonies honoring the kachinas. Americans, viewing this custom in terms of their own culture, have come to regard the Hopi figures as dolls. They are commonly referred to as kachina dolls, and readers of popular magazines are sometimes told how Hopi give these dolls to children, just as American children receive dolls at Christmas. Actually, though small Hopi children sometimes play with kachina figures, they are not made for that purpose and they are not accurately viewed as dolls. They are not even decorative dolls; instead, they are provided so the children will become familiar with the appearance of different kachina costumes worn by Hopi men as they impersonate the supernaturals in their ceremonial dances. Rather than being given to children to play with, the images are hung from the rafters in the child's home (Colton 1969:5).

Misperceptions across cultural boundaries have many ramifications. Among other things, they affect what we find interesting about other cultures, and this, in turn, affects our descriptions of alien customs. In *ethnographies,* which are the descriptions anthropologists write of the cultures they have studied, many examples of this can be found. One observer reported that the women of the society he was studying carried unbelievably heavy loads. That was an unwitting misrepresentation of the custom in question, since the loads were not unbelievably heavy to the people carrying them. The anthropologist was reacting in terms of culturally conditioned frames of references that he, as an American, shares with other Americans. The statement reflects that, in American culture, women normally carry light loads and are regarded as incapable of carrying very heavy loads, which results in our perception of the heavy loads carried by women of some other cultures as being "unbelievable."

The only way such cross-cultural, culturally biased misinterpretation could be completely avoided would be for the observer to abandon completely his native culture and experience everything just as the cultural aliens do. In the first place, that is impossible, and, in the second place, it would eliminate the possibility of members of one society understanding anything about those of culturally different groups. Thus it is that American anthropologists, in order to describe other cultures to Americans, must write their ethnographies in English. But since American English is designed to express American rather than other cultures, the description must remain something of a distortion of what the culture is like.

If we desire the most accurate possible perception of alien cultures, our alternative is to force ourselves to understand the customs by viewing them in terms of the culture in which they occur and to relate them to the other customs and ecosystem circumstances to which they are functionally linked. Much of the time this will require us to admit that we know too little about a custom's context to perceive it in any way like the people who practice it, but in many other cases we will be able to learn enough about the indigenous context and viewpoint to eliminate much of the distortion from our perceptions. In some cases it may be relatively easy. Only a little care and objective observation are needed to determine how the Hopi kachina images are related to their cultural context. In other cases, the nature of a trait or cultural complex and how it fits into the culture requires more careful anthropological analysis. James Downs has provided such an analysis for the sheep-breeding practices of the Navajo Indians. The Navajo permitted their sheep to breed early in the fall, with the result that the lambs were born during the worst winter weather. Americans argued, from the stance of American cultural practice, that it would be better for the sheep to breed late in the fall, so that the lambs would arrive during better weather and have improved chances of survival. To some Americans it was quite irrational of the Navajo to refuse to follow a practice that could minimize the death rate of newly born animals. But an inside look at the cultural and ecological context yields a less ethnocentric, more accurate view. For one thing, the Navajo knew that the dropping of lambs in winter made it possible for the ewes to utilize the new spring grass to produce milk during the lambs' most important growth period. The Navajo preferred to exert the extra effort to keep the newborn lambs alive during the bitter winter weather. Moreover, the Navajo have other work to do, both on and off the reservation, during the times of better weather, while winter is a time free for the work of caring for new lambs. Actually, the lamb losses are very low and, due to their earlier birth, there is more time for the lambs to reach full market weight. Finally, to the Navajo, a herd of sheep is an important symbol of the family. The worst period of winter is a time when the family members cooperate closely to protect and enlarge the herd, and their work has great meaning to them as a symbol of the unity and continuity of the family (Downs 1975:113). From this analysis it becomes apparent that Navajo sheep-breeding practices have functions not apparent to the culture-bound outsider and that a contextual analysis is required to understand Navajo custom better and reduce the distortions of ethnocentrism.

Beginning anthropology students are unlikely to conduct anthropological analyses to counteract cross-cultural misinterpretations, but they can increase their capacity to understand other cultures by watching themselves for reactions which are clearly governed by their native reference frames and asking themselves whether a more complete understanding of a custom's meaning to the people and its place in their culture and ecosystem might alter the reaction. Strangeness, quaintness, and ridiculousness are not the only bases for interest in alien lifeways; it can also be enjoyable to discover how a custom fits into people's lives and what it does for them.

In anthropological theory the problem of understanding other cultures has crystalized around the *emic* and *etic* approaches. Anthropologists have long issued calls to understand cultures in their own terms rather than by imposing our own biases, but it was not until the 1950s that a movement arose to develop more refined methods for determining how a given culture classifies phenomena of which people are aware and to which they respond. The terms emic and etic were coined by linguist Kenneth Pike (1954:8). Pike stressed that the *emic* approach applies only to attempts to describe the pattern of a single language or culture in terms of its own structure, while the *etic* approach applies concepts and categories of phenomena developed in advance of the study of the culture in question.

Emic categories for understanding and reacting to the world are those which the people of a particular group are aware of or which govern their behavior. Karl Heider is viewing things emically when he describes the Dani concept of *edai-agen* (1970:227). To the Dani this is something located within the body just below the base of the sternum when one is in good condition but which withdraws toward the backbone and becomes small when one is ill, injured, or in mourning. Heider reports that the Dani think of the *edai-agen* as the heart, the seat of the personality, one's goodness, or the essence of a person. Though some distortion is intro-

Figure 2–3 *Dani mourning at a funeral pyre. Heider describes the Dani belief that there is something called edai-agen which is located just below the base of the sternum when one is in good condition but which withdraws toward the backbone and becomes small when one is ill, injured, or in mourning.*

duced by using English rather than Dani, the description is basically emic. Heider is trying to define the concept as the Dani perceive it, avoiding the distortion that would result from imposing the English category, soul.

For one American subculture, that of tramps, a researcher obtained from one informant the information that there are different kinds: bindle stiffs, mission stiffs, box car tramps, home guard tramps, and rubber tramps (Spradley 1970:273). For both the Dani and the American tramps the investigators were trying to discover the *emics* of the group, that is, the categories and organization of categories that are meaningful to the people themselves and that affect how they behave.

The movement in anthropology to develop more adequate methods of discovering the *emics* of cultures has emerged in a speciality known as *cognitive anthropology,* or, *ethnoscience.* Cognitive anthropologists object to the uncritical, culture-bound use of Euroamerican categories such as witchcraft, religion, marketing, education, and law to classify phenomena of other cultures because they may not correspond with the categories used by the people themselves. In trying to understand a culture, Tyler suggests, there are "two ways of bringing order out of apparent chaos—*impose* a preexisting order on it, or *discover* the order underlying it" (1969:11). Cognitive anthropologists prefer the second approach and believe that cultural order is reflected in language. Much of ethnoscience, accordingly, has been the exploration of how various societies classify and organize their experience linguistically. The cognitive anthropologist may seek to identify a *semantic domain,* which is a category of things all of which share at least one feature in common that differentiates them from other semantic domains (Tyler 1969:8). One of the semantic domains of American tramps is *hustling,* which is made up of a variety of ways of obtaining, while in jail, the cash, cigarettes and other things that they need. The components of this domain, as ascertained by the anthropologist, are conning, peddling, kissing ass, making a run, taking a rake-off, playing cards, bumming, running a game, making a pay-off, and making a phone-call (Spradley 1970:247). Of course, this is only one of many semantic domains in the tramp culture of Seattle, Washington, but it is emic because it is the way the tramps see things and their behavior is affected by this and other ways they classify and relate experience.

Though the study of semantic domains is significant in cognitive anthropology, it is only one basic part of it. For example, semantic domains with a feature or features in common may be grouped into more inclusive domains, and this may be done at two or more levels to form *taxonomies.* Folk taxonomies of a number of cultures have been studied for a variety of cultural aspects of limited scope, such as diseases (Frake 1961), color (e.g., Conklin 1955), foods (e.g., Perchonock and Werner 1969), animals (e.g., Hunn 1977), plants (e.g., Berlin, Breedlove and Raven 1974), firewood (e.g., Metzger and Williams 1966) and land tenure (Pospisil 1965). Semantic domains are also organized in nontaxonomic ways not described here. The methods and findings of cognitive anthropology are significant for the study of cultural differences because they provide effective ways of seeing a culture as the people experience it. They also reveal that no two cultures are alike in all semantic domains, the features of meaning by which the domains are distinguished from one another, or the ways that they organize domains and features.

The emic approach certainly yields superior perceptions of how people in particular societies experience life, but this is not enough. A major goal of anthropology is to generalize about human nature, and this requires comparing cultures with one another. Such comparisons are impossible if we have only emic categories; we must have etic categories. Scientifically useful etic categories can be developed from two kinds of sources: phenomena of the external world that do not vary culturally, or the body of similarities among cultures revealed by comparing emic studies. The former is illustrated by the color spectrum, a phenomenon external to all cultures, but which can be used with all groups to discover what portions of the spectrum people react to and how they react. The comparison of emic concepts of different cultures to establish etic categories is illustrated by the observation that many cultures include the concept of injuring another human as a purely psychic act. Once it is established that various cultures are similar to one another in this respect, we can call the phenomenon witchcraft or something else and use the newly formed category as a thought tool by which we can compare cultures. Presently, anthropologists are using a variety of etic categories, such as witchcraft, clan, divorce, suicide, and animism, which are of incompletely determined scientific value for comparing cultures. They repeatedly encounter trouble in trying to apply such concepts to specific cultures. Some, for example, have defined a sib as a common ancestor group whose members acknowledge descent from the common ancestor in the paternal line or in the maternal line, though they are unable to trace all the links. But Heider found that the Dani have kinship groups that meet all the criteria for a sib except the clear acknowledgement of common descent (1970:66). For purposes of comparing the Dani with other cultures, is it better to say that they lack sibs or to stretch the definition and say that they have a different kind of sib? Heider's solution was to include the Dani kinship groups under the already established etic category, sib, since he did not want to add another term to the already complex kinship literature. The development of etic categories for comparing cultures in all their vast diversity is so difficult that some anthropologists have seemed to neglect it. Carol Ewber feels that among the cognitive anthropologists the emphasis on emic description has inhibited comparison, partly because they have been so busy describing and partly because of a feeling that cultures cannot be compared until we have many accurate descriptions and can be sure that the things compared are properly comparable (1977:34). Since cross-cultural comparison is indispensable to anthropology's goal of understanding human nature, the best solution is to continue to use what etic categories we have, abandoning or revising them as their inadequacies become apparent in the light of more accurate emic descriptions, and adding more useful etic categories as new findings permit.

EVALUATING CULTURAL DIFFERENCES

Students of humankind have long been impressed with the tendency of people to think their own culture is superior to others. The noted sociologist, William Graham Sumner, developed the concept of *ethnocentrism,* which he defined as the "view of things in which one's own group is the center of everything, and all others are scaled and rated with reference to it." (1906:13). The term caught on both with social scientists and the educated public. It has come to be used not only as a term for thinking one's own culture to be superior to others but, as a put-down term used by some anthropologists and others to condemn those who think their lifeways are better than others. Anthropologists can be ethnocentric exponents of their own subculture, regarding other subgroups as being inferior because they are ethnocentric. As noted earlier, this text uses ethnocentrism in a broader sense (see page 37).

Judgmental reactions to the customs of other cultures commonly stem from ethnocentric misinterpretation of alien customs. In many black African societies a man and his relatives pay a bride price of cattle, iron hoes, or other items. In American culture paying for something is the equivalent of acquiring property, and supposedly people do largely as they please with what they own. Accordingly, Euroamericans have misinterpreted bride purchase to be treating women as property; this observation is then accompanied by the judgment that it is an inferior way to treat women. Such misjudgments are potentially correctable by perceiving the custom as the African experiences it. He is not purchasing property in our sense but compensating her relatives for her loss and the loss of her children. The compensation, in fact, may be thought of as evidence of respect for the bride and the valuable contributions women make to family life. Without question, humans everywhere repeatedly misunderstand and misjudge the customs of alien societies. For those who value accuracy and fairness, the answer is to view those customs in the context of the culture within which they exist and to discern the values they have for the people who practice them.

Anthropologists disagree as to whether customs and cultures can be evaluated by scientific standards. The prevailing view, an extension of *cultural relativism,* is that customs are to be evaluated only in relation to the culture in which they exist. If the people value them, then they are good in that sense, but there is no supracultural standard of goodness. What is good in one culture may be bad in another and vice versa. Another view says that all cultures are equally good. A number of anthropologists, however, reject these positions because of what they see as overtones of absolutism. They object on the grounds that to say that something is good because people value it or that all cultures are good implies some standard of goodness which cannot be scientifically established. What scientific principle justifies the assertion that something is good because members of some society regard it as good; why would it not be just as valid to declare that all cultures are equally bad? A prominent American anthropologist once suggested that we should respect the dignity inherent in every culture, but, assuming that dignity is inherent in cultures, what scientific finding obliges us to respect it? Many anthropologists feel that the only tenable view is that cultures and customs cannot be scientifically evaluated. One must remain neutral or, at least, agnostic, about the goodness or badness of customs and cultures, since science is not equipped to judge goodness and badness. Someone or some group can state goals that they value, and science may be able to determine that some customs are more effective for reaching or maintaining those goals than others; but science, according to the neutralist view under discussion, is unable to determine the goodness or badness of the goals.

In addition to these relativistic and neutralistic positions, some anthropologists suggest that people everywhere have certain basic desires; that this is the reason that standards of value are found in all cultures; and that it would be reasonable to treat these basic desires as value standards. If such universal desires exist they have, of course, been so modified and concealed by the diversity of cultural specifics that it is difficult to determine what they might be. The entire question of cultural evaluation is difficult also because it becomes so quickly entangled with philosophical presuppositions that people often disagree about. While cultural relativism is strongly supported by anthropologists, it is significant that they disagree on the possibility of evaluating customs and cultures. (Additional remarks on this issue are included in the discussion of values and ethical principles in Chapter 12.)

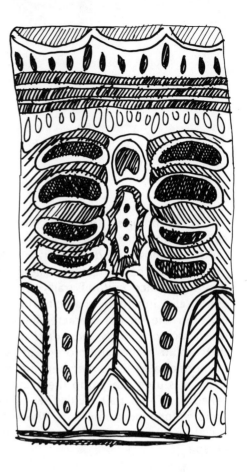

3

CUSTOMS
AND
CULTURES

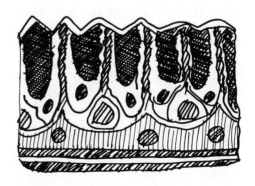

Anthropologists think of cultures as being composed of customs, or cultural traits. They disagree somewhat on the fundamental nature of these traits, but most anthropologists emphasize two characteristics of cultural phenomena. The first is that *customs are learned—they are not biologically inherited.* Since cultural traits are acquired, it is important to exclude genetically inherited characteristics when dealing with the content of cultures. The second characteristic of cultural traits is that *they are social, or shared, not solely individual.* If customs were unique to individuals, they would be nothing more than personality traits. When, however, two or more of a society's members manifest closely similar learned personality traits, it is useful to group these individual customs into a single category called a cultural trait. With few exceptions, then, anthropological usages limit cultural phenomena to those that are learned and those that are social, excluding traits that are genetically inherited or unique to a single person.

INDIVIDUAL AND MULTI-INDIVIDUAL CUSTOMS

The culture concept delineates a domain of phenomena for cultural anthropologists to research and draw conclusions about, but there is some disagreement about how to define culture and whether or not the concept provides a suitable foundation for significant theory building. Some assert that culture is only an abstraction, but it is well to remember that we live in terms of abstractions. Concepts such as "person," "book," "love," "money," and "full' certainly are abstractions in the sense that they are only incomplete and, in the sense of their incompleteness, inaccurate indicators of the phenomena that we suppose exist in the "real world." Even concepts such as "my husband," or "that fly on my plate" are abstractions, since no wife really knows accurately all there is to her husband, and our knowledge of any particular fly is general and incomplete. Even at supposedly specific, concrete levels, we have no choice but to deal with our experiences by means of abstractions that we formulate in our minds. For the culture concept, as well as the concept of any given culture such as that of the Nuer of Africa or the Miskito of Central America, the question is not whether or not they are abstractions—

they are! The question is how well our concept of culture or of a given culture match our most concrete experiences of what we are trying to know and understand. For this purpose some concepts are more useful than others, and we seek a culture concept that is highly productive for understanding the learned, multi-individual (shared) lifeways of human groups. For culture, then, we ask, "What is really there as humans experience it?" We realize that we cannot know totally but that some concepts will take us farther toward accuracy and completeness than others.

This requires that we base our concepts of culture as carefully as we can on how humans experience things. An inescapable prerequisite to the culture concept is our notion that individuals have customary behaviors. We can observe anyone's actions and listen to his or her utterances, in our own society or another, and find many of them repeated. Every person behaves at different times in ways that we experience as similar or, in some cases, identical. Each time one of the Samoan girls observed by Margaret Mead was asked to dance she did so negligently (Mead 1928:154). It was her customary way of dancing. An economics professor at a West Coast university in the United States misses few opportunities to point out the flaws of lâissez fâire capitalism as he

Figure 3–1 *Young Samoan dancers entertaining visitors. Individuals have customary behaviors. Each time one of the Samoan girls observed by Margaret Mead was asked to dance she did so negligently.*

lectures to his classes. It is his custom to do so, and observers arrive at such a conclusion by experiencing his classroom utterances at different times as being similar. From what we experience as similarities in a person's behavior at one time and another, we conclude that there is stability, continuity, or the like in his or her actions and utterances. No normal individual has been found in any human society for which this is not true. In fact, the idea of people whose actions and utterances are at all times different from all their past behaviors is so foreign to human experience that we can hardly conceive of it.

The concept of social or multi-individual customs is based on the idea of individual customs. It derives from the observer's experience of similarities and identities among the customs of different members of particular societies. Not only will the Dani, Oklia, tell us that the military alliance to which his village belongs has a most influential person or "big man," but so will Asikhandedlek and other Dani. It is the custom of all normal Dani to be aware of the presence of such persons in their society and to make utterances which reveal that awareness when there is an occasion for it. It is customary for Dani to recognize the presence of such influentials and to subject themselves to their authority.

Any social custom or, alternatively, cultural trait, is composed of the individual customs of people who behave in such closely similar ways that observers regard their customs as identical, or, at least, so closely similar that they belong to the same category. Whatever else it is, *a cultural trait is a set of customs of different individuals that are experienced as being closely similar or identical.* The total lifeway or culture of a human society is composed of all these sets of personal customs—that is, all the cultural traits of the group in question. This, basically, is what we mean when we speak of Miskito culture, Nuer culture, or any other culture. There are other important things to be said about the nature of cultural phenomena, but these elementary points are foundational and necessary to remember if our abstractions about culture are to kept sufficiently anchored to how humans characteristically experience one another.

THE ESSENTIAL NATURE OF CULTURAL PHENOMENA

A difficulty in defining culture has emerged because of our realization that people who are performing various actions and utterances do so because of something inside them. When Dani rub pig fat on themselves, it is the immediate result of their ideas of doing so and the associated mental and/or physiological skills. They may have learned their ideas and skills about applying pig fat from seeing others do it and hearing what they say about it, but we are not concerned here with why ideas and behaviors become part of one's makeup, but why people repeat actions and utterances. At the given moment they perform the custom, the Dani do not think of rubbing on pig fat as the result of their act of rubbing it on. It is the other way around. People repeat actions and utterances because they carry within them conscious and unconscious mental and physiological traces or forces that have continuity through time, and when a person is appropriately stimulated, those traces are the immediate source of the actions and utterances that we observe.

In line with this, some suggest that cultural traits are essentially multi-individual (social) ideas (Barnett 1953:110), and many anthropologists (especially cognitive anthropologists) now like to define a group's culture as a "design for living" or a set of conscious and unconscious rules that govern the people's behavior and reactions to the world. Of course, no one sees, feels, or hears these designs or rules. Since they reside within people's minds, we only infer their existence by observing repeated actions of the body and hearing repeated utterances that are similar from one society member to another. Other anthropologists feel that culture must be defined to include what we can experience empirically (by the senses) rather than through what we must infer from what we observe, and definitions of culture as learned and shared behavior are common. In addition to mental forces and behaviors, there are *artifacts,* the material objects, such as arrows and automobiles, that result from some sets of actions. Accordingly, we can distinguish three categories of phenomena that have been included in various definitions of culture: ideas (or other internal forces), behaviors (actions and utterances), and artifacts. The view favored in this book is that whether or not behaviors and artifacts are included in culture, the internal, learned mental and physiological conditions which cause them and which must be inferred from them are the essential elements of culture. These may be ideas, motivations, and the like of which we are conscious, or they may include internally carried mental rules or physiological skills that we are not conscious of. An observer's concepts of their existence can be formed only from sensing their manifestations, which may be called *empirical indicators* of customs. These empirical indicators are *actions, utterances,* and *artifacts.* We learn that Dani have in their minds the idea of rubbing pig fat on their bodies and the learned physiological skills for performing the act by seeing the actions and, perhaps, by hearing Dani talk about them. From actions and utterances we infer the internal mental-physiological continuities they express, and from artifacts we infer the set of acts which produced them and the images and other mental factors which resulted in the actional performances which produced the artifacts.

There is no English noun which covers both conscious and unconscious mental conditions and both mental and physiological factors, although a more flexible term would be helpful. Trait, which indicates a characteristic of something, and the prefix *eso-,* which means "inner," form the word *esotrait,* meaning "inner characteristic" or "internal trait." An esotrait is defined here as any learned, continuous force or condition within a person that is expressed through his or her customary utterances and actions. Different members of a society behave in a number of closely similar ways because they carry within them closely similar eso-traits. The Dani rub their bodies with pig fat because they carry within them closely similar esotraits (ideas and other mental conditions and physiological skills) relating to the desirability and ability to do so. Using the concept of esotrait, a cultural trait may be defined as any set of esotraits of different members of a group whose manifestation observers experience as being closely similar or identical. Some esotraits are peculiar to one person, but many are social, and cultures are composed basically of learned, multi-individual esotraits.

Though few social scientists have adopted the notion that cultural traits are basically multi-individual esotraits, they can still discuss cultural phenomena with those who have accepted the idea by using the neutral terms of *custom* or *cultural trait*. When it is said that lingering to flirt with plantation workers to whom they have brought food is a part of the culture of Miskito girls, one anthropologist may mean the actual behavior and another may mean the multi-individual esotraits that produce the behavior. In this book, the reader may assume that terms such as cultural trait, social custom, or cultural elements refer to multi-individual esotraits.

CUSTOMS IN CONTEXT

We face in anthropology a difficulty that afficts us in our daily lives and troubles the world of science. This problem is that the world of phenomena within which we live and move is very much a unity or continuum, and difficulties result from our attempts to distinguish one thing from another. We have claimed that a group's culture is composed of traits, though anthropologists agree that any culture is a unit or a functioning whole. But in describing and discussing a culture it is impossible for either the anthropologist or a member of the society under study to cope with the whole assemblage at once. A culture must be analyzed, consciously or unconsciously, into parts or elements, an act which forces us to treat those elements as distinct from one another in ways they probably are not in reality. But there is no choice, so we must ask how we identify a cultural trait to distinguish it from other traits in the culture being studied.

The culture trait is commonly thought of as the smallest, most basic element of a culture, but it is important to realize that many cultural elements anthropologists refer to as traits can be subdivided into culturally significant parts which, in turn, might be called cultural traits. The Crow practice of smoking a ceremonial pipe as a symbol of peace would seem to be a minimal unit of culture, but it can be analyzed into several parts meaningful to the Crow, such as the formation of a circle, passing the pipe in a clockwise direction, singing and dancing, and a number of other elements (Lowie 1935:29).

Some anthropologists have suggested that we identify cultural traits as elements that cannot be analyzed into such meaningful parts. This has not proven very useful for the simple reason that people may treat a given element as an indivisible unit in some cases and, under other conditions, may divide it into parts, one or more of which they may regard as indivisible. It is clear that what a cultural trait is depends on how people are viewing it at a given moment. In terms of its scope, then, it seems most useful to distinguish a cultural trait as one which at some time, in some context, is customarily viewed by the people as an indivisible unit. Clearly the scope of a trait is determined by its context at given times rather than by any objective quality of the trait itself.

But another difficulty is that people ordinarily live their culture without thinking about it or analyzing it into elements to any significant degree. In fact, this has proved to be one of the weaknesses of cognitive anthropology. The fact that most of us who have learned English as our native language would have trouble explaining the grammatical rules governing our speech behavior illustrates the problem. The result is that anthropologists are forced to view a culture in some ways that the people themselves do not. They can hope for two things, however; first, that the elements they see as making up a culture correspond to categories the people are aware of or which govern their behavior; and, second, that their conclusions make the behavior more understandable and form a sound basis for generalizations about human nature. This vexing difficulty of anthropological methodology will not be pursued further here, but the student should be aware of it.

Functionalism

A basic doctrine of cultural anthropology is *functionalism*. While the doctrine has taken various forms, its essential feature is the idea that a culture's traits are interrelated with one another and with noncultural factors. In anthropology functionalism is closely associated with Bronislaw Malinowski and A. R. Radcliffe-Brown. Beginning in the 1920s Malinowski vigorously attacked the tendency of some anthropologists to view cultures as little more than aggregations of unrelated traits. He emphasized the importance of explaining any cultural element in terms of its relationship to other elements of the culture and its contribution to the operation of the culture of which it is a part (1944:150). Malinowski also viewed the ultimate function of culture as the satisfaction of biological needs. Radcliffe-Brown also emphasized the contribution made by a custom to the lifeway which it is a part of, but his concern was mainly with how customs contribute to the stability of a system of social relationships and the solidarity of societies (1952:180). Unlike Malinowski, Radcliffe-Brown was uninterested in the relationships of social customs to biological and psychological factors.

In the broad sense, then, functionalism consists of two aspects. One is that *any culture is a system of functionally interdependent parts* rather than a collection of unrelated customs. The other is that *any culture is a component of a larger system* that includes features of alien cultures and, also, biological, habitat, and population characteristics. In more current terms, the culture is part of an ecosystem (see page 29).

Any system, as noted previously, is a set of interrelated parts that forms a whole. Textures of interdependent customs that illustrate the *systemic* nature of cultures are described in any good ethnography. Heider, in fact, stated that his purpose was to write a holistic description of Dani culture—an exploration of the interrelationships of traits within Dani culture (1970:3). Both ritual warfare (a complex of customs) and belief in ghosts were major elements of Dani culture when Karl Heider studied the people in the 1960s. These two elements were linked to one another by the Dani beliefs that the ghosts would be angry if they did not kill an enemy and the angry ghosts would afflict them with poor health, economic misfortune, and, perhaps, death (1970:130). Warfare also was interdependent with land use, since the Dani were unable to use cultivable land in the broad strips of no-man's-land between enemy alliances. Marriage was affected by the death rate of males in war, which, in combination with the ideal of polygyny, resulted in a large percentage of the men having more than one wife. Political leadership was interdependent with war in that no one could become a leader without proving himself in battle.

As anthropologists trace the links from one custom to another, they are led into various areas of the total lifeway. The traditional division of cultures into aspects such as technology, economics, social organization, political organization, religion, art, education, and the like is an artificial device for organizing the great diversity of customs in any culture for purposes of description. Because it is artificial—a set of etic categories, in fact—classification obscures the indivisibility of cultures as whole systems. In the foregoing example the tracing of intracultural links led from war to religious beliefs, a techno-economic factor, a social practice, and a political custom. In American society the custom of attending church on Sunday, a religious custom, may be linked to belief in God, another religious custom. But it also may be related to a technique for gaining political influence, that is, by showing oneself to be morally respectable. Attending church may also be linked to educational elements (if one regards religious instruction as an effective avenue to character development) or recreation (if one attends church for the opportunities to socialize). The fundamental point here is that customs put in different aspects of culture by our etic categories may be just as firmly interdependent with one another as customs within the same aspect. This is an elementary point which, nevertheless, is often overlooked in practical affairs. Every element of a culture has a function in relation to some other element in the culture.

Themes

A custom that is related to a significant number of other traits in a given culture is sometimes called a *theme*. A theme may be defined as a multi-individual value or orientation, with or without emotional content, which is linked to a significant plurality of other traits in the culture. Morris E. Opler, who proposed this concept, regarded a theme as a "postulate or position," either implicit or explicit, that usually controls behavior or stimulates activity (1945:198). It seems appropriate to think of themes as linking together the various traits they control and stimulate.

A major theme of the culture of the East African Nuer is their concern with cattle. Not only do they depend on their herds for many of life's necessities, but their entire world view is integrated around their high valuation of cattle. The Nuer risk their lives to defend their herds and to raid those of neighboring societies. Cattle are used to compensate for injuries and killings during disputes. Families and households co-operate with one another to protect and herd their cattle. Marriage involves a bride price of cattle, and every aspect of the marriage ritual is marked by their transfer or sacrifice. Nuer men are named according to the colors and markings of their favorite oxen, and a woman may take a name from a cow that she milks. A Nuer gets in touch with the spirits and ghosts of the dead by rubbing ashes on the back of a cow or ox, and many Nuer ceremonies require the sacrifice of an ox. The Nuer talk so much about their cattle that Evans-Pritchard was sometimes driven to despair that the young men would never talk with him about anything but livestock and women, and even the subject of women inevitably led to a discussion of cattle (1940:19).

A major theme of American culture is the acquiring of weath and the material signs of economic success. American readers will have little difficulty thinking of examples: driving late model cars, attending a fashionable church, living in a fine house, and many others. That some have questioned this value does not alter its dominance in the thoughts of many Americans and its great influence on their daily lives.

One of the most impressive aspects of cultural variability is that societies differ greatly in what themes they emphasize. In her widely read classic, *Patterns of Culture,* Ruth Benedict suggested that the Plains Indian cultures manifested a *Dionysian* quality, in contrast with the *Apollonian* orientation of the Pueblo tribes of the American Southwest. The Plains tribes, she said, emphasized emotional and physical exuberance, excess aggressiveness, and reckless activism (1934:79). Fasting and torture were used to bring on supernatural visions; men gained prestige by daring and reckless risking of their lives in war; death resulted in uninhibited and prolonged expression of grief. But the Hopi and other Pueblo groups emphasized emotional control and moderation in all aspects of life.

Many anthropologists think Benedict went too far in leaving the impression that a whole culture might be dominated by a single theme or *ethos*. It is now felt that there are few cultures in which a single theme prevails over all others; most cultures manifest several themes of varying importance. In Lipan Apache culture, for example, Opler discovered twenty major themes. Benedict also gave insufficient attention to the presence of Apollonian elements in some aspects of Plains Indian life and evidences of aggression and conflict in Pueblo life. Nevertheless, she called attention to the significant cultural differences in ethos and world view and stimulated wide interest in anthropology.

Reasons for Interdependence

As previously indicated, members of a society under study may not view their culture as consisting of the same customs that the ethnographer perceives. Yet they distinguish items of belief or behavior from one another and, implicitly or explicitly, relate them to one another. Samoans, for example, entertain in their minds the concept of long life and, undoubtedly, can discuss it in various contexts. They also have the notion of hard work, and most of them explicitly relate hard work to great longevity (Holmes 1974:89). The anthropologist's concepts of hard work and long life as separate elements of Samoan culture, as well as the idea that they are functionally linked to one another, apparently matches the Samoan view well. But Marshall's statement to the effect that the !Kung of southern Africa avoid exchanging insults and sexual jokes with relatives on their parents' generation and their children's generation cannot be said to match the !Kung view. Using the etic category, generation difference, the statement is true enough, but it is not part of !Kung culture to distinguish joking and generation differences as customs and conceive of them as interdependent with one another (Marshall 1976:208). So, when anthropologists discuss functional relationships among customs the linkages will sometimes be between customs distinguished by the anthropologist rather than by the people. If the people were social scientists trying to analyze and understand their own culture, they might develop analyses similar to those of the anthropologist, but much of any culture goes unanalyzed by those who participate in it.

Whether or not customs and their connections in the culture are recognized by a people, many relationships among cultural traits are "just there" in the sense that no particular reason for them can be found. No one remembers how the customs became interdependent, and they are related to one another merely as a part of a person's cultural heritage. In Samoan culture cooking has traditionally been a male activity (Holmes 1974:48). While this seems linked to the role of a men's association as servants to the chiefs, there is no way to establish for sure why men rather than women cook for chiefs, or why their cooking prerogatives include household as well as ceremonial cooking. Most of the customs of all cultures, including the ways they are interdependent, have resulted from specific circumstances and events in the culture's history which are unrecoverable (see page 36–37).

Extracultural *physical interdependence* is among the most obvious causes for relationships among customs. In some cases there is direct contact between artifacts. There is an obvious linkage between the Dani's knowledge of techniques for binding an arrowhead in its shaft and their idea of the shape of the arrowhead. Their ideas about these items are governed by the relationships among the materials themselves. In other cases interdependence is a matter of space-time relations without contact. In the United States, for example, there is a linkage between air transportation and major league baseball scheduling. It is possible for baseball teams three thousand miles apart to maintain acceptable game schedules.

A second explanation for relationships among customs seems to be the existence of *psychological tendencies or forces common to the inherited nature of people everywhere.* People's minds appear to be so constituted that under specific circumstances they tend to make certain associations. It seems natural, for example, for humans to assume connections between things or events experienced as similar to one another. For instance, many groups appear to see a relationship between sexual intercourse and the fertility of plants, animals, and humans. Roscoe reported that after having sown seed, a woman of the Nyoro would have sexual intercourse with her husband that night to make the seed germinate (1923:202).

There also is a universal tendency for behavior toward relatives to be linked to the terms used for them. Among the Nyoro of Africa not only does a male refer to his male parent as his father, but the term includes the father's brothers as well. A Munyoro is expected to respect his father. He does not use his father's personal name, may not sit on a chair or stool in his father's presence, may not whistle in his father's presence, and so forth. Such treatment applies also to his other fathers (Beattie 1957:330). There appears to be something about human psychological makeup that disposes people to behave in similar ways toward persons called by the same term, and under some circumstances to call people toward whom they behave in similar ways by a common term. It is of great importance to understand that this sort of thing does not imply genetic inheritance of specific cultural traits. Linkages of this kind are merely evidence of inherited tendencies, which may find specific cultural manifestations in diverse forms and which may be weakened or cancelled by other influences.

Social interdependence is another major cause of linkages between traits. Linking customs and other traits originate and are maintained because people must establish satisfactory ways of dealing with one another to achieve their goals. In the Samoan village of Fitiuta the custom by which untitled men share their income with the extended family as a whole is linked to the practice of having a titled man of high prestige and responsibility as head of the extended family. The relationship is maintained by the fact that serving the family by making donations is a form of service which the contributors hope will qualify them to be selected as a family head in the future (Holmes 1974:23). Social interdependence binds the customs to one another.

Many cultural traits are linked into complexes because they *occur in the same context*. The customs brought into play at a machinist's lathe may be linked in the minds of machinists and others because they occur in the same context. Or consider the tavern drinking complex among some Americans. Elements of this complex include always having a drink in front of you, taking turns paying for rounds of drinks, adapting the drinking pace to that of the person who has paid for the drinks, playing games to determine who will pay, regulation of the behavior of other regular patrons, and a number of other features (Clinard 1962:282). Both participants and observers may be expected to experience these elements as interdependent.

A fifth way that customs may become linked is through their *contributions to the same goal*. They become linked in the minds of a society's members through recognition that they help reach an objective or complete a task. In our own society there is a courtship complex of many specific traits which may be considered interrelated because they have to do with winning a spouse. The customs in a courtship complex vary from generation to generation and from one American subculture to another, but in each time and group they are associated in people's minds because they have to do with winning a spouse.

In describing cultures, social scientists also group customs into complexes because they see them as contributing to some goal they envision. The institutions dealt with by sociologists, such as education, the family, economics, and the like, and the basically similar aspects of culture into which the anthropologists divide their written descriptions of cultures appear to be vast complexes of customs linked with one another around what the describer sees as basic purposes in the life of societies everywhere. These institutions and aspects, however, are etic concepts that ordinarily do not coincide with categories people in most cultures are aware of. The linking goals are largely imposed by the social scientist to order the data.

Form Associated Linkage

In every society the people carry in their minds perceptions of their artifacts and behaviors. For example, Americans share with one another mental images of the form of a Frisbee, the aerodynamically shaped plastic disk that many Americans use to play catch. The Nuer share with one another the image of the spear. The images of these forms are part of American and Nuer cultures, respectively.

In all cultures there are other customs attached to or related to such form esotraits. In some cases the form may have been invented to accomplish some purpose in the people's minds; in other cases certain uses, consequences, or meanings associated with the objects may have developed at some time after its invention. In any case, a form and the multi-individual perception of it do not stand alone, but are linked with other esotraits in the people's minds. The prominent anthropologist, Ralph Linton, introduced the idea that a cultural trait may consist of its form, use, function, and meaning (1936:402). Here, instead of aspects of single traits, they are presented as distinct though interrelated customs. Linton proposed the concepts as aids in understanding the significance of a cultural trait for the total culture of which it is a part.

The *use* of any cultural element consists of its intended consequences for things outside the culture—in other words, its effects on noncultural elements of the ecosystem. A Frisbee is used to provide physical activity and psychological release, although it may also be used in a pinch for protecting one's head from rain. The Nuer use spears, among other things, to kill people and to cut notches in the ears of cattle. In fact, the spear is the only thing the Nuer have which cuts (Evans-Pritchard 1956:233).

A *function* is the consequence of the use of an artifact or the practice of a behavior for an element within the culture in question. The image of the form which the people share is related to another esotrait through this consequence. One of the functions of the Frisbee is to satisfy American cultural desires such as having something to do at a picnic and relaxation between stints of sedentary effort, while the Nuer spear functions as an object to brandish as a man delivers an oration to a deity. Thus picnicking and work breaks are associated with the image of the Frisbee, and ceremonial speechmaking is linked to the idea of the spear.

A *meaning* is an implicit or subjective association of a form esotrait. For many Americans the Frisbee seems to symbolize readiness to have fun at a moment's notice; to be willing to take a break from onerous responsibilities rather than to be a slave to work. In line with this meaning, a Frisbee is something that can be taken into many situations, since it is easy to stow in a bag or on a nearby shelf for retrieval as needed. For some Americans the meaning of the Frisbee is irresponsibility, since they conceive of hippies and others who do not work regularly or who are not highly productive economically as the ones who use Frisbees most. For the Nuer the meaning of the spear is masculine strength, virility, and vitality.

To sum up, then, not only do cultures include ideas about forms, but also multi-individual ideas about the uses to which the forms are put, ideas about the functions or consequences of using the forms in various

Figure 3–2 *American university student playing with Frisbee on his way to class. A meaning* is *an implicit or subjective association of a form esotrait. For many Americans the Frisbee seems to symbolize readiness to have fun at a moment's notice.*

ways, and implicit and explicit feelings about the meanings or significance of those forms. Description of a culture in these terms can do much to reveal its wholeness as a system of interrelated elements.

CULTURES AND INTRACULTURAL DIFFERENCES

The discussion of cultural traits (see page 48), revealed that each is a category of individual customs, that the individual customs that make up each social custom are actually slightly different from person to person, and that they are regarded as the same custom because they are so closely similar that they appear identical or so little different that the variation is insignificant. These differences that people ignore for the sake of talking about what groups are like may become recognized cultural differences within societies. If one person's way of doing something differs sufficiently from that of others, they may brand him as eccentric or idiosyncratic. But if others begin to behave in closely similar ways, the custom is no longer an idiosyncrasy: it has become multi-individual, and therefore, cultural. Multi-individual customs also differ in certain important ways from one custom to another. Certain significant aspects of this intra-cultural variation from person to person and from custom to custom comprise the topic of this section.

Universals, Alternatives, and Specialties

Anthropologists are more keenly aware now than before that even small-scale cultures are not uniform; there are individual and subgroup differences in the body of custom of every group. Relatively early recognition of this is seen in Ralph Linton's threefold distinction among cultural traits in terms of who participates in them (1936:273), a scheme that has been rather widely used in the social sciences. *Universals* are customs practiced by all normal adult members of a society. *Alternatives* are traits that people can choose among, for example, different modes of transportation or different kinds of footwear. *Specialties* are customs associated with a particular subcategory of people. For example, there are customs associated with being a woman, man, child, policeman, carpenter, canoe maker, medicine man, or a military society member.

There are probably few true universals in any culture. The easiest example is probably that of linguistic customs. Presumably all the Miskito of Asang, Nicaragua engage in many of the same linguistic habits. And apparently all or nearly all of the Miskito attribute special significance to dreams (Helms 1971:186). But it is useless to try to determine from most ethnographies which customs are truly universal. Since it is impossible to examine completely the personal customs of every member of the society, the investigator cannot be sure. The significant point is that some customs are especially consequential because they are practiced by nearly everyone in the group.

Cognitive Diversity

The research of cognitive anthropologists has revealed even greater intracultural diversity than can be fully covered by Linton's scheme. As they sought to determine what exeriences people included in various semantic domains cognitive anthropologists learned that they might contradict themselves from one time to another and that there might be several different views of the scope of a domain in the same society. Eleanor Heider's research on the color system of the Dani nicely indicates the nature of this diversity. Only 20 percent of her informants used a color term roughly equivalent to the English term "red," 45 percent used a term designating "yellow," 28 percent had a term for blue, and 23 percent used all three terms (E. Heider 1972:451). There were also a number of terms used by only one person. Heider also found that the Dani did not fully realize that they differed in their color terminology. Informants tended to believe that all other Dani used the same terms they did. In one instance a husband and wife argued about whether certain terms could be used for various colors, and each appeared to be surprised at the other's opinions.

Covertness and Overtness

A culture's customs differ from one another in the ease with which their existence can be detected accurately by an outside observer or a member of the society not familiar with a given trait. A custom is highly *overt* if it is manifested in artifacts that are kept in public view or in actions and utterances that are performed with sufficient frequency that the observer has plenty of opportunity to experience them. The headband worn by some American young men to keep their long hair in place is a good example. A person seeing the headband immediately forms a mental image of it which is undoubtedly very similar to that in the mind of the wearer. As for behavior, it does not take an outsider long to learn that cattle are highly valued by the Nuer, since they constantly talk about their cattle and direct many of their actions toward them.

In all cultures, however, many traits are highly *covert*. This may apply particularly to ideas that can be communicated only by utterances, notably abstract ideas that are difficult to express and, perhaps, are expressed infrequently. Such customs are among the last detected by field anthropologists, or they may never discover some of them. They also may be the last and most difficult of the native customs to be learned by a child or young person. The meanings and functions related to artifacts and other forms are among these customs. Heider's investigation of ritual warfare among the Dani indicated its great importance: the Dani had to kill the enemy to maintain good relationships with the ghosts, since the ghosts would afflict the people until they righted matters by killing an enemy in revenge for the slaying of a member of the group. Heider felt that there would be an increase in ghost anxiety, within-group fighting, and suicides when the Dutch authorities forced the Dani to stop their fighting. He was wrong, however. The Dani's ritual warfare did not have the intensity of meaning the ethnographer had supposed (K. Heider 1970:123). The difficulty stemmed in part from Heider's great difficulty in getting the Dani to share fully about their warfare. Much of the meaning and function of this easily observable ritual activity was covert, making it difficult to determine its full nature and strength.

Implicitness and Explicitness

A custom is *explicit* if the people are aware of its existence and can talk about it. If they are unaware or only dimly aware of its existence, it is strongly *implicit*. Implicitness and explicitness concern the experience of the people possessing the custom, while covertness and overtness have to do with the view of the observer. The Nuer interest in cattle is both overt (easy for an observer to detect) and explicit. The Nuer are clearly aware of their interest and can be very explicit in expressing the importance of cattle. Members of every society are strongly aware of and can be highly explicit about many of their customs.

Every culture also consists of many learned, multi-individual esotraits of which the people are not aware, and they often are unaware of many of the actions and utterances by which they express those esotraits. Evans-Pritchard suggests that the Nuer are only dimly aware or, in some instances, wholly unaware of some of the deeper symbolism of the spear (1956:252). An element of their implicit culture appears to be a left-right polarity based on the association of the spear with the right hand. Evans-Pritchard was not told this by the Nuer, presumably because of their low level of awareness of it. The principle emerged as he discovered that the Nuer erect a sacred pole to the right of the entrance to their windscreens; a Nuer husband sleeps on the right side of the hut; the people identify east with life and the right; a Nuer youth puts the left arm out of action for several months or a year or two by mutilating it, and so on.

Many motor and speech habits also are highly implicit. University lecturers are almost inevitably surprised when they first see a videotape of their lecturing, since people tend to be unaware of many of their habitual mannerisms. Americans are also unaware of their walking modes, and are surprised when an alien visitor comments on how Americans walk. As for linguistic habits, Americans are often astonished when Englishmen tell them that they speak with an accent.

Ideality and Performance in Culture

Every culture consists of many shared notions about what the members of the society in question think and do, or what they ought to think and do. But only some of the customs as actually performed are in harmony with these ideals and rules. Among the nineteenth-century Crow a stable marital relationship marked by deep and enduring emotional attachment was certainly the ideal, and in many cases the ideal was fairly well matched by performance (Lowie 1935:59). Yet the ideal was often violated; there were many cases of trouble in marriage and divorce was frequent. The Miskito of Asang, Nicaragua, regard rice and beans mainly as items to be exchanged for money or foreign goods rather than as food. But they are actually their most important foods, and since they conceive of them primarily as cash crops, they do not grow enough to provide a year-long supply (Helms 1971:139).

It is common for people either to be unaware of or to fail to attend to discrepancies between their rules and ideals and their customary performance. When such contradictions are forced on their attention, they either deny them or rationalize. Within two hours after being told by one of his informants that Dusun of Borneo never beat their wives, the anthropologist saw the same man hit his wife in the face six times, knock her out the door, across the porch and down the steps, where he kicked her repeatedly while she screamed in anger and pain. When the ethnographer asked about the difference between what he said and what he did, the man answered in a way reminiscent of Euroamerican rationalizations, "Well, that is the way we are supposed to do things. This is a special case for she needs to be hit to make her learn" (Williams 1965:91). A similar discrepancy seems to exist in American culture. In spite of the general condemnation of wife-beating, it occurs in many families, and American humor sometimes manifests a fascination with the idea. American audiences roar with laughter when Jackie Gleason (Ralph on "The Honeymooners") threatens to lose his patience someday and hit his wife, Alice, "Pow! Right on the kisser!" But the same Americans who find this amusing may profess abhorrence for the idea of wife-beating.

4

OBTAINING AND PROCESSING CULTURAL DATA

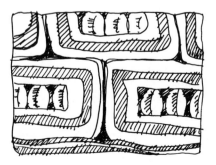

A particular culture consists of all the learned, multi-individual customs of the society, including those which tie them together into a whole cultural system. *Ethnography* is the study of particular cultures by entering living groups, observing their customs, and recording the information for the use of those who generalize about human behavior. Ethnographers carefully observe and record the people's utterances, actions, and artifacts. Among the vast number of empirical indicators observed, the ethnographer must be sure, first, that they are repeated—that is, customary, rather than one-time or aberrant events—and second, that they are multi-individual rather than idiosyncratic.

While in the field ethnographers do all they can to detect customs and learn how they are related to one another. They try to learn how widely spread the customs are in the society. They take into account that many of the customs are either covert to observers or implicit to the people and, consequently, they must make special efforts to detect and understand them. They try to distinguish ideals and rules from performance, since this is so important in understanding human behavior. Ethnographers make some of their decisions about the nature of a culture after leaving the field, but this can be done only if they keep excellent field notes. The anthropologist's ultimate goal as an ethnographer is to prepare a written *ethnography*—a description of the culture he or she has studied that can be used by ethnologists in generalizing about human nature and behavior.

PARTICIPANT OBSERVATION

The basic field methods used by anthropologists are *participant observation* and *interviewing informants*. Participant observation—learning about a culture by participating in the customs to some degree and, while participating, observing—is a cardinal practice of ethnography. This ordinarily means that anthropologists live among the people and make themselves as much like them culturally as they will permit and as is compatible with the maintenance of mental and physical health and scientific objectivity.

Participant observation has several advantages, one of which is that it may help an investigator establish good relationships with the people,

Figure 4–1 *Ethnographer Martin Ottenheimer in Comoro Island Costume. Participant observation —learning about a culture by participating in the customs to some degree and, while participating, observing—is a cardinal practice of ethnography.*

opening channels of communication. Second, by trying to experience the culture as the people do, one gets an inside view not possible otherwise. Finally, by constantly being among the people the ethnographer has opportunity to learn much that would ordinarily be missed. Making close friends and overhearing and participating in a multitude of casual conversations yield a wealth of clues, many of them subtle, by which the investigator can infer the existence of highly covert customs (see page 60).

For several reasons these advantages are never fully realized. For one thing, some groups will not permit participation, or they limit it severely. Second, too much participation may provide poor relationships with some groups, arousing suspicion and inhibiting communication. Third, ethnographers are likely to find participation disturbing. They may experience mental stress as the result of the ambiguity and insecurity of having to live in an unfamiliar cultural environment, a state known as *cultural shock*. Some ethnographers can stand more of this stress than others. A fourth difficulty is that participation (taking local foods and drinks, for example) may adversely affect the anthropologist's physical health. There is no choice but to take some risks, which prompted one writer to characterize anthropologists as people who refuse to believe in the germ theory of disease (Service 1958:v).

Another major difficulty with participant observation is that an investigator may begin to identify with local values and lose the detachment necessary to achieve accurate, objective descriptions of the culture. This is handled by remaining aware of the danger and limiting participation. One effective way to limit participation is to leave the community for a short time, a device that serves also to restore mental or physical health. Many ethnographers have found that an absence improves relationships with the people, since they often are favorably impressed that the anthropologist would return to be with them again.

The nature of the task is such that there are no perfect participant observers, but the advantages are so great that participant observation remains a primary and highly productive ethnographic technique. To minimize disadvantages, investigators explore cautiously, governing their behavior by the people's reactions to their presence and work, as well as according to what they wish to learn about the culture. Anthropologists are not all endowed with equal sensitivity, nor are they all of equal ability in controlling their own prejudices and reactions so as to conduct themselves most effectively. Clearly some anthropologists are better field workers than others, and the value of their reports reflects their abilities. Over the years anthropologists have come to realize this more completely, and increasing numbers are reporting in detail their experiences and modes of operation in the field so that others may more readily evaluate the results. A few illustrations from these reports will elucidate the foregoing points.

The prominent British social anthropologist E. E. Evans-Pritchard found the Nuer of East Africa profoundly hostile, especially since they were, at the time, on poor terms with the British. They would not assist him in any way and refused to provide satisfactory answers to the simplest questions. Evans-Pritchard expressed his frustration by commenting that "after a few weeks of associating solely with the Nuer, one displays, if the pun be allowed, the most evident symptoms of 'Nuerosis' " (1940:13). Between 1930 and 1936 Evans-Pritchard managed to accumulate a year of residence among the Nuer, but serious illness during both the 1935 and 1936 trips brought his work to a premature end.

When, eventually, Evans-Pritchard overcame the hostility of the Nuer, effective field work was greaty hindered by their insistence that he live as one of them, a full-fledged member of the community. Such forced intimacy made it impossible for him to escape their everyday life enough to hold confidential interviews with trained informants. He became competent in their language, but the compelled participation meant that information came to him in small fragments and, in spite of the intimacy (or because of it) he learned less about them than he had hoped to. The need for balance between participant observation and other field methods is illustrated by the fact that Evans-Pritchard learned much more about the culture of the Azande, who required him to live as a stranger outside the community, than he did about the Nuer.

Mary Helms had to limit her participation in Miskito culture for somewhat different reasons. As a woman she had limited access to studying the activities of men, and as a single woman she was culturally defined as a subadult in some respects and not expected to involve herself in the full range of home and village activities. As an English-speaking foreigner, she was thought to be above certain everyday matters, such as working in the fields, lagoon fishing, and so on. When her participation in things defined as improper to her position as an unmarried American women threatened to affect adversely her relationships with the Miskito, Helms had no choice but to curb it (1971:3).

Some anthropologists enjoy and can achieve greater participation than others. In referring to his work among the Kaska, a hunting and trapping Indian group in the cold interior of northern British Columbia, John Honigmann commented on the great personal satisfaction of the experience: "Both my wife and I were caught up in another culture as we never have been again. . . . My chief pleasure lay in actively participating in the Indians' cultural activities. . . ." (1970:45, 50). He accepted invitations to home-brew parties and crashed them with his Indian companions when not invited. He wore moccasins and bought snowshoes, fish, and game. He helped the Kaska set fish nets and repair houses, visited them extensively, exchanged Christmas gifts with some, and participated in their stick gambling. Often, he assumed leadership roles, such as organizing a dance, and frequently he made known his opinions about recreational plans. He also came to hold many of the same points of view as those he was studying. He was so deeply and personally involved that leaving the community was, in his words, "acutely painful." The contrast with Evans-Pritchard's experience with the Nuer is apparent. In spite of the depth of his personal involvement, Honigmann indicated that his research among the Kaska was the most ethnographically productive he had done. His work among them formed the basis for a widely used ethnography, *Culture and Ethos of Kaska Society*.

Honigmann was explicit about the possible personal reasons for his favorable reaction to the Kaska lifeway. He noted that he may have been working off some rebellion against his own culture and that there were, perhaps, other personal needs met by the experience. Such personal involvement is unavoidable in participant observation, and to the extent that ethnographers deny it, they cut themselves off from the necessity for controlling it and reducing its distorting effects on their field data.

INTERVIEWING

Participant observation remains of basic importance, but it is time-consuming, and it fails to reveal some things the ethnographer does not have the opportunity to observe. Many things in a culture are covert and can be detected and understood adequately only by questioning people who have relationships of mutual trust with the ethnographer. Also, the ethnographer must depend on informants to learn about things that occur infrequently, perhaps only at certain times of year, or only at certain places not easily accessible to the investigator.

A number of principles are observed in informant use. For one thing, it is important to use multiple informants so that their statements can be compared and any discrepancies checked or clues gotten from one person can be explored with another. A second principle is that the informants should represent various ages, both sexes, and other categories of the society. Third, it is important to check the internal consistency of a given informant's testimony, since there are a number of reasons that informants give anthropologists false information. Informants, for example, some- times tell ethnographers what they think they want to hear. Or, like the Nuer, they may think the questions are none of the anthropologist's business. There are also informants who take pleasure in fooling anthro- pologists. It is said that informants in one community delighted in getting the ethnographer drunk and regaling her with all kinds of false stories, some of which may have found their way into her ethnography.

Another reason for checking an informant's statements against one another is that it may reveal contradictions between ideals and rules on one hand, and performance, on the other. Anthropologists often find that an informant's generalizations are out of harmony with his or her descrip- tions of events. In such cases the task is to determine whether a generaliza- tion is a shared ideal or rule, therefore part of the culture, or just an idio- syncratic falsification. Lowie's Crow informants emphasized bravery above all else, and told him of what an honor it was to be elected an officer of the Foxes, Lumpwoods, or other military association, since it required them to be especially brave and distinguished them from the rank and file by certain emblems and standards of honor. But the same men who had distinguished themselves this way, apparently unaware of the contradiction, told of how they begged to be excused when selected for the honor of office (Lowie 1959:54). In this case, Lowie found, the practice of avoiding a high honor which gave the warrior a chance to display his courage by risking death in battle did not harmonize with the professions of bravery because the Crow also highly valued long life.

If informants understand and accept it, the anthropologist may take complete notes in their presence. Beattie apparently had little difficulty in this respect with the Nyoro, many of whom were educated and literate. Often, however—and this is most frequently true of those situations in which much participation is demanded—the ethnographer must keep the notebook out of sight or take sketchy notes in casual fashion so as not to destroy rapport. Many anthropologists have resorted to heavy reliance on their memories, escaping to a latrine or elsewhere at the earliest feasible time to get information recorded before forgetting it. In a few cases the issue is more than the danger of destroying good rapport: the whole field project could end suddenly if it became known that notes were taken.

For the same reason that caution may be necessary with the use of a notebook, it is often impossible to go through a list of questions with an informant or to use anything like a sociological schedule. Beattie was able to use questionnaires among the Nyoro (1965:37), but in many societies such a procedure dries up the flow of information, or the informant intentionally gives false information. Heider attempted to question Dani informants systematically, but the yield was small (K. Heider 1970:18). The Dani are not introspective, and they learn their culture more by observation than from instruction. Heider was given much freedom to observe, however, and he spent much of his time sitting in the people's homes and gardens, watching them and listening to their conversations. Many anthropologists use questionnaires and schedules to permit statistical treatment of their data when they can, but often the only alternative is to engage in casual conversation with informants, trying to follow up crucial points when they appear and, for the rest, taking what comes.

Ethnographers who use the ethnosemantic approach of cognitive anthropology employ *controlled eliciting* techniques with their informants. Using controlled eliciting the ethnographer asks questions that are taken from the language of the culture under study and are selected so as to avoid the imposition of etic categories. They are designed to elicit responses from the informants which reflect or reveal their own categories of thought and the criteria they use to distinguish those categories. The first step is to ask general questions to discover what semantic domains are meaningful to the informants, then the ethnographer can proceed to the more specific questions about those domains. *Structural questions* reveal how the informants classify things together into categories (Spradley and McCurdy 1972:67). Once the ethnographer has determined that "supernatural" is a meaningful category, it is appropriate to ask the structural question, "What different kinds of supernaturals are there?" The answer or answers (since a series of questions may be needed to elicit all kinds of supernaturals) may be "souls," "spirits," "demons," and "gods" (Frake 1964:117). *Attribute questions* are designed to elicit the criteria by which people distinguish among categories. An appropriate attribute question would be, "What is the difference between a 'soul' and a 'spirit?' " By such eliciting procedures the ethnograper learns of the culture's semantic domains, how they are ordered into taxonomies, and how the people distinguish the categories.

OTHER TECHNIQUES AND PROBLEMS

The foregoing review of a few important principles and problems of the two basic ethnographic techniques, participant observation and interviewing informants, provides some notion of how ethnographic data come to us. As increasing numbers of anthropologists have practiced ethnography, they have learned from failures and successes of the past. Now, not only are participant observation and informant use conducted with greater sophistication, but additional and related approaches have been refined. A complete account of all the problems and techniques of field work is not attempted here, but a few more matters of interest are noted.

Length of Term

An ethnographer usually tries to spend at least a year in the field to learn about the many customs of only seasonal occurence. Frequently, field workers have only a year's leave for their research, although they prefer a longer time since the first weeks or months are rarely as productive as later periods. Unless the ethnographer has worked in a community before there must be a period of getting settled, establishing good relationships, and acquiring adequate language proficiency. If, as sometimes happens, six months takes care of most of this activity, a total of at least eighteen months is needed for adequate observation of the year's cultural cycle.

This time frame represents ideal minimums. Every culture is so complex that much will remain unobserved and unrecorded after only a year's effective investigation. In spite of such limitations, the techniques of ethnography are so superior to those of casual observation that in a few months an anthropologist can acquire more reliable information about a culture than some administrators, missionaries, or others who have spent decades with a people.

Gathering Nonsensitive Data

Ethnographers often collect relatively nonsensitive data to establish good rapport or, at least, to minimize the chances of suspicion and hostility. *Village mapping* brings familiarity with the locations of dwellings and other places people frequent and the routes they use, and the investigator inevitably observes new things and comes into contact with many people in this way.

Census-taking, like mapping, provides a way of contacting many people, giving the ethnographer a better knowledge of the kinds of people who live in the community. This is valuable information for locating informants and making other decisions. The technological, economic, demographic, and other information obtained this way is susceptible to statistical treatment.

Artifact study is usually a good nonsensitive technique. Many people appreciate an outsider's interest in the objects they make with their hands, and such study may establish relationships with people who later may also provide information about religion, sexual behavior, and other sensitive topics.

Language study is similar in its effect to artifact study, since people often appreciate efforts to learn their language. This places them in an enjoyable teaching role in relation to the ethnographer. So the ethnographer's need to learn the local language supports the need to establish good relationships with the people. In fact, language study is a major form of participant observation.

The *genealogical method* involves interviewing informants to find out who their relatives are, how they are related to them, and by what term they refer to each kind of relative. In many societies, though not in all, informants are interested in supplying such information. When used with a number of informants, this method can enable a student of kinship to work out the system by which the people classify their relatives. This system supplies important clues to how relatives behave toward one another.

Collecting biographies and autobiographies has been used by a number of ethnographers, since it is not unusual to find people willing to relate their life story. Since any individual's personality is significantly similar to those of many other members of the society, life histories provide rich and vivid views of people participating in their culture.

Psychological Testing

Rorschach ink blot tests, Thematic Apperception Tests, and other projective tests provide a means to obtain information about implicit or covert aspects of personality and culture. In such tests subjects are presented with a stimulus sufficiently ambiguous to prompt them to use their imaginations in trying to give meaning to blots, figures, or pictures. In 1961 Kaplan estimated that projective tests had been used in about seventy-five societies (1961:235), but a number of difficult-to-resolve questions have resulted in a decline in their use. Many of the issues involve difficulties of interpreting the data and questions as to whether the test results can be usefully compared from culture to culture.

Audiovisual Techniques

Still pictures, movie films, and tape recordings are of great value in reporting a society's customs to others, provided they are well integrated with written descriptions. Audiovisual devices, however, are no substitute for human observers in gathering cultural information. Ethnographers can listen to tapes and look at pictures to find things they might otherwise overlook, but this is miniscule compared to what cameras and tape recorders miss. The eyes and ears of a trained human detect a range of stimuli, many of them extremely subtle, that cannot be approached by machines.

Written Records

Ethnographers increasingly find themselves working where written documents are available. Records of various kinds have been kept on a number of nonliterate and peasant groups, in some cases since early colonial days. In studying the Nyoro, Beattie used mission records, government reports, police files, coroner's reports, reports of court proceedings, and other official records. From the court records he obtained valuable data on sorcery, witchcraft, marriage disputes, divorce, inheritance, debt, Nyoro moral and legal norms, and the like (Beattie 1965:35). Anthropologists often work where newspapers and other publications with articles of value appear. Another field activity, then, may be development of a file of written sources.

Cooperative Research

There has long been a kind of romanticism attached to the anthropologist who goes off alone to study the customs of some remote society.

Figure 4–2   *Ethnographer Richard B. Lee, student of !Kung Culture. A most successful example of continuing cooperative research is that of the Kalahari Research Group. The work was begun by anthropologists Richard Lee and Irvine DeVore in 1963.*

But with increase in the numbers of anthropologists and improved appreciation of the merits of restudies and cooperation, joint research projects have become more common. A number of ethnographers use student assistants, which both increases the number of observations and provides training for students. In other cases anthropologists of somewhat different areas of specialization have cooperated in the study of a single society. A most successful example of continuing cooperative research is that of the Kalahari Research Group. The work was begun by anthropologists Richard Lee and Irvine Devore in 1963, and between then and 1976 at least sixteen investigators, most of them anthropologists, pursued various studies among the !Kung. Members of the group have published over a hundred articles, and a book-length treatment of their work was published in 1976 (Lee and DeVore).

A common practice that has long been used is hiring members of the group being studied, or a culturally related group, and training them as field assistants. This approach proved of considerable value to Beattie in his study of the Nyoro (1965:27).

ETHNOGRAPHY AND THEORY

Sometimes field work has been regarded as nothing more than the collection of cultural facts, but anthropologists are now quite aware that some kind of theory or orientation toward the field task, explicit or implicit, is always present and influences the nature of all investigation. If ethnographers regard themselves as fact-collectors ungoverned by the goal of testing a hypothesis, this view is itself a theoretical orientation, one which many feel has led to describing cultures as though they were collections of unrelated customs. In contrast, Karl Heider, governed by the theoretical assumption that every culture is a wholistic system—a unity—sought to discover how Dani customs were interrelated (1970:3). Theoretical positions governing the data-collection process are often stated (as Heider does) in the introductory chapter, and a final section may state the implications of the research results for theoretical positions taken.

A major theoretical position underlying much of the research of cognitive anthropologists is that a culture is a set of rules reflected in a society's semantic domains and how they are organized. Others, including several cognitive anthropologists, have suggested that there are problems with this theoretical position, since accumulating evidence shows that many linguistic categories are not as neatly distinguishable from one another or as clearly organized as some have believed (M. Harris 1974b). This probably varies from one aspect of life to another, but there are no linguistic terms for some concepts and percepts that influence people's behavior, many categories and criteria for defining them are quite fuzzy and changeable in people's minds, and members of the same society often disagree about them. The theory that cultures are rather ambiguous, loosely organized, and extensively implicit systems results in rather different field approaches than the view that most of the culture is semantically and systemically neat. Many anthropologists have begun to work on the development of better ways of studying intracultural variation and the ambiguity and implicitness of the conceptual categories that govern human behavior. Perchonock and Werner, for example, found the conventional eliciting techniques of ethnoscience inadequate in the study of Navajo concepts of food. So they developed a card-sorting technique that revealed some of the overlapping of categories and application of similar criteria in more than one area of life (1969). Changing theories of the nature of culture will continue to affect ethnographic techniques.

Comparison and Generalization

Anthropologists must go beyond accurate emic descriptions of cultures. They must compare cultures in order to generalize, and comparison requires etic categories that can be applied cross-culturally. One of the major devices for comparing cultures is the Human Relations Area Files, which includes cultural data on over 300 societies. These data are classified into over eighty general categories, which are further subdivided to yield a total of some 600 specific categories of cultural phenomena. Among the general categories are language, finance, property, fine arts, armed forces, death, sex, socialization, and living standards and routines. Some of the specific categories under the latter heading are sleeping, elimination, postures, and leisure-time activities (Murdock 1971). The files are organized according to the numbered categories, with the file for each culture containing the relevant pages from the books and articles on that culture. If a scholar wishes to compare postures in a number of societies, for example, it is only necessary to locate the numbered category for postures for each culture.

The most adequate generalizations must be based on a truly representative sample of all known cultures, and as it stands, the Human Relations Area File does not constitute such a sample. Consequently, the Cross-Cultural Cumulative Coding Center , which uses the Human Relations Area Files material, has been established at the University of Pittsburgh (Murdock and White, 1969). Murdock and White considered it important to divide the approximately 1,250 cultures on which data are available into clusters of those so similar to one another culturally that a representative world sample should include only one culture from each cluster. After some additional refinements, the world was divided into 200 sampling provinces, twenty-four of which could not be drawn on for various reasons. From the remaining provinces the best described and/or most distinctive culture was selected to be part of a standard world sample of 186 cultures. Naroll and his associates developed a sixty-culture sample based on geographical factors and the quality of the ethnographic literature, which is known as the Human Relations Area Files Probability Sample Files (Lagacé 1977:vi). Basically it is a sample of the world's preindustrial, rural cultures.

The difficulties of constructing and using a representative sample of the world's cultures for statistical testing of hypotheses about human culture are so complex and formidable that many anthropologists have serious reservations about the use of the two just mentioned. But efforts to solve these difficulties continue, and studies employing the samples are useful to anthropological efforts to compare cultures and generalize about humankind.

A common approach in many studies is simply to test hypotheses using a sample of cultures for which sufficient data are available. Kang wanted to test the widespread theory that, in those societies in which people belong to a variety of groups and social categories, the resulting conflicts of loyalty insure a low level of feuding and such internal troubles. The idea is that an individual who belongs to different groups or categories with contrary goals and interests will behave in ways which promote resolution of disputes and the maintenance of law and order. If this is true the frequency of feuding should be low in societies characterized by such divided loyalties. Kang chose to test the notion by using an already existing feuding sample of fifty societies, some of which are included in the Human Relations Area Files and some of which are not (1976:203). The results of the statistical testing showed no significantly lower incidence of feuding in societies with many conflicting loyalties than in those with few. The findings based on this comparison, then, require anthropologists to rethink and reformulate their hypotheses about the causes of law and order. This kind of comparative activity, whether statistically based as in this instance or not, illustrates the anthropological use of the material collected through ethnography.

5

LANGUAGE
IN CULTURE

Every natural language is a functioning aspect of some culture. Speech customs are learned just as surely as other kinds of cultural traits, and they are shared rather than solely individual. A language occupies a special place in its culture, however, since it is the vehicle by which people transmit most of the culture to those of their own and succeeding generations. Many implicit customs are transmitted mainly by certain kinds of actions, but most multi-individual esotraits probably are or can be expressed by utterances.

The human mind and vocal apparatus are such that a great diversity of languages exists; moreover, all human groups have the biological equipment for learning any language in existence. As a result, linguistic phenomena can be understood best by considering the range and variety of languages in all kinds of cultures. The following review does not attempt to teach techniques of linguistic analysis. Technical concepts and data are introduced only enough to show how cultures vary from one another in the linguistic customs used in social interaction.

MICROLINGUISTICS

Linguists, linguistic anthropologists, and others have long been interested in describing the sound and grammatical features of languages and comparing them to classify languages and study their historical development and relationships. The former endeavor is called *descriptive linguistics,* and the latter is *comparative* and *historical linguistics*. Both are aspects of what the linguistic anthropologist George Trager has proposed to call *microlinguistics*.

Many of the peoples studied by anthropologists lack writing systems, so the most effective way to study cultures is to learn the native language and use it. This field practice has led anthropologists to study the sounds and combinations of sounds in many languages and how they are employed to communicate. Descriptive linguistics, therefore, is part of both anthropology and general linguistics, and the results of descriptive studies furnish us with a knowledge of how cultures vary from one another linguistically.

Phonological Variation

The sound systems of the world's languages differ from one another both phonetically and phonemically. *Phonetics* has to do with the sounds and categories of sounds that a linguist can distinguish in people's speech, while *phonemics* is concerned with the sound differences that the people under study recognize and which affect the meanings of their utterances. Pike coined the terms *etic* and *emic* by dropping the *phon-* from each and applying *etic* to categories not meaningful to the people under study and *emic* to those that actually operate in their lives (see page 40).

When linguists begin to record the utterances of an unfamiliar language, what they hear is determined by a set of etic sound distinctions and categories they have acquired from their previous experience and training. At the beginning of a study, a linguist has no way of knowing which sound differences are recognized and used by the people and which are not. The only alternative, therefore, is to begin the study using sound distinctions formulated by linguistic science. Using a phonetic alphabet devised by linguists, a linguist records each distinguishable sound that occurs repeatedly in the people's utterances. Each of these basic sounds is called a *phone,* which may be defined as a *minimal unit of sound consistently employed by the speakers of a given language and distinguishable by a linguist from other such sounds in the language.*

English writing is not phonetic; that is, the alphabet does not include a letter for each phone that is used in speech. To study any language, including English and others for which writing systems exist, linguists use a special phonetic alphabet that makes it possible for them to record all the different sounds they hear. In English linguists hear more than one sound that we use the letter *t* for, since the *t* varies according to whether or not a puff of air accompanies it and in other ways. They also will notice and record the glottal stop, which is produced by complete closure of the vocal cords to stop the flow of air through the glottis. The glottal stop is often the first sound in words such as *eat* and *on*.

Some English phones are not found in some other languages, and other languages use sounds not found in English. English uses bilabial stops, such as *b* and *p,* which involve the closing of both lips to stop the flow of air and sound, but not bilabial fricatives. The latter differ from stops in that the lips are not closed tightly enough to stop the flow but are brought close enough together to produce a friction sound as the stream of air passes between them. Some other languages also make use of certain voiceless sounds not found in English. *M* and *n,* for example are "whispered," that is, voiceless, in some languages. Among the voiceless sounds of English are *p, t, k,* and *s,* which may be contrasted with their voiced counterparts, *b, d, g,* and *z.* !Kung and other San languages employ click sounds made with an ingressive air stream and sharp withdrawal of the tongue away from points on the roof of the mouth (Lee and DeVore 1976:xix). The exclamation point in !Kung indicates a click made by sudden retraction of the tongue from the area behind the upper teeth, and there are three other clicks in the !Kung language.

Vowel sounds are etically distinguished by position and shape of the tongue and lips. The long e in words such as *beat* and *see,* used in many languages, is produced with unrounded lips and the front portion of the tongue in a very high position. German and some other languages include a vowel almost like it, different only in that the lips are rounded (pursed) rather than unrounded, giving a quite different quality. Voiceless vowels are also found in a number of languages.

All humans can learn to pronounce phones of other languages by learning how the various organs used in sound production are positioned and by governing their own organs accordingly. Sometimes this can be done by forming a familiar sound differing only slightly from the alien phone and modifying it appropriately. One can learn to produce a voiced bilabial fricative by placing the lips in position for *b,* then opening them just enough to barely let the flow of air escape with friction and forcing the air between the lips. Phonetic study of alien sounds can help one learn to speak a foreign language with a minimum of accent.

No language uses more than a fraction of the sounds the human organism can produce. Normal infants utter at random a number of sounds that adult members of their society do not produce. As they grow older and, by imitation and inculcation, acquire the ability to make sounds they did not use as infants, they lose the ability to make sounds that are not used in the language they are learning. The specific sounds normal individuals can use in speech depend not on race or genetic background but on the phonetic customs learned as members of the group in which they were reared. Phonetic abilities are acquired, multi-individual customs just as certainly as other kinds of cultural elements, and societies differ from one another in the phones they use.

As noted earlier, native speakers are unable to distinguish all the phones trained linguists can hear in their speech, and a linguist does not know which sound distinctions they recognize and use. Therefore, it is necessary to keep the phones separate from one another until certain procedures reveal how they are grouped into phonemes. The linguist uses a body of etic data, the phones, to learn the emic distinctions in the linguistic aspect of the culture.

Linguists have developed a set of procedures for determining which sound variations make a difference in meaning and which do not. These procedures reveal that there are groups of closely similar sounds which seem to the native speakers to be the same sound. They use one sound one time and a different one another time, with no change in the meaning of the utterance. Such a category of interchangeable phones is a *phoneme,* which may be defined as a *set of alternative sounds, the phonetic differences among which make no difference in meaning.* The voiced bilabial stop *b* and the voiceless bilabial stop *p* are common in the world's languages, but in some languages this variation in sound makes a difference in meaning, and in others it does not. In English using one of these instead of the other either changes or destroys the meaning. For example, *batting* a dog's head is hardly the same as *patting* it, and to tell someone that there is a monkey in the *parn* might fail to indicate that there is a monkey in the barn. The *b* sound and the *p* sounds belong to different phonemes. In the Gorge dialect of Dani, however, the *b* sound and the unaspirated *p* (pronounced without a puff of air) may be substituted one for the other without changing the meaning of an utterance. Since the Dani regard the two sounds as the same and may use them interchangeably, they are members of the same phoneme (Bromley 1961:16). But if speakers of the Gorge dialect use an aspirated *p* instead of an unaspirated *p* or a *b,* they thereby change or destroy the meaning of the utterance. Accordingly, the *b* and unaspirated *p* are placed in one phoneme, while the aspirated *p* belongs in a different phoneme.

When phonetic differences do not affect meaning, speakers tend to be unaware of the differences. The Dani are unaware of the difference between *b* and unaspirated *p,* just as English speakers are usually unaware that there are different sounds in their *p* phoneme. The English *p* is accompanied by a puff of air in words like *pan, pill,* and *pray,* but lacks it in words beginning in *s,* such as *span, spill,* and *spray.* To emphasize the word, a puff of air could be added to the *p* in a word like *spill,* and it would sound unusual, but the meaning of the word would not change. English speakers automatically use the correct sound: the one with the puff of air in initial positions, and the one without it following an *s.*

Since some sound differences make no difference in meaning and the speakers may be unaware of the differences, a linguist who is constructing an alphabet needs a letter only for each phoneme, not for each phone. In a phonetic alphabet there would not only be more letters than necessary, but the native speakers would be puzzled by the presence of more than one letter for what seem to them to be the same sound. English speakers do not need separate letters for the two kinds of *p,* and Gorge Dani speakers do not need separate letters for the *b* and unaspirated *p* phones. A phonemic alphabet, having a symbol for each phoneme, is easily learned by native speakers for both reading and writing their language.

In line with the theme of cultural variability, anthropologists and linguists have learned that cultures differ phonologically from one another in a variety of specifics. While many languages utilize many of the same sounds because of the similarity of human vocal mechanisms everywhere, a number of phones inevitably differ from society to society. And even languages with mostly the same phones categorize them differently according to which sound differences affect the meanings of their utterances —that is, they have different phonemes.

Grammatical Variation

Remember that a phoneme does not have a specific meaning; it merely makes a difference in meaning. The smallest unit of language that has a specific meaning is the *morpheme*. It may be defined as *a linguistic unit composed of either a single phoneme or a combination of phonemes plus a specific meaning*. A morpheme cannot be divided without destroying or greatly modifying its meaning. To avoid confusing a morpheme with a phoneme, it may be helpful to note that a phoneme is never a combination of sounds; it is only a class of interchangeable sounds. Morphemes are usually combinations of phonemes. In addition, as noted before, a morpheme has a meaning, while phonemes only affect meanings.

Morphemes can either stand alone as words or combine with other morphemes to form words. *Man* in English is a morpheme consisting of three phonemes and the meaning "adult male human." By itself it functions as a word, but it can be combined with other independent units or with units that must always be used with other morphemes. It can be combined with *gentle* to form the word, *gentleman;* with *ly* to form *manly;* or with both to yield *gentlemanly*. If the morpheme *un* is prefixed to the latter, the result is a four-morpheme word meaning "not having the qualities of good breeding, kindness, courtesy and moderation" (referring to an adult male). Each of the four morphemes is a combination of phonemes, but, as the definition allows, there are also morphemes consisting of a single phoneme.

A morpheme may consist of phonetically similar alternatives, which are known as *allomorphs*. While allomorphs may differ slightly in pronunciation, the meaning remains the same. The sounds *s* and *z* differ in that one is voiceless and the other voiced, but they both mean "more than one" when suffixed to a word. The allomorph *s*, meaning plural, is used with *bat, book,* and *turnip* to produce *bats, books,* and *turnips;* and the allomorph *z*, meaning plural, may be used with *bag, song,* or *telephone* to yield *bags, songs,* and *telephones*. The prefixes *in, im,* and *il* are phonetically similar allomorphs meaning "not," as in *inflexible, impossible,* and *illogical*. The three two-phoneme allomorphs, plus any other phonetically similar prefixes with the same meaning, constitute one of the many morphemes used in building English words.

Morphemes, and the allomorphs they may be composed of, are combinations of phonemes plus a meaning, and a word may be either one morpheme or a combination of morphemes. Languages differ from one another in what combinations of phonemes are used with which meanings to comprise a stock of morphemes. Languages also differ in the ways that the morphemes are combined. The *morphology* of a language consists of the stock of morphemes and the ways they are used to build words.

Some morphemes may be called *root morphemes;* they are basic morphemes with important meanings; they are altered or added to in various ways to form words that use basic meanings. The several ways root morphemes are altered to form words are called *morphological processes. Prefixation* is the process of adding a morpheme to the beginning of another unit to form a word. *Trans-* is a prefix widely used in English, and *transport* is an example of its use. *Suffixation* is the addition of a unit to the end of the unit, the *-ly* in quickly, for example. *Infixation* is the insertion of a morpheme within another morpheme to modify its meaning. The Sioux word *cheti* means "to build a fire." *Chewati* means "I build a fire," since *wa* is a morpheme indicating first person. Some languages are *tonal;* the meanings of words are regularly modified by shifting the voice pitch of one or more syllables. Other morphological processes are *vowel change, consonantal change, reduplication* of a morpheme, and *accent shift.* Some morphological processes are absent from some languages. Tone shift and infixation, for example, are not used in forming English words. Cultures vary extensively in the kinds of morphological processes used and the degree to which they use them.

   Syntax concerns the arrangement of words to form phrases and sentences. Languages differ syntactically, so it is not possible to substitute word equivalents from one to another. In the Nbaka language of the northern Congo, to say, "I will never make a home with you," one must say, "Not I make will house with you" (Nida 1957:165). A number of syntactic processes are universal or widespread, such as *conjoining,* which is combining two simple sentences into one by means of a conjunction (such as *and* or *but)* or in some other way, and *embedding,* which means modification of a sentence or a part of it with a qualifying word or phrase (Lehmann 1976:191, 192). *Topicalization,* the use of special syntactic devices for singling out important elements of sentences, is more significant in some languages than others. Chinese, for example, has been referred to as a topic-prominent language, since the topic of a sentence is placed at its beginning. Syntax is an especially complex subject, and in the interests of brevity, no further discussion of it is provided here. It is another important aspect of cultural variability.

Aspects of Descriptive Analysis

   When a linguist has analyzed a language in terms of the various elements discussed above, the product is a full picture of its structure and the functional relationships among its parts. Descriptive analysis consists of four phases corresponding with the aspects of variability just reviewed: (1) *phonetic description* to determine what phones are consistently used in the people's speech; (2) *phonemic analysis* to determine how the phones can be classified into the meaningful units known as phonemes; (3) *morphological analysis* to identify the smallest units in the

Figure 5–1 *Applied linguist working with Cheyenne informant. When a linguist has analyzed a language he has a full picture of its structure and can assign symbols to each phoneme to construct an alphabet. Knowing the structure and processes of their language, he can compose or translate a wide variety of treatises of value to the people.*

language that have meaning, which are known as morphemes, and how they are used to form words; and (4) *syntactical analysis* to determine how words are combined with one another to form phrases and sentences.

Applied linguists carry out such analysis of a language and assign symbols to each phoneme to construct an alphabet. Then people can be taught to read and write, and, knowing the structure and processes of their language, the linguist can compose or translate history, sacred writings, agricultural instructions, fiction, or a wide variety of treatises of value to the people.

Comparative and Historical Linguistics

Careful comparisons of languages in terms of their phonetic, phonemic, morphological, and syntactical characteristics enable linguists to classify them into families according to their degrees of similarity. About nine language families are spoken by close to 90 percent of the world's population (Nida 1954:203). One of these is Dravidian, which includes Tamil, Malayalam, Telegu, and Brahui, all languages of the subcontinent of South Asia. Another is Indo-European, which includes Hindi, Sanskrit,

Greek, Russian, French, German, English, and a number of others. The nomadic Basseri of Iran speak Persian, which belongs to the Iranian family. The Nuer language of East Africa belongs to the Nilotic division of the Eastern Sudanic family, while the Nyoro of East Central Africa speak one of the far-flung Bantu languages. The !Kung speak one of about forty-eight languages of the Khoisan family of southern Africa, which, according to some authorities, includes the Hottentot languages. Miskito is one of only three languages in its family, Misumalpan, which are spoken only in portions of Nicaragua and Honduras. The Crow speak a Siouan language, with other languages of the Siouan family found over much of the northern Plains of North America but also scattered as far south as Mississippi and Louisiana, and as far east as Virginia. Samoan is one of about twenty-seven Polynesian languages, while Dani is classified among the eleven languages of the West New Guinea Highlands family (Voegelin and Voegelin 1977).

Some areas of the world are far more variable linguistically than others. A recent classification indicated seventy-three linguistic families for aboriginal North America, thirty-one represented by only one language each. It has been alleged that there are more than eighty families in South America, many represented by only a few hundred speakers.

When linguists compare words from different languages to determine whether or not the languages are related, they are looking for *cognates:* words that are similar because they have a common ancestry. But one difficulty is distinguishing cognates from words that are similar due either to borrowing or accident. Making such judgments requires expert application of several criteria; it is not a task for amateurs. For one thing, a linguist must take into account that some linguistic features are more easily borrowed across cultural boundaries than others, so if similarities between two languages are mainly in the area of easily diffused characteristics, they will be discounted as evidence of common origin (Swadesh 1964:578). The linguist must be proficient in making judgments of this kind, and this is only one of a number of factors that must be expertly considered.

Some historical linguists have tried to determine whether or not vocabulary and grammatical changes occur at constant rates, hoping to determine how long ago similar languages separated from one another. *Glottochronology* is such a method. It is based on research into the history of written languages, which suggests that the "basic vocabulary" of a language may be expected to change at a rate of 19 percent every thousand years. This basic vocabulary consists of words for a sample of a hundred concepts regarded as universal in human culture. Glotto-chronology, for example, indicates that the nomadic, buffalo-hunting Crow spoke the same language as their settled, horticultural neighbors, the Hidatsa, until about 771 A.D. (Pierce 1954:134). Though glottochronology continues to be used, there is controversy over the question of the constancy of language change rates and other aspects of the method, and a number of leading linguists have abandoned glottochronology as a valid technique of much significance.

METALINGUISTICS

While microlinguistics focuses on the phonetic, phonemic, morpho-logical and syntactical aspects of language, metalinguistics concentrates on the relationships between language customs and other aspects of culture. These relationships are explored by anthropologists, philosophers, psychologists, sociologists, general linguists, and others under headings such as ethnolinguistics, sociolinguistics, and psycholinguistics. The issues they examine are so overlapping and difficult to distinguish that the inclusive term metalinguistics seems useful.

Many metalinguistic studies have emphasized the notion that lan-guage influences people's thought and experience to a greater degree than generally recognized. This simple idea has been dignified by the term, *Sapir-Whorf hypothesis,* for it was promoted extensively by anthro-pologist-linguist Edward Sapir and a former engineer, Benjamin L. Whorf. Whorf became interested in this concept as a result of observing that behavior is influenced by the words people use. He noted that a workman handling barrels of gasoline was very careful about his matches and cigarettes, but after the barrels were emptied—that is, when they could be defined linguistically as *empty*—he was no longer careful (1941:75); and this carelessness often led to explosions. Such observations prompted Whorf to study other languages to see whether there were many cross-cultural differences of this kind. From a study of Hopi, for example, he reported that temporary events, such as lightning, wave, flame, meteor, pulsation, and the like, are referred to with verbs, thus clearly indicating short duration. In English, however, we express these phenomena by nouns, disposing us to think of them as having more stability and per-manence than the Hopi attribute to them (1956:215).

The Nuer of Africa differ from Euroamerican societies in their lack of a word or expression for time, and their language provides them with no way to refer to time as something which passes, can be wasted, can be saved, and so on (Evans-Pritchard 1940:103). Probably they never feel the pressure of fighting against time or having to arrange their lives ac-cording to time divisions. Their lives are coordinated in reference to herding, agricultural and other economic activities, which are mostly leisurely in nature. To communicate with his readers, Evans-Pritchard spoke of units of time, but this is a culture-bound convention of our language. When Nuer orient themselves with reference to what Euro-americans would think of as time, they say "I'll be back at milking," or "I'll leave when the calves get home."

The Dani language lacks ways of comparing things. The Dani can say that something is big, or very big; good, or very good; but there is no effective way of saying that something is bigger or better than something else. Karl Heider's conclusion is that they have few ways of comparing things in terms of their attributes (1970:170). Such examples of the relationship between language and experience suggest the importance of knowing the native language if one wishes to understand a culture and, also, knowing the culture as an aid to analyzing a language.

Under the influence of the Sapir-Whorf hypothesis, ethnolinguists long tended to neglect the effects of nonlinguistic customs on a language. But this has changed in recent decades as anthropologists have developed greater appreciation of the language-in-culture approach. Dell Hymes, for example, has called for an "ethnography of speaking," an approach to languages not just as systems of utterance units but in terms of culturally defined meanings, behavioral contexts, and social functions of utterances (1962:13). A number of social scientists have engaged in studies they often call *sociolinguistics,* in which there is relatively strong emphasis on the effect of social arrangements on language. Psychologist Joshua Fishman advocates what he calls a "sociology of language," which would include studying how language determines social behavior, how language behavior varies with social behavior, and the linguistic consequences of social behavior (1968:6). This proposal seems very similar to Hyme's ethnography of speaking. Both proposals illustrate the continuing advocacy of a well-balanced investigation of language in culture by representatives of the various disciplines concerned with sociocultural phenomena. Linguistic anthropologists, then, join with nonanthropologists in investigating metalinguistic problems.

Ethnoscience, or cognitive anthropology, is itself a major example of the exploration of relationships between language and the rest of culture. Cognitive anthropologists have suggested that most of a society's customs can be discovered by identifying all the linguistic terms used and ascertaining their total range of meanings, although there are increasingly frequent suggestions that people lack terms for some of their most significant cultural experiences. Perhaps the area of kinship terminology illustrates especially well the cognitive anthropologist's study of the connections between language and social behavior. Just one point from Goodenough's analysis of Yankee kinship terminology, using himself as informant, will exemplify this. One of the characteristics of the kinship aspect of many Americans' lives is that all relationships that fall within two degrees of collaterality (those with spouses, parents, children, brothers and sisters, grandparents, grandchildren, uncles and aunts, nieces and nephews and step- and in-law derivatives of some of these) are associated with lifelong responsibilities to one another, while all more distant relatives (cousins) are subject to no obligations other than expressions of cordiality (1965:279). An American's culture-bound reaction to this might be that it is obvious, but the point is that mutual obligations are distributed differently among relatives in many other societies. One of the aims of this kind of study in any culture may be to discover how linguistic terms for relatives are associated with how people behave toward one another.

The question of the relationship between language and behavior is intimately linked to the matter of status and role. The basic notion of the status-role concept, developed by anthropologist Ralph Linton, is that people have certain rights and duties in relation to one another (1936:-113). According to Linton, such a collection of rights and duties is a *status,* while a *role* is how one actually behaves according to status. Social scientists have distinguished status from role in various ways, but the two words are frequently used interchangeably in actual discussions of how different kinds of people and categories of people are expected to behave toward one another and how they actually behave. The rights and duties are *reciprocal* and, commonly, *complementary.* The head of a Samoan extended family has the duty of contributing from his wealth to members of his family at times of economic need or when they have wedding, funeral, church, or other such obligations (Holmes 1974:23). But this is related to the duty of the members of the family to build up their family head's wealth by making gifts to him. From the members' standpoint this is a duty, and from the family head's position, it is his right to receive those gifts. A reciprocal or two-way relationship is involved. The respective statuses are complementary in that they are not identical in all respects. It is the family head's duty to settle disputes among the people, but the people have no responsibility to settle the headman's disputes. Their obligation is to grant him the right to intervene.

Sociolinguistics relates to status-role in that statuses have to be identified, and this is ordinarily done linguistically. Statuses are often labeled by terms such as father, mother, parent, child, philosophy professor, anthropology major, big man, sash-owner (a leader of a Crow military club), blood brother, or expert bonito fisherman. Whatever roles the person or group so labeled is expected to perform in relation to others are associated with that identifying label, and when the label is used the society's members can specify the expected rights and duties. Yet there appear to be some statuses that are not labeled. Karl Heider found that the Dani apparently had no label for the only man with the authority to initiate a pig feast, which is an important part of all funerals and the only time that people can marry and boys can be initiated (1970:162). The people know who the man is and what his rights and duties are, but his status is informally rather than formally designated.

Since language is the main vehicle by which culture is expressed and communicated, the types of relationships are manifold, the research possibilities virtually infinite, and the practical significance of the resulting findings considerable. The social functions of the street language of American blacks, the effects of having to learn a second language without first learning to read and write one's native language, linguistic differences between people of different prestige level, language as a play device,

Figure 5–2   *Gutelo, the only leader in his Confederation of Dani with the authority to initiate a Pig Feast. There appear to be some statuses that are not labeled. The Dani apparently had no label for the only man with the authority to initiate a pig feast. His status is informally rather than informally designated.*

international conflict and language, and the relationships between linguistic borrowing and cultural change are among the many problem areas that are being investigated. Metalinguistic studies are a significant aspect of anthropology and several other fields concerned with human behavior.

COMPARATIVE EVALUATION OF LANGUAGES

As one might expect, languages vary in grammatical complexity and in the number of words in the vocabulary. Actually, no simple language has been found, and some unwritten languages seem more complex in many ways than those of some literate societies. During World War II, the United States used Navajo as an unbreakable secret code system. It is one of the most difficult languages for an adult of many Euroamerican societies to learn, partly because it is tonal, but also because many aspects of its grammar are difficult for Euroamericans.

Actually, no satisfactory way of measuring the complexity of languages for sake of comparison has been developed, and statements made about complexity remain largely impressionistic and relative to a number of criteria. One language can be seen to be more complex than another in rather specific ways, but the broader comparisons remain difficult. Even vocabulary comparisons may be misleading. Since civilizations have large numbers of customs, they may be expected to have a larger number of words than other cultures. It would be unfair, however, to compare the personal vocabularies of nonliterate people with the vocabularies represented in our dictionaries, since none of us know, much less use, more than a fraction of the words in a dictionary. But a nonliterate person, not having dictionaries, must be able to use the vocabulary. Dictionary counts are said to indicate that literary-minded people in Western society know some 30,000 words, although they may actually use less than half of these in speech. Word counts by missionaries and others suggest that members of some North American Indian and black African groups know and use at least as many words. It seems safe to say that people in every society know and use at least several thousand words.

Sometimes the assertion is made that all languages are equally adequate, but there is no way of substantiating such a statement. It may be that most, if not all, languages are more adequate for communication and cooperation among the members of the society in question than any other language would be, but even this has not been demonstrated. Some kinds of concepts are more effectively communicated by some languages than others; and languages are of unequal effectiveness in specific areas. These are difficult and unanswered questions because of the lack of adequate ways of measuring overall language effectiveness, but the available evidence does suggest that all languages are fully developed in all basic ways. There is no way of categorizing them into evolutionary levels, or anything of the sort, and all seem to include the grammatical mechanisms and word-building modes necessary to adapt to cultural changes, including the complexities of modern Euroamerican science and technology.

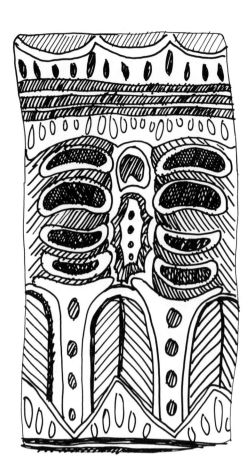

6

TECHNOLOGY

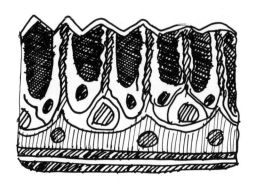

As a cultural term *technology* refers to all of the multi-individual customs for manipulating material entities and substances. It includes techniques of manipulating raw materials to produce artifacts, ways of handling or modifying artifacts, and means of manipulating animal and human bodies, including one's own body (Honigmann 1959:290). Technology, therefore, extends into all aspects of life. The way water is applied in baptism, kissing the hand in greeting a respected elder, a way of mixing art pigments, and the means of holding a saxophone are all techniques.

Conventionally, anthropologists confine technology as an aspect of culture mainly to the production and use of foodstuffs, shelter, clothing, and the containers and implements that satisfy physical wants. These topics are the main concern of this chapter.

EVALUATION OF TECHNOLOGIES

Europeans and Americans, with their extremely complex technologies and pride in their ingenuity, often hold that cultures of simple technology are inferior. But a dispassionate and careful look at the techniques of small-scale cultures provides occasions for admiration, even by the standards of Western civilization. Herskovits has noted that nonliterate peoples utilize a very large proportion of the fundamental principles of engineering (1952:241). Moreover, many techniques which seem to be crude are far from it if the skills and intelligence required are taken into account. Actually, so-called primitives manifest ingenuity and proficiency in dealing directly with sometimes rather harsh environments that most civilized persons are unable to match. In Euroamerican societies most of the technology has been turned over to specialists, many people actually being much less accomplished technologically than those with technologically simpler cultures. And a given Euroamerican specialist may be ignorant and unskilled outside his or her own area of specialization.

By the criterion of insuring human survival the complex technologies now dominating the world may be inferior to some of the simpler ones. Spiraling production of more gadgets and goods has depleted natural resources and despoiled the habitat to the point that some fear humanity will not endure. Euroamericans transcend the limitations of human and animal power by exploiting oil and coal, but as the easily available sources of fossil fuels are depleted, vastly greater quantities of energy must be expended in wresting them from the earth. The day of shallow, relatively low-cost oil wells, for example, is past, and we are digging deeper wells in more remote areas than before. Some think, in fact, that the persistence of monetary inflation on a world-wide scale may be due to the greater proportion of energy that now goes into the energy-getting process (Odum 1971:193). If energy-based technology brings such difficulties and threatens human survival, there may be some question about its humaneness. Cultures with simpler technologies are either more con-servation-oriented or incapable of damaging their habitats so extensively. Undoubtedly our complex technologies bring us satisfactions we would not enjoy otherwise, but it seems out of order to dismiss other techno-logical systems only because they are less complex.

ARTIFACTS: THEIR PRODUCTION AND VARIETY

Handicrafts

No human culture is so simple as to lack planned production of tools, weapons, implements, containers, and other artifacts. The raw materials exploited, of course, differ some from group to group, but taking the nonliterate world as a whole, there is great variety. Stone, wood, bone and horn, animal skins, wool and hair, sheets of bark, basketry materials such as grass, roots, twigs and leaf strips, clay, and metal ores are the major items that nonliterate groups have utilized.

A wide variety of objects is manufactured from stone: knives, scrapers, axe heads, lance and projectile points, drills, and many other things. Some are made by *chipping,* taking flakes from hunks of stone that can be fractured easily without disintegrating, such as flint or obsidian. But most groups who make stone tools manufacture them by a combination of *pecking and grinding,* which takes more time than chipping but results in a more durable tool and permits a greater variety of shapes and sizes. Pecking off small pieces with another stone gives the basic shape; grinding, usually with the aid of sand and water, yields the final shape. American Indians, using what is basically the grinding process, made tobacco pipes by drilling holes through stone cylinders, thereby preparing a stone tube. One end was placed in the mouth and tobacco stuffed in the other.

Archaeological research indicates a long period when humans made stone tools by the chipping process only. Many of the hunting and gathering cultures of the Lower and Middle Pleistocene (Glacial Age) were characterized by use of the stone core left after the chips were removed and the flakes discarded. During Upper Pleistocene times humans produced a variety of items from the chips or flakes themselves, often discarding the cores. As the glaciers subsided and the forests crept northward, the variety of stone items previously produced declined. In many places this was a time of transition, a time of developments leading to the post-glacial coming of agricultural technologies. Stone axes and other woodcutting tools were important during this transition, and the *microlith* is the most distinctive form in the Old World. Microliths are tiny stone chips of triangular and other geometric shapes. They were fixed in rows along the edges of bone or wooden implements to provide effective and lasting cutting edges on sickles, swords, and other tools. After this period, as plant domestication developed, pecking and grinding became the dominant stone technique.

Currently, virtually all of the world's peoples have abandoned stone tools in favor of the metal implements they have learned about from Europeans and Americans. For many years most ethnographies which mention the matter at all have reported that the people have forsaken the working of stone. Lowie was unable to obtain information on how the Crow made stone arrowheads during the first decade of this century. In 1960 the Dani of New Guinea were still making stone tools, the stone adze being their basic tool, but before the decade was over they were substituting the metal blades that had begun to trickle into the valley (K. Heider 1970:272).

It is not quite accurate to picture a "stone age" in which all prehistoric societies made most of their tools from stone. In many places easily worked stone was unavailable or in limited supply, and wood, bone, or other raw materials were more important.

Artifacts of wood are very common in nonliterate cultures, and woodworkers of a number of nonindustrial groups are highly skilled. The Maori of New Zealand produced extremely intricate carvings on the panels and posts of some of their council houses and storage buildings. Some of the Indians of British Columbia made a wide variety of highly crafted items, mainly of cedar. They smoothed large planks with adzes and polished them with stones and dogfish skin. To make a box from a single piece of wood, they heated and steamed it until it could be bent to the desired shape. They sometimes stitched together the edges of planks and worked them in such a way that the joints could hardly be noticed (Drucker 1965:30). The basic woodworking tools, so skillfully wielded by nonliterates in several parts of the world, are the *axe,* the *adze* (in which the blade runs at right angles to the length of the handle), and the *knife.*

Animal skins are of considerable importance in many of the world's cultures. They are used to make bags, bottles, shields, pouches, food storage cases, clothing, and many other items. Some things are made of rawhide, but many nonliterate groups also tan hides to make leather. Urine, brain substances, flour and sour milk mush, and bark tannin are among the substances which have been used to treat skins. Crow Indian women, who made a variety of items from buffalo and deer skins, tanned

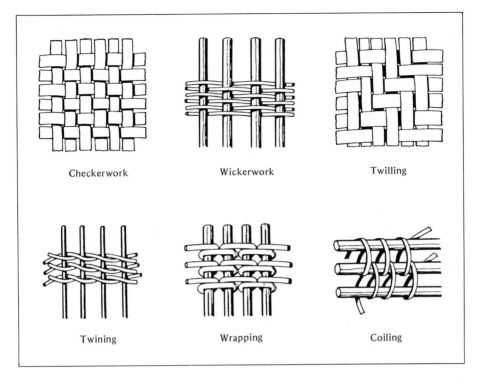

| Checkerwork | Wickerwork | Twilling |

| Twining | Wrapping | Coiling |

Figure 6–1 *Basketry weaves. Many nonliterate groups produce exceedingly excellent basketry containers, hats, sandals, and so on.*

a hide by working in an oily compound of buffalo brains and liver (Lowie 1935:76).

Objects of bone and horn are employed extensively, especially by herders and hunters. Needles, awls, hide scrapers, arrowheads, hoe blades and necklaces are only a few of them.

Felt is sometimes important in pastoral nomadic groups, since they have an adequate supply of wool and hair. The fibers are rolled, beaten, and pressed together into compact, even sheets of criss-crossing filaments. The Basseri of Iran produce their felt from lamb's wool. *Bark cloth* is made in parts of Africa, Central and South America, Indonesia, and Oceania by a process somewhat similar to felting. The inner bark of suitable trees is beaten with mallets, usually grooved, so the bark will be worked into a thin mat of intersecting fibers. The commonest use of bark cloth is for clothing. The cloth made in Samoa and other Polynesian cultures from the bark of the paper mulberry tree is pure white and somewhat like soft, tough paper. If it gets wet, it falls apart, but dry it is quite durable. Bark cloth is often decorated. The Miskito Indians of Asang use both purchased cotton cloth and sheets of bark cloth for bed covers. Before the twentieth century, they used bark cloth for clothing (Helms 1971:119).

Containers and mats are often produced by interlacing splints of

Figure 6–2 *Miskito weaving a basket.*

grass, roots, twigs, or strips of leaf. The techniques of interweaving the splints, whether for baskets or other items, is known as *basketry*. Mats and baskets of flexible material are often made by hand weaving pliant, flat strips of about equal flexibility crossing each strip over one and under the next to produce what is known as *checkerwork*. If the elements going one direction are notably larger or stiffer than the others, forming foundation rods across which the more flexible strands are woven, a strong, prominently ridged basketry known as *wickerwork* results. *Twined basketry* is made by handweaving two or more flexible strands at a time across the base, or warp, strands. One of a pair is passed on one side of one base splint and the other side of the next, while the other is woven around the opposite side of each base splint, and at the same time the strands are given a half twist between the base splints. *Wrapped basketry* is made by winding all the strands going in one direction at least once around the usually more rigid warp splints. Wrapping and twining may be combined in the same basket. *Coiled* basketry is made by forming a thick strand into a spiral and binding the coils into one another. Pliant elements may be looped around two or more coils, or the coils may be sewn together. Many nonliterate groups produce especially excellent basketry containers, hats, sandals, and so on. Some groups produce baskets so tightly woven that they hold water.

Loom weaving differs from basketry in that the *warp* threads are divided into two sets of alternate threads that can be raised and lowered in relation to one another to permit insertion of *woof* threads between and across them in one movement. Each set of warp threads is raised and lowered by means of a *heddle,* a rod attached by short threads to every second warp strand. The woof threads can be inserted by hand or by means of a *shuttle.* Reversing the two sets of warp threads secures the woof thread and makes it possible to insert the next one in the opposite direction. A bar or *batten* may be used to pack the woof threads tightly against one another. A common type of loom in nonliterate groups is the *belt* or *tension* loom, in which the warp is stretched between a bar attached to a stationary object and one fastened to a belt around the weaver's waist. Looms with full frames are also found in many places. Weaving is widespread among sedentary societies in the nonliterate world, and a number of them have produced especially fine textiles.

Threads used in weaving and for string are spun, either by rolling fibers between the hand and the thigh, or by means of a spindle whorl. The speed with which some can produce string or yarn using the hand and thigh is remarkable to Euroamericans, but using the spindle whorl ordinarily produces better yarns more quickly. The spinner twists a little fiber into a short length and fastens it to a slender rod which has a disk of clay or wood attached near the bottom. Spinners of the old world twirl the rod to twist the fibers, with the whorl acting as a flywheel. By adding fiber and manipulating it into the previously spun yarn, the spinner produces a continuous, tightly twisted thread. The pre-Columbian peoples of the New World seem to have twisted the yarn with their fingers and use the disc as a guard for keeping the thread from slipping off.

Pottery-making is a highly developed skill. The clays must include the proper proportions of substances so the pot will not crack during drying and firing. Tempers of various kinds—sand, pulverized pieces of broken pots, and the like—are commonly added for this purpose. The pot must also be properly shaped to avoid breaking during firing or use. Sometimes this is done by *molding,* applying clay to a mold such as an old pot or basket. Shaping a lump of clay with the fingers, without benefit of a mold, is known as *modeling.* The *coiling method* of shaping pots uses spirals of rolled clay. The rolls are pinched together, and shaping is completed by rubbing or scraping the inner and outer surfaces. Wheel-made pottery is limited to literate cultures of Europe and Asia. After shaping, pottery is dried and fired, which requires much skill. Some groups fire ceramic items in open fireplaces, but many use a furnace or kiln to attain greater control and higher temperatures. Some waterproof their pots and improve their appearance by adding a thin coating of clay containing a mineral and firing them a second time, which is called *glazing.* Pots may also be waterproofed by applying a *slip,* a surface coat of finer clay, by rubbing on melted resin, or by smoking them and smearing them with fat. Pots may be painted or incised before firing, and bases, legs, handles or other elements may be added. Many groups produce relatively crude, undecorated ware, but others exercise more care and produce a superior product.

In modern times machine-produced metal containers have widely replaced those of fired clay. True metallurgy, however, was known before modern times in both hemispheres. *Metallurgy* involves smelting metals from ore rather than using them in their natural state. Ironworking was not well developed in the New World, but it is outstanding in most cultures of black Africa and among nonliterate peoples of southern and eastern Asia. The industry was so highly developed in Africa that some felt it was an independent development, but it is now generally thought that the basic concept of ironworking diffused to Africa during the first millenium before Christ (Clark 1970:214). Many African groups both smelted and smithed iron before contact with Europeans, though some tribes with blacksmithing secured their iron in the form of spades or hoe blades from groups who specialized in mining and smelting.

Fires

All peoples use fire, and only a rare few were unable to produce it at the time of European contact. The Andaman Islanders, who lacked fire-making techniques, were very careful to keep fires going in the villages and carried fire with them on hunting trips or other moves (Radcliffe-Brown 1932:474). They knew what kind of wood would smolder for a long time rather than going out or bursting into flame. Some groups find fire-making difficult and prefer to keep their fires going rather than produce them. The Siuai of the Solomon Islands regard fire-making as a long, strenuous job, and they have been seen to give up in exhaustion and disgust (Oliver, 13).

Some societies use the percussion method to strike a spark and thereby ignite tinder. Others use one of three basic friction methods: the *fire drill, fire saw,* or *fire plow.* With the drill the end of a wooden rod is placed in a depression in another piece of wood and the rod is twirled between the palms or turned by a bow string or other cord arrangement. The fire saw involves drawing a stick or withe back and forth across another piece of wood. The fire plow differs from the saw in that the end of a stick is rubbed back and forth along a groove in the direction of the wood grain. South Pacific groups can produce a fire in about a minute by rubbing a small pointed stick rapidly up and down in another piece of wood until the sawdust so produced begins to burn.

Clothing and Ornamentation

Most anthropologists feel that social identification and adornment are the basic functions of clothing. People of all cultures ornament themselves by attaching aesthetically pleasing objects or by mutilating their bodies. Clothing and other ornamentation, being highly visible, also serve well to emphasize social differences. All societies distinguish the sexes through clothing and ornaments, though no specific way of doing this is universal. In some societies, Samoa, for example, men wear skirts; and in others women wear trousers. Dress and ornament may indicate age, marital status, social class, occupation, religious or political office, and other social positions. The same person, of course, may wear different clothing and ornaments at different times, depending on his or her role at the moment. Special ceremonial attire, for example, is virtually universal.

Concealment of portions of the body and *protection* of the body are also important uses of clothing, but there are so many exceptions that neither appears to be the basic reason for wearing clothing, taking the world as a whole. In some societies, among the Nuer, for example, neither sex conceals any of the body nor feels embarrassment at exposure. Those groups accustomed to seeing people with little or nothing on are not ordinarily aroused sexually by the sight of bodies of persons of the opposite sex. Other stimuli, such as certain postures or expressions, are usually necessary. Many groups, however, including the scantily clad Dani, keep portions of their bodies covered due to feelings of sexual modesty.

In the very coldest environments clothing is necessary for survival, but many groups get along with far less than others consider adequate. Humans are flexible in regard to how much cold they can learn to stand or are willing to put up with; moreover, some in hot climates wear far more clothes than necessary. How much protection is needed is culturally defined, and within limits, human physiology adjusts to these definitions.

Animal skins, basketry, woven fabrics, felt, grass or other vegetal materials, and bark have been used for clothing. A basic garment in many groups is the *breechclout,* which covers the pelvic region, other parts being covered only for weather protection or ceremonial purposes. Skirts and aprons of varying lengths are widely used. Capes, blouses, and other short garments draped from one or both shoulders may be used in combination with other garments, and some drape themselves in long robes. Tailored clothing, such as sleeved shirts and trousers, is shaped to the body. In pre-Columbian time it was restricted to northern North America, northern Asia, and Europe. Sandals, moccasins, or boots are worn in many societies, but barefootedness is also common, especially in warm, wet areas. Hats of several kinds are found among nonliterates, but not as often as footgear.

Many kinds of objects are attached to the body to ornament or identify people. There are necklaces, anklets, armbands, leg bands, and headbands; and plugs, rings, pins, feathers, bones, precious stones, and the like may be worn in the nose, lips, or ears. The body's appearance may be modified by staining the skin or teeth, plucking body hair, tatooing or scarifying the skin, stretching the ear lobes, binding the feet, deforming the head, or severing fingers. Again, the rule is cultural diversity, which illustrates the large number of cultural alternatives that inherited human nature allows.

Housing

For shelter, everything from natural places to large architecturally elaborate structures have been used by nonliterate societies. Some have used caves, even in recent times. Many nomadic peoples use a simple windbreak, commonly with a fire on one side to permit sleeping between the wind screen and the fire. Many shapes and materials have been used. Many houses are rectangular with vertical walls; some are cylindrical, some cone-shaped, and a few octagonal. Some have flat roofs; others have cone-shaped, domed, or gabled roofs. Some houses have roofs but no walls, with the eaves virtually sitting on the ground. Brush, poles, planks, bamboo, stone, brick, reeds, felt, and hide are among the many materials used. There are so many house types that a full treatment of all basic kinds would take too much space for this brief survey, but to emphasize the diversity further, it is of interest that Driver mentions no less than fifteen basic types of dwellings for the aboriginal peoples of North America alone (1969:116).

Neither housing shapes nor materials are completely determined by the natural habitat, for different sorts of houses are often found within the same habitat. The Crow and other buffalo hunters of the plains live in large, hide-covered tipis, while their neighbors, the Hidatsa, Mandan, and Arikara dwell in large lodges covered with earth.

Protection is the obvious function of housing, but other functions, such as privacy, aesthetic satisfaction, social identification, and modes of interaction are involved. Most Nyoro dwellings, which are rectangular with thatched roofs or beehive-shaped, shelter a man and his wife and children (Beattie 1960:51); but among the Dani the men and boys sleep and spend much of their time in a separate house, while the women have separate dwellings in which one or, sometimes, two of them live (K. Heider 1970:264). Much of the family activity takes place in a long, rectangular communal cook house.

House furnishings vary so much from society to society that a great deal of space would be necessary to give an adequate picture of their diversity. Nonliterate groups generally use the ground as the floor, though various kinds of mats and blankets are used. Larger dwellings commonly have raised banks or benches against the walls for sleeping. A fireplace usually is found near the center of such dwellings. Raised bedsteads, tables, and chairs are uncommon. Goods are usually kept in baskets hung from the supporting structures of the roof, hung on wall fixtures, or placed on the benches.

Transportation Technology

Wheeled vehicles are not found in nonliterate cultures, so people move themselves and other things about on foot, on animals, or on watercraft. Some people wear footgear regularly, whereas others use footwear only when traveling. Perhaps the most specialized footgear in nonindustrial cultures is the snowshoe of the Indians of subarctic North America. Devices for carrying loads on the person include head rings for transporting large or heavy objects on top of the head, containers carried on the back, and balance poles. Bags, packs, baskets and other containers carried on the back often are held in place by a carrying band which passes across the forehead, chest or shoulder. Such an arrangement is called the *tumpline*. Loads may also be hung from each end of a *balance pole,* which passes across one shoulder.

Various kinds of pack gear are employed on camels, horses, donkeys, reindeer, llamas and other animals. The *travois* consists of two poles tied to the sides of an animal with the ends dragging behind on the ground. The Indians of the Great Plains used them on dogs and later, transferred them to horses. Dogs and reindeer have been used extensively with sleds. All large domesticated animals, including reindeer, are ridden by one group or another.

Rafts have been used in many places. An interesting type is the *balsa,* which consists of several bundles of reeds tied together to form a cigar-shaped craft. The two main types of air-buoyant craft used by non-literates are dugouts and those built by stretching skins or bark over a frame. The birchbark canoe made by the Indians of Canada is so light it can be portaged with ease. The skin *kayak* is one of the most finely engineered boats made by nonliterates. The *dugout,* made from a log hollowed with fire and an adze, is the most widely used type of water craft. The Polynesians may be the most expert navigators, having settled the Pacific islands by traversing long distances across water. They observed the stars and ocean currents and made navigation charts.

FOOD TECHNOLOGY

No society lives a life of complete leisure, simply plucking luscious food from trees or bushes at will. Some work much harder than others, but all groups work for a living.

Several major kinds of *subsistence modes* are distinguished. *Collecting* involves gathering wild plant items, primarily, though insects and, sometimes, smaller forms of animal life can be included. *Hunting, fishing, agriculture,* and *stock-raising* are the other major modes. It is important to remember that these are the etic categories of the anthropologist, for a given subsistence system is a blend of two or more of them. Hunting, fishing, and collecting are frequently combined among those who gather animals and plants from the natural environment rather than produce them as in agriculture and stock-raising. Even those who produce foodstuffs (cultivating plants or tending animals) often employ one or more of the techniques for collecting wild foods as well. Though the Nuer value their herds of cattle above all as a source of food, the production of millet, corn, and beans, as well as fishing are also important food sources. In addition, they hunt occasionally and collect a few wild plant foods (Evans-Pritchard 1940:69). In many groups, down through the millennia, horticulture has been secondary to other subsistence modes.

Collecting

Simple collection of wild foods seems crude to peoples having technologically elaborated cultures, but competence is required for success. Knowledge of where and when to find plant foods, including the ability to distinguish edible from poisonous species, and the means of obtaining them, is transmitted from generation to generation. The !Kung San are fine botanists. They are able to identify plants not only when they are in bloom but in the dry season as well, when only a dead leaf or a thin, threadlike fragment of vine among the grass stems is all they have to reveal where a root is and whether it is poisonous or edible (Marshall 1976:95). The San are amused at the outsider's inability to distinguish valuable roots from useless ones. Knowledge of this kind, collected by ethnographers, has been incorporated into survival manuals for military or other personnel who might become lost in an alien habitat (Kluckhohn, 1949:173).

Digging sticks and *containers* of some kind are among the most important items of equipment for collectors. *Beaters,* often made of basketry, may be used to gather seeds, and long, *hooked poles* may be employed to secure nuts, cones, and fruit from trees. *Knives,* of course are useful, and *nets* may be used for catching insects or birds.

Hunting and Trapping

Large, strong animals such as bison, deer, bears, guanacos, kangaroos, caribou, or whales are ordinarily brought down with substantial weapons that are thrown or by missiles propelled by mechanical contrivances. A *club, knife* or *lance* can be used to dispatch game after they have been brought down by an arrow or spear, but they require the hunter to approach the animal more closely than is usually safe or possible for the initial attack. Some groups use knives or clubs specially designed for throwing, making close approach unnecessary. *Spears* are commonly propelled by a *spear thrower,* also known as an *atlatl.* This is simply a stick with a hook or other arrangement at one end to receive the base of the spear shaft. In throwing, the spearman retains the front end of the spear thrower in his hand, using the device as an extension of his arm. The *harpoon* has a point to which a cord is attached and which separates from the shaft when it penetrates the animal. It can either be thrust like the lance or thrown like the spear. The *boomerang* is a flattish, angular throwing stick, with some rare models being designed for return. The *bola* consists of several weights connected by cords, which wrap around an animal's legs when thrown.

The most widespread device for propelling a missle is the *bow,* sometimes used with pellets but, usually, with the *arrow.* A *compound bow,* one which is built of layers of wood, bone or sinew, has considerable power if it is skillfully made. Considerable muscular control and coordination are required for such a bow, but a properly sent arrow plunges into a beast with great force, inflicting a lethal wound. The !Kung and other San groups have relatively weak bows and rely on arrow poison to bring down the animal. There are many different techniques for handling bows and arrows. Different groups hold the string and arrow in different ways, and some use special devices to pull back the string and arrow against the tension of powerful bows.

The *sling* is a fairly widely used device for flinging pellets or stones. The *blowgun* uses concentrated air power to propel darts. Poisons are used on the points of spears, arrows, or blowgun darts in many places. In modern times the gun has replaced many aboriginal weapons.

Traps differ from weapons in that they can operate in the absence of the user. The common types of trap are the *pitfall, snare,* and *deadfall.* Animals which fall into camouflaged pits may be impaled on sharp stakes set in the bottom. A snare consists of a loop that tightens around the animal that trips it and tries to pull free. The common procedure is to attach one end of a cord to a bent sapling, though there are other means. A deadfall consists of a weight which falls on the animal and holds it down. The weight may have a spear mounted in it.

Anyone who studies in detail the hunting and trapping activities of any group turns up a rich variety of specific techniques not indicated by the foregoing summary. Various lures and disguises are common. Hunters often reproduce an animal's call or masquerade in its skin to approach it closely. The nineteenth-century Crow disguised themselves in horned buckskin masks to stalk deer at their watering places (Lowie 1935:72). Grazing animals are often driven into a pen or cornered in the V of converging fences or at the end of a blind canyon. Animals may be driven over cliffs or into rivers and lakes, where they can be killed more easily, sometimes from canoes. They are also driven into the open or into ambush by setting fires. The Eskimos place a bloody knife in the ground, blade up. A wolf licks the knife, cuts his tongue, and excitedly gorges himself to death on his own blood. The !Kung take the nocturnal springhare by running a long pole with a hook on the end into the burrow, and when they have hooked the sleeping animal, they measure the distance that the pole has been inserted and dig the sand away to secure the animal (Lee 1972:344). Anthropologists are impressed with the keen observation and ingenuity employed in the game-taking techniques of nonliterate peoples.

Fishing

Fishing is commonly secondary to some other subsistence mode, though some groups depend mainly on fishing. It is of major importance to groups living by oceans, rivers, or lakes in all parts of the world, though not all people who live by water fish. The tribes of coastal British Columbia depend on fishing to an unusual degree. Salmon, herring, cod, candlefish, and so on are taken with traps, hooks, harpoons, nets, spears, and rakes. They keep busy taking fish or other forms of water life most of the year, though during the coldest winter months they devote most of their time to feasts, potlatches, and shaman's dances. The modern Samoans fish regularly by a variety of methods, but they spend perhaps ten times as much time in agricultural work. They may have spent more time fishing in the past than they do now, but argiculture has always been much more important than fishing on many Polynesian islands (Holmes 1974:46). As illustrated by the Nuer, fishing is commonly a seasonal endeavor. Fish become an important supplement to Nuer groups during the dry season (Evans-Pritchard 1940:70).

A number of the hunting techniques already mentioned are used for fish, such as the bow and arrow or multi-pronged spears. A fish trap may be a cone-shaped cage with an opening at the small end where the fish enter easily but cannot locate the way out. Many groups set traps in weirs or dams. Poisons placed in water stupefy the fish so they can be gathered at will. Fishing with nets is widespread; the nets are either thrown or fixed where the fish will become entangled in them. The hook and line also are widely used. Hooks are made from wood, bone, or metal, and both barbed and unbarbed types are found.

Plant Cultivation

Horticulture, plant production by hand, is widely found among non-literates, and many kinds of crops are grown. Aboriginal America is noted for the large number of plants domesticated there: maize (Indian corn), beans, squash, pumpkins, white potatoes, sweet potatoes, manioc (from which tapioca is derived) peanuts, pineapples, tomatoes, and more. New World Crops are now grown extensively by groups in Africa and Asia and by Euroamericans. The white potato, in fact, was grown so extensively in Europe before being brought to North America by English-speaking whites that many are unaware that it originated in South America. From the Old World, mainly Asia, have come wheat, barley, oats, rye, peas, several fruits, soy beans, millet, rice, and sugarcane. Coconut, taro, yams, and breadfruit are grown extensively in the islands of the Pacific. It is significant that all these crops were domesticated by so-called primitives.

Civilized cultures are the beneficiaries of the keen observation and experimental activities of nonliterate peoples.

Nonliterate peoples in all parts of the world use *slash-and-burn* techniques, sometimes known as *shifting* or *swidden* cultivation. This involves cutting and burning trees and other vegetation to clear a field or garden. When a plot's fertility is exhausted, the process is repeated in another place. Deforestation and erosion have been the consequences in many regions. In some places land may be renewed by floods or by artificial means. The Dani and other New Guinea societies use the slash-and-burn technique on the forested hills, but in the wet bottomlands they renew their fields annually by cleaning the mud from a system of ditches and spreading it over their gardens (K. Heider 1970:40). Techniques other than slash-and-burn are used wherever fertility levels and the availability of water, either by rains or irrigation, permit. One of the most striking examples is the extensive terracing of mountain slopes for wet rice paddies in much of southeastern Asia. This provides an impressive example of the alteration of the habitat by cultural means.

The *digging stick,* also used in gathering, and the *hoe* are the most widely found soil preparation and planting implements among horticultural peoples. The digging stick is used to loosen the soil or poke a hole for seed. A few groups have added a foot bar to gain added leverage. Hoe blades are of stone, bone, wood, or metal. African farmers use a short-handled hoe with an iron blade. Many American Indian groups attached a bison's shoulder blade to a stick to make a hoe. In modern times, of course, many groups have adopted the plow and other animal-drawn equipment, but plow agriculture was indigenous only to Europe, North Africa, and parts of Asia before Euroamerican exploration.

The technological contrast between American agribusiness and farming and the slash-and-burn horticulture are impressive, and our ethnocentric reaction to them is that they are very inefficient. In this case we overlook the total context of farming in our own society, which, if fully considered, reveals that our farming is not as efficient as we suppose. We are fond of reminding ourselves that less than 5 percent of our people are farmers, which implies to us that it takes only one American to feed twenty others, plus many more in other countries. As Marvin Harris reminds us, this overlooks the fact that our agribusiness farmers carry out only a limited number of operations midway in a food production sequence that begins in the oil fields and coal mines and on the automotive and farm equipment assembly lines and does not end until truckers, carhops, and supermarket cashiers have been involved (1978:10). Harris also remarks that it requires 2,790 calories, mostly in nonrenewable resources such as oil and coal, to produce a can of corn that yields only 270 calories. From the standpoint of the amount of energy expended in relation to energy produced, a number of so-called primitive systems may be more efficient than our own.

Domesticated Animals

The most widespread domesticated animal is the dog. Dogs are eaten in some places and are sometimes raised for food, but no group, apparently, raises dogs as a basic food source. In North America some groups eat dog flesh only for ceremonies or when they are starving.

Among the main domesticated herd animals are sheep, goats, cattle, horses, donkeys, camels, and reindeer. These are raised extensively by pastoral nomads, who secure crop foods and manufactured items by trading the products of their herds. The main pastoral area of the Old World is the belt of desert and grassland including parts of North Africa, Arabia, the central Asiatic steppes, and portions of southern Siberia and Mongolia. The Basseri of southern Iran herd a variety of animals, sheep and goats being the most important. They also keep donkeys for transportation and wool, and dogs as camp watchers. The same animals are found with other southwest Asian groups and in North Africa, though the camel is more important among many of them. Reindeer are important in northern Siberia, and cattle in much of black Africa, especially in the east. It has already been noted that, for the Nuer of the Upper Nile, the main concerns of life revolve around cattle. Rather than being herded

Figure 6–3 *A Basseri camp in migration. The Basseri of southern Iran herd a variety of animals, sheep and goats being the most important.*

by nomadic peoples, pigs and chickens and other fowl are tended by sedentary peoples. In New Guinea and other parts of Oceania pigs have become important as ceremonial and display animals. The Dani of New Guinea feed their pigs on sweet potatoes and account them as important items of ceremonial exchange. Although they are now found all over the world, pigs and chickens were domesticated in Southeast Asia.

Though many plants were domesticated in the Americas, few animals were domesticated there. Only the llamas and alpacas of the Andean region—where they supplement a basically nonpastoral subsistence system—are of significance.

Foods

The several subsistence modes make available a great variety of items for human ingestion. Societies, however, have been selective about what foodstuffs they secure and how they prepare them. Even the sometimes hungry San of southern Africa fail to eat all the natural plant and animal foods available. Lee found that the !Kung of the Dobe region systematically hunt only 17 of the 54 animal species classified as edible, and they know of 220 species (1972:345). They also make only negligible use of insects and seek only a few of the many snakes, lizards and amphibians as food. Because the belief that hunting and gathering "primitives'" live so close to starvation that they eat everything available has come to be a part of American culture, many observers conclude without adequate evidence that this is true of certain groups they come into contact with.

Of course, what is thought to be edible is a matter of cultural definition. Some North American Indians eat acorns, and some do not. Boiled grasshoppers, lizards, and angleworm soup are consumed in some societies. !Kung San eat ostrich eggs and Americans consume chicken eggs, but some peoples of Asia regard eggs as excrement and unfit for human consumption. Such differences from society to society are not the result of genetic differences but a consequence of cultural conditioning, the original reasons in most cases being lost in antiquity.

Only some foodstuffs are eaten without modification, and all cultures include customs for modifying foods before eating. Some foods, such as acorns and bitter manioc, are not fit to eat until certain elements are removed. People who produce grains or collect seeds pulverize them with a *mortar and pestle* or use *grinding stones*. The flour then may be made into gruel, cakes, or incorporated into a mixture. Meat and fish commonly are cut into small strips or chunks and dried by air or over the fire. Either may be smoked. A number of plant items must be scraped, peeled, or cut open before use. Cooking is done with or without vessels. Many peoples broil meat or other food by placing pieces on a stick or otherwise arranging them over or near a fire. Many things are baked in hot ashes or heated sand. A number of societies, notably in Oceania, steam or bake food in pit ovens. The Dani dig a pit and lay in alternating layers of heated rocks, ferns, meat, and leaves. People without pottery may boil food in wooden, hide, or basketry containers by placing red hot stones in the water. The Crow had no pottery, but they boiled foods in rawhide containers by the stone-boiling method. Some Indonesians cook their food in bamboo tubes.

Techniques of serving and consuming food also vary cross-culturally. Some people eat with their fingers, others with implements. Many have only two meals a day or, perhaps, one big meal and snacking at other times. Some like their food hot, and others like it cold. The Nootka Indians of Vancouver Island allow all their food to cool before eating, since they believe that hot food is unhealthy. Then, as they eat, each bite is dipped in oil. But all such cross-cultural differences are learned, for inherited human nature does not dictate precisely what, how, or when we eat.

TECHNOLOGY IN THE ECOSYSTEM

Techniques for manipulating and modifying the natural habitat and for making and using tools, houses, clothing, food, and so on are interdependent with one another, with religious and other nontechnological customs, and with extracultural features of the ecosystem. This chapter illustrates relationships mostly between techniques and artificial objects, and within the natural habitat, but linkages within the total system cannot be neglected. The impact of habitat factors on social life is nicely illustrated by the Nuer. For part of the year they live in villages which may reach a population of several hundred people, but at other times of year they live in camps which, during the early part of the dry season, are occupied by only a few young people (Evans-Pritchard 1940:63). This is because during the flood season, only a few high areas are dry enough for house sites, horticulture, and avoidance of hoof diseases, while during the dry season the people are forced to scatter into camps by the barrenness of plant life and for fishing. The young people take the cattle to the first camps because the rest of the people must remain behind to finish the work in the gardens and homesteads. During this time a girl may make known her desire to marry one of the young men, who parade and leap behind their favorite oxen while chanting poems (Evans-Pritchard 1951:56).

A negative relationship between the social system and the habitat is seen among the Basseri (Barth 1961:102). In the southern part of the Basseri range there are several large pastures that the people are unable to use because of lack of water. This problem could be solved by digging a well, but the Basseri lack the type of social organization that would permit them to organize for such a communal work project. Among the Samoans of Fitiuta there is a strong interdependence between bonito fishing and religion. Each evening as the fishing fleets return the boats assemble just outside the reef, where the fleet chief offers thanks to God for the day's catch (Holmes, 1974:48). Both the families of crewmen and the boat owners are expected to remain idle and pray for the fishing while the fleet is out.

The interdependence of features in various parts of an ecosystem can be illustrated further by a look at one aspect of American culture: air pollution in Los Angeles (Duncan 1961:145). Some of the linkages among elements of the habitat, population, technology, and social organization have been traced for this situation. Technology (automobile emissions, industrial smoke, household waste incineration) has contributed to the habitat changes (dimmer light, irritating air, and fewer plants). These changes are linked to social organization in that they stimulated organizational activity (appointment of abatement officers, passing control ordinances, and research programs.) These features of Los Angeles social organization have led to technological changes designed to change the habitat back to its previous state. Abatement devices in factories, emission-control devices in autos, and elimination of backyard incinerators presumably reduce smog levels, which allows for more sunlight, permits the vegetation to grow better, and so on.

The broad question of the relationship between technology and habitat, on one hand, and technology to social and ideological customs, on the other, must involve thorough exploration of many specifics such as those mentioned in the preceding paragraphs. As noted earlier, this is being undertaken in anthropology under the heading of cultural ecology. Much anthropological debate has turned on the question of whether or not technology is dominant over social arrangements and ideological customs in accounting for cultural change and cultural differences. Marvin Harris, for example, advocates *cultural materialism* as the proper approach to the study of culture. Cultural materialism holds that "material factors" (environmental, technological, economic and demographic) in large part determine the nature of social and ideological aspects of life (M. Harris 1979:52, 55–56). But cultural materialism does not deny that social and ideological elements influence material conditions; it only states that material factors are primary.

According to views of this kind, primitive (primeval) humans, having few customs to exploit their habitat, would do so initially by taking the available wild plants and animals from the environment for food, shelter, warmth, and so forth. Customs for acquiring these things would differ from one place to another, as they do among hunting and collecting peoples today, but regardless of the climatic, botanical, and zoological differences, all these hunting and collecting cultures would of necessity be basically similar. This similarily would exist because, except in the richest habitats, reliance on hunting or gathering makes possible some kinds of cultural development and discourages or prohibits others. For example, all such societies must be on the move to some extent, since they cannot remain in one place permanently and adequately satisfy their needs for food and fiber. Therefore, material goods must be limited in number and size, since they must be moved so often. The result is that hunting and gathering societies are unable to develop the elaborate technological customs that would permit them to utilize their habitat more completely and become more independent of its limitations. Such a simple technology does not produce large populations, and the elaborate legal, governmental, and other social mechanisms for coping with the problems of large populations do not develop. Relationships among the society's members are regulated as part of ordinary family and kinship obligations. Political, religious, and economic functions are handled mainly by the family and, to some degree, by bands—the small collections of families who move about together. By this view, then, the nontechnological aspects of the culture are accounted for largely by the nature of the technology interacting with the habitat. According to cultural materialism, habitat and technological factors initially give rise to social and ideological factors rather than vice versa.

It is difficult to say with confidence what it is in the culture of a food-collecting society that gives rise to plant cultivation or stock-raising. In harmony with the interest in the interdependence of ideological and social customs with technological traits, we may suppose that some societies' social interaction and life-view customs make it more likely for people to think of planting seeds to produce more plants or keeping animals to use them more effectively. A notion explored by a leading specialist on Near Eastern archaeology illustrates this. Robert Braidwood has suggested that a nonagricultural society which had developed an extensive complex of woodworking and other techniques in response to increasing forests and other habitat changes might develop a more experimental orientation to life (1967:88, 91). This is not unreasonable, for we know that cultures of the present differ from one another in their willingness to experiment and their general receptiveness to change (Barnett 1953:56). Should the kind of thing Braidwood suggests take place, it would be an example of the habitat (increased forests, changed animal life, etc.) influencing the technology (woodworking techniques, new hunting and trapping methods), which would in turn contribute to a receptive rather than traditionalist ideology and, possibly, lead to experimentation with plants and animals.

Because they need not go where the wild plants and animals are but must settle down to give their crops proper attention (except for pastoral nomadic groups), food-producing societies can accumulate more and larger artifacts. These enable them to modify their habitat to a degree not possible in most food-collecting groups. Food production thereby overcomes some of the limitations imposed by habitat on nonproducing societies. Since food production can provide more food than collecting, there may be enough to support a variety of specialists. The more abundant food supply will support more people, which both permits and requires more elaborate social and political arrangements. There are more groups in a food-producing society than in a collecting one, including kinship groups. Clans, sibs, and lineages, as well as more complex kinship arrangements, are often of greater importance in food-producing cultures than in food-collecting groups. Obviously the cultures of some producing societies are more complex than those of others, but the general difference between hunting-gathering and food-producing cultures stands. In each case the same kinds of links among habitat, population, technology, social organization, and ideology occurs, as previously discussed.

Anthropologists agree on the importance of interdependence within an ecosystem, though the implications of the idea are not yet fully explored. They also agree that technology interacting with the habitat heavily influences social and ideological aspects of the culture. There are many, nevertheless, who feel that cultural materialism gives too little credit to the power of ideas to influence technological and economic forms. The argument is sufficiently complex that it will not be pursued here at any length. Suffice it to say that it is also possible to argue that once the social and ideological components of a culture have become sufficiently developed, they may influence technology as much or more than the technology influences them.

7

ECONOMIC
ORGANIZATION

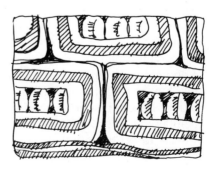

The term *economics* is sometimes used to include subsistence technology, but it is commonly employed by anthropologists to refer to the ways people, time, and materials are organized to produce, distribute, and consume goods and services. Linkages between technological and economic customs, which, of course, are etic categories, are numerous and strong. It is quite impossible to discuss one area without frequently mentioning the other, as illustrated by the frequent references to economic matters in the previous chapter.

With economic organization we move more surely into the area of social organization, since we are more concerned with how people relate to one another—specifically for the production, distribution, and use of technological items. In technology, by contrast, the main concern is how people relate to substances and objects.

FORMALISM AND SUBSTANTIVISM

The *formalist* tradition in anthropology has long used etic distinctions derived from Western economics, treating non-western groups as though their economic systems operate by many of the same principles as Euroamerican systems. In the late 1950s this position was sharply challenged by economist Karl Polanyi, who insisted that Western economic systems are so basically different from those of nonliterates that it is essential to avoid using the same concepts to analyze both. Those who took up and developed Polanyi's position have come to be called *substantivists*. They stress the idea that Western economic systems are dominated by the *market principle,* which they insist is absent from nonliterate cultures. Market systems feature general purpose money (used for purposes in addition to buying and selling, especially as a standard of value and for discharging obligations); prices are regulated by supply and demand; and economic activities are dominated by the goal of gaining the greatest possible benefit from limited resources. By contrast, other cultures are said to be dominated by reciprocal exchanges based on establishing and maintaining social relationships and, perhaps, a flow of economic resources to central points from which they are redistributed to the society's members.

The formalists admit a difference in emphasis and the possible distortions from ethnocentrically forcing nonliterate behavior to fit into Euroamerican economic concepts, but they choose to believe that a significant number of behavioral principles underlie all economic systems. Some also contend that the differences between Euroamerican and other economic systems are not as profound as substantivists allege, and that the market principle operates in a few nonliterate cultures. The debate has been somewhat inconclusive. In terms of the distinction between etic and emic approaches, there is disagreement about what etic categories are most helpful in exploring the emic distinctions of different economic systems. No attempt to settle the issue is made here. Instead, this chapter indicates and illustrates the range and variety of economic modes.

ORGANIZATION OF WORK

A significant feature of work in nonindustrial cultures is the lack of time orientation. The times work is begun and abandoned vary from day to day. On some days work may last only a couple of hours, while at other times it may last most of the day. There may also be interruptions of varying duration for rest or for nonproductive activity such as conversation. The number and length of breaks may depend on how demanding the work is, the physical condition of the worker, and similar factors. This contrasts sharply with the Western concept of working regularly for so many hours a day, so many days a week, with scheduled breaks for rest, refreshment, and vacations. Some Euroamericans find this difficult to understand, but they may not realize that the notion that time has monetary or economic value is largely a peculiarity of industrialized societies. Many cultures lack machine technology, which must be employed efficiently to realize a return from investments in expensive equipment (Dalton 1961:8).

Western machine technology is linked to and has consequences for other aspects of the culture. For one thing, the existence of an extreme variety of machine-made items encourages a highly monetized economy, since the most efficient possible means of distributing items among consumers is desired. A monetary system's effectiveness can be increased by credit modes that allow producers, merchants, and consumers the greatest possible flexibility in using money. Thus, financial institutions have come into being to facilitate payment, storage of weath, investment, borrowing against future profits, and for other economic reasons. Underlying all of this is what Jules Henry, who has studied both American culture and the Kaingang of the Brazilian jungles, calls *technological driveness,* the perceived necessity for continuing expansion of capacities to extract raw materials and produce and consume artifacts. Americans must buy things; otherwise, producers will not make the money to buy the goods and services of others and to pay people to develop, operate, and maintain their machines or advertise and distribute their products. Development must go on, or the economy will grind to a halt and people will be reduced to a material level they would find wretched. Henry suggests that the type of person most suited to such a system is the individualistically oriented man or woman, willing to do whatever is necessary to get ahead. He points out that it is easy in American society to locate jobs that require interest in achieving, competing, and making money but difficult to find employment that calls for "love, kindness, quietness, contentment, fun, frankness, and simplicity" (1963:14). Machine technology and social values are functionally interdependent in American society.

One of the most common notions about so-called primitives is that they work only to survive, but the truth is that people everywhere have desires that prompt them to go beyond mere survival needs. They adjust the volume of work to meet those desires. The potter works to produce a useful container and, at the same time, one pleasing to the eye, as well as for the sheer satisfaction of manipulating materials. In a number of South Pacific groups a grower of yams works for more than a food supply. He also desires to produce enough to put on large displays which enhance his prestige. In the 1920s a Samoan girl would spend up to two years weaving a *finemat* woven of the best quality of pandanus, which was soaked, baked, and scraped to yield golden white, paper-thin strands (Mead 1928:32). The *finemat* was part of a girl's dowry, a testimony to her industry and manual skill rather than an item of survival.

It is the combination of available resources, technological efficiency, and culturally defined desires that makes people work as hard as they do. In a harsh habitat it may be necessary for people to work rather steadily to survive, at least at times, and starvation is not unknown to a number of groups. Still, the traditional idea of "primitives" as constantly at work for food applies only to a few groups, and hunters and gatherers characteristically enjoy considerable leisure time. Though the food supply available to the aborigines of Pulykara in western Australia is very limited, for part of the year they can collect an entire day's food in a short time, and the women spend most of their days talking or sleeping while the men are free to engage in the generally unproductive activity of hunting. Their diet is meager, but they desire little more, and more labor could hardly improve much in that severely limited habitat (Gould 1970:63). The !Kung San of the Dobe region of the Kalahari Desert have an abundant food supply, and they are not malnourished. Most of them seem to operate on their own schedules and spend less than half of their time obtaining food (Lee 1968:37). In one camp Lee noted that on a given day usually from one-fifth to one-half of the able-bodied members were out getting food (1972:347). The others would be resting, cleaning house, and making tools, clothing, and jewelry. During July 1964 the women worked only two or three days a week getting food, and the men hunted on an average of only three or four days per week. By contrast, the horticultural Dani of New Guinea work hard. Gardner and Heider tell us that there is seldom a day, unless it is miserable weather or a ceremonial time, that Dani women are not in their gardens for several hours (1968:40); the Dani men are constantly occupied with a variety of tasks, though many of them have little to do with securing food. The notion that hunting and gathering is inevitably the tough life and that agricultural peoples enjoy more leisure is false, and many would choose the hunting and gathering life over the agricultural if given the choice. And some have so chosen, the Crow being among them, since their ancestors were horticulturalists. It is clear that some nonliterate groups work as hard as people anywhere, while others enjoy a good deal of leisure. Societies differ in how hard they work according to a variety of factors, many, if not most of them, having to do with matters other than survival.

Cooperative work is rather common in nonindustrial cultures. Ordinarily this occurs as the informal working, side by side, of family members, relatives, or neighbors as they clear their gardens, pursue game, or accomplish whatever task is at hand. !Kung cooperate to locate and kill game, and the members of the Basseri household cooperate informally in the striking of camp, the packing and unpacking and loading and unloading of the animals (Barth 1961:16). Cooperative labor by large groups ordinarily is confined to special occasions, such as harvesting a large crop or building a house. Typically, a host invites large numbers to help with such jobs and rewards them with a feast. Some cultures even have permanently organized cooperative work groups. For example, the untitled men of a Samoan village are organized into a cooperative work group called the *aumaga* (Holmes 1974:31). They plan and provide most of the labor for cutting copra, repairing village paths, building houses, ferrying people and freight to boats anchored beyond the reef, planting and harvesting taro, group fishing on the reef flat, and similar village enterprises.

The obvious reason for cooperative labor is to accomplish jobs almost impossible for one or a few people. Beyond that, it may be more efficient, even for relatively easy tasks. This may be due to the enjoyment of working with others, since an ordinarily tedious task may be undertaken with greater will by a group. Some groups work in rhythm to music or a chant, and people may work harder in anticipation of feasting and recreation to follow. It is also true, however, that group labor sometimes is inefficient, especially if the social function interferes with the technological purpose, and some cooperative labor is arranged more for recreational than technological reasons.

The practice of paying wages to others is unimportant or absent in nonliterate groups. Assistance with a major task may be rewarded in some way, but laborers do not regard themselves as selling their services. Dani who have helped their neighbors in cooperative garden work have the

Figure 7–1 *Two teams of Miskito Indians take turns sawing a log into planks. Cooperative work is rather common in nonindustrial cultures.*

right to call on them for help with similar work in their own gardens (K. Heider 1970:39). Wage labor is characteristic of cultures, such as our own, that have market economies.

SPECIALIZATION

Economic specialization of some kind is found in every culture, but *sexual division of labor* is the salient feature among nonliterates. This is largely an extension of kinship organization, especially of the family. The husband is ordinarily concerned with tasks requiring greater strength and mobility or those that are more dangerous. Women are commonly less muscular than men and generally less mobile due to the physiology of reproduction. Accordingly, women are most often involved in tasks that make it possible for them to stay fairly close to home and children. The men hunt in hunting and gathering cultures, and women collect wild plant foods and, possibly, a few small animals. Among agricultural peoples men usually do only the heaviest work, and women commonly take care of the bulk of the field tasks. In herding cultures men usually care for the animals. In many societies the women work more steadily than the men, who often follow more of a stop-and-go rhythm.

It is important not to overemphasize the biological distinction as a basis for sexual division of work. Biology urges differentiation, but there are other reasons for the association of specific pursuits with one sex or the other that seem to be more a result of unique cultural-historical factors than biological. It has been suggested, for example, that women usually take the main responsibility for crops because they were the plant gatherers at the hunting and gathering level. Yet in some groups, the Pueblo Indian tribes, for example, the men do the farming. Many kinds of tasks assigned to one sex in a given society are assigned to the other sex in another society. In some cases historical evidence explains the division; in other cases the possible reason may be inferred; in still others there is no way of knowing or inferring the reason. The biological explanation seems least applicable to crafts, where one sex is as physiologically adequate for the task as the other. Functionally, the important thing about sexual division of labor is not which sex does what, but that the division maintains reciprocal dependence between men and women, providing a strong bond between husband and wife (Levis-Strauss 1956: 277). Some degree of economic interdependence between the sexes is present in every known culture.

Sometimes ethnographers report sexual division of labor by listing male work in one column and female work in another. By itself, this is an oversimplification, since the division is worked out with varying degrees of flexibility as husband and wife interact day by day. The Basseri women do most of the milking of the sheep and goats, but the men do some (Barth 1961:16). Among the Dani the women are supposed to do the planting, and unmarried men ask a female relative to plant for them. Actually, however, Karl Heider saw men engaged in planting a number of times (1970:39).

Age difference is another universal physiological factor associated with division of labor. Obviously, there are some tasks for which the youngest and oldest members of a society lack the strength, endurance, or other qualifications. In Samoa the elderly make sennit and do light agricultural work. The old women care for children, make mats and barkcloths, sew, and weed yards while the men fish on the reef. The old men also help their wives with domestic tasks and child care (Holmes 1974:91). In most cultures children either assist occasionally or take full responsibility for a variety of technological activities. Dani children are often assigned to herd the pigs, and the Samoan children of the 1920s would gather small land crabs. Children are often assigned tasks that prepare them for adult economic responsibilities.

Many cultures manifest little specialization beyond sexual and age differentiation. Though voluntary or part-time specialists may be found,

full-time groups of specialists are uncommon. Some Dani men are especially good at making arrow tips or removing them from wounded men.
Both men and women may specialize in curing, and some women serve
as midwives. These are only spare-time activities (K. Heider 1970:24).
Even the political leaders participate fully in the garden work. The Samoans
have much more specialization than the Dani, but everyone is first of all
a farmer. Even the tatooers, housebuilders, canoe builders, and master
fishermen spend some of their time in the fields (Holmes 1974:45). Even
among the twentieth-century Miskito, who have long been in a purchase
relationship with industrial cultures, there are no full-time craftsmen
(Helms 1971:153).

In some cultures there is community and regional specialization. The
Dugum Dani prepare bundles of hard, ashy salt from a nearby brine pool
and trade it for other things they desire, such as the fine nets that are
made by the neighboring Jale. In and around the Oaxaca Valley, which
lies about 350 miles southeast of Mexico City, the towns of the Zapotec,
Mixtec, and other Indian groups specialize in activities such as carpentry,
blanket-weaving, mining salt, making hats, making rope, or raising sheep.
A certain type of black pottery, for example, is produced in only one
town. This community specialization underlies a system whereby on
certain weekdays people from various communities display their products
for sale in some central market town, such as the capital city of Oaxaca
or the Sunday market at nearby Tlacolula. There is some full-time specialization in some of these communities, though much is half-time or less.

PROPERTY

Land, products of exploitive activities, and intangibles constitute the
property of both literate and nonliterate groups. Westerners err, however,
when they suppose that property is owned in the same way in all societies.
This led whites into trouble with the American Indians, since the latter
did not realize that the whites expected permanent possession and exclusive use of the land they paid for.

Ownership must be understood primarily as a matter of one's relationships with others, for one never has absolute ownership: there is
never complete freedom to do whatever one desires with something.
Even when there is a right to destroy a possession, there are limitations
on what can be done with it, and those limitations are imposed by other
people. *Ownership* refers to a person's or a group's rights to use, exploit,
or dispose of something and to exclude or control its use by others, as
well as limitations on those rights. Rights and limitations to property are
so different among nonliterate societies that only a a few basic generalizations are offered here.

Land among nonliterate and other traditional cultures is often owned
communally, that is, by the community or tribe as a whole rather than

by individuals or subgroups. This is especially true among hunters and gatherers. Territories may even lack precise boundaries, since they are defined in terms other than imaginary lines. !Kung band territories are not clearly defined and not defended, and there is no single term for them in the language (Yellen 1976:54). In each of the !Kung bands of the Nyae Nyae region there is a man known as the "big owner" who personifies the band's rights to the plant foods and water holes of the territory within which they live (Marshall 1976:192). The rights are conceived of in terms of resources rather than territory.

It is incorrect to assume that a society's territory is for the use of that group's members only. !Kung band territories overlap and some bands move about within the same territory. The White Knives and other Shoshoni groups of the American West entered one another's territories regularly. This was fully accepted by all, with no danger of attack from those ordinarily identified with an area (J. Harris 1940:43). Because of their highly possessive property concepts, Westerners may fail to recognize that many communities and tribes permit outsiders to enter and use their land, sometimes without permission.

Farming groups tend to hold land by *usufruct*. The land is owned basically by the community or tribe; so it is, in this sense, another form of communal land ownership. But the society grants families, kinship groups, or individuals the right to use the land as long as they cultivate

Figure 7–2 *King of Bunyoro. All the land of the Nyoro of Africa belonged, before British administration came, to the king.*

it. The users may not have the right to sell the land or otherwise transfer it, since ultimate ownership is communal. When a user stops cultivating the land for a period of time, it may be assigned by the tribe or community to someone else. All the land of the Nyoro of Africa belonged, before British administration came, to the king, and no one held permanent, irrevocable rights to any of it (Beattie 1971:168). A landholder had the right to build a house, cultivate the soil, graze livestock, and to pass those rights on to an heir. The rights were retained unless the owner abandoned the plot, failed to cultivate it for a long time, or was driven out for being a sorcerer, habitual thief, or was otherwise objectionable. Vacant lands were reallocated by the senior man of the clan.

Many herding groups emphasize possession of animals and pasture and the water and migration rights necessary to maintain them, rather than ownership of the land itself. Boundaries are not rigid, and there may be other groups occasionally or regularly using parts of the areas, though not always without bloodshed. An important tribal property of the Basseri is their migration route between the northern pastures and the southern pastures. It is the "tribal road", invested with considerable ritual significance. The Basseri leave the southern winter area at the spring equinox and follow a route northward over a series of ridges and passes that separate a succession of large flat valleys. Most of the tribe arrive in the Kur valley to the north in June. The tribal road includes rights to travel over certain roads and uncultivated lands, to draw water everywhere except from private wells, and to graze their herds outside the cultivated fields. These rights are recognized by the local populations and their authorities, but apply only at those times of year that the tribe migrates (Barth 1961:5). At the end of August a rapid return to the south is made, taking only forty to fifty days. The total distance is well over 200 miles. For their grazing rights the Basseri use a system similar to usufruct. Ideally they are under the control of the tribal chief, who has the ultimate right to allocate grazing privileges. Yet Basseri households and camps maintain their rights over generations without interference from the chief unless unusual circumstances justify it.

Land and other property may also be owned *jointly,* that is by a group smaller than the tribe or community, such as a kinship group or family. In Samoa the land is owned by the extended families; there is almost no individual land ownership (Holmes 1974:22). The titled man who serves as family head administers the land in behalf of his family. The oxen of the Nuer are owned by families rather than by individuals (Evans-Pritchard 1940:17), and so are the sheep and goats of the Basseri (Barth 1961:13).

Usage seems to be the basic criterion of ownership for food and artifacts, which are usually held individually or jointly. Many groups are generous with food and other items, sharing with relatives and others and, perhaps, giving away their possessions readily. But this sharing should not be confused with communal ownership, since the shared items may be borrowed without ownership transfer or individual or joint ownership retained until they are given away. !Kung artifacts are owned outright by the individual (Marshall 1976:188). Every arrow, bag, bead and so on, is the personal property of a man, woman, or child. But the !Kung do not keep things long, soon giving them away to express generosity and friendliness; one person gives something he or she owns to another person, who then becomes its new owner. Individual property is universal among human cultures.

Intangibles are considered as property in all kinds of cultures. Knowledge of curing processes, technical skills, religious knowledge, myths, songs, and dances are examples. Individuals often own such property, but kinship and other groups also may own it. Among the Crow Indians the privilege of mixing tobacco seeds with water and other ingredients was the property of a Tobacco Society official known as the Mixer (Lowie 1935:287), and the right was transferred by the rules of inheritance.

At death a person's rights and obligations concerning property must be transferred. In many cases inheritance is determined by *custom* or *law,* and in others it may be transferred by *testament.* Customary and legal rules of inheritance differ from one culture to another, and rules for different kinds of property may differ within the same culture. Ordinarily, a male's property rights are acquired by another male, such as a son, sister's son, or brother, while a female's are passed on to another female. Murdock's *Ethnographic Atlas* lists several alternatives. Property may be inherited through males, usually by a son or sons (*patrilineal* inheritance); or it may be inherited through females, ordinarily by a sister's son or sons. It also may be divided among the children of either or both sexes, sometimes with the sons receiving more than the daughters. In a minority of cases, either the oldest son receives the property (*primogeniture*) or the youngest acquires it (*ultimogeniture*). In cultures which lack inheritance rules a testament, by which the individual declares his will as to the disposition of his property, may be important. There also are societies which practice the destruction, burial, or giving away of movable property (Murdock 1967:167).

CAPITAL, CREDIT, AND INTEREST

Substantivists have objected to the application of these terms to nonliterate economics, but there are some practices which seem rather parallel to some of our own in these areas. Nonliterate societies do use certain types of goods to produce other goods, and it may be appropriate to say they have capital, as long as we avoid thinking that their attitudes about it are identical to our own. Of course, nonindustrial groups are very limited in capital goods as compared to industrial civilizations. Hunting peoples have their weapons; farmers have their implements and storage facilities; but some fishing groups, notably Indian groups along the northwest coast of North America, maintain more capital goods than most agriculturalists, pastoralists, or hunters. Ocean-going groups, especially, have various kinds of water craft, elaborate netting and trapping devices, hooks and lines, and other items which represent a great investment of labor and time and give long-lasting service.

The investment of goods with the notion of getting a return also occurs in nonliterate cultures. The Nuer sometimes loan cattle, for which they expect to receive a more valuable animal than they loaned when they are paid back (Evans-Pritchard 1940:91). Yet this is more of a social than economic practice, since a Nuer lends cattle only to someone with whom he has an established social relationship. Among the Ekagi (Kapauku), who live some 150 to 200 miles west of the Dani, a borrower of shell money may pledge to return extra shells when he repays the loan, though there is no legal mechanism to enforce the interest payment (Pospisil 1963b:26). A Nigerian Nupe with capital may entrust some of his money to a trader for a specific commercial venture, such as a trading expedition. The trader combines the money with his own, and if the enterprise is successful, he returns the investment with the profit (Nadel 1942:311). There are other examples of these kinds among nonliterates, but more widespread by far is the notion of lending without interest.

DISTRIBUTION AND EXCHANGE

The substantivists have contributed significantly to the study of economic systems by investigating the variety of modes of allocating goods and services. They have stressed three major modes, which may occur in combination with one another but one of which may be dominant in a given economic system. *Reciprocity* is the exchange of items between units of similar type, for example, between individuals, households, kinship groups, or communities. *Redistribution* is the flow of economic items to some central point from which they are redistributed to the society. The *market system* of allocation is characterized by economy-wide operation of general purpose money and prices governed by supply and demand.

Reciprocity

This exchange mode is fundamental in the economies of most cultures and present in all. In many cultures most items are transferred by a form of reciprocity known as *gift exchange*. Distribution of goods is not the main purpose of gift exchange, rather, the items are distributed as a result and as a part of the reciprocal social and ceremonial obligations that people have toward one another. Though the economic consequences are extensive, the main reason for the exchanges is to establish or maintain social bonds important to those involved. Here is another illustration of the systemic interrelationships within culture, since gift exchange, conceived economically, is embedded in a culture's network of social relationships. Food-sharing is a case in point. One person maintains good social relationships with another and gains respect or prestige by sharing food, and as the occasion arises, recipients are expected to respond in kind. Marshall reports that the !Kung are fully aware of the great social value of sharing meat (1976:295). When the !Kung have killed a large animal, the first distribution is to the hunters and to the owner of the arrow that killed the animal, but the second distribution is along kinship lines. The hunter gives meat, first to his wife's parents, then to his own parents, his wife, his children, his brothers and sisters, his wife's brothers and sisters and to other friends and relatives who are present. Visitors will also receive some. Each receiver of meat gives again, and such waves of sharing continue. In the later waves of sharing the act definitely has the quality of giving, and the person who has received meat must reciprocate at a future time. From the killing and distribution of the meat of one animal, then, all receive meat, and a tight network of social bonds is maintained.

Marriage arrangements are frequently accompanied by transfer of gifts. Often a groom and his relatives must make substantial gifts to the bride's family. Sometimes there is a two-way exchange, both before the wedding and at designated times during the early period of married life. A vast amount of property changes hands at Samoan weddings as well as on other important occasions (Holmes 1974:83). Some observers have stressed how this promotes equal distribution of economic resources throughout the community, but others have emphasized the good will between individuals and between families that is affirmed by such extensive gift exchanges.

It is sometimes important to exchange gifts of identical kind or equivalent value. Many an American feels disturbed at receiving a Christmas gift of much greater value than the one given. In a number of societies, prestige depends greatly on how much has been given and received.

Trade in its various forms is another kind of economic reciprocity. Face-to-face barter is the most common form, but some societies have what is known as *silent trade* or, sometimes, *dumb barter*. One party leaves the items to be traded at a designated spot and withdraws, sometimes to watch unobserved. The other party then comes, examines the goods and, if satisfied, leaves items in their place. The fact that this system has been known in several parts of the world for hundreds of years demonstrates its workability.

Face-to-face barter may or may not be accompanied by bargaining and haggling. The stereotype that prices in peasant and nonliterate markets are invariably established in this way for each individual sale is false. In many societies where bargaining is practiced, both buyer and seller already know about what price they will come to when they begin, and the bargaining is more a social activity than an economic procedure. In some places the native vendors take advantage of the visitor's false stereotypes about bargaining and ignorance of local set prices.

Trade may or may not occur at special market sites. Hunters and collectors, especially, lack marketplaces, and their trade is occasional and, usually, individual. Among peoples with enough occupational specialization, marketplaces facilitate exchange between communities, for within the community trade can often be handled adequately without a special assembly point. Markets have been important in several places among nonliterates, but their presence does not mean that the market principle of exchange dominates the economy. The markets that are so striking a feature of West Africa are important as trading places, but the market system of economic allocation (see page 124) is minor and could disappear without disrupting the economic system or the activities of the marketplaces. West African markets are also places where people meet to exchange news and gossip with friends and relatives, make political decisions or engage in recreational and religious activities (Bohannan 1963:242).

Trading occasions vary from accidental encounters between individuals to elaborate, permanent markets, with most being between these polar extremes. Culturally different groups who want one another's products often arrange trading occasions. Tswana pastoralists would annually leave their towns on hunting and grazing expeditions and rendezvous with groups of !Kung for several weeks of hunting, dancing, and trading. !Kung traded furs, hides, honey, and ostrich eggshell beadwork for tobacco, clay pots, iron implements, and European items (Lee 1976: 92). The Basseri, who depend on trade with sedentary groups for a great part of their daily necessities, either enter the marketplaces in the towns and cities to buy and sell or establish relationships with trading partners (Barth 1961:98). They pitch their camps several miles from town and ride in, some bringing money and others bringing livestock to exchange for cash. Livestock buyers meet them at the edge of town and much haggling ensues before the deal is closed. But most goods are obtained through trading partners in smaller villages and from itinerant peddlers. Each Basseri has an enduring relationship with a number of such partners in villages scattered along the migration route and, also, in the winter pasture area. Usually the villager comes to the Basseri camp with his donkeys loaded with a variety of goods, and the nomad invites his partner into his tent for tea and the arrangement of the purchase.

In many places goods are reciprocally transferred between communities and tribes over long distances, often through chains of trading partners. The Kula ring of Melanesia as reported by Malinowski in his noted ethnography, *Argonauts of the Western Pacific,* has become a classic anthropological example of intercommunity trading partner chains. The trading requires long canoe trips among islands lying off the east end of New Guinea. Two basic items are traded around the large circle

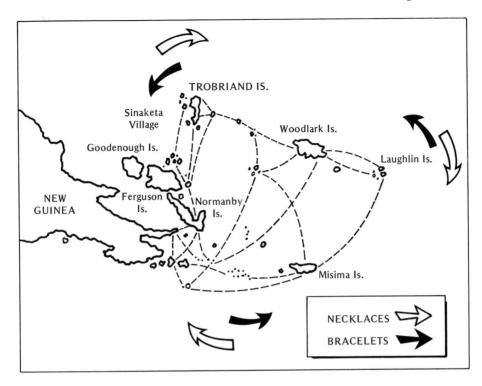

NECKLACES
BRACELETS

Figure 7–3 *The Kula ring of the South Pacific.*

of islands. Long necklaces of red shell move clockwise around the circle of islands, and white shell bracelets move in the other direction. As items pass around the ring and are kept for a while by different persons, they acquire increasing sentimental value and accumulate a freight of stories about their history: whom they have belonged to, the adventures of the expedition by which they were transferred, and so forth. No participant knows or can describe the entire Kula system, but the result is that bracelets going counterclockwise pass entirely around the ring of islands in two to ten years, depending on how many traders possess them or how long each keeps them. In addition to the ritual exchange of necklaces and bracelets, many items of economic importance are traded, such as axe blades, baskets, combs, clay pots, sago, and coconuts. Trade in such practical items takes place not between the partners in the Kula relationship but between accompanying members of an expedition and the local residents (Malinowski 1929:32).

In the highlands of western New Guinea, the Dani participate in an extensive network of informal trade contacts (K. Heider 1970:27). The Dani have salt, which is desired by other groups, but the forests around them have been exhausted of many resources the Dani depend upon. From the Jalemo, for example, they receive bush fibers, bark for net making, bamboo for knives, and other items. The trading parties move back and forth between neighboring groups, since the constant warfare makes it dangerous for people to travel beyond familiar territory. Men in different areas often form informal trading-friendship relationships, and goods move rather long distances through such links. At least two kinds of ocean shells, for example, have found their way into every part of the highlands.

There are enough examples of these kinds from all over the world to indicate that, over the long run at least, trading has significantly affected the world's nonliterate cultures. Economic reciprocity between communities and tribes appears to be a major type of intercultural contact, but its significance in cultural change and the extent of its role in accounting for cultural similarities over rather large areas has yet to be fully worked out.

Redistribution

This mode of economic allocation has been strongly emphasized by Polanyi (1944:54). It is particularly important in a number of nonliterate societies, especially those with centralized political control (Service 1978: 7). The controlling center serves also as a focus of economic redistribution of the goods and services that are received from the population. Redistribution, for example, is important in many African chiefdoms and monarchies, the chief or king being expected to give generously to his subjects on ceremonial and other occasions, thereby maintaining political loyalty. In turn, a chief's subjects pay tribute to him, with the result that he is provided with the goods to bestow on his people. In this way economic items are allocated and inequalities of production within the chiefdom are evened out. The people realize that if they have met their obligations to contribute their surpluses to the chief's granary, they will be provided what they need in case of scarcity. Among the traditional Nyoro, the king delegated authority to territorial chiefs of various ranks. From their subjects the chiefs received tribute in foodstuffs, beer, and labor, and a portion of this was passed on from time to time to the king. The king in turn would reciprocate with feasts and gifts for his chiefs and the people (Beattie 1971:136). Also, in return for their donations and their loyalty, the people expected a chief to provide feasts, protection, and help in time of need. If he failed they would move to another district and offer their goods and services to another chief. It is apparent that both economic and political functions are intertwined in this institution, illustrating again the relationships between the aspects of culture into which social scientists divide cultural phenomena.

While redistribution is central in some cultures, as among the Nyoro, it occurs as a secondary mode in many types of cultures from urban industrial groups to hunting and gathering societies. In American and other politically elaborated cultures, citizens are taxed by the government, which uses the income to provide goods and services such as highways, medical research, and compensation for victims of discrimination, unemployment, and natural disasters. Redistribution among the !Kung is illustrated by the assignment of responsibility for distributing the meat from a newly killed game animal to the owner of the arrow that killed it. As in other examples of redistribution, the item is directed to a central point from which it is redistributed.

The Market System

This system is the main allocation mode in Euroamerican and other urbanized cultures. It should not be confused with markets, the sites where people assemble for trade, since markets are found in many cultures that lack a market economy, and exchanges in societies with an economy-wide market system frequently take place without the exchanging parties meeting or directly communicating with one another.

Market systems are associated with what has been called *general purpose money*. This does not mean that money is used to buy many or all kinds of goods and services, but that money serves more than one basic purpose. One purpose is to provide a medium of exchange for *buying and selling*. A second is the *discharge of obligations,* such as taxes, fines, and debts. Third, money may provide a *standard of value*: a way of comparing the value of different kinds of goods and services. There are other functions, but these are considered the three main ones. Money is general purpose if it serves all of these basic functions; if it serves only one or two, it may be called *limited purpose money* (Dalton 1965:48). Apparently, general purpose money is found among only a few nonliterate groups. A number of traditional and rural societies use the general purpose money of the civilization with which they are integrated.

The money objects used by societies operating by the market system and having general purpose money serve most effectively if they manifest certain kinds of physical characteristics and relationships. These are *homogeneity, divisibility, portability,* and *durability* (Gregory 1933:602). Euroamerican coinage exhibits these features, and a few nonliterate groups with money forms meeting these criteria have been found. Cowry shells have been used in a number of places, and dog's teeth have been used in the Admiralty Islands. Among the Ekagi, remote New Guinea neighbors of the Dani, a cowry shell of angular shape, uneven surface, and yellowish coloring is the most important denomination. Two of these equal one larger cowry similar in appearance, and ten to twelve of them equal one large, angular, uneven cowry. It takes fifteen small-smooth cowries to equal this basic denomination (Pospisil 1963a:301). Ekagi money is used to buy and sell food, domesticated animals, growing crops, land, garden labor, surgical services, magical curing, pig breeding, and so on. It also is used in discharging obligations, as in damage settlements and payment of fines. Finally it serves as the standard of value for Ekagi goods and services.

Limited purpose money that fails to manifest all four physical characteristics and relationships is found in a fair proportion of nonliterate cultures and in widely scattered places. In addition, money seldom functions to purchase more than a limited number of exchangeable items. By contrast, in modern civilized cultures money is used for a great variety of things. Even the money of Euroamerican societies, however, is not used for buying and selling all goods and services exchanged; acts of hospitality are an example (Burling 1962:820).

Formalists allege that there are some nonliterate cultures with market economies and general purpose money used for a wide variety of exchangeable items. Pospisil insists that the Ekagi have general purpose money, savings, operation of the law of supply and demand, exchange of commodities through sale, paid labor, and lease contracts (1963a:300). Substantivists have suggested that those who report such cases have read more into the situation than is actually there and do not sufficiently appreciate the crucial differences between Western and nonliterate economic processes.

Cultures differ in the relative importance of the three modes of allocation. It has been suggested that reciprocity dominates in band and tribal level cultures (see pp. 26–28); "archaic" cultures (those with the simpler types of state political systems) are redistributive; and modern Western cultures are pervaded by the market principle. The validity of this scheme is debated. It is enough to say, first, that two or three allocation modes commonly exist in the same culture. Second, reciprocity is universal; it has economic consequences in all cultures. Third, reciprocity is the dominant allocation mode in a great many cultures, particularly in kinship-oriented societies. Fourth, redistribution is present in many cultures as an important means of distribution and exchange, but its importance differs from culture to culture, and it is the dominant mode in only some. Finally, the market principle of allocation is characteristic of modern civilizations and, possibly, a few nonliterate cultures.

CONSUMPTION

The unit of consumption is not always identical to the unit of production in nonliterate societies. For instance, a given family may not consume all that its members produce and may consume items it did not produce. This is true even of the relatively simple hunting and collecting groups, for they may share food and other things rather extensively. A !Kung arrow, for example, had passed from one person to another five times before it was used in killing an eland (Marshall 1976:301). The !Kung value the artifacts in which they invest time and effort, but they constantly circulate within and among the various bands. The pastoral-agricultural Nuer must always share a surplus with neighbors; in fact, no Nuer ever has a surplus (Evans-Pritchard 1940:183).

The common notion that nonliterate peoples lack the discipline necessary to save for lean times must be rejected. Their technology embodies few effective techniques for preserving and storing most foods, and people often find themselves having to consume great quantities within a short period if they are to consume them at all. The assumption of natural improvidence of "primitives" is further invalidated by the fact that many do what they can with the preservation techniques available. The nineteenth-century Crow dried meat and used it in the preparation of pemmican, which was stored in rawhide cases for future use (Lowie 1935:74).

Consumption is for more than biological maintenance and has a number of functions in all cultures. For some the preparation and consumption of food is something of an art, and the enjoyment of taste may be highly emphasized. In addition to this aesthetic function, sociability may be important. *Prestige consumption* is also of considerable significance in many societies. This can be most highly developed in cultures having the necessary surpluses, but it is common among such cultures. Upper-class members of American society, for example, commonly exhibit their social position by means of their cars, houses, clothing, and fine art objects, and spending money on parties, vacations, and philanthropy. Some Oceanian peoples, we noted earlier, produce great public displays of yams which, though they are left to rot, bring prestige to the owner.

Perhaps the best-known example of prestige consumption in ethnographic literature is the *potlatch* of some of the tribes of North America's Northwest Coast. These sometimes spectacular giveaway ceremonies were made famous by Ruth Benedict's dramatic account in *Patterns of Culture* of the potlatches of Kwakiutl chiefs, who tried to destroy one another's reputations by seeing who could give away or destroy the most property. This extreme practice has no close counterpart in most North American groups and may have developed after contact with Europeans. The Nootka potlatch is probably more typical. At the main ceremony the host brought out his property and announced whom the potlatch was honoring, the occasion for giving it, how much he would give away, and where it came from. He indicated what he got from the potlatches where he had been a guest, how much came from the various rights he owned, what his family and tribesmen had contributed, and so on. After some ritual display of his titles, dances, songs, and other privileges, he distributed goods among the guests in the order of their rank. By this ceremony a man's hereditary claims and his right to transmit them to his heirs were publicly acknowledged, the prestige of the host and his group was validated and enhanced, and the social bonds between the host group and the guests were strengthened. In contrast with their neighbors, the Kwakiutl, the Nootka were careful not to humiliate former hosts by giving them more than they received when the guest-host roles were reversed. In fact, less might be returned.

WEALTH

The wealth concept implies that some members of the society have more of some valued kind of property than others. In a culture like that of the !Kung everyone is approximately on the same level; there is very little to be accumulated and little opportunity to accumulate it. Some !Kung are better hunters than others and bring home more meat, but the family without meat receives plenty as the result of !Kung meat-sharing customs. From this kind of dead-level economic equality, cultures vary from those with insignificant wealth differences to those in which differences are marked. Cultures also differ in how wealth is used and what it stands for. Perhaps it is obvious that cultures differ in what constitutes wealth. For the Basseri of Iran wealth includes herds of sheep and goats; for the Nuer it is cattle; and for the Samoans it is houses, canoes, food, bark cloth, and mats.

There is a fundamental contrast between the use of wealth in American society and its use in many others. For Americans the possession of wealth and its use for themselves is a road to prestige; whereas in many other cultures it is the giving of wealth to others that brings prestige and influence. In traditional Samoa the road to prestige for an ordinary person was through the contribution of goods and labor to the extended family, and a titled man gained respect and influence by plowing his wealth back into the family pool for the benefit of the people (Holmes 1974:21). Many cultures have *leveling mechanisms* (of which the Samoan practice is an example) which ensure that the community's wealth will serve many people rather than piling up in the hands of a few individuals or groups. Basseri polygyny and the custom of giving a patrimony to sons at their marriage militate against extreme accumulation of wealth by one person. By the time a man has accumulated much, he probably has a son ready for marriage, which drains off a large portion of his herds, and if he has several sons, the effect is even greater. And the practice by which a wealthy man takes an additional, younger wife, may add to the number of sons who will have to receive a patrimony, equal to those of the sons of the first wife. Only childless men can accumulate wealth throughout their lives, but they lack the labor supply in the form of sons to expand their herds rapidly (Barth 1961:106).

8

SOCIAL
ORGANIZATION:
KINSHIP

Social organization is variously defined by anthropologists to designate several categories of customs that most extensively involve interpersonal relations and the groups that result from them. Inevitably included are marriage and family relations; kinship groups such as the lineage, clan, phratry, and kindred; age groups; and a variety of nonkinship groupings such as clubs and secret societies. Sometimes economic organization, political organization, legal customs, and social stratification are included. It is important to remember that, since any culture is a system of inter-dependent customs, it is impossible to carve it into mutually exclusive categories without doing violence to its wholeness.

Social units are formed as people are stimulated to establish and maintain social identities and their associated statuses. A basic reason that people relate to one another according to various statuses is *kinship*. The relationship between a mother and child is the most important of all, and all over the world the ties between them are characteristically close. The tie with the father may also be important, and siblings (children of the same parents), grandparents, aunts and uncles, cousins, grandchildren, and more remote kin are apt to relate to one another by virtue of the parent-child link. But not all cultures define kin in just the same way, and people who, by scientifically derived etic concepts, are defined as genetically related may be nonkin in some societies. Many cultures, for example, define an offspring of one's mother's brother and of the father's sister as unrelated and, therefore, a potential spouse, while an offspring of one's mother's sister and father's brother is a relative and, consequently, not a marriage prospect. Anthropologists refer to people who are sup-posed to be biologically related as *consanguineal* relatives.

Sex identity is, of course, another basic factor in the formation of social units. Marriage, which establishes families and many other kinship links, is a world-wide response to sex identity. Anthropologists refer to people who are linked through marriage as *affinal* relatives. *Residence* is significant in group formation primarily because of the inevitability of responses to proximity of other humans. Often, of course, residing to-gether is a consequence of kinship, marriage, or some other factor. *Mutual interest,* for whatever reason, and having *special purposes* in common often result in the development of interaction customs and group formation. Finally, *age differentiation* is a factor in the formation of some social units.

MARRIAGE

Marriage designates the socially recognized, specially intimate relationship between a man and a woman which is expected to involve the sexual, economic, and other forms of interaction thought necessary to a full life. It is one of the major means by which new groups are formed and new relationships between existing groups are established and maintained.

Spouse Selection

No culture allows complete freedom in selection of a marital partner. The universally found incest taboo, for example, prohibits sexual congress between siblings or between parent and child, although the proscription usually extends to other relatives also. This results in marrying outside the family. Certain exceptions are found, such as the brother-sister marriage in Hawaii or ancient Egypt, but these are special cases. In both Hawaii and Egypt brother and sister marriages occurred only in the royal family so as to maintain the purity of the royal line. Incest among family members also occurs in many societies as unapproved and unusual deviations. In spite of exceptions and violations, the incest taboo is found in all societies.

Marriage in many cultures is far more than the business of two people. It is often a union of social groups, namely the relatives of the bride and groom. Relatives affected by the union—parents, brothers and sisters, uncles, aunts, and cousins—may have a right to influence who will marry whom. In some societies specified relatives, commonly the parents, negotiate with another family without consulting the future spouses; in a few cases the decision is made while the children are still infants, or even before they are born. If a Nyoro man wants to make such an arrangement, he might say to a close friend, "My wife is pregnant; I give her child to you!" (Beattie 1960:56). This is understood to mean that, if the child is a girl, she will be available to marry the friend's son, but there will be no marriage if the child turns out to be a boy. In many societies young people are free to choose their own spouses within culturally defined bounds. Once the decision is made, the two families make whatever arrangements are defined or permitted in the culture in question.

The immediate family is not the only group within which marriage may be prohibited. *Exogamy,* the term for taking a spouse from a group other than one's own, may apply to clans and other groups of relatives larger than the family as well as to the members of communities and other territorial units. A socially significant effect of exogamy is to link the married couple's respective groups, establishing between them a set of ties that may have economic, political, or other functions. These inter-group linkages contribute significantly to the unity of a society. Frequently this unity emerges from the marriage of various members of a clan or other kinship group with men or women from the several other kinship groups of which the society is composed. For example, members of the Whistling Water clan of the nineteenth-century Crow took their spouses from one of the other twelve clans found among the Crow, and there might be marriage links between Whistling Water people and several, if not all, of the rest of the clans. In some other societies social solidarity is augmented by the existence of pairs of spouse-exchanging groups. The Dani are divided into two exogamous categories of relatives, who are bound to one another by the membership of the husband in one of them and the wife in the other. Each of these halves of Dani society are, in turn, divided into clans. In a few societies the rule is that a person can take a spouse from only one of the several other kinship groups that make up the community or tribe. If, hypothetically, the tribe consists of five clans, men of the first clan marry only women of the second clan, but men of the second clan do not marry women of the first. Men of the second clan marry women from the third; men of the third marry women of the fourth; men of the fourth marry women of the fifth; and men of the fifth marry women of the first clan. Thus each man marries a woman of his mother's clan and a closed chain binds the kinship groups together. Marriage exchanges between two groups and through chains of kinship groups have been discussed at length by the noted French anthropologist Claude Levi-Strauss (1969:178).

The opposite of exogamy is *endogamy,* which is marriage within one's own group. Obviously, the family cannot be endogamous, though some larger kinship groups are. It is fairly common for communities to be endogamous. The nomadic camps of the Basseri of Iran are strongly endogamous, since the headmen try to maintain or augment their influence within the camp by promoting marriages between members (Barth 1961:35). Both exogamy and endogamy may be either *required* or *preferred.* Groups which are neither exogamous or endogamous are said to be *agamous.*

Often, it is preferred that one marry a certain kind of relative. Many societies, for example, require any person (Ego) to marry a *cross cousin,* that is, one related to him or her through the mother and her brother or through the father and his sister, as diagrammed in Figure 8–1. Cross cousins, then, are related through siblings of the opposite sex. Many groups distinguish cross cousins from *parallel cousins,* children of siblings of the same sex, that is, children of sisters or children of brothers. Examine Figure 8–2 for a clarification of the difference between cross cousins and parallel cousins. In most cultures parallel cousins may not marry one

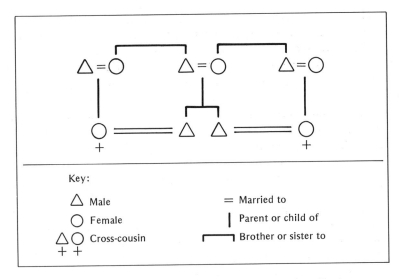

Figure 8–1 *Cross cousin marriage. Many societies require (Ego) to marry one related to him or her through the mother and her brother or through the father and his sister.*

another, though in some Islamic groups, including the Basseri, there is a tendency for a man to marry his father's brother's daughter.

The distinction between parallel and cross cousins is functionally interdependent with group membership and statuses (see page 88). In many societies a person's parallel cousins on one side of the family belong to one's own kinship group, while the cross cousins belong to some other group. If the kinship group is exogamous, its members must find their spouses in a different kinship group from their own, and they

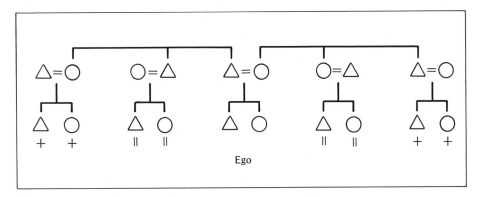

Figure 8–2 *Parallel cousins and cross cousins. The distinction between cross cousins and parallel cousins is important to understanding kinship arrangements.*

may be allowed to marry a cross cousin. In addition, one status label may be applied to the parallel cousins and a different one to the cross cousins. Under one common mode of labeling relatives, a person refers to parallel cousins by the same term used for brothers and sisters, which harmonizes well with the prohibition against marrying people who belong to his or her kinship group (see page 135). The distinction between cross cousins and parallel cousins is so important to understanding kinship arrangements that those unfamiliar with the concept will profit from mastering it before going on.

Two kinds of widely found secondary marriage illustrate that marriage establishes a relationship between groups. In some cultures a man who loses his wife by death may replace her by marrying her sister, a custom known as the *sororate*. The *levirate* is marriage of a widow to her late husband's brother. The Crow have both the sororate and the levirate, since some men would marry a brother's widow, and a man had the right to replace a deceased wife with a younger sister. The Crow referred to the sororate by a term meaning "keeping a sister-in-law," while their term for the levirate is translated as "keeping a brother's wife" (Lowie 1935:51). Both the levirate and the sororate continue the union between the two sets of relatives which were joined when the original partners married. The terms are also used to include the fairly frequent cases in which a dead spouse is not replaced by an actual sibling, but by a close kinsman, such as a cousin who belongs to the same kinship group as the deceased. This also might occur among the Crow.

Marriage Ratification

In most societies some kind of wedding ceremony marks the initiation of a marriage. The specific rituals take such a diversity of forms in various cultures that no attempt is made here to delineate their variety. In some cultures the ceremonies last several days, while in other places the couple need only live together to establish the marriage. Among the Kaingang of Brazil the beginning of marriage is marked simply by the couple's announcement that they are "sitting together." In some communities the ceremony takes place sometime after the couple begins to reside together, perhaps after the first child has arrived.

Aside from wedding ceremonies, there are many other means of ratifying a marriage. Some kind of property transfer is found in all parts of the world, frequently as what anthropologists call either *bride price* or *bride wealth*. This is paid by the groom's kin to the bride's relatives, not only in compensation for the woman's loss but also for the loss of the children she will bear. This transaction reinforces the principle that marriages are often more group than individual affairs, especially since the wealth is received and used by the parents or other relatives of the bride, not by the bride herself. This is almost never correctly viewed as the purchase of property, since the woman is not thought of as a possession in the same sense as the items exchanged for her. The Nyoro say that no bridewealth can be large enough to compensate for the value of a woman who, though her labor is important, will above all bear children to continue her husband's line (Beattie 1960:56). A husband among the Nyoro is expected to feel gratitude and respect toward his wife's clan, since they have given him a wife.

The bride price differs from society to society according to what is regarded as wealth. Among the cattle-raising tribes of eastern and southern Africa the bride price is cattle, forty or more head among the Nuer of the Upper Nile. Among the Basseri the bride price is comprised of sheep; the Crow paid horses; and the modern Nyoro contribute money, though the bride wealth was formerly cattle. In many cultures the bride price contributes significantly to marital stability, since it may have to be returned if the relationship is dissolved.

The *dowry* is a substantial transfer of property from the bridal group to that of the groom, just the opposite of bride price. The practice is rare among nonliterate cultures. It is reported for one or two groups in Australia and for a number of literate communities.

Another widely found mode of ratifying marriages is a major *gift exchange* between the pair's relatives. The gifts seem to symbolize the unity between the two groups that are establishing an alliance by the marriage. It has been suggested that it is similar to the exchange of Christmas gifts among those who maintain valued social relationships. As part of the lavish exchange of property at a Samoan wedding the Talking Chiefs of each kinship group present the gifts, which consist mostly of pig meat and other foods from the groom's relatives, and fine-mats, floor mats, and other textiles from the bride's kin (Holmes 1974:50, 83; Mead 1969:96). This exchange is an excellent example of economic reciprocity operating within a social context.

In some groups the groom is required to work for the bride's family before or after co-residence begins, or at both times. This mode of ratifying marriages is known as *bride service* or, sometimes, *suitor service*. As with the bride price, the notion of compensation to the bride's relatives is involved. A !Kung man serves his wife's parents and their dependents by hunting for them. The people say that this service should continue until three children have been born, and since !Kung men may marry little girls and have to wait until they mature to live with them, they sometimes have to serve her family for ten years or more (Marshall 1976: 170). The Miskito formerly might betroth a girl before puberty, with her husband-to-be residing in her parents' home until she was old enough to marry, which may have involved bride service (Helms 1971:25).

Another arrangement, functionally more like the bride price and bride service than it may seem, is *brother-sister exchange*. The family of the groom may give one of his sisters to his bride's relatives to be the wife of one of their men, perhaps the bride's brother. The Yạnomamö

Figure 8–3   *Basseri preparing a marriage contract. Many Basseri marriages are sister exchange marriages.*

of Brazil and Venezuela follow brother-sister exchange so faithfully that some of their villages are made up of only two kinship groups, whose members take their spouses from the other group (Chagnon 1977:55), and many of the Basseri marriages are sister exchange marriages, the term for which means "cow-for-cow" (Barth 1961:33).

Marriage by *capture* is not the usual or approved way for securing a wife in any community, though it occurs some among warlike groups and as a minor mode in some other cases. The !Kung often mention marriage by capture, but this is apparently no more than fantasy (Marshall 1976:266). Mock capture is sometimes a feature of weddings and may be a ritual means of expressing the reluctance of the bride and her relatives to initiate the new relationship.

There are few cultures in which *elopement* is the main way of getting a spouse, but elopements do occur in most societies. It seems to be a way out sometimes used when one is unhappy with the partner chosen by the parents, when a strongly desired marriage is not approved by one of the families, or when standard marriage rules are otherwise viewed as too burdensome. Miskito couples sometimes elope, but the custom has disadvantages, especially for the woman, since her family may disown her, thereby depriving her of support if the marriage develops problems (Helms

1971:87). A Miskito man is expected to secure permission from a woman's parents before marrying her.

Inheritance is another way of receiving a wife, some cases of levirate and sororate being examples. A very few groups permit a son to inherit the wife of his father, provided she is not his biological mother. If an elderly Nuer man dies who has recently acquired a young wife who has either no children or only one, a son may receive her as his own wife, but this is rare (Evans-Pritchard 1951:112). In other cultures a man may acquire a wife by being adopted into her family, whereby he becomes both the woman's husband and the legal heir of his in-laws.

Marital Stability

Cultures vary widely in the degree of marital stability. In many non-literate groups the relationship is quite brittle, and a person may have several spouses during a lifetime. Also, the act of divorce is often quite simple, termination of co-residence being all that is required. Divorce among the nineteenth-century Crow was frequent and required no ceremony (Lowie 1935:55). A man might divorce his wife for adultery, for having a bad disposition, or just because he felt like it. A Crow woman could also divorce her husband. Nevertheless, the Crow ideal was one of stable, faithful companionship, and a number of Crow marriages approached that ideal. In many societies the marriages are rather brittle until the first child is born, after which the relationship is apt to be enduring. Evans-Pritchard found that the Nuer thought of marriage as incomplete until a child was born, and that most broken marriages occurred either during or shortly after the marriage ceremonies. But after a wife had borne her first child and had lived with her husband for a year or two, divorce was quite unusual (1951:94). In some cultures, as previously mentioned, bride price may contribute to the stability of marriages, since the bride's relatives may have to repay the wealth if the woman and her husband separate. Evans-Pritchard feels that, while the bride price is considered by the Nuer, it is not the major factor contributing to stability.

FAMILIES

Traditionally, Westerners have thought of the family as the social unit established by a man and a woman who live together, cooperate economically, and produce and rear children. But anthropologists have found units in a number of cultures which function like families but lack husband and father. In some cases among black groups of Guyana a man may father children, but instead of residing with his wife, he continues in his mother's household, since he may have responsibilities to her. The mother of his children, then, may set up a household consisting only of herself and her children (R. Smith 1956:257), and this husbandless household carries out most of the functions of two-parent families. Units of this kind occur as an alternative arrangement in enough cultures that social scientists have come to call them *matrifocal* families. It seems most useful to define the family as a group consisting of at least one parent with offspring and providing for the physical care, affectional support, and socialization of its members.

Most families in most societies consist of at least one husband and wife with children. Many anthropologists refer to this unit as the *nuclear family,* since it may be viewed as a basic unit expandable in various ways to form larger families consisting of more than one nuclear component. *Independent nuclear families* prevail in Euroamerican and many other societies. They result from the practice of *neolocal residence,* whereby a newly married couple establishes a household separate from those of parents or other relatives. Residence of husband and wife in separate households, which occurs in a few societies, is known as *duolocal residence.*

Nuclear families may be expanded or combined with one another to form larger units in at least three ways. Residence practices may result in the combining of related nuclear families of different generations; related families of the same generation may join together; or husband or wife may add an additional spouse or spouses. An *extended family* consists of three or more generations of related nuclear families. Extended families are formed through a residence rule that provides for a bride and groom to join either the family of one of the parents or the groom's maternal uncle. If the rule is for the groom to bring his bride into the family into which he was born, *patrilocal residence* prevails and a *patrilocal extended family* is formed, consisting of the older parents, their unmarried children, if any, and their married sons with their spouses and children. A *matrilocal extended family* is created when daughters remain with their parents at marriage, bringing their husbands into the group and rearing their children as members of the larger unit. *Ambilocal extended families* result when both sons and daughters bring their spouses into the parental family, since *ambilocal residence* allows choice as to which family the married couple lives with. An *avunculocal extended family* is formed when a man living with his maternal uncle brings his wife into the uncle's family, but *avunculocal residence* is unusual. The four types of families are diagrammed in Figure 8–4.

Anthropologists also apply these residence terms to cases in which the bride and groom are from different villages or other territories, and the question is which spouse's territory they will reside in rather than which spouse's family they will join. Patrilocal residence, then, refers to either joining the groom's parental family or taking up residence in the groom's territory instead of the bride's. The same distinction applies in reverse to matrilocal residence. With avunculocal residence, also, the

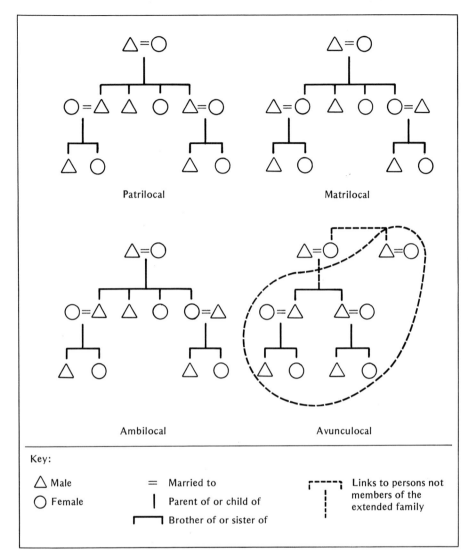

Figure 8–4 *Four types of extended families. An* extended family *is one which consists of three or more generations of related nuclear families.*

couple may either become part of the groom's mother's brother's family or only reside in the uncle's village or territory. So patrilocal, matrilocal, and avunculocal residence may involve living either *with* or *near* a parental or avuncular family.

Those using ethnological literature will also encounter the terms *virilocal* and *uxorilocal*. In 1947 Adam proposed that the terms replace patrilocal and matrilocal, respectively (1947:678), but since he coined them several different usages of the new terms have been proposed. In spite of the confusion, their wide usage justifies noting that virilocal residence, whether or not one distinguishes it from patrilocal residence, places the couple in the vicinity of the groom's family. Uxorilocal residence, like matrilocal residence, places the couple in the vicinity of the bride's family. Residence practices actually are much more variable than the terms above would indicate.

A second way of forming families larger than the nuclear unit is through the joining of the families of siblings or cousins to produce *joint* or *agnatic* families. Joint families often result from the death of both elderly parents in an extended family, leaving brothers with their spouses and children as the functioning unit. Such units become extended families again when the children marry and have offspring. If more than one pair of elderly parents with their children and children's children function together as a domestic unit, they comprise a combination extended and joint family.

Another way that a family may be expanded beyond the simple nuclear unit is by adding one or more spouses to produce a *polygamous family*. Logically, there are three kinds of *polygamy*, which is marriage involving multiple spouses. *Polygyny* is the term for marriage of a male to two or more females. A minority arrangement, it is often found as the ideal, and it is encouraged or permitted in over three-fourths of the

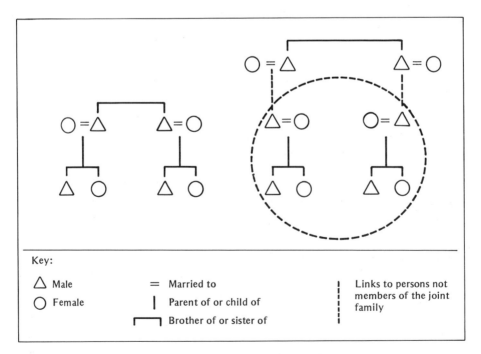

Figure 8–5   *Joint or agnatic families. Joint families often result from the death of both elderly parents in an extended family, leaving brothers with their spouses and children as the functioning unit.*

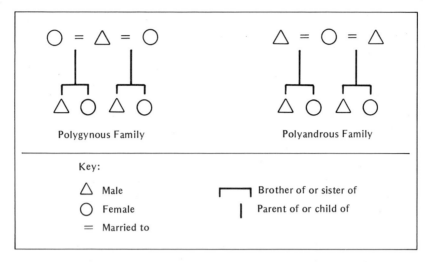

Polygynous Family   Polyandrous Family

Key:

△ Male   ⌐‾‾⌐ Brother of or sister of
○ Female | Parent of or child of
= Married to

Figure 8–6 *Polygamous families. A family may be expanded beyond the simple nuclear unit by adding one or more spouses.*

world's cultures. Another form of polygamy is *polyandry,* the marriage of a woman to two or more men. This occurs with much less frequency than monogamy or polygyny, being reported as the preferred form of marriage in less than 1 percent of one sample. Yet it has become clear that polyandrous marriages occur intermittently in a much higher proportion of the world's societies than anthropologists once realized. It tends to disappear readily when the rather special conditions that bring it into being are relaxed. The third logical form of polygamy is marriage of more than one woman to more than one man, sometimes called *group marriage.* Cases have been reported to have occurred, but only rarely and never as a standard alternative.

Actually, most of the world's marriages are monogamous. For most of the marriages in a society to involve more than one person of one sex would require either a very unbalanced sex ratio, a division of the society into men with plural wives and women with plural husbands, or many of one sex going without a spouse. The last alternative actually exists in a few societies. Among the Tiwi of Australia a rather unique system of infant betrothal and widow remarriage makes it possible for a few successful old men to corral most of the women as their wives, while most of the young men go without spouses (Hart and Pilling 1969:51). In large part due to a shortage of males from war and other violence, nearly half of the men of the Dugum Dani had more than one wife when Karl Heider worked among them in the 1960s (1970:72). Nevertheless, the notion of societies in which each male has several wives is improbable simply because there are seldom enough women. Monogamous families, then, are far more common than polygamous units.

Polyandry and polygyny yield rather different family arrangements.

In a polygynous family the husband participates in two or more nuclear families, which sometimes operate as rather separate units. For the Dani, Heider distinguishes between full polygyny, where the husband lives and works with all his wives, and displaced polygyny, where the co-wives live in different compounds and the husband spends time with each in turn (1970:72). With polyandry the result is a single unit of mother with her children, with two or more men serving as husbands and fathers for that family. In many societies a man marries sisters, which is called *sororal polygyny;* and most polyandry is *fraternal,* resulting in a family incorporating brothers who are also co-husbands.

Europeans and Americans easily think of a variety of difficulties for polygynous families, but these may be less than expected if we remember that the people have learned to view polygyny as a normal or ideal arrangement. A first wife may welcome the help and companionship of another woman, and the problem of jealousy can be reduced by having each wife with her children in a separate hut or sleeping quarters. Sororal polygyny is also said to reduce jealousy, since sisters are already accustomed to one another. Problems also may be reduced by putting one wife, usually the first, in a position of authority over the others. Polygyny also has the advantage of relieving a woman of sexual demands during pregnancy and from having children so frequently. In societies where the women gather or raise most of the food, polygynous families may be wealthier than monogamous families. Of course, polygynous families do have their difficulties. Jealousy is troublesome at times. Senior wives may abuse junior wives, and a husband sometimes wishes he had stopped with one because of the trouble among his spouses. The point is that the life of a polygynist is somewhat different from the Euroamerican's ethnocentric notions of it.

Various combinations of residence and marriage occur within the same society to produce different family arrangements. It is possible, for example, to have families which are extended in the sense of including at least three generations, joint in that brothers are retaining membership in the same unit, and polygynous in that some of the males have more than one wife. Ordinarily, less comprehensive combinations are found, such as the combining of three generations with polygyny, or polygyny with agnatic arrangements. Among the !Kung San there are independent nuclear families alongside polygynous and extended families (Marshall 1976:171). When a !Kung girl marries, her husband, who may already have been living with and hunting for her parents, continues to live there until they have children. It thereby becomes a matrilocal extended family. If the father and grandfather has taken a second wife, it is also a polygynous family. When, after children have been born, the younger man and his wife leave her parents and join his parents' family, a patrilocal extended family results; or if a daughter and her husband with their small children are still with her parents and a son has returned with his wife and children, the equivalent of an ambilocal family exists for a time. Anthropolo-

Figure 8–7 *!Kung matrilocal extended family. Among the !Kung San when a girl marries, her husband, who may already have been living with and hunting for her parents, continues to live there until they have children. It thereby becomes a matrilocal extended family.*

gists say that the residence practice of the !Kung is matri-patrilocal, which has the potential of producing matrilocal, patrilocal and, perhaps, ambilocal extended families. In addition, smaller units may split off to form independent monogamous or polygynous two-generation families. When the father in an extended family dies it does not become a joint family, since the component monogamous and polygynous units break apart.

Some kind of combination family arrangement (extended, joint or polygynous) prevails among humankind rather than the independent nuclear unit. The economic and technological activities are carried out collectively to some degree and are commonly directed by the older members. The group provides its members secure status and affection, and it operates as a unit in the care and training of children. It is able to do things more effectively than the independent nuclear type because it contains a greater number of persons to fall back on in times of sickness or other failure. If a mother becomes ill, other women, perhaps her sisters and her mother, will care for her and her children. If the elderly father is no longer able to carry his share of the workload, others will compensate. The circle of intimacy is larger in a composite family, and the strains of sustained and intense interaction with a small number of people (so common in independent nuclear families) are avoided. The functional value of an extended family seems borne out by the fact that it prevails in six times as many societies as those in which independent nuclear families dominate (Murdock 1967:170).

The prominent French student of social structure, Claude Levi-Strauss, prefers not to view the larger family types as combinations of nuclear units; he alleges that it is more realistic to think of the nuclear group as a *restricted* family, which appears in societies where the family is given little functional value. Further restriction, by eliminating the male parent, does away with the nuclear family, and the evidence like that from Guyana (see page 141) has prompted many to abandon the once-held belief in the universality of the nuclear family. But such cases do not detract from the significance of the near universality of some type of family group incorporating co-resident husband and wife. Apparently, certain functions or combinations of functions are performed more satisfactorily in the long run by a unit that includes both parents and children than by any other arrangement. Sexual satisfaction, economic cooperation, rearing children, and emotional gratification may be regarded as the family's main functions. Investigation shows that any one of these needs may be provided by arrangements other than the family, but formation of family groups, most commonly composite units, seems to be the most effective way of serving all of these functions together.

KINSHIP AND DESCENT

Bilateral Relationships

Bilateral kinship relationships are those which ramify through both males and females in each generation. People who reckon their ancestry bilaterally, then, count themselves equally related to both parents, all four grandparents, each of their eight great-grandparents, and so on through the ascending generations as far as they remember or are concerned to extend the reckoning. Laterally they may include both uncles and aunts on both sides of the family and all their descendants of both sexes. And among their own descendants both sexes in each generation are included.

From one point of view an independent nuclear family of parents and offspring is a bilateral unit, since, within that unit, the children may regard themselves as related to both the male and female parents. If someone includes the relatives of both the mother and father as relatives and the descendants of those relatives and of themselves, it yields a kinship unit which is strictly Ego-focused—more like a category than a group. This unit is known to anthropologists as a *kindred*. While full brothers and sisters share the same persons as members of their kindred, their

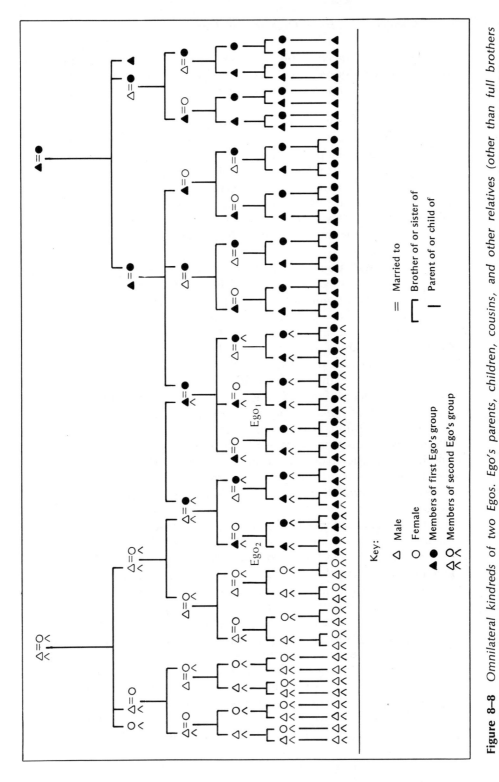

Figure 8-8 *Omnilateral kindreds of two Egos. Ego's parents, children, cousins, and other relatives (other than full brothers and sisters) will have among their consanguineal relatives some persons in common with Ego and his siblings and others not related to Ego.*

Key:

△ Male

○ Female

▲ Members of first Ego's group

▲< ○< Members of second Ego's group

= Married to

⌐ Brother of or sister of

| Parent of or child of

149

parents, children, cousins, and other relatives—considered as individuals having their own kindreds—will have among their consanguineal relatives some persons in common with Ego and his siblings and others not related to Ego (see Figure 8–8).

Since it differs from person to person, one's kindred is not a group of people who interact regularly with one another in well-defined ways. Usually a kindred is simply a category of relatives who have some interest in Ego because of their relationship to him or her, and this carries with it the possibility that interaction will occur. Also, members of a person's kindred may cooperate with one another occasionally in Ego's behalf. As an Ego-focused unit, a kindred cannot be a residential group as such, though many of the members may live near one another for various reasons.

From one standpoint the kindred consists of everyone to whom a person is related through all male and female links. But such a kindred, sometimes called an *omnilateral kindred,* rarely if ever functions as a unit in any known society. Ordinarily the functioning bilateral kinship unit consists of only some of the relatives: those who interact with Ego and, perhaps, other relatives because the culture so defines their rights and obligations or because of personal interest. Relatives who actually enter into a relationship with Ego because of bilateral links may be said to compose a *restricted kindred.* Restricted kindreds probably occur frequently, and are of considerable importance in many of the societies in which they are found. They consist of the people who may concern themselves with Ego as he or she passes from one phase of the life-cycle to another, and who may provide aid in culturally defined circumstances. For example, they may bring gifts at marriage, participate in one's initiation ceremonies, provide for a person's burial, or give financial assistance as needed.

Kindreds among the Nuer of East Africa conform fairly well to the foregoing observations. In one sense the Nuer kindred includes every person with whom one has a consanguineal relationship, except for siblings and parents. Evans-Pritchard suggests that it is like a circular elastic band that can be stretched to accommodate any number of social contacts (1951:156). More important than this apparently omnilateral unit is a restricted kindred consisting of one's mother's and father's brothers and sisters and their offspring and one's brother's and sister's children. They assist Ego with the most difficult work, provide care during sickness, supply food when hunger strikes, attend personal rituals, help one get married, dash to one's assistance in danger, give support in quarrels, and allow one to behave naturally when with them.

Many Americans have functioning bilateral kindreds of the restricted type, and these often overlap one another to form intermittently functioning groups of relatives. Perhaps there is some tendency for American kindreds to be omnilateral in that any person to whom one can trace a consanguineal relationship may establish a role relationship with Ego. But the functioning category is restricted, for only a portion of the relatives have anything to do with Ego. There are Americans linked with one another through either males or females or both who tend to assemble for occasions such as weddings, christenings, funerals, and holiday celebrations; and they visit and aid one another in varying degrees. As an occasionally functioning group, this unit appears to consist of those who belong to the overlapping kindreds of more than one Ego—first cousins, for example—plus some of the spouses. As a youngster you may have been a member of a functioning group of relatives who visited in one another's homes, who appeared at your high school graduation, or who assembled for summer picnics and holiday dinners. The group was not focused on you only, however, for the same people might attend the graduation ceremonies, baptisms, and so forth of your cousins and others to whom they were related. It was simply a group of relatives built on the foundation of bilateral Ego-focused relationships.

Many societies, especially hunters and gatherers with little in the way of political organization and, also, large populations with elaborate technologies and political systems, are strictly bilateral. They have small domestic units, independent nuclear families, for example, as well as kindreds of various kinds. As you would expect, the use of bilateral descent is tied to the classification of relatives by status labels. With the parents-children unit being so strong, one's brothers and sisters and parents are much more important than cousins, aunts, and uncles. A person tends to interact much more intensively with brothers and sisters than with cousins and in different statuses. Consequently, there is a strong tendency to use one label or set of labels for siblings (possibly allowing for sex difference) and different terms for cousins. This produces what anthropologists call *Eskimo terminology* for Ego's generation, which is the kind of sibling-cousin terminology found in American society (see Figure 8–9,A). Americans refer to a sibling as "my brother" or "my sister" and offspring of a parent's brother or sister as "my cousin." Complementary and mutual status relationships are extensive among brothers and sisters in American society, whereas cousins may interact very little.

!Kung of southern Africa also use an Eskimo system. They use three terms for siblings; one for an older brother, one for an older sister, and another for a younger sibling, regardless of sex (Marshall 1976:215). All cousins, whether paternal or maternal or the offspring of an uncle or aunt, are lumped together under a term for female cousins and another for male cousins. One of the status differences between sibling relationships and cousin relationships is that a !Kung may joke (exchange sexually tinged insults) only with a sibling of the same sex—brother with brother or sister with sister—but one may joke with a cousin of either sex.

In using Eskimo terminology, Ego separates those in his own line of descent (siblings) from those in collateral lines (cousins in this case). The same distinction may be made in Ego's parental generation, and it applies in both !Kung and American culture. In both cultures parents are separated from uncles and aunts, the parents being in Ego's line of descent and the uncles and aunts in a different line. Anthropologists call this *lineal*

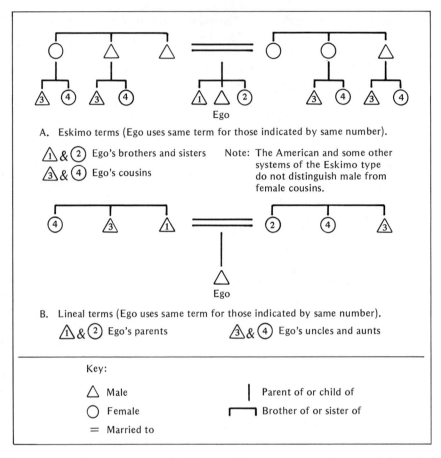

A. Eskimo terms (Ego uses same term for those indicated by same number).

△&② Ego's brothers and sisters   Note: The American and some other
                                         systems of the Eskimo type
△&④ Ego's cousins   do not distinguish male from
                                         female cousins.

B. Lineal terms (Ego uses same term for those indicated by same number).

△&② Ego's parents   △&④ Ego's uncles and aunts

Key:

△ Male | Parent of or child of

○ Female   ⌐ Brother of or sister of

= Married to

Figure 8–9 *Eskimo and lineal kinship terms. Societies emphasizing bilateral descent often use kinship terms which separate those in one's nuclear
family from other relatives. This applies in both !Kung and American
cultures.*

terminology (see Figure 8–9,B). Both the lineal and the Eskimo systems are
in harmony with the fact that the independent nuclear family is a strong,
discrete unit of daily importance to its members. Though the uncles,
aunts, and cousins are members of Ego's kindred, the latter, since they
compose an Ego-focused unit, perform their roles toward Ego only occasionally. Its members are not bound to Ego by ties nearly as strong as
those with the members of the immediate family, and there is a differentiation of statuses within the family from those with others.

Ambilineal Descent Units

Instead of reckoning descent bilaterally, it is possible to trace one's
descent line through only one person in each generation, that is, *lineally*.

This is much simpler than bilateral descent, since one only has to remember one person in each generation rather than doubling the number for each as in bilateral reckoning. In some societies everyone traces descent through people of one sex only, which is known as *unilineal descent*. In some unilineal societies, all trace their descent lines through a mother in each generation, whereas in other societies, all trace their ancestry through a father in each. In societies that are neither unilineal or bilateral it does not matter absolutely whether descent is traced through a man or a woman, with the result that one may trace his or her ancestry through a woman in some generations and a man in others. This is *ambilineal* or *optative descent*.

Some cultures have common ancestor groups of putatively consanguineal relatives which people become members of by affiliating through either the mother or the father. Some members of these groups may trace their ancestry through a male in one generation and a female in another, while still others may have only male ancestors and some, conceivably, females in every generation. The result is an *ambilineal descent group,* a unit of relatives all of whom trace descent through only one person in a given generation but who may have differing combinations of the sexes in their descent lines. A hypothetical result of ambilineal descent is shown in Figure 8–10. If the ambilineal group is of shallow genealogical depth, with the members able to trace their relationships back to the common ancestor and to one another, it may be called a *ramage*. Ambilineal groups that go back so many generations that members are unable to remember how all are related are also found, but there is no standardized term to designate them.

Ambilineal groups are consanguineal in that a person can be affiliated through either male kin or female kin, but nonkinship factors of different sorts determine which. On the western Pacific island of Nukuoro the first child becomes a member of the father's group, the second a member of the mother's and so on in alternation (Fischer and Fischer 1957:130). In some societies there seems to be a unilineal preference, with people having the freedom to let residence desires, advantages in property inheritance, availability of prestigious titles, and the like decide whether or not they will conform with the unilineal preference. Among the Samoans a child would ordinarily become a member of the father's kin group, but in a high proportion of cases people are permitted to establish themselves as members of a different descent group. Anyone who can trace a lineal relationship, through either males or females or both, to a holder of the title after which the descent group is named, and who has maintained various obligations to the group, may claim membership (M. Ember 1959: 574). In fact, a Samoan normally claims membership in several ambilineal groups. This is what produces common ancestor groups which include members who trace their ancestry through men in most generations, but through women in some of them.

There seems to be a tendency for ambilineal descent and ambilocal extended families to occur in the same society (Murdock 1960:13). Both

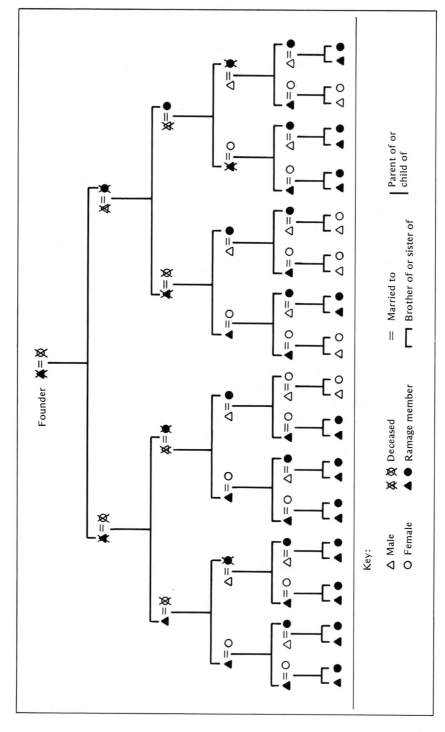

Figure 8–10 *Hypothetical ambilineal descent group (Ramage. A unit of relatives, all of whom trace descent through only one person in a given generation but who may have differing combinations of the sexes in their descent lines.*

Key:

△ Male   ⊠ ⊠ Deceased   = Married to

○ Female   ▲ ● Ramage member   ⎾⎤ Brother of or sister of

│ Parent of or child of

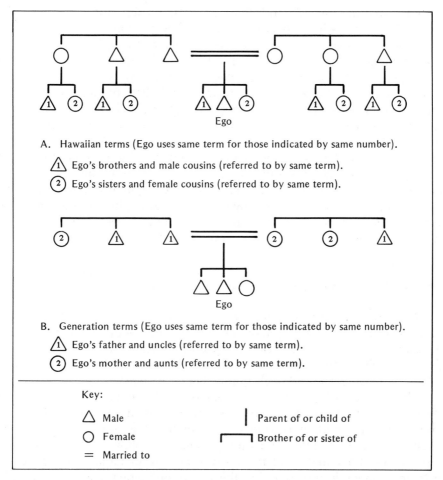

A. Hawaiian terms (Ego uses same term for those indicated by same number).

⚠1 Ego's brothers and male cousins (referred to by same term).

② Ego's sisters and female cousins (referred to by same term).

B. Generation terms (Ego uses same term for those indicated by same number).

⚠1 Ego's father and uncles (referred to by same term).

② Ego's mother and aunts (referred to by same term).

Key:

△ Male | Parent of or child of

○ Female   ⌐⌐   Brother of or sister of

= Married to

Figure 8–11 *Hawaiian and generation kinship terms. It is as though people refer to their siblings and all their cousins as "my brother" or "my sister" and their parents, uncles, and aunts as "my mother" or "my father."*

ambilocal families and ambilineal groups bring siblings, parallel cousins, and cross cousins together in functioning units of the societal type, and the nuclear family is not notably independent. Siblings interact with one another and with many of their cousins in roughly similar ways and to a somewhat similar degree. Accordingly, *Hawaiian* sibling-cousin terms, by which a person refers to siblings and cousins by the same terms or set of terms (see Figure 8–11), are common in ambilineal societies.

This terminology lumps people in Ego's line of descent with those in collateral lines: the cousins. This also may be done on Ego's parental generation, yielding what anthropologists call *generation* terms. Under this system one uses the same terms for uncles and aunts as for mother and father (see Figure 8–11,B). Under Hawaiian-generation terminology it is as though people refer to their siblings and all their cousins as "my brother" or "my sister," and their parents, uncles, and aunts as "my mother" or "my father." It is often misleading to translate Hawaiian and generation terms this way, since the people's terms may have quite different meanings from our terms for brother, sister, father, and mother. Yet it is significant that many of the roles of siblings toward one another are notably similar to those between cousins and that interaction of nieces and nephews with their aunts and uncles often resembles that between offspring and parents. On Samoa, for example, where the terms for cousins are the same as those for siblings, cousins as well as siblings must abide by a set of "brother-sister avoidances." Samoan cousins and siblings of the opposite sex must avoid suggestive or salacious language in one another's presence, they must not remain alone together in a house, dance on the same dance floor, or do anything else that might smack of intimacy (Holmes 1974:20). So there is some correspondence between the use of the same status labels for cousins as for siblings.

Unilineal Descent Groups

Many societies are divided into a number of groups of consanguineal relatives who are, ordinarily, supposed to have descended from a common ancestor through forebears of one sex only. These kinship groups are generally fully or strongly exogamous, which results in husband and wife belonging to different unilineal groups. Under whichever unilineal descent rule the society follows, all of a couple's children are assigned to the common ancestor group of only one parent, with the result that one parent and the children belong to one unilineal group while the other parent belongs to a different group. In societies following the *matrilineal* descent rule, both male and female offspring in all families are assigned to their mother's group. Ignoring the exceptions which can occur in any society, this produces groups whose members have descended from a common ancestor through mothers only. They are *matrilineal descent groups,* often referred to in anthropology as *matrigroups.* In societies that follow the *patrilineal* descent rule, both male and female offspring in all families are assigned to their father's group, which produces *patrigroups,* whose members have descended from a common ancestor through fathers only.

Many find it virtually indispensable to use a kinship chart to understand unilineal descent groups. Figure 8–12 shows a number of relatives who are consanguineally related to one another by descent from the same ancestress, with the symbols for those matrilineally (through mothers) related to one another blackened. Figure 8–13 also shows a number of relatives who are consanguineally related to one another by descent from the same ancestor, but the blackened symbols here indicate those who are patrilineally (through fathers) related. In Figure 8–12 note that no child of a male member of the group is a member of his group. In a sense, one has reached the boundary of a matrilineal group when considering

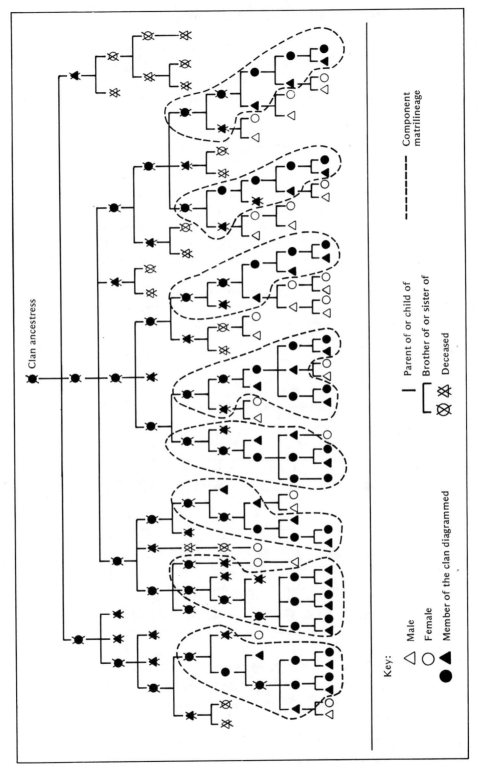

Figure 8–12 *Hypothetical matrilineal clan, incorporating lineages. One has reached the boundary of a matrilineal group when considering any male. He is a member, but his children belong to a different matrigroup.*

Key:

△ Male
○ Female
● Member of the clan diagrammed

| Parent of or child of
⌐ Brother of or sister of
⊗ ⊗⊗ Deceased

------- Component matrilineage

157

any male. He is a member, but his children belong to a different matri-group. The same principle applies to female members of patrigroups, as can be seen in Figure 8–13. One has come to the boundary of a patri-group when considering a female member, since she is a member and her children are not. This is because it is the sex of the parent that deter-mines membership, not the child's sex, and both male and female new-born are assigned·to the unilineal group of the same parent.

The members of unilineal groups of shallow genealogical depth (few generations). are supposed to be able to trace their relationships to one another and back to the relatively recent common ancestor through known consanguineal links. Such groups are commonly referred to by anthro-pologists as *lineages*. If they are matrilineal they may be called *matri-lineages,* and if patrilineal, *patrilineages.* Many confuse this usage of lineage with a line of descent, but the term refers here to a kind of kin-ship group.

There are unilineal groups of greater genealogical depth than line-ages. The common ancestors lived so many generations back that they may have been forgotten and may have become mythological. And the

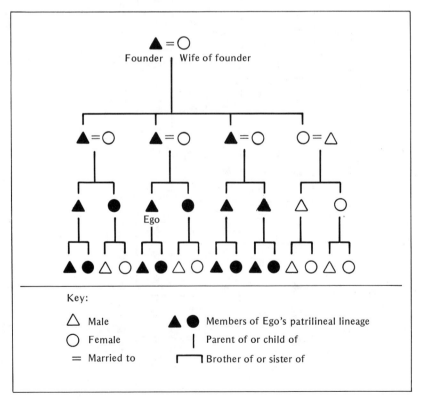

Figure 8–13 *Patrilineal lineage. One has come to the boundary of a patrigroup when considering a female member, since she is a member and her children are not.*

number of people, living and/or deceased, who have belonged to the group through the generations are so numerous that the consanguineal ties among many and the links back to the common ancestors are no longer known. While the matrilineal or patrilineal descent rule is used to determine membership, the group consists of people who have only a tradition of belonging to the same unilineal group rather than being able to tell just how all members are related. In Figure 8–12, for example, living members of the lineages would not be aware of the ancestors indicated for the most remote generations. Some anthropologists call these groups of relatively great genealogical depth *clans,* while others call them *sibs*. Both terms are used enough that it is advisable to be familiar with them. Some societies have clans without lineages, some lineages without clans, and others clans that are subdivided into lineages (see Figure 8–12).

Figure 8–14 *Crow Indian couple. The matrilineal descent rule prescribed that each Crow newborn, whether boy or girl, was assigned to the mother's clan rather than to the father's, thereby separating the father from his wife and children with regard to unilineal group membership.*

Each Crow Indian of the second half of the nineteenth century belonged to one of thirteen matrilineal clans (or sibs) (Lowie 1912:193). Members of the same matriclan were not supposed to marry, with the result that husband and wife nearly always belonged to different clans. The matrilineal descent rule prescribed that each Crow newborn, whether boy or girl, was assigned to the mother's clan rather than to the father's, thereby separating the father from his wife and children with regard to unilineal group membership. Crow clans were clearly consanguineal rather than residential or family groups, since a given clan's members were scattered among the three territorial groups into which the Crow were divided. Exogamy was the ideal and was generally practiced, and the few who married within their clan were ridiculed. Lowie's informant Gray-bull was greatly amused at the fact that the children of such disapproved unions belonged to their father's and mother's clan at the same time (Lowie 1912:189).

The Nuer are patrilineal rather than matrilineal; they have both clans and lineages, and the lineages are subdivisions of the clans. There also is a four-level hierarchy of lineages within each clan, which is unusual in the world's cultures. Evans-Pritchard calls the largest lineages "maximal lineages"; the subdivisions of a maximal lineage, "major lineages"; the subdivisions of a major lineage, "minor lineages;" and the subdivisions of a minor lineage, "minimal lineages" (1940:6). The Nuer usually give the name of their minimal lineage if asked about their lineage membership, and they are able to tell a questioner how they are related to all other members of the lineage. Lineage members are scattered among different villages and, as for the immediate family, the father with his children of both sexes belongs to one patrilineage and patriclan, while the mother belongs to another one.

When the basic notion of what matrilineal and patrilineal lineages and clans (or sibs) are is understood, four points should be given special attention. First, one's unilineal descent group does not include all of the relatives on one side of the family, a misunderstanding that must be avoided if the nature of the group is to be correctly discerned. A matrilineal descent group, whether lineage or clan, incorporates only a portion of Ego's maternal relatives, and a patrilineage or patriclan includes only some of the paternal relatives. Note how this applies for Ego in Figure 8–13. The cross cousins, for example, are excluded.

The second point is that membership of one unilineal group does not overlap with any other descent group of the same type and magnitude. Each Crow belongs to only one of the thirteen patriclans, and each Nuer belongs to only one of the various minimal lineages of his society. This differs from the situation so frequent in ambilineal societies, whereby a person may belong to several ambilineal descent groups.

Third, the consanguineal unilineal group is not a residential unit. A territory need not be occupied by all members of the group and no members of other such groups. In fact, this is impossible if husband and wife live together, since by exogamy they belong to different unilineal groups. Frequently, many members of a certain group reside in the same territory, but members of other unilineal groups virtually always reside among them. Most of the Nuer living in a particular village may belong to one lineage, but that lineage also has members in other Nuer villages, and there are members of other lineages in the village. Similarly, each of the three Crow territorial units contains members of several of the thirteen clans. Confusion can be avoided by remembering that the terms patrilineal and matrilineal pertain to descent, while patrilocal and matrilocal refer to residence.

Finally, since this type of group is both unilineal and consanguineal, membership is theoretically for life, remaining unchanged by marriage, residence, or other nongenetic factors. Whatever the ideals, of course, they are sometimes violated. The Dani are patrilineal, which means that they automatically become members of their father's clan for life. But it is reported that some men who moved into the Dugum neighborhood as a result of a fight in their former community dropped their original clan membership and joined a different one (K. Heider 1970:69). Examples from many cultures illustrate that it is relatively easy for people to define relationships as consanguineal in ways that violate either their ideas or the genetic realities. Still, such departures are so infrequent that it is appropriate to regard unilineal groups as essentially consanguineal.

While it is important to understand the composition of unilineal groups, how they affect people's lives and relationships is the ultimate concern. Though they may have several functions, anthropologists generally recognize two main ones. One is the *regulation of marriage* through exogamy. This is structurally important because, if exogamy were not practiced with sufficient frequency, the composition of the group would change until it ceased to exist and function. Though a few cases of marriage within the matriclans were known among the nineteenth-century Crow, there were not enough to disturb the composition and functioning of the clans.

The second main function of many unilineal descent groups is *mutual aid*. The group is often a kind of second line of defense for its members in time of need, and it supports them on important occasions in the life cycle. Those who get into trouble or have a legitimate need that cannot be handled otherwise may turn to other members of their unilineal group, or the others may come to their aid voluntarily out of recognition of their kinship. If one member of the group is murdered or injured, it ordinarily is the duty of his lineage or clan to see that restitution or revenge is obtained, if necessary, by killing or injuring a member of the assailant's group.

The mutual aid function of nineteenth-century Crow clans was strong. Spotted-fish's favorite horse was stolen by the Piegan Indians and, later, recovered by four Crow warriors, and the other members of the clan collected a large amount of property to buy the horse back for him. If a

Crow killed someone in a different clan, the murderer's clan sometimes paid an indemnity. Otherwise there was likely to be a feud. After Fire-bear killed Wraps-up-his-tail, the latter's fellow clansmen repeatedly tried to kill Fire-Bear. When Birds-all-over-the-ground killed another Crow to get his horse, the victim's clan prepared to avenge his death. But members of Birds-all-over-the-ground's clan offered a pipe and horses loaded with presents to the grieving father and asked for peace. The leaders of the two clans deliberated at length and agreed to the proposal, and the bereaved father accepted the gifts and distributed them among the members of his clan (Lowie 1912:188).

Beyond marriage regulation and mutual aid, clans and lineages may assume a member of other functions. They often have *ceremonial and religious concerns*. They may have their own gods, priests, and peculiar rituals and ceremonial paraphernalia for dealing with the supernatural. The ceremonial functions may have to do with *totemism,* for a unilineal group, especially a clan, often has a totem. The *totem* is an animal or plant species or some other object or class of objects with which the group believes they have a special mystical relationship. It may be a mythological common ancestor, and it may be taboo to kill or eat a member of the totem species. Ceremonial and religious functions may involve ownership of songs, rituals, myths, or totemic symbols.

In a number of societies clans and/or lineages *own land and other economically valuable property* and control its use and inheritance. In this sense they are what many anthropologists call *corporate* groups. In addition, the chief or other government functionary may come mainly or exclusively from a certain unilineal group.

Ceremonial-religious functions are important for Nuer patriclans and patrilineages. The role of God (Kwoth) as creator is sometimes recognized by an allegorical inclusion of God as the ultimate clan or lineage ancestor (Evans-Pritchard 1956:7). After tracing his line of descent back to the clan founder, a member of the Jinaca clan may go on to say that the clan founder was the son of the first Leopard-skin priest, who was a son of man, who was a son of the universe, who was a son of God. Each Nuer lineage and clan has a spear name, which the leader of a patrigroup ceremony shouts out as he brandishes a spear. The spear represents the group's ancestor and symbolizes the group as a whole. The spear name is shouted as the opening words of the invocation made in preparation for the sacrifice of an ox or other animal at weddings, in war, at funerals, at initiations, at blood-feud settlements, and on other occasions that concern the entire descent group.

Both the Nuer and the Dugum Dani patrigroups have totems. Various Nuer patrilineages have special mystical relationships with the lion, monitor lizard, crocodile, python, spitting viper, ostrich, cattle, egret, tamarind tree, gourd, the Nyanding River, and so forth. The Leng lineage of the Jinaca clan say that their founder, Gilgil, was born a twin to a lion. When they sacrifice to the lion spirit, they throw a token piece of meat into the bush, calling on the lions to come and eat their share. The lion spirit is apt to take revenge if a Leng injures or kills a lion, and there are even stories of how trouble came to the lineage as a resulting of the killing of a lion by an outsider who used a Leng member's spear. Punishment also may come if the Leng fail to dedicate sacrifices to the lion totem. In one case, the lion spirit caused hysterics in a Leng girl, who was then cured by the sacrifice of a sheep.

Each Dani patriclan is mystically related to a bird and to a topographical feature, usually a hill. A clan member cannot eat the clan bird; it is one's brother. There apparently is economic significance to some of the clan hills, since several are mountains where clan members have special hunting privileges and rights to pandanus trees (K. Heider 1970:68).

Another kind of kinship grouping found in many places is the *phratry,* which is a combination of two or more clans. Some phratries seem to do little more than regulate marriage through exogamy, but in some societies phratries are not exogamous. There also may be other specific functions, but these are quite variable and sometimes not very important. The Crow had seven phratries, five of them consisting of two clans and one of them composed of three. Some of them were rather strongly exogamous and others were not. Clans within the same phratry were on more intimate terms than with those of other phratries. They tended to feast and camp together on appropriate occasions and helped one another in various ways.

Some communities or larger units are divided into halves which have certain relationships with one another that vary from culture to culture, and each half is referred to by anthropologists as a *moiety.* Moieties are of various kinds; they may be paired unilineal descent groups or paired phratries. They are widely found among nonliterate cultures, the Dani being among those which have them. The Dani moieties are exogamous and patrilineal. The patrimoiety members are scattered among many Dani communities, and they are so large that some members may never have seen one another. Yet, within a particular community the two moieties are of significance in people's lives. The rule of exogamy is seldom violated; kinship terms may be extended to include all of a certain kind in the moiety; certain roles and rituals are prescribed by moiety membership; and several food taboos are based on moiety distinctions. A Dani refers to his or her father or a father's brother as *opase,* but *opase* may also be used to refer to any male of the older generation and to the speaker's own moiety. Similarly, *ami,* which refers basically to one's mother's brothers, can be used also to refer to any male of the older generation in the other moiety. Since the moieties are patrilineal, a Dani's mother's brother belongs to the opposite moiety. At a funeral the members of the dead person's moiety are supposed to bring pigs, which are eaten during the ceremony, and the members of the mother's moiety bring cowrie shell bands and other shell goods, some of which are used in the ceremony and others of which are given to those who brought pigs (K. Heider 1970:150). As for food taboos, there is one kind of banana and a kind of bird that members of one moiety are not supposed to eat, and two kinds of bananas and over a dozen kinds of birds and mammals are forbidden to those of the other moiety. If these taboos are broken the Dani say that the ghosts will punish them by causing stomach swelling and death. Nevertheless, Heider found that Dani would often eat a forbidden food when alone with him (1970:64).

Certain kinds of status labels occur frequently in unilineal societies. Under *Iroquois* terminology, as shown in Figure 8–15, A, a person refers

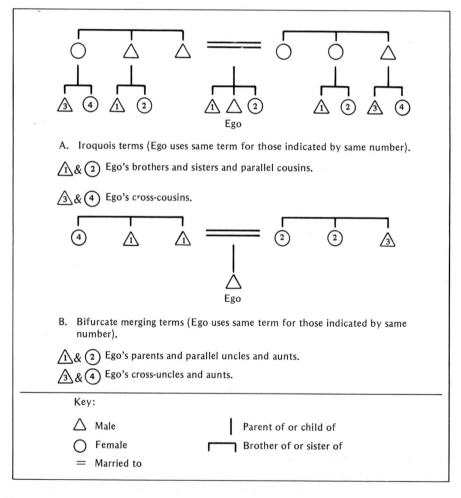

A. Iroquois terms (Ego uses same term for those indicated by same number).

△1 & ② Ego's brothers and sisters and parallel cousins.

△3 & ④ Ego's cross-cousins.

B. Bifurcate merging terms (Ego uses same term for those indicated by same number).

△1 & ② Ego's parents and parallel uncles and aunts.
△3 & ④ Ego's cross-uncles and aunts.

Key:

△ Male | Parent of or child of
○ Female   ⌐⌐ Brother of or sister of
= Married to

Figure 8–15 *Iroquois and bifurcate merging terms. Though Iroquois sibling-cousin terms are found in a number of societies without unilineal groups, they are common in unilineal cultures. On the parental generation bifurcate merging terms replicate the pattern of Iroquois terms.*

to brothers and sisters and parallel cousins by one term or set of terms, but uses different terms for cross cousins. Americans limit the set of terms for siblings (one for brothers and another for sisters) to those having the same parents, but under the Iroquois system, the terms for brother and sister are also used for parallel cousins. Though Iroquois sibling-cousin terms are found in a number of societies without unilineal groups, the Miskito of the nineteenth century being an example, Iroquois terms are common in unilineal cultures. While unilineality may not cause the terms, they are quite compatible with them. Notice in Figure 8–13 that, on one side of the family, Ego's parallel cousins belong to his own unilineal group, while cross cousins belong to a different one. On the parental generation *bifurcate merging terms* replicate the pattern of Iroquois terms, since one uses the same term for one's parent and his or her sibling, who is one of the parents of the parallel cousins. That is, one's father and father's brother are referred to by the same term, as are one's mother and mother's sister (see Figure 8–15, B).

Omaha and Crow terminological systems are much more closely associated with unilineality than Iroquois terms. They are similar to one another, but Omaha terms are found in many patrilineal societies, whereas Crow terms may be associated with matrilineality. *Omaha* nomenclature for one's own generation employs the same terms for maternal cross cousins as for maternal uncles and aunts, thereby lumping people of different generations under the same terms. For example, if people refer to a mother's sister as "my mother," the mother's brother's daughter is also referred to as "my mother," and the mother's brother's son is referred to as a mother's brother. The Omaha system is the consequence of extending the terms for the aunts and uncles in one's *mother's patrilineal group* to include those in the group's descending generations. The result is that, at least from Ego's parents' generation down, all the males are referred to by one term and the females by another (see Figure 8–16). It is as though Ego is treating all members of the mother's patrilineal group as the same. It is not one's own patrilineal group, but since it is the mother's group, it is of importance in one's life (see Figure 8–16). A key point is that the terms for the mother's sister and the mother's brother are the ones used for the patrigroup's members in descending generations, though they may differ from society to society. The basic Nyoro term for all members of anyone's mother's patrilineal group is *nyina,* which means "mother or person who 'gave birth' to Ego." Any female member of one's mother's clan is *nyinento,* or "little mother," and any male member of the same clan is *nyinarumi,* or "male mother" (Beattie 1957:331). Accordingly, a person's mother's patriclan from the first ascending generation down consists of a mother, little mothers, and male mothers. From Ego's perspective it is a kind of group of mothers; and each member of that group refers to Ego as his or her child. It is from the mothers that Nyoro generally expect love and indulgence, and any "little mother," even if younger than Ego, will have maternal feelings and behave in maternal

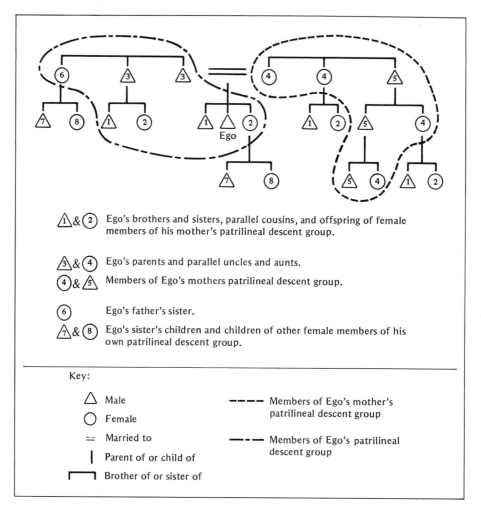

Figure 8–16 *Omaha kinship terms. The terms for the aunts and uncles in one's mother's patrilineal group are extended to include those in the group's descending generations. It is as though Ego is treating all members of the mother's patrilineal group as the same.*

ways toward her "child." The mother's brothers and younger "male mothers" also occupy a special place in the life of a Nyoro. Nyoro enjoy a number of privileges in a male mother's house, including taking food uninvited, borrowing things without asking, and joking in familiar ways with the male mother's wives. Nyoro often remark about what good times they had in their mothers' houses as children.

The "motherly" nature of Ego's mother's patrilineal clan or lineage does not emerge in all Omaha societies with the strength that it does among the Nyoro, but the idea of the unity of the mother's group in relation to their child, Ego, is basic. From Ego's perspective this unity may also apply to other clans or lineages that are important because one's close relatives belong to them. In addition to a group of mothers, the clan of a grandparent is a group of grandparents to Ego, and the clan of his wife a group of siblings-in-law. Generalizing for all Omaha cultures with unilineal groups, the practice of referring to all members of Ego's mother's patrigroup by basically two terms regardless of generation, one for males and another for females, reflects a person's attitudes and behaviors toward and expectations from people who are not members of his own group but who are nevertheless, as a group, important.

Omaha terminologies have sometimes produced ethnocentric reactions among early explorers, missionaries, and colonial administrators who, having learned what a grown man called his mother, would discover that there were also little girls that he would refer to by the same term. If the status label for one's biological mother is translated as "my mother," it is apparent why Westerners might be astounded that a man would refer to a female infant in arms as "my mother." In many groups it would be more accurate, perhaps, to translate the word for Ego's mother and other female members of her patrigroup as "female member of my mother's patrilineage," or something of the sort. For those above the parental generation, incidentally, the grandparent terms are usually retained.

Matrilineal societies often use Crow terminology, which got its name from its use by the Crow Indians. It is similar to Omaha terminology, but the emphasis on group membership at the expense of generation differences occurs within *Ego's father's matrilineal* group rather than in the mother's patrilineal group. The members of the father's matrilineal group from the parental generation down may be referred to by two kinds of terms only, one for males and one for females. The term meaning "my father" may also be used for the rest of the male members of the group, while the term for father's sister is used for each female member. In those groups in which the terms can reasonably be translated as "my father" and "my paternal aunt," it is apparent that a person will be using the terms for the father's sister's son as well as for males of younger generations (see Figure 8–17, p. 166) Lowie heard his informant Gray-bull, then about sixty-five years old, address as father a man in his twenties (1935:19). The nineteenth-century Crow treated those in their father's matrilineal clan with great respect. For example, they were careful not to walk in front of a "father" without giving a present, and it was considered good for people to feast members of their father's matriclan. Anthropological literature contains many such examples of the relationship between status terms and social behavior.

Double Unilineal Descent

Ordinarily a unilineal society has only patrigroups or only matrigroups, but some societies have both. In such cases each member of the society belongs to both a matrilineal group and a patrilineal group, and

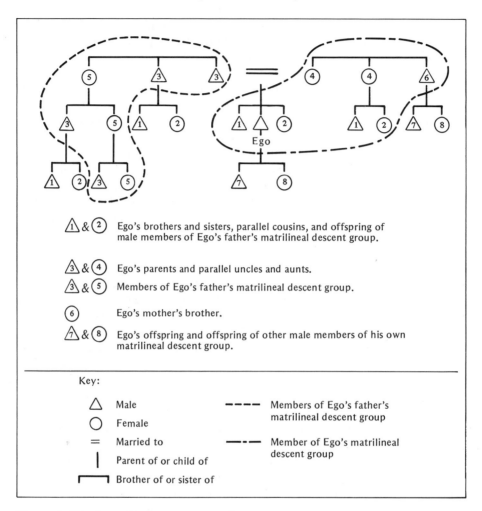

Key:

△ Male

○ Female

= Married to

| Parent of or child of

⌐¬ Brother of or sister of

- - - - Members of Ego's father's matrilineal descent group

—··— Member of Ego's matrilineal descent group

Figure 8–17 *Crow kinship terms. Emphasis on group membership at the expense of generation differences occurs within Ego's father's matrilineal group.*

each matrilineal group overlaps partially with a patrilineal group to form a category called a *double descent group, bilinear kin group,* or *section.* Each such category is composed of people who belong to the same matrigroup and patrigroup.

Initially some people confuse double descent with either bilateral or ambilineal descent. Double descent differs from bilateral descent in that one is related to *only a portion* of the relatives on each side of the family. A look at Figure 8–18 will reveal that cross cousins on both sides of the family are excluded in double descent, whereas in bilateral descent all relatives on both sides of the family are included (see Figure 8–8). The members of a particular matrigroup or patrigroup in a double descent

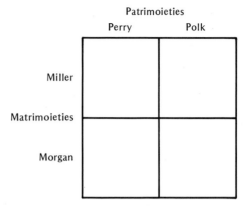

Figure 8–18 *Double descent: Four-section system. Some societies divide all their members into two patrilineal moieties and two matrilineal groups, each person belonging to one patrilineal group and, also, one matrilineal group. This results in four* marriage *sections, a person being permitted to take a spouse from only one of the other three sections.*

society trace descent through one sex only just as surely as if they had only one of the two descent rules, whereas members of an ambilineal descent group may trace their ancestry through either or both males and females.

The full structural variety and range of functions of double unilineal descent are not yet fully known, but marriage regulation seems important in several cultures. Some societies divide all their members into two patrilineal moieties and two matrilineal groups, each person belonging to one patrilineal group and also one matrilineal group. If the groups are firmly exogamous this results in four *marriage sections,* a person being permitted to take a spouse from only one of the four sections. This arrangement is also referred to as either a *four-section system* or a *four-class system.* Using Perry and Polk for the two patrimoieties, and Miller and Morgan for the two matrimoieties, a person belonging to the Perry patrimoiety and the Miller matrimoiety may be called a Perry-Miller. The other three categories or sections, formed by the overlapping of the four groups, would be Perry-Morgan, Polk-Miller, and Polk-Morgan, as indicated in Figure 8–18. (The hyphenated names are used only to aid in understanding the system; category names used by nonliterates with such groups may consist of single terms.) A Perry-Miller would not be able to marry a Perry-Morgan because both belong to the Perry patrilineal group. Nor would a Perry-Miller be permitted to marry a Polk-Miller, since both belong to the Miller matrigroup. Only a Polk-Morgan is an eligible spouse for a Perry-Miller. If Ego is a Perry-Miller man married to a Polk-Morgan woman, the children will belong to the Perry-Morgan section, that is, the Perry patrimoiety to which their father belongs and the Morgan matrimoiety of their mother. If Ego is a Perry-Miller woman married to a Polk-Morgan man, the children will be Polk-Miller. Readers can trace the rest of the possibilities for themselves.

The four-section system is associated with the exchange of spouses between cross cousins and, usually, kinship terms that separate parallel from cross cousins. Also, parents and children belong to different mar-

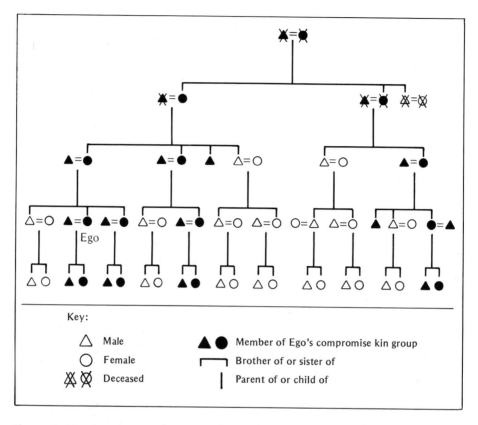

Figure 8–19 *Compromise kin group based on matrilineal descent and matrilocal residence. A combination of matrilineal descent with matrilocal residence can produce a residential group composed of a core of people of both sexes who belong to a single matrigroup, plus females from other purely matrilineal groups who reside with the core group because of the matrilocal rule.*

riage sections, while a man and his son's children or a woman and her daughter's children belong to the same section. There also are cultures with more than four marriage classes; some have six, some have eight, and even twelve-section systems have been found (Layard 1942:143). Double descent systems, though uncommon, are interesting as examples of the wide variety of ways that human beings can relate themselves to one another.

Localization and Descent Groups

Anthropologists often speak of *localized* clans, sibs, or lineages. These are formed by the joint operation of a unilineal descent rule and a corresponding marriage residence rule. But while both rules affect the group's formation, they are partially incompatible and result in a compromise arrangement. A purely unilineal group cannot be a residential group if husband and wife reside together and if married brothers and sisters live apart due to residence rules, for husband and wife belong to different exogamous groups, and brother and sister belong to the same unilineal group. Consequently, members of a purely consanguineal patrigroup or matrigroup are unavoidably scattered among the members of other unilineal groups.

A residential group, however, can consist of a *core* of unilineally related people plus the spouses of the married members of that core. Examination of Figure 8–19 will show how a combination of matrilineal descent with matrilocal residence can produce a residential group composed of a core of people of both sexes who belong to a single matrigroup, plus males from other purely matrilineal groups who reside with the core group because of the matrilocal rule. This also means that men matrilineally related to the core of this local group move away when they get married. This kind of group emphasizes the matrilineal relationships among the women and those men who are still there because they have not married, but men who marry lose their membership in that residential group when they move away.

A given society may have both purely unilineal and the localized type of groups. The Nuer, for example, have patrilineal lineages with a high incidence of patrilocal residence, which produces villages that are identified with a patrilineage because they are associated with a core or nucleus of patrilineally related people (Evans-Pritchard 1940:203). Some members of the lineage are scattered among other Nuer villages, and members of several lineages live together in the same village. Yet the Nuer think of the village itself as a patrilineal group—a lineage. Only in regard to exogamy, certain rituals, and homicide responsibility do they take care to distinguish among the different lineages represented there. While doing fieldwork, Evans-Pritchard had difficulty getting the Nuer to separate their lineage affiliations from their community relationships.

Variability in Kinship Arrangements

The foregoing discussion of kinship is oversimplified, for in actual situations things are seldom so neat. For example, unilineal groups are not always completely exogamous, and some are even preferentially endogamous. In such cultures the unilineal rule for membership is useful only if the parents belong to different descent groups. Also, in some societies provision may be made for changing consanguineal group membership, perhaps by adoption of a child into a different clan from that of its birth.

In regard to kinship terminology the emic distinctions may be different from generation to generation and from one side of the family to the other. If people use Hawaiian terms for siblings and cousins the same degree of lumping in the parental generation would yield generation terms; that is, there could be a female term for all sisters and female cousins and a male term for all brothers and male cousins, as well as a female term for one's mother and all aunts and a male term to cover one's father and all uncles. The Miskito of Asang have Hawaiian sibling-cousin terms but bifurcate collateral terms for the parents and their siblings. A female Ego, then, would refer to her mother as *Yapti,* her mother's sister as *Anti,* her mother's brother as *Tahti,* her father as *Alsa,* her father's brother as *Rapia,* and her father's sister as *Tahka* (Helms 1971:64). Finally, we have not begun to describe the variety based on several other distinctions that affect kin terms. In addition to distinguishing parallel from cross relatives, collateral relatives from those in Ego's own line of descent, and those in Ego's own descent group from those in the other parent's descent group (as in the Omaha and Crow systems), kinship terms *may or may not* distinguish living from dead relatives, relatives who are older than the speaker from those who are younger, those of the same sex as the speaker from those of opposite sex, those spoken to by a female from those being spoken to by a male, male relatives from female relatives, relatives of the same generation as the speaker from those of a different generation, and consanguineal relatives from affinal relatives.

FICTIVE KINSHIP

There are various arrangements by which unrelated people establish interaction similar to that of kin. *Fictive kinship* relationships are formed for reasons other than kinship but are granted the strength and permanence ordinarily thought appropriate between close relatives.

Adoption is one widespread form of fictive kinship. Adoption of persons born in one unilineal descent group into another is a common form. Theoretically, all members of a purely unilineal group are biologically related, but frequently a few persons have been adopted into the group and, therefore, are only fictive unilineal kin. Adoption of persons from other tribes is found in a number of groups also. The Nuer scorn their Dinka neighbors and raid them regularly, but captive Dinka are adopted into the tribe. Dinka males are nearly always admitted into the lineage of their captors by the rite of adoption, and they enjoy the same legal rights as a free-born Nuer. Females are not adopted into the lineage, but they have full marriage rights. At least half of most Nuer tribes are people of Dinka descent (Evans-Pritchard 1940:221).

Some groups kill male war captives and adopt the women and children. In many societies adoption of women and orphans or other children by another family is common, and in others childless couples may adopt children. A few cultures provide for adoption of a child by a maternal uncle. In societies with unilineal groups an orphan or other child deprived of proper care by the parents is adopted by other members of the descent group. Adoption occurs in a variety of other contexts, also.

Another common type of fictive kinship is *institutionalized friendship*. This practice binds together unrelated persons, perhaps for life. Two people, for example, may pledge themselves to lifelong comradeship and mutual support. Two Miskito who decide to become special friends exchange articles of clothing or ornaments to seal the agreement and, then, follow kinship obligations toward one another insofar as they can (Helms 1971:96). Such relationships, varying in specific content, have been reported in many other groups, including the Crow and the !Kung.

The *godparent-godchild relationship* is also found as a form of fictive kinship in some cultures. The *compadrazgo* system of much of Latin America is a well-known example. On occasions such as baptism or confirmation the parents select godparents for their children, thus forming for life a special relationship between the godparent and child and between the parent and godparent. The co-parents refer to one another as "compadres"; the godparents have special obligations to one another; and all parties are supposed to stand together in times of difficulty or need.

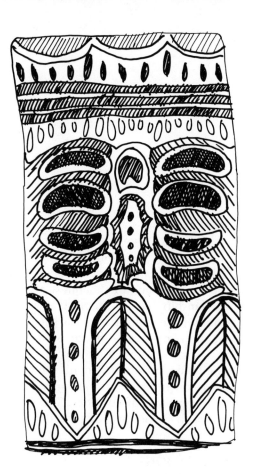

9

SOCIAL ORGANIZATION: ASSOCIATION, RANK, AND SOCIAL ORDER

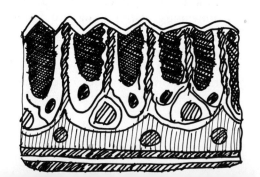

Kinship is so important in most nonliterate cultures that it is often thought of as their most characteristic feature. But more than one type of factor enters into the formation and maintenance of social units, and non-Western cultures manifest a variety of categories and groups in which non-kinship factors are just as important as kinship, or more so. Many groups have units based on special purposes, mutual interest, age differentiation, prestige differences, or territorial considerations. Associations, classes and castes, and territorial groups are of sufficient importance in nonliterate groups to merit separate attention. In addition, every group faces the problem of maintaining acceptable order among the individuals and subgroups of societies. These are conventionally treated under headings such as political organization, law, and social control.

ASSOCIATIONS

Associations are basically non-kin groups formed because of special purposes or interests the members share. Most members may be kin, but this is not the reason for the group's existence. A number of small-scale cultures are completely without associations, but several kinds are of importance in many places. A number of cultures have a *pan-societal association,* which is for all adults of the community or tribe. The *kachina cult* of the Hopi Indians of Arizona is an example, since all Hopi are initiated into it as young people and remain members as adults. Initiation confers on both boys and girls the right to join ceremonial associations, whose activities are regarded as essential to the welfare of the Hopi and the world in which they live (Titiev 1944:106).

More common among nonliterates is the *pan-societal fraternity,* an organization to which all the men belong. Not infrequently, manhood is synonymous with joining the fraternity. Commonly the group is set in opposition to the women, and the club's activities are kept secret from women and children. Men's clubs that have clubhouses may exclude women from them. In a clubhouse the men may work together on crafts, eat, tell stories, conduct ceremonies, hold councils, play games, and so forth. The Dani lack *pan-societal fraternities,* though they have at least one men's house in each compound from which women are normally excluded (K. Heider 1970:252).

There are a variety of other kinds of associations among nonliterates, more often for men only than for women or for both sexes. In many societies domestic responsibilities leave women little time for club life. There are women's associations here and there, but they often are weak and relatively insignificant.

Mutual aid is the dominant function of some associations. In fact, it is the typical association of the Dahomeans of West Africa. In many other associations mutual aid is one of several significant functions. *Community service* may be mentioned as an important function of some groups, such as the Samoan cooperative work group known as the *aumaga*. This voluntary association of untitled men not only plans and provides most of the labor force for many economically important tasks,

Figure 9–1   *Member of Samoan* Aumaga *society processing kava root. This voluntary association of untitled men (among other things) cooks and serves food at council meetings and ceremonial occasions.*

it also cooks and serves food at council meetings and on ceremonial occasions (Holmes 1974:32).

Organizations with *healing* as an important function are found in some places, the Grand Medicine Society of the Ojibwa Indians being an outstanding example. A man purchased curing knowledge from one of the society's members, and when he was knowledgeable enough he could be initiated into the society. The instruction took years, but as a society member a man enjoyed curing and other powers (Hoffman 1891: 156). The Nyoro of East Africa, until recently at least, have had spirit possession cults. A person who became ill from ghostly affliction could be healed by undergoing a lengthy initiation into the cult (Beattie 1960:77).

Associations with *military* significance exist in some societies, such as the social-police-military clubs of the American Plains Indians. The nineteenth-century Crow had several military groups, though they were not battle units, since war parties were formed independently of a man's association membership. The club's officers had to behave in certain ways in battle or they would bring shame on themselves or their club. The clubs would parade occasionally, and the officers might recite their war successes in public.

Associations in nonliterate cultures may also have *political* and *police* functions. Each year one of the Crow military clubs was selected to police the communal bison hunt, which involved preventing overanxious hunters and small groups from scaring off the bison before the camp as a whole was ready to attack the herd (Lowie 1935:5). The Crow military club chosen to serve as a police unit also had political significance, since they stopped ill-advised war parties, directed camp movements, and tried to settle disputes and maintain order. The Samoan association of untitled men also serves police functions, since they enforce all the legal pronouncements of the village council.

It is usual for societies to recognize categories of people distinguished from one another by age, such as the child, adolescent, and adult categories of the Miskito of Asang (Helms 1971:60), but clubs or associations that form people into groups on age criteria seem relatively uncommon in peasant and nonliterate societies. Often the prevalence of people of a particular age category is incidental to some group purpose. This is the case with the training and service organizations in Samoa. The *aumaga* is basically a society of untitled men, most of whom hope to qualify for a title through successful participation in the *aumaga*. Since many leave the organization some years later to accept a title, and since they are inducted into it as young men, it tends to be a society of young men. The woman's service organization in Samoa also includes mostly young people, since it consists in large part of unmarried girls. But it is not strictly an age group, for widows of various ages and, in some communities, wives of untitled men are members (Holmes 1974:82).

A special kind of age association, commonly referred to as an *age set,* occurs in a few cultures. The age set ordinarily is formed from young men, or young women in some cases, of about the same age category, and the members remain together as they pass through the life-cycle. Among the Nuer of East Africa, for example, there are annual initiations of boys into manhood. After about ten years an official closes the set's membership, and all boys initiated after that must enter the next youngest set. At the time of his initiation into the age set a young Nuer assumes the rights and obligations of manhood. He no longer milks cows; he becomes a warrior; he owns cattle; and so on. Members of the same set joke, play, and eat with one another, share their possessions, associate in war, duel with one another, and grant special hospitality to one another (Evans-Pritchard 1940:257). They should be respectful toward members of older sets in a variety of ways; the sets are segregated at sacrificial feasts; and a deceased member must be buried by someone in another set. One has special relationships with his father's age set, since they are all "fathers" to him in a sense. The set ceases to exist when the last member dies.

In many societies with age sets the sets are graded. This means that the life-cycle or a portion of it is divided into well-defined *age grades* or age brackets for which there are culturally prescribed statuses and behaviors, and the sets pass intact from grade to grade with their statuses changing as they do. The Galla of Ethiopia differ from the Nuer in this respect. There are five grades, and the members of each set change grades every eighth year. The class of men occupying the next to the highest grade exercises political power and responsibility, and those in the highest grade serve as advisers. They are retired from the system at the same time their sons enter the lowest grade (Prins 1953:58). The Hidatsa of the nineteenth century were one with the Crow, who, many centuries before, had age-graded age associations for both men and women (Bowers 1965: 174).

One of the most unique age systems is the age village arrangement of the Nyakyusa of what is now Tanzania. All of the boys of about ten or eleven years of age leave their parent's village and establish a new one a quarter of a mile or so away. There they sleep and spend their spare time, though they return to their mother's huts for meals. For a few years additional boys join the new village until, when the first members are about fifteen or sixteen, admission to the group is closed. The residence unit so formed continues throughout life. When the boys marry, they bring their wives to the village; and when the last member dies, the village dies (Wilson 1959:32, 158).

RANKED CATEGORIES AND GROUPS

Differentiation in prestige among individuals or groups within communities or larger units is a universal of human culture, but most societies lack the well-defined categories or groups of different prestige generally called *social classes*. There are always prestige differences based on skill, wisdom, bravery, supernatural ability, and other personal characteristics, and even minor wealth differences, but these usually remain individual and family matters. Nonliterate societies are relatively homogeneous in many ways, and wealth and resources ordinarily are rather evenly distributed. The result is that many nonliterate cultures lack significant class distinctions, and classes are nearly absent in hunting and gathering cultures (Murdock 1949:88).

Division into a hereditary nobility and a commoner class is the most frequent arrangement among nonliterate cultures having classes. Among the Nyoro, people who can show that they are patrilineal descendents of a king within, usually, three or four generations consitute a hereditary aristocracy (Beattie 1971:96). Before British influence changed things, this aristocracy was both wealthy and powerful. Its members still claim special prestige and privileges, and they sometimes act as a group. Commoners only occasionally show resentment of the demands and occasional arrogance of members of the aristocracy.

The second most frequent type of class system among nonliterates is based on wealth distinctions, and a number of cultures, literate and nonliterate, enable ambitious, talented, or fortunate persons to enhance their power and prestige through the assembling or manipulating of wealth. The top-ranked Basseri of Iran are a class apart from the rest of their tribe. They are free to associate with any corporate herding unit within the tribe, but most of them participate little in nomadic life. In fact, the Basseri chief and his brothers before the chieftainship was ended by Iranian authority were members of the national Iranian elite, who maintained homes in Shiraz and traveled extensively both within and outside the country. Each member of the elite owned several villages and many thousands of sheep and goats (Barth 1961:74).

In a few nonliterate cultures and many literate societies classes are based on occupational diversity and ranking of occupations. This may stem to a significant degree from the felt need to motivate people to undertake occupations perceived as greatly important to achieving highly valued goals. Those who respond by carrying out the functionally most valued and most difficult occupations are rewarded with wealth and other privileges. American physicians, for example, are permitted to charge high rates, since their highly skilled services require much training and are thought to be especially important to the welfare of society. Some social scientists have suggested that there are five or six classes in most American communities, with the main criteria of differentiation being occupation and wealth. In the late 1950s citizens of Kansas City, Missouri, were asked to rate one another. Their ratings were by residential neighborhood, occupation, income, housing quality, amount and kind of schooling, club and association membership, ethnic background, and church affiliation (Coleman and Neugarten 1971:56). Though most Kansas Citians were unable to say how many classes existed, the study of how distinctions were made led the investigators to formulate five dominant classes composed of thirteen substrata. Life-style features, such as participation in organizations and material standard of living, are more often used by Kansas Citians to rate one another than occupation, but the latter is significant at many levels. The investigators found that the perceptions were significant in determining which families interacted with one another.

In a small minority of cultures elite groups have gained ascendancy by acquiring control of scarce resources. These kinds of classes are rare among nonliterates and apparently emerge under rather special circumstances. Control of irrigation water is one basis for the development of such elites.

Castes are ranked categories whose members are assigned to the category at birth, are kept from moving into higher categories by the rules of the society, and must marry only members of their own category. They are quite unusual in nonliterate societies. Caste distinctions sometimes emerge when groups become culturally or occupationally dependent on one another, and one of them has the desire and the power to prohibit or severely limit intermarriage or other forms of passing from one group to the other.

Slavery is found in a substantial minority of nonliterate groups, but few of them have integrated a servile class into the social system so effectively as to be significantly dependent on it. At one time the Nyoro had slaves they had acquired in battle, purchased, or inherited (Roscoe 1923:11). Household slaves were of higher status than others. A man could marry a slave woman, and if she had a child the mother was freed. In most societies slaves have been war captives, and their sudden removal would have little effect on the overall structure of the society.

LOCAL AND OTHER TERRITORIAL GROUPS

A *community* may be defined as the smallest territorial unit in which member individuals and families can carry out most of the activities thought important and necessary for daily life. This means that the community is the basic unit with a *relatively complete culture*. It incorporates technological, economic, social, political, religious, recreational and aesthetic customs in sufficient balance to enable people to live well-rounded lives within its scope. Only rarely, if ever, can the community be said to be equivalent to the family.

The type of community characteristic of hunting and collecting or herding cultures is the *band*. The band is a nomadic group of families moving about within some territory, which may or may not exclude other bands. A band may be very small, consisting of no more than two or three families, and most bands appear to average around fifty persons. Marshall describes a !Kung band of forty-one persons as typical of that society. It consisted basically of the leading man with his two wives, his four young children, his younger brother and family, one of his younger sisters with her husband and children, and his elderly, widowed mother. In addition, at the leader's request, the band was joined by his first wife's father with his wife and child, two of his younger sons, his wife's sister and her son, and finally, sixteen other persons tied to the group through one of them doing bride service for the relatives of the leader's first wife's father (1965:268). The !Kung are regarded as having permanent membership rights in the bands into which they are born. They may become members of another band, but they always have the right to return to the natal band.

The *village* is a sedentary community, with the families occupying a cluster of dwellings, commonly near the ecological center of an area they exploit. Villages are characteristic of farming groups, and Murdock suggests that they average around 300 persons (1949:81). A number of specifics affect the composition and flavor of life in a village, even within the same tribe. Some villages of the Miskito of Nicaragua and Honduras are located along a river on top of a mud and grass river bank well above the flood line and must be reached by narrow, winding, slippery trails (Helms 1971:43). Others, where the land level is lower and flooding more severe must be located farther inland. Some have a police station, small stores, and Spanish-speaking members, while others lack commercial features and are almost entirely Miskito. Asang, a village of about 665 Miskito living on the Nicaraguan side of the Rio Coco, is located atop a fifteen-foot high bank separated from the river by a creek and a spit of sand and stones covered with trees and bushes. The ninety thatched dwellings, raised on four-foot high pilings, are arranged in three approximately parallel rows in line with the bank. A school, a commissary, two churches, a cemetery, a grazing area, and benches along the river bank complete the physical assemblage. Not only do the Miskito think of Asang as a physical place but they also see it as a political entity, a social unit, and a set of religious congregations (Helms 1971:52). Politically it consists of all those born in Asang and still living there, those who have married into the community, and people who are temporarily absent. Socially it is composed of people related to each other through kinship, and religiously the community is the Moravian congregation, which consists of most of Asang's families, and the smaller Church of God.

Another kind of sedentary community is the *neighborhood*, whose families are scattered in semi-isolated homesteads. They are found in fewer societies than villages and are generally somewhat smaller in population. The homesteads of the Nyoro, which usually consist of one or two mud-and-wattle huts around a courtyard surrounded by gardens and banana groves, are somewhat scattered in neighborhood clusters, with the homes usually within shouting distance of one another (Beattie 1960:1). Even though they do not live in compact village clusters, the Nyoro are interested in their nearest neighbors and attach great value to being neighborly. Within the Nyoro neighborhood community, people help one another, have communal beer parties and feasts, and adjudicate minor disputes through an informal neighborhood court. Each community, which consists of a hundred or so people living in from forty to sixty or more homes, is led by a headman.

The size at which a village becomes a town or city is problematical. The 2,500 figure sometimes used in the United States is arbitrary. Very few nonliterate communities have indigenous towns or cities of over a thousand persons or communities that feature the occupational diversity typical of urban societies. West Africa was one of the most urban areas of the nonliterate world, with large cities being a pre-European tradition in some groups. One of the smaller pre-European cities was surrounded by an earthen wall enclosing an area of 400 square miles. Though these cities of tens of thousands of people were basically farming places, there was also a great deal of occupational specialization. It is of interest that urban Yoruba would look down upon and ridicule the rural people as unsophisticated yokels.

The members of some communities intermarry so much that they become the localized consanguineal unit which Murdock refers to as a *deme* (1949:63). The deme is a strongly endogamous community whose members are genetically related to all or nearly all the rest of the group. The demes of the Basseri nomads of south Iran are communities of ten to forty tents. The headman's authority over his camp depends on the strength of his influence over the others in his camp, and there is constant occasion for dispute. In order to hold the group together, a headman promotes marriages within the camp, and in two camps where the ethnographer took a census, 66 percent of the marriages were endogamous (Barth 1961:35).

Demes are not the only communities which either are or come close to being kinship groups. As already indicated, unilineal groups may be localized in a sense. A Nuer village is composed of a core of patrilineally related lineage-mates, plus wives the men of the core have brought into the village, as well as members of other lineages who have moved into the community (see page 171).

The largest territorial unit common among nonliterate peoples is the *tribe,* a term used here to refer to a group of culturally similar communities within a given territory whose members think of themselves as belonging to the same cultural unit (Mandelbaum 1956:295). Often a tribe has a name which distinguishes it as a unit, and this name frequently means "people." Not all !Kung groups use that name for themselves, but some do and it is their word for "person" or "people."

A tribe may or may not be politically organized. The nineteenth-century Crow Indians recognized themselves as belonging to a cultural unit distinct from others, but the Crow were not politically unified (Lowie 1935:4). By contrast, the Nyoro tribe is governed by a hierarchy of chiefs and other officials, with the Mukama, or king, as the top tribal ruler (Beattie 1971:7).

POLITICAL ORGANIZATION

Anthropologists have had difficulty deciding whether all cultures have government or political organization. The answer depends in part on how such terms are defined, and they have been defined in many ways. It is clear that some nonliterate groups lack full-time specialists who order group affairs, so they can be said to be without a government. But this does not mean that they are not governed by some culturally established procedures. Government is defined here as the process of administration, however informally it may be done, of the affairs of a territorially based unit, such as a band, village, neighborhood, city, localized kinship group, or tribe. The *administrative process* consists of making decisions for the group, putting decisions into action, and appraising current circumstances and the results of previous actions as the basis for future decisions (Litchfield 1956:12). Decisions have to do with two areas: relationships among the individuals and subgroups composing the society, and relationships with other societies. Stated this way, it appears that nearly all known cultures exhibit government (not necessarily a government) over either the tribe or over smaller territorial units.

To say that a tribe is not politically organized means that there is no governmental mechanism for the tribe as a unit, but it does not mean that the tribe's members are not subject to political regulation. Though the Crow were not tribally organized, there were political mechanisms in operation at the band level, with each band having a headman (Lowie 1935:5). The headman decided when and where his followers were to move and place their tipis and appointed one of the military societies as a police force, but he had very little power or responsibility otherwise. Some other American Indian groups, including the Cheyenne, had true tribal government.

Administrative arrangements among the world's cultures differ in a variety of dimensions and in their complexity. The simplest type of political arrangement is here referred to as *informal local group administration*. It is characteristic of many societies at the band level of social integration (see page 26). Three characteristics of this type of political organization may be emphasized. First, the communities in the society are independent of one another politically; they are not combined or integrated on a higher level. Second, leadership is informal; administrative responsibility is granted primarily on the basis of experience and success in terms of culturally accepted standards. Third, political decisions cannot be distinguished from family, kinship, economic, moral, and other such decisions; those who make the decisions are the same persons in all areas of life.

The man most often looked to for advice by the members of a local group is commonly referred to by anthropologists as a *headman*. In many bands a headman may operate as little more than a convener of the group or the most senior or influential member of the group. In a few societies the elders serve with the headman as a kind of advisory council. Government by such informal councils of old men sometimes is called *gerontocracy*.

Informal local group administration is apt to occur among peoples who spend much of their time moving about in small groups, specifically hunting and collecting societies. In many cases the groups have small and shifting memberships, and the most influential person lacks coercive authority. In each !Kung band there is a man who is thought of by the people as the owner of the food and water resources in the band's territory. His position is passed from father to son, and he is the one outsiders should talk to if they want to draw on the band's water or plant resources. (Marshall 1976:193). But he is not an administrator of group affairs and possesses no political authority. He has no responsibility to organize hunting parties, gathering expeditions, trading trips, visits, craft work, or gift-exchanges, nor does he have any authority over marriage arrangements. These and other such affairs are planned by discussion among the members of a !Kung band, and their plans are carried out with a minimum of controversy. In some !Kung bands the "owner of resources" may come to be a leader, but someone else may emerge as a leader, or there may be none. So, whether or not a !Kung band has a headman depends on whether a person with strong qualities of leadership emerges informally. If such a person exists, he still lacks coercive authority and is simply one sufficiently respected that people look to him for advice, seek his help, and tend to fall in with his plans. The administration or government of a !Kung band's affairs, then, is basically in the hands of the band as a group, sometimes with an informally functioning leader and sometimes with none.

Other groups, such as the Crow and the Basseri, manifest more permanent administrative leadership, but even in these cases the headman is an adviser rather than a dictator. If he can discern, crystalize, and express the feelings of the band, its members draw together and move toward their goal. In this way a headman promotes harmony within the band and facilitates its objectives. Although the Basseri once had a tribal chief with great authority, he did not delegate any of his authority to the band headmen. A Basseri headman must depend on his personal ability to formulate and guide public opinion in his camp, just as the typical headman of other societies must operate, and this is linked to the network of kinship within the band (Barth 1961:29).

In many societies headmanship tends to be hereditary, but not at the expense of effective leadership. Sometimes a man in line for a headmanship yields the position to someone else because he lacks interest or ability, and sometimes a headman is replaced simply by people's refusal to follow him. The headman of a Crow band might remain in his position until he resigned, but Lowie was also informed that a headman might serve only as long as the people had good luck under him (1935:6). The Basseri also claim that they have the right to depose a headman whenever

Figure 9–2 / Toma, the most influential person in one of the approximately six-teen !Kung bands. Whether or not a !Kung band has a headman depends on whether a person with strong qualities of leadership emerges. Administration is basically in the hands of the band as a group.

they wish, and this is apparently acceptable to the tribal chief. The common American assumption that "primitive" communities have "chiefs" who tell their followers what to do has little or no validity.

Consistently used criteria governing usage of the terms *headman* and *chief* have not been developed. As previously noted, most anthropologists refer to the informal leaders of small local groups as headmen. The political leaders of larger units or individuals who exercise their administrative prerogatives with greater formality and authority than most headmen are frequently called chiefs.

Societies with large bands or which assemble in substantial population units frequently for long periods of time often manifest a second type of government: *multicentric administration*. Multicentric administration is government as the by-product or extension of the activities of various nongovernmental, nonfamily subgroups of the society. These subgroups may be kinship units, secret societies, ceremonial associations, military fraternities, age sets, or territorial subdivisions such as wards and hamlets. Basically such groups are concerned with administering their own affairs, but when there is a felt need for administration for the larger society, leaders of the various groups can work together to cope with governmental matters, or one of the groups can extend its administrative operations to represent the general society. In some cases the leaders form temporary or permanent councils, sometimes with officers. Such councils organize and operate in a variety of ways, and the basic point is that their administrative work for the larger society is an extension of their own internal operations.

Multicentric administration is common at the tribal level of social integration (see page 27), and many tribal societies are farming groups with unilineal or other descent units. For example, the tribal council of the Hidatsa Indians was composed of prominent members of the matrilineal clans (Bowers 1965:27). Age set membership was also important to Hidatsa government, since the top leaders were supposed to have advanced beyond the Black Mouth age grade. There were no tribal officials charged only with tribal administration, but the administrative leaders of the lineages and advanced age sets combined forces to handle tribal affairs as needed.

One of the more unusual types of political arrangements is the *segmentary lineage system*. It is multicentric in the sense that administrative questions are resolved by component subgroups, the lineages, but without defined political leadership. The Nuer, who are classified by Service as an example of the tribal level of social integration (1978:5), are among those having this type of system. Among the Nuer, if two minimal lineages within the same minor lineage have a disagreement, matters are resolved at that level. But if the two minimal lineages belong to different minor lineages, the other minimal lineages support their "brother" lineages, with the result that the disagreement is raised to the "minor" level of the lineage hierarchy—that is, minor lineage against minor lineage. Through this same pattern, as when the dispute is between minimal lineages of different clans, the argument escalates through the minor, major, and maximal lineage levels to the clan level (see page 160) until it is clan against clan. Or if the quarrel is between minimal lineages of different tribes, one Nuer tribe will be fighting with another (Evans-Pritchard 1940:143). The Nuer have ritual mediators who are important to them in the settlement of feuds, but they lack rulers, councils, or other governmental entities. The segmentary system of lineages, however strange it may seem to outsiders, serves to integrate tribes made up of tens of thousands of people.

A measure of political centralization exists when the leaders of a society's component kinship groups, associations, or territorial subdivisions form an administrative council. Even so, the political process may remain basically multicentric, since the council members are acting primarily as leaders of their respective groups. Fully *centralized government* may be said to exist when there is a segment of the society which has as its main function the administration of the whole group's affairs. At this level the society must produce enough of a food surplus to justify having one or more persons spending most or all of their time on administrative matters. Centralized government has been associated with the chiefdom level of social integration among nonliterate groups in which the monopoly of force that characterizes political states is lacking (Service 1978:8). Centralized governments tend to occur in societies with a fair amount of social differentiation and economic specialization and economic redistribution (see page 128) as a dominant mode of allocating goods and services. On the Samoan island of Manua, a village is governed by a council of chiefs, each of which holds a title as the elected head of a household and a chieftainship as head of an ambilineal descent group. One or more of the council chiefs holds the position of High Chief. A High Chief presides over the village council, maintains a special house for entertaining important visitors, and enjoys a number of ritual privileges. If a village has more than one High Chief, they share responsibility as a group of "brother chiefs" (Holmes 1974:26). Some of the Samoan chiefs are known as *talking chiefs,* who characteristically have special responsibilities as spokesmen for the other chiefs and as ceremonial leaders. The Samoans have traditionally had a redistributive economy, and much of this still pertains. The village council of chiefs retains ultimate control over the village lands, and all landholders are subject to assessments against their crops and their labor (Mead 1969:70). On ceremonial occasions, at feasts, and during community projects of various kinds, food and other products are redistributed to the participating villagers and laborers and the craftsmen who are being compensated for their services.

Many literate and some nonliterate societies have centralized governments which possess the official right to establish and enforce the rules of social order (Sahlins 1968:6). Such a government is known to political anthropologists and other specialists in political organization as a *state.* The kingdom of Bunyoro, for example, was a state. The king prohibited private war, and blood revenge could be undertaken only with his consent.

The various factors by which political systems differ from one another appear in a variety of combinations in particular societies, so much so that it often is difficult to characterize a culture as having one type of government or another. The Crow Indians, for example, had informal administration at the local level, but there was a multicentric element also, since the leaders of the various military and other associations exercised considerable political influence. And the monopoly of force which distinguishes states from other types of administrations nevertheless allows for a good deal of democratic and informal decision making in many contexts. Though the Basseri chief monopolized the right to command before he was deposed by the Iranian government, the camp headmen still operated informally and noncoercively. In one sense the government of the United States is less centralized than that of the Bunyoro and some other nonliterate governments. The Bunyoro chiefs were directly responsible to the central government, but governors of the American states are not under the central administration, since the states are not administrative subunits of the national government. Each American has a dual citizenship, national and state, for the American Constitution reserves certain functions for the states.

The governments of some nonliterate societies are highly elaborated. Black Africa, especially, is outstanding for its variety of political systems and the complexity of many of them. In pre-European Africa there were true monarchs heading confederacies of territorial subunits, each with its own political structure. Some African rulers had large numbers of ministers and retinues of major and minor officials of many kinds. They commonly used authority symbols extensively, such as palaces, escorts, and special clothing. Many African governments used force rather extensively to maintain order, though a good deal of authority was democratically exercised. Rulers were identified symbolically with their kingdoms and empires, and they were accorded a great deal of respect. But seldom were they able to do as they wished without consulting their ministers and members of councils, who commonly were the chiefs or headmen of the component territorial units. Pre-European African states conducted wars of conquest by which they overcame and incorporated other nations, thus forming empires. Some were strongly based on kinship groups or associations, but the leaders had greater power over and independence of those units than in fully multicentric systems. Other pre-European African societies developed governments significantly independent of nonpolitical groups. The difficulties of today's African governments have reinforced a stereotype of blacks as unable to govern themselves, but the pre-European story reveals a strong flair for the development and maintenance of orderly, effective political arrangements. The complex monarchy of Bunyoro is only one of many examples.

DIPLOMACY AND WARFARE

Relations between political units, whether communities or tribes, are regulated either by peaceful means (diplomacy) or by warfare. Governmental authorities in nonliterate societies do conduct diplomatic relations, but anthropologists have given little systematic attention to this area. The investigations of Numelin, a Finnish diplomat, have shown that the use of diplomatic functionaries as messengers, envoys, negotiators, and ambassadors is common among band and tribal peoples (1950). Local groups in

Australia have been known to negotiate with one another for borrowing ceremonial objects. The aboriginal Maori of New Zealand were famed for their vicious intertribal wars, but they negotiated for peace and solidarity as well. It is reported that a Maori chief might choose a high-ranking woman as an envoy, since women were permitted to visit other tribes in complete safety. Samoan villages sometimes warred against one another (Mead 1969:168), but frequent ceremonial interaction between villages was much more important, and remains so (Holmes 1974:28). The village High Talking Chief is especially significant on Manua, in Samoa, as the leader of an official party of titled men who visit another village for various reasons, such as requesting mat-making materials, engaging in sports, exchanging marriage property, and the like. Dani political alliances arrange for payments to secure certain rights of access. The leader of the Gutelu alliance receives payments of pigs from members of other alliances for access to the brine pool from which they obtain their salt (K. Heider 1970:87). The Nuba tribes of the African Sudan have hereditary ambassadors who meet to arrange and conduct ceremonies of reconciliation after a blood feud. And some Nuba communities had ambassadors assigned to several enemy groups, their function being to negotiate ransoms for captives (Nadel 1947:158, 259).

Many anthropological references to diplomacy seem to occur within discussions of war. This may or may not indicate an unconscious ethnocentric concern with war on the part of Euroamerican anthropologists. It has been suggested that societies frequently reject the ideal of war as a way of life even when the record indicates its importance. Turney-High listed sixteen wars for the United States during its 190-year history, an inception of hostilities on an average of about every twelve years (1968: 383).

Anthropologists commonly use the term war to refer to any kind of intergroup combat, but combat among nonliterates is not of the kind carried out by modern nations. Sustained, well-organized combat conducted by formally organized governments is uncommon among non-literate groups, though it certainly existed among the Nyoro and other African states as well as among other well-elaborated aboriginal cultures in various parts of the world. It is not always easy to distinguish warfare from the more organized kinds of raiding and feuding. Feuding is usually thought of as sustained mutual enmity between groups which results in intermittent armed clashes or raids. Participation in raids was a common way of obtaining presige and validating manhood among the Crow and many other American Indian groups. Trophies—such as scalps, heads, or other body parts—were taken, either to gain prestige or for supernatural or ceremonial reasons. Intergroup combat in the form of feuds and raids is common and is found in all parts of the globe.

The Dani lack formal governments and standing armies, but warfare between confederations of adjacent residential compounds and neighborhoods was a regular part of their lives before it was stopped by the Dutch in the early 1960s. Alliances of several confederations considered them-selves at war with one another, but the actual one-day battles which occurred from time to time were ordinarily fought by confederations belonging to different alliances (K. Heider 1970:80). Most of the warfare was ritual, the purpose being to kill a member of the enemy group so as to maintain or restore good relationships with the ghosts and, thereby, to maintain or restore group well-being. An alliance which had suffered a loss at the hands of an enemy had to take revenge for this purpose, and whichever group had last inflicted a death had to defend itself against the enemy's attempts to change the balance. A desired death might occur either in the course of an arranged battle or a surprise raid. Sometimes tensions grew to the point that short, bloody, nonritual wars with major political and economic consequences would break out, but the ritual warfare, which prevailed most of the time, was casual, conducted almost like a sport.

Some take the high incidence of intergroup combat among the world's peoples as evidence that humans are incurably warlike, but the fact that there are some cultures without war and with a nearly complete absence of internal violence demonstrates that we are not dealing with an instinct. The !Kung are strongly opposed to fighting and think it both dangerous and dishonorable. To have to fight is evidence of failure to find a solution by more intelligent means. There are no stories of battles and no songs of praise for war heroes, past or present (Marshall 1976:53). Marshall found no !Kung who could remember a war between bands over resources or for any other reason, nor any who had been told of such wars by their parents or grandparents (1976:182). There are a number of other societies in various parts of the world which have developed satisfy-ing cultures that do not include war. It remains to be seen whether modern humans can invent complex cultural systems that exclude warfare.

SOCIAL CONTROL

One form of social control, *law,* is ordinarily thought by Euroamer-icans to consist of written regulations produced and enforced by special governmental units such as police forces and courts. This would mean that nonliterate cultures lack law. But anthropologists generally prefer a broad definition that recognizes the functional similarity among the social control systems of all kinds of societies. One approach suggests that law exists in a society whenever violation of a behavior standard brings about community-authorized exercise of force or threat of force to punish or bring the violator into line (Hoebel 1954:28). Hoebel specified community-authorized physical force, but it seems reasonable to accept Pospisil's suggestion that the effectiveness of force is the functionally significant criterion, which would include psychologically coercive force.

Though many societies rely on police and courts to administer law, community-authorized coercion, either physical and/or psychological, may do as well. Evans-Pritchard speaks of law among the Nuer as a moral obligation to settle disagreements by conventional mechanisms (1940:168). There are no law enforcement agencies and no formal legal procedures; the community as a whole does not punish violators. Instead, those who are strong enough and have enough backing from their relatives can take matters into their own hands; and if they are in the right, the offenders do not resist. A man who feels that someone owes him cattle will simply enter the debtor's cattle byre, corral, or pastures and take what he is owed, knowing that the community will approve if he is in the right. If the issue is unclear there may be prolonged and repeated discussion or a fight, but in many cases Nuer law operates in the form of community-approved self-help. This is law enforcement just as surely as if it were carried out by police and courts. If this broad concept is accepted, it can be said that virtually all cultures include law in one form or another.

Law and political procedures overlap, but some political decisions are not law. Laws, ideally, are applicable to many similar cases, while many political decisions are specific and nonrepetitive (Pospisil 1958:257).

Many societies have *mediators* who aid in the resolution of legal matters. They may not be able to force compliance, but they can often direct consideration toward relevant issues or successfully propose solu-

Figure 9–3 *Nuer leopard-skin priest. The leopard-skin priest may hear a dipute and render an opinion, though his verdict is accepted only if both parties agree to the solution.*

tions. The leopard-skin priest among the Nuer may hear a dispute and render an opinion, though his verdict is accepted only if both parties desire peaceful settlement and agree to the solution (Evans-Pritchard 1940:164). The use of the *ordeal* to legally identify a culprit or determine guilt is also widespread. The accused are required to undergo some procedure that ordinarily would kill or injure, and a person who escapes is adjudged innocent. In many societies *testimony* is taken from the litigants or witnesses. This is especially true of some African cultures, which are noted for their emphasis on law. Many, in fact, have highly developed legal systems with courts to hear statements from witnesses and to apply in behalf of the community a complex of well-standardized legal principles. The Nyoro formerly had a central court presided over by a chief justice, four county chief's courts, and twenty-five sub-county chief's courts. They also had informal neighborhood courts, which dealt with minor disputes. A group of neighbors would gather informally to hear the case; the disputants stated their positions; witnesses were heard; and the group discussed the matter and rendered a decision. If the neighborhood court could not resolve matters, the case would go to a higher court.

The notion that legal norms may originate from sources other than special legislative bodies has precedent in European and American cultures, which recognize common law. This consists of customary and legally enforceable norms of remote and unknown origin, and many laws in nonliterate cultures are of this kind. On the other hand, the origin of legal norms in some small-scale groups has been observed. In the very process of resolving interpersonal and intergroup disputes, headmen, chiefs, monarchs, and councils may propose and pronounce norms that are sanctioned from then on by the whole community. African councils occasionally set forth new laws to deal with new situations; and the Plains Indians developed legal norms to cope with horse theft, one result of the adoption of horses by Plains societies (Hoebel 1978:60).

Cultures differ from one another in the content of their legal norms and the kinds and severity of sanctions applied. In some societies premarital intercourse is a serious violation, whereas in others it is tolerated as long as the rules against incest are observed. Personal property may be taken without permission in some cultures as long as the borrower is known, but in other cultures this would be considered theft. Among the infractions recognized by the Samoans of the island of Manua are spreading scandal about one's own village, distributing kava incorrectly, incest, habitual theft, adultery, the use of insulting words in quarrels, and trying to stir up trouble between two titled men (Mead 1969:169). The Nyoro initiate legal action for insulting political leaders, failure to plant anti-famine food crops, fouling drinking water sources, excessive drunkenness, sorcery, adultery, failure to repay a brideprice after divorce, theft, failure to pay taxes, and many other offenses (Beattie, 1971:220). In spite of diversity there remain a number of basic similarities among cultures in what kinds of behaviors they define as illegal or criminal. Virtually all have legal regulations concerning the taking of human life, the use of material objects, or sexual activity.

Law may be universal, or nearly so, but there are other ways of maintaining a reasonable degree of conformity which lack the coerciveness and community authority usually associated with law. It is not always easy to decide whether a given instance is law or some other mode of social control, but success in classification is less important than understanding something of the range of ways societies encourage conformity to their norms.

A major element of social control in all societies is *reciprocity,* which operates in both legal and nonlegal relationships. Positively stated, the fundamental idea is that people are prompted to conform to what others expect of them because they realize that they can thereby expect others to observe their rights. Negatively stated, reciprocity may be withheld when someone does not conform. It is the realization that one may be cut off from the support and daily cooperation of others that keeps many a person in line.

Another extensively used means of social control is bringing *shame* on the violator. Through education and other socialization, people are conditioned to feel embarrassed and chagrined when the members of the group discover that they have violated accepted norms. The technique is to let the violator know, by ridicule or some other means, that the behavior is disapproved of, for the purpose of stimulating a sense of shame. It operates well, of course, only if the society's members have been effectively conditioned to feel ashamed under such circumstances. This also functions to educate young people to their society's expectations.

Some people feel ashamed of violating a norm whether they are found out or not and whether or not there is any expression of disapproval. In fact, some writers have distinguished cultures that condition people to feel guilty about violations and so to control their own behavior without external disapproval from cultures that condition people to feel ashamed only when they are found out (Benedict 1946:222). In either case exposure or condemnation evokes or intensifies feelings of shame.

The specific techniques of evoking shame are highly variable. Ridicule and gossip are among the most common practices. The Crow Indians unmercifully ridiculed anyone who broke their rule against marrying someone of the same matrilineal clan. The offender's nephews and nieces, who had joking privileges with their uncle, would tell him that his buttock was his brother-in-law, which was a way of saying that he actually had no brother-in-law. According to Crow kinship terms, men of the same clan were brothers, and by marrying a woman of his own clan a man left himself without brothers-in-law (Lowie 1935:282). When this and other techniques used by the Crow are considered, it becomes understandable that a Crow would think twice before enduring the ridicule that came from marrying a clan-mate.

Gossip is the most powerful means of informal social control in the Miskito village of Asang. Though the Asang Miskito do not admire gossip, they engage in it extensively, and people are sensitive about the possibility of being the subject of negative gossip. Helms was frequently asked by her informants, "Why haven't you visited me lately, did you hear something bad about me?" (1971:161).

Avoidance, public insult, reprimand, self-deprivation, and physical violence are among other means of evoking shame. If the !Kung disapprove of someone's behavior they may either criticize it directly or sing a song of disapproval. They compose a special song concerning the bad behavior, and they may sing it in camp during the dark of night (Marshall 1976:289). Even suicide or its threat may be used to shame people. An abused Iroquois woman, for example, might commit suicide as a way of striking back, which would encourage restraint among those who might offend women (Fenton 1941:124). Physical violence to evoke shame applies to the relationships between parents and children on the South Pacific island of Tikopia. Physical blows against a child are thought of as an infliction of shame more than physical suffering, and there is probably an element of shame in the corporal punishment of children in many societies.

In addition to reciprocity and shame, *affective reinforcement* is a major means of social control. This is the evoking of a sense of pride by expression of approval, and it is applicable particularly to those who go beyond what is prescribed or who abide by cultural prescriptions with unusual consistency. A person may be rewarded by being publicly honored, by appointment or election to positions of prestige-bearing responsibility, or by being provided with various psychologically gratifying experiences. Not only does this encourage the rewarded individual to abide by the norms, but it presumably has a motivational and educational effect upon those who honor, admire, or witness the person's good fortune. The Plains Indians of North America made extensive use of praise to encourage young men to distinguish themselves in raiding.

Another technique of social control is what has been called *logic* (Honigmann 1959:500). Violators or potential violators are reminded that the violation is incompatible with beliefs that they share with the other members of the society. There may be argument, and a person of much influence may pressure one of lesser position to accept his or her point of view. When one !Kung man seized another already angry man and began to shake him, increasing his anger to the point that he nearly became violent, one of the peacemakers led him away saying, "If you want to help people, don't get angry with them. Keep calm. Don't increase anger . . ." (Thomas 1958:186). This was clearly an appeal to the general !Kung concern with maintaining cooperative, peaceful relationships, and an expression of their fear of fighting. In like vein, a Yurok Indian who failed to take immediate steps against a violator of his rights was reminded that his behavior was inconsistent with a belief he shared with the rest of the Yurok, namely, that justice and good social relations cannot be maintained without careful adherence to the principle of quick retribution for all offenses (Spott and Kroeber 1943:198).

These are only a few of the significant ways of keeping violations of cultural norms at a minimum and avoiding the consequent disorganization of social relations. When norm violations are so frequent that a society's members are unable to predict and count on the behavior of their fellows, it becomes difficult or impossible for the people to reach their culturally defined goals—a state some sociologists have called *social disorganization*. Every society, no matter how dimly aware its members are of the issue, must maintain some kind of effective compromise between the stultification and frustration of absolute regulation at one extreme and the social disorganization and psychological disorientation of total freedom on the other. Every culture's system of social control has been developed in response to that necessity. More careful, more objective comparison of the world's systems of social control than we now have may help us solve some of the problems of freedom and conformity in the modern world.

10

RITUAL

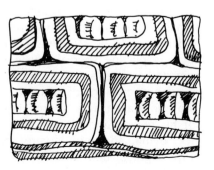

Ritual is of great functional significance in every aspect of life and occurs in much more of daily life than many recognize. Much ritual is religious, but a great deal occurs in technological, economic, kinship, political, and other activities. It seems advisable, then, to avoid the common practice of treating ritual as an aspect of religion. *Ritual* is defined here as the symbolic affirmation of values by means of culturally standardized utterances and actions. A ritual may be considered a unit of such symbolic expression. A *ceremony* is a given complex of rituals associated with a specific occasion.

Any society's members have culturally defined feelings about all kinds of things, and people in all societies are inclined to symbolize these feelings in conventional ways. Ritual behavior is an effective means of expressing or reinforcing important sentiments. To the Nuer it is a matter of great pride for the kinsmen of a man who has been killed to insist on a death in revenge, and a matter of dishonor if they do not. If both kin groups want to avoid hostilities, they permit a leopard-skin priest to mediate, but their pride must be ritually expressed in a refusal of the mediator's efforts until the last possible moment. The priest might threaten to curse them. He would rub ashes on an ox's back, declaring to the ox that if the dead man's kinsmen refused to accept compensation and insisted on revenge, many would be killed and they would throw their spears at enemies in vain. He would then raise his spear to kill the ox, whereupon one of the dead man's people would grab his arm to prevent him from stabbing the ox and declare their intention to accept compensation (Evans-Pritchard 1940:175). By such last-minute obstinacy was pride of kin ritually manifested and strengthened.

In state societies, especially, political leaders are recognized as functionally important persons who must maintain some degree of authority and respect to be effective. Certain behavior ritually emphasizes this fact, such as playing special music when a president arrives, a genuflection executed before approaching a monarch, and many other specifics that occur on occasions of contact between political leaders and their people. The importance of a Nyoro king was emphasized by a special vocabulary for his person and his acts. His eating, sleeping, bathing, laughing, being sick, dying, and burial were referred to by special words, as were his corpse, grave, bed, drums, spears, the milking of his special cows, and other persons and objects associated with him (Beattie 1971:109). The Samoans used a special courtesy language when they were talking to or about titled people (Mead 1969:114), though they lack the state.

The techniques and objects employed in rituals are highly diverse. Manipulation of the body is frequent, and nearly any movement or physiological activity may have ritual significance, such as folding the hands to show reverence for God, weeping to express solidarity, spitting to show contempt, clapping the hands to show approval, and bowing to manifest subordination. Various dance movements are also used in ritual symbolism.

Cultures differ in the meanings of specific ritual actions. Placing the palms together indicates an attitude of prayer in some places, but elsewhere it may be a gesture of respect. Such rituals are verbal or actional or both without involvement of objects; and when objects are of ritual significance, they may be either manipulated or simply present as a meaningful part of the ritual setting. Cultures also differ in the substances and materials employed for ritual and in the frequency of their use. Cattle, for example, are much more extensively employed in the ceremonies of the Nuer and other East African cultures than in some other groups who raise them. The meanings of bodily movements, musical and other sounds, utterances, and materials are commonly so well standardized that their employment not only expresses but also stimulates the feelings that are supposed to be experienced on given ritual occasions. For example, partakers of Christian communion not only ritually remember Christ's broken body and shed blood, they often find that taking the bread and wine makes them feel closer to God.

Anthropologists have given a great amount of attention to *rites of passage* and *calendrical rites*. Rites of passage occur when individuals or groups move from one status to another. Naming ceremonies, baptisms, initiation rites, graduation exercises, investiture ceremonies, and funerals are examples. There has been considerable description and analysis of the rituals that mark passage from childhood to adulthood, which usually occur about at puberty. The initiation of Nuer boys into manhood takes place at about fourteen years of age or within the next few years. The main feature is the making of six long cuts across the forehead from one ear to the other, which leaves prominent, life-long scars. Many of the ceremony's elements symbolize a newly intimate and mystical relationship between a male and oxen. The initiates may have no contact with cattle during the initiation period, including the daily practice of all men and boys of rubbing the ashes of cattle dung over their bodies. At the end of the period the boys are smeared with cattle dung, after which they wash in a stream, beat the cattle with wild rice, and rub themselves with cattle-dung ashes. They also chant and leap behind the oxen their fathers have given them, which are the first ones they can call their own (Evans-Pritchard 1956:255). These rituals clearly emphasize the boys' change of status concerning the dominant theme of Nuer life, the concern with cattle.

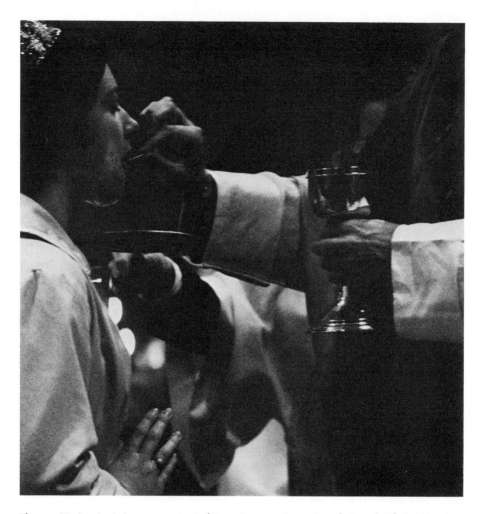

Figure 10–1   *American woman taking Communion. Partakers of Christian communion not only ritually remember Christ's broken body and shed blood, they often find that taking the bread and wine makes them feel closer to God.*

Passage rituals are by no means absent from American life, baptism and confirmation being among them. Puberty rituals are less important in the United States than in some other cultures, but informal rituals of passage occur at various points during the teenage years. A number of habits developed by teenagers ritually symbolize either their desire to become adults, their urge to be independent of their parents, or solidarity with their peers. During the 1960s, long hair became for some teenage boys a symbol of rejection of their parents' authority, but as the custom spread, it became for many little more than a mark of conformity and security in being like one's age-mates.

Calendrical rites are associated with events that recur in the society in question: annually, seasonally, monthly, weekly, etc. The Aztecs and other Mesoamerican groups performed world renewal ceremonies every 52 years, since it required that much time for the 365-day calendar and the 260-day calendar to return to the point at which the first days for each would coincide. In the United States calendrical rites occur on holidays such as Independence Day, Thanksgiving, Christmas, and so on. Many of these rites reaffirm solidarity or identification with the past, but many other values are registered, too. Memorial Day rites symbolize for many people appreciation of the patriotic sacrifices made by men and women who have died in American wars, and the specific elements of those rites (such as wearing a red poppy) represent the blood of those sacrifices in the minds of some (Warner 1953:5).

The experiences of a group can change its attitude toward some of its traditional rites. Armistice Day (November 11) was a major ceremonial occasion in the lives of older readers of this book, since it symbolized sentiments about World War I. As the proportion of the population who remembered that war and valued what it stood for decreased, and later wars superseded it in the consciousness of many, fewer communities celebrated the day until, finally, it was converted into Veterans Day and the date was changed.

Contrasting rituals within a society may be anchored to the conflicting sentiments of different groups. With the wave of criticism of the motives of the United States government and the questioning of the value of war which developed during the 1960s a polarization in attitudes centered on flag ritual. At one extreme the flag was burned or worn upside down on the seat of denim trousers to stand for rejection of the country's motives and alleged warlikeness. Others purchased flagpoles and expensive flags, which they devotedly displayed as a reaffirmation of a continued commitment to their idea of the American way of life, and their rejection of those who ritually and otherwise criticize it.

It is clear that passage and calendrical rites are not the only kinds of rituals, but anthropologists have had limited success in developing mutually exclusive, comprehensive, ritual categories. Accordingly, we will turn our attention to the functions of rituals.

Validation and reinforcement of values is one of the most obvious ritual functions; in fact, this is basic in the definition of ritual. On ceremonial occasions such as Independence Day, the investiture of governmental officials, or weddings, speeches may be delivered which allude to group values in conventional statements reminding the people of their commitments and, perhaps, even praising people for their correct attitudes and behaviors. In this sense, ritual has a social control function.

Ritual also *provides reassurance* and feelings of security in the face of the psychological disturbances of everyday life. Magical rituals comfort the person in that he feels he is doing something to overcome his problems, and the praying person who has put his problems in God's hands feels comforted and renewed. Many ritual activities reassure one by providing a sense of having conformed to the requirements of powers beyond, with a consequent feeling that all will be well. Much religious worship is of this nature. Ritual also may be viewed as providing reassurance in the sense that it is a ready-made solution to problems that are poorly understood and difficult to solve. In the face of danger and uncertainty it is comforting to cross oneself, utter a standardized prayer, or sing a song with the group.

Much ritual, obviously, is conducted in group situations. Simply the enjoyment of doing things together provides the participant with a sense of belonging. Beyond this, ritual may be designed specifically to express and reinforce group ties. Whichever way it works, ritual has the function of *unifying groups*.

Ritual also *aids status change*. Passage rituals, particularly, may be concerned with acquainting people with the roles they are to perform in their new status and motivating them to perform them well. Political leaders assuming office and young people entering married life are often adjured to acquit themselves well and advised how they are to behave. At a Miskito wedding of three couples observed by Helms, the Moravian lay pastor conducted a lengthy session of admonition on the proper behavior for husbands and wives (1971:89). He discussed at length the need for the men to respect and remain with their wives. He stressed that marriage was for life rather than just a few years, that it is not easy, and that the men could not run around any more. He stressed that the husbands now belonged to their wive's families, and that their wive's homes, parents, brothers and sisters, and cousins were to be their concern. The women were told to obey their husbands; to cook and to iron. He noted that husbands sometimes turn out bad, but that it was the wife's responsibility to endure and to seek God's help.

One aspect of ritual status change is what semiotic anthropologist Victor Turner refers to as *ritual liminality* (1974:241). As individuals pass from one social status and its component roles to another, there may be a period between the two conditions when they are free from the expectations and requirements of both their previous condition and the new stage of life they are entering. During this time they are able to stand apart from normal life, gain new perspectives, and prepare for the new life to come. Nuer boys, for example, are in seclusion from the time the cuts are made across their foreheads until they have healed. (Evans-Pritchard 1956:255). They no longer help the women milk the cows, and they never will again. All contact with cattle is prohibited until they return from seclusion. During the liminal (threshold) period between boyhood and manhood the initiates are subject to various taboos and enjoy license from some of the usual sexual restrictions. It is a time of preparation for the new stage of life they are about to enter.

Another significant function of ritual is *relief of psychological tensions,* many of which are culturally induced in the first place. Often merely the

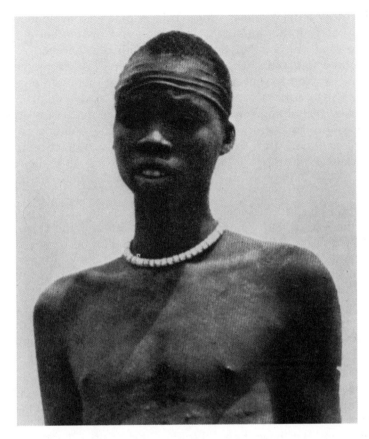

Figure 10–2 *Nuer young man with initiation scars. Nuer boys are in seclusion from the time the cuts are made across their foreheads until they have healed. It is a time of preparation for the new stage of life they are about to enter.*

act of participating in meaningful ritual relieves emotional strain, but of particular interest are what Gluckman has called "rites of reversal," in which people are permitted to do the opposite of what is culturally proscribed. By such ritual license the prescriptions are actually strengthened (Gluckman 1955:109). Among some African groups where the monarch enjoys great power there are occasions when the king's subjects are allowed to insult him to his face. Presumably, this makes it easier for them to bear the normal burdens of obedience to the king by affording them an opportunity to discharge some of their hostility toward him. Many groups have times when they permit sexual relations that ordinarily are proscribed, possibly because it makes it easier to observe the prohibitions the rest of the time.

Tension reduction probably is one of the commonest functions of rituals. It is a major element of avoidance ritual and joking relationships.

Both the Crow Indians and the Miskito have practiced avoidance between son-in-law and mother-in-law. A Crow man and his mother-in-law could neither look at one another nor converse with one another. A man was also supposed to avoid saying any word that is part of his mother-in-law's name, and a woman never used the name of her son-in-law (Lowie 1935:30). Early Moravian missionaries to the Miskito complained about the difficulty of holding services in an Indian's home because mother-in-law and son-in-law were not allowed in the same building at the same time. Helms found that in-law avoidance is now practiced by Asang Miskito only if necessary to maintain family peace after the birth of a child, since the child is an object of possible conflict between parents and grandparents (Helms 1971:130). Avoidance may both express the strain of a relationship and provide a way of reducing it.

On the other hand, among both the Miskito and the Crow, a joking relationship may exist between a woman and her husband's brother. A nineteenth-century Crow man could treat his wife's sister with great license, including raising her dress to expose her, and she could joke with him in similar fashion (Lowie 1935:28). A Crow referred to his wife's younger sister by a term meaning "my young wife," and according to the customs known as the sororate (see page 138) and sororal polygyny the wife's sister was a potential wife. Such ritual license between potiential spouses is found in a number of cultures. A joking relationship also sometimes develops between an American male and his wife's sister. It may involve teasing or good natured argument or one-upmanship, which may be a response to sexual or other tension in the relationship.

Some have suggested that rituals exist as ways of restabilizing patterns of interaction that have been disturbed by crisis (Chapple and Coon 1942:398). It seems that all five of the functions just reviewed fit this concept and may be interpreted in terms of either maintaining stability in the face of potential disturbance or adjustment to such disturbances. Ceremonies commonly strengthen the group for dealing with all kinds of crises by reinforcing the sense of commitment to cultural values, draining off tensions that might threaten social stability, bolstering feelings of confidence and security, or by providing stronger feelings of unity. Passage rites occur in the life-cycle at points when physiological and other changes have disturbed the stable patterns of adjustment to which people are accustomed. Birth and death, growth changes, sexual maturity, and the decrepitude of old age inevitably upset established and satisfying modes of interaction. Rituals function to maintain and restore people at such emotionally disturbing times.

Ritual seems to have negative function, too, judging by the fact that some people find ceremonies wearisome and wonder why they must be endured. Thus it is that ritual may *cause tension* as well as reduce it. Rituals of dedication are common in American life. Celebrations of dam completions, store openings, academic year openings, and many others are announced and reported daily in newspapers all over the nation.

Large numbers of Americans attend such ceremonies, but many find them tedious, which indicates, in part, that their sentiments lie elsewhere. Some groups have clowns to provide release in the midst of boring ceremonies, and Americans generally appreciate the preacher or speaker who includes some good jokes in his or her presentation.

But it is not only the tedium of long ceremonies that causes difficulties. Some rituals are difficult to execute, and if precise performance is required for the success of magical or other instrumental rites, both performer and concerned observer may feel strain. Yet, the fact that ritual customs are so common and continue to be observed is evidence that positive functions generally override undesired consequences.

11

IDEOLOGY

All cultural traits are ideological to the extent that they are ideas, but *ideology* is here limited to several categories of beliefs and knowledge about the nature of people and the universe, time and space, animal and plant life, and how things ought to be. In these areas there is a high proportion of multi-individual notions that lack direct expression in actions or artifacts and, consequently, are most often communicated verbally. It should be clear that religion, especially, incorporates many customs that are ideological in this sense, but they are found in all other aspects of culture as well.

REASON AND SCIENCE

The *scientific method* consists of at least two essential components, the *rational* and the *empirical*. Determining which is basic is as difficult as deciding whether the chicken or the egg comes first. The important thing is to realize that both are essential. What is empirical (what can be experienced by the senses or some extension of them) must be present. However, facts do not speak for themselves; people must interpret empirical data, which is where rational processes apply. They reason to determine what empirical phenomena they will experience or collect and what meanings these have for them.

Science began with ideas about natural phenomena derived from everyday empirical observations. From these ideas, observers formulated various hypotheses about relationships among phenomena. Setting up hypotheses is a rational (reasoning) process. Once they are set up, empirical data are gathered; then it is rationally determined whether they increase or decrease our confidence that the hypotheses are true. In modern technologically elaborated cultures this procedure has been highly formalized and named the scientific method, but nonscientific, nonliterate peoples reason and interpret empirical data in basically the same ways.

The notions that so-called primitives have a kind of prelogical mentality or that they only feel in some mystical fashion rather than employ the same reasoning processes as Euroamericans are not supported by the evidence. It is clear that people in all societies employ the same thought processes as Europeans and Americans. Also, both Euroamericans and nonliterates often violate the rules of logic; and both can and do think logically part of the time. One thing to remember is that the ideas of one culture seem illogical to people of another culture because they are based on different assumptions. For example, it seems illogical to many Americans to think of the past as lying in front of us and the future behind us as some groups do (Nida 1954:206). Americans think of themselves as moving forward into the future, and in terms of this notion it is obviously appropriate to conceive of the future as lying in front of one. However, if we begin with the assumption that the past can be seen—in the sense that it is known—and that the future cannot be seen; and, moreover, we remember that our eyes are in the front of our heads, it becomes quite reasonable to think of the future as being behind us. What seems logical or illogical is often relative to the context of culturally defined assumptions or premises.

Shifting the emphasis to the empirical approach, there is abundant evidence that nonliterates are keen observers. A detailed study of the subsistence technology of any nonliterate culture will reveal that the people have apprehended the "real" nature of many phenomena and have acted logically to get results. The !Kung San possess extensive knowledge of the habits of the animals they hunt and act faithfully and reasonably on all this knowledge to locate, track, and kill those animals. The very fact that a culture is different in various ways from those of adjacent groups implies that the society's members have reasoned, observed, and invented. Oliver asks why the Siuai of the Solomon Islands let their gardens lie fallow for six years instead of three or ten, and he suggests that the practice is based on the same empirical observations that can be made by an observer today. The Siuai are aware that crops are apt to fail if land is replanted too soon, and they know that the trees are about the right size for building fences after about six years of growth. Also, there is not yet so much jungle growth or so many oversized trees to remove as there would be if they waited much longer (Oliver 1955:23). However informally, the Siuai have developed hypotheses about the relationships between the length of time land is fallow and factors like productivity, ease of clearing land, and availability of the right sizes of trees for fences. They established the time length by checking their hypotheses against their observations, and they check their conclusions against experiences each season.

Americans have often attributed mystical or animal-like instincts to nonliterates when, actually, they detect and reason about empirical clues that a cultural alien is not trained to notice. Such was the case with an event shown on American television, in which Australian aboriginals located a grave where, as far as the American explorer knew, all surface traces had been destroyed by natural events. In the interest of accuracy, it is important to be careful about attributing mystical instincts to people who operate with data we are not prepared to be aware of or understand. Nonliterate societies may not have formalized the processes of logic or

Figure 11–1   *!Kung men reviewing successful hunting excursion. The !Kung San possess extensive knowledge of the habits of the animals they hunt and act faithfully and reasonably on all this knowledge to locate, track, and kill those animals.*

the method of setting up hypotheses and testing them by empirical data; they nevertheless reason logically and check their notions against empirical evidence. Many groups studied by ethnographers do enough of this that some anthropologists have used the term science for it.

KNOWLEDGE

Knowledge here refers to rather specific ideas about relatively concrete elements of the universe. Such ideas are knowledge in the sense that they are assumed to be correct by the people who hold them. Obviously, many peoples lack the resources for obtaining the knowledge of cosmic and other phenomena that Western cultures have. Some are actually uninterested in cosmic phenomena. The Dani manifest little interest in the stars and planets and other cosmological elements, and Heider found that many of his informants were uncertain in this area and that there were many differences from person to person. The Dani lack an elaborate mythology about the origin of the universe and its components (K. Heider 1970:140). Mead reports that the mountain Arapesh of New Guinea have no cosmology and no myths for the origin of the earth or the sky and its bodies (1940:340). By contrast the Samoans and a number of other nonliterate groups had well developed cosmological beliefs reflected in elaborate creation myths.

Many societies regard the earth as the center of the universe, as a flat expanse covered by the sky, across which the heavenly bodies move. Also common is the notion that the earth is bounded by waters. The Ekagi, who live in the same part of New Guinea as the Dani, think of the world as a flat block of stone and soil surrounded with water. The sky is a solid bowl of blue that defines the edge of the known world at the horizon. The sun traverses the underside of the bowl during the day, slips under the bowl's edge, and travels above it at night. The stars are sunlight shining through perforations in the sky (Pospisil 1963b:84).

Constellations are named in many cultures, though some groups ignore them. The Dani prefer to stay inside on cold, dark nights when the ghosts are abroad, and they pay little attention to the stars, but the San tribes of southern Africa are much interested in them. One observer reported the /Gwi San story that Orion represents three zebras and an arrow which a god has shot at them. The arrow is what, to Euroamericans, is Orion's sword, and the three star's of Orion's belt are the zebras (Thomas 1958:121).

Culturally standardized responses to eclipses are virtually universal, with many peoples regarding them as due to attacks on the sun or moon by an evil being. The aboriginal Sumu, close neighbors of the Miskito, thought a moon eclipse occurred when a jaguar tried to devour it (Conzemius 1932:136). The Miskito, however, said that a lunar eclipse occurred when the moon had caught his mother-in-law.

Culturally standardized reactions to weather are found everywhere. Many societies associate thunder with a bird. Among the Crow, thunder usually appears in the shape of an eagle (Lowie, 1935:252). The Nuer associate thunder and lighting storms with God and pray to God to come to earth gently rather than in fury (Evans-Pritchard 1956:124). Means of forecasting weather seem universal, and a number probably enjoy some reliability. The Teotitlán Zapotecs say it is going to rain when they hear the *chachalacas* (a kind of bird) calling repeatedly from the foothills (Taylor 1960:296).

Groups living near oceans, lakes, and rivers may accumulate extensive knowledge about currents, tides, water temperatures, and other such factors. The Samoans and other Polynesians use knowledge of both the stars and ocean currents in navigation.

Handicraft technology requires extensive knowledge of physical and chemical properties, though, of course, exactly what happens in scientific terms is unknown to many groups. Though the Dani are fairly indifferent technologists, they understand that the application of water increases the grinding power of the sandstone they use to sharpen their adzes and axes, and Eskimo know better than to blow their damp breath on the tinder when starting a fire in the cold Arctic air. The Dani have also found that a certain abrasive, grassy reed serves as a fine-grained sandpaper for smoothing their bows and spear shafts (K. Heider 1970:280).

Nonliterates also have well-formulated ideas about time and space. All peoples, of course, order time according to the daily appearance of the sun. Periods corresponding roughly to a month, indicated by the appearance and disappearance of the moon, are also common. Many groups recognize years, even if their systems entail no more than counting the number of winters since some event. Usually nonliterates keep track of different times of the year according to weather changes and variations in the position of the sun or the stars and planets. The !Kung divide the year into five seasons, primarily in terms of rain or dry spells and temperature and/or wind conditions (Yellen and Lee 1976:32). The Havasupai of the southwestern United States stand at a specific place at sunrise to observe the solstices (L. Spier 1928:168). Still other groups note where the sun rises each morning along a ridge of hills or mountains having a distinctive outline. Such observations may be viewed as comprising a kind of crude calender.

Some may be surprised that many nonliterate groups keep track of the movement of the stars, but groups who spend much time in the open at night may be expected to make such observations. The Dani spend little time outdoors at night and pay little attention to the stars, but the !Kung and other San groups of southern Africa are keen observers of the movements of the stars and planets. They observe the seasonal rising of the stars Sirius and Canopus and keep track of their later positions as a way of reckoning the passage of winter (Leach 1954:116). Many groups have not developed concepts as precise as hours and minutes, but various kinds of markers for certain times of day may be well standardized. The Nuer use two systems of marking the times of day, one geared to the position of the sun and the other to the daily pastoral tasks. It is common for the Nuer to indicate when something will occur by pointing to where the sun will be (Evans-Pritchard 1940:101). They have quite a number of expressions designating such points, but the most frequently used are dawn, sunrise, noon, and sunset. By far more important than sun positions, however, is what Evans-Pritchard refers to as the "cattle clock." The main points are the removal of the cattle from barn to corral; milking; driving the adult herd to pasture; milking the goats and sheep; driving the flocks and calves to pasture; the return of the adult herd; the evening milking and the return of the animals to the barns.

Nonliterate people ordinarily do not think in terms of the greatest distances, such as thousands of miles or more. Yet a number of groups, (e.g. Eskimos), move about over hundreds of miles and even make maps of the areas. Directions are often important to nonliterate peoples, and some think in terms of six directions rather than four: north, east, south, west, nadir, and zenith. It is not unusual for nonliterates to be far more interested in spatial features than time. The Rapans of the South Pacific, for example, are careful to specify the location of all events when they are conversing or telling stories (Hanson 1970:46), but they have little interest in just when or in what sequence things occur. Obviously the precise nature of a group's spatial orientation depends on a number of specifics that are highly variable from one place to another. The South Pacific island of Tikopia, for example, is so small that one is seldom out of sight or sound of the ocean. This has a direct bearing on the Tikopia feeling for space. They are highly isolated from other places and find it nearly impossible to imagine a very large land area or a country where the surf cannot be heard. In locating any item, whether a point on the island or an artifact on the ground, they employ the expressions "inland" and "seaward." Firth once heard one man tell another that he had a spot of mud on his "seaward cheek" (1936:19).

Distances and dimensions frequently are measured by bodily dimensions. Capacities and weights, however, are seldom measured by nonliterates.

Ethnobotany and *ethnozoology* are terms used by anthropologists to refer to ideas about plant life and animal life, respectively. Much of this knowledge is highly practical. Samoans know how to prepare a bright yellow dye by mixing the reddish-brown dye made from one kind of bark and a dull yellow dye made from turmeric root (Buck 1930:299). The pre-Christian Miskito knew what kind of palm tree seeds to use to make an oil that would soften their hair (Conzemius 1932:27). Some knowledge about plant and animal life is inaccurate, of course. The Miskito also believed that they would become forgetful if they ate the flesh of a certain speckled tortoise. In spite of many such erroneous ideas, a thorough study of the botanical and zoological notions of nonliterates provides impressive evidence of their powers of observation. Nonliterates, of course, suppose that their ideas are correct, just as Euroamericans assume their knowledge to be true. But it seems a fair assumption that many Euroamerican ideas about the nature of the physical and biological environment, even some of the scientifically derived ones, are incorrect also. Euroamericans may have acquired a higher proportion of correct ideas than nonliterates, but it would be only a relative difference.

Some nonliterate peoples have a notably accurate knowledge of human physical structure. A number have words for various organs such as the lungs, stomach, heart, liver, spleen, kidneys, and many of the bones. Less common is the Alaskan Aleuts' accurate and detailed knowledge of the internal organs. The Aleuts preserve bodies by removing the viscera and stuffing the cavities with dry moss and grass and drying the cadaver. Aleut medicine men dissect the bodies of dead enemies and serfs to learn about the internal organs in preparation for surgery. They can identify nearly all viscera and internal organs, many bones, and some of the musculature; and they know, among other things, that the soft bone in the tip of an infant's finger hardens and the locations of the body's pulse points (Marsh and Laughlin 1956:41). The knowledge about inanimate objects, plants, animals, and people is far greater among nonliterates than many of us realize.

PHILOSOPHY AND WORLD VIEW

Anthropologists have given somewhat less attention than they might to explicit philosophical systems as part of nonliterate cultures. This may be partly because many groups have few specialists who reflect about ultimate problems. Moreover, the governing premises, assumptions, tenets, and axioms about life and the universe tend to be more implicit than explicit for a high proportion of a society's members. In addition, philosophical customs are part of the covert culture and must be transmitted verbally. Coupled with this is the fact that philosophical issues can be communicated effectively only in the native language. Consequently, ethnographers who are unable to speak and understand the indigenous language well are unlikely to learn much about them.

That many groups may have unsuspected philosophical systems is illustrated by the experience of ethnographer Vincenzo Petrullo while studying among the technologically simple and highly nomadic Yaruro of Venezuela. Petrullo became seriously ill and was largely immobilized for some time. The Yaruro remained with him and cared for him until he could leave, and during long conversations with them, he discovered that they had an elaborate philosophy concerning the nature of the universe (1939:190). Most of it was what scientifically oriented societies would label as mythological, but the point is that they did speculate about ultimate questions and they had developed socially standardized notions— an explicit world and life view.

Philosophy is ordinarily thought to involve rather explicit notions. Currently, anthropologists make rather extensive use of the concept, *world view,* which includes both explicit ideas and implicit assumptions and orientations about life and the universe. The implicit, of course, must be inferred by the investigator from his or her observations, since such eso-traits and seldom expressed directly and clearly.

World views differ notably from culture to culture. Some societies think of the universe as a mechanism. It has been suggested that the American middle class treats the universe as a mechanism which, therefore, can be mastered by humans. It is a machine that can be exploited by science and technology for material benefit. This has sometimes been associated with a highly exploitive orientation, and only recently have modern Americans been giving careful thought to working in harmony with nature rather than conquering it. Many blame the destructive exploitation of the habitat on the Christian doctrine of human dominion over nature, while others call for a rediscovery of the Christian principle that all of nature is to be honored as God's creation (Schaeffer 1971:74). Some of the societies which see the universe as a mechanism use the notion differently. According to Hoebel, the Cheyenne view the universe in a mechanistic way, with a limited amount of energy which is dissipated gradually through time. This energy supply, however, is rechargeable by magic. Each aspect of the universe is governed by a spiritual being who knows how things work, and the main function of supernaturals is to instruct people how to magically renew the world's fund of energy and get the most out of life (Hoebel 1978:89). The main tribal observances of the Cheyenne are world renewal ceremonies.

Other cultures find the universe a more capricious place and see little possibility of control. The Kaingang of Brazil feel that they dwell in a hostile and dangerous universe inhabited by people and supernaturals who are more often sources of trouble than help. The typical reaction of the Kaingang is a kind of desperate anger and striking back in revenge. When an infant dies, the Kaingang abandon the camp, since the ghost may want to take someone with it or may kill again. When thunder is heard in the distance, the Kaingang scowl and grumble back in anger. When the wind, thunder, and lightning roar and crash about them, they shout at the storm to go away, and they may utter insults to shame it into leaving. The Kaingang experience little of the comfort of scientific or magical control of a reliable mechanism. Instead they strike back in angry desperation at a capricious universe and flee.

Some world views emphasize equality; others inequality. The Nuer are egalitarian in the extreme, so much so that each man counts himself as good as anyone else and no formal authority system exists (Evans-Pritchard 1940:134). Along with this attitude the Nuer tend to be gruff and curt with one another and readily respond with violence when they feel that someone is trying to dominate them. In contrast, the Nyoro feel that inequality is of the essence of social order: the king rules his subjects, fathers rule their children, and men rule women (Beattie 1960:8).

World views differ in many other specific ways. Some societies regard the universe as highly personal, that is, animistic, while others seem to take rather impersonal views. Some people manifest great concern with cosmic forces, whereas others are more interested in relationships among people. Some world views include elaborate concern with sexuality, and others do not. The Crow Indians of the nineteenth century often manifested a casual and opportunistic orientation toward premarital and extramarital sex, while the Dani of New Guinea seem so little concerned with acquiring sexual experiences that men will abstain from sexual intercourse for years without apparent psychological distress (K. Heider 1976:190). There is such a variety of ways that people differ in their views of and reactions to life, that a description of the total range and variety of known

Figure 11-2   *Nuer at a dance. The Nuer are egalitarian in the extreme and readily respond with violence when they feel that someone is trying to dominate them. Playful brandishing of spears during dances appears, in part, to symbolize Nuer readiness to defend their position.*

world views would require the spilling of a great deal of ink. Perhaps this is among the most fascinating aspects of cross-cultural variation.

VALUES AND ETHICAL PRINCIPLES

Sometimes anthropologists single out the values and ethics of a culture for separate treatment. Values, of course, have already been mentioned repeatedly. It is difficult to imagine a cultural element that carries no overtones of either negative or positive sentiment, however weak. The very fact that a social custom is continued may be taken as evidence that people value it. Obviously, some values are far stronger than others, and cultures differ considerably in what is greatly valued. *Ethical principles* are values concerning conduct, especially in relation to other people.

Some anthropologists allege that there are no universal ethical principles. Some insist that, since a culture must be understood in terms of its own categories and concepts, a search for universal principles of human behavior is misleading. Ethics may be seen as one of those etic categories (see page 40) which distorts what is "really there" in a culture. An extreme view seems to intrude in Mead's suggestion that the modern world is changing so fast that elders no longer have moral imperatives they can pass on with certainty to the young (1978:75). The implied assumption of such positions is that when ethical systems differ, whether the ethics of different societies or ethics of different generations of the same society, there is no way to determine that one is superior to another—they are simply different. Ethical differences between cultures in different places and between generations are presented to support either a strong ethical neutralism or the opinion that the value of an ethical system is completely relative to the society's particular circumstances. The ultimate expression of ethical neutralism is a recent statement to the effect that the only thing we know for sure is that all our facts and theories are false and, accordingly, there is no ethical basis for social action.

Without question, the diversity of ethical beliefs around the world is significant. In some cultures, for example, ethical principles prescribe a strong standard of truth; while in others, such as traditional Samoan culture, it is appropriate in ordinary social intercourse to tell people whatever they wish to hear. Personal property rights of some kind are universal, but in some cultures a person may take another's possessions as long as it is known who has them, and it may not be necessary to return them until asked. Premarital sexual activity is acceptable in many societies, and cultures differ in what kinds of sexual behavior they forbid.

While virtually no *specific* ethical or moral value is universal, humans show remarkable similarity in the *kinds* of ethical norms they are concerned with. Ralph Linton mentions, among other things, the rule against incest, rejection of promiscuity, valuation of marriage, mutual obligations of parents and children, family loyalty, private property, standards of truth, and proscriptions against killing and maiming as examples of universal kinds of ethical values (1952). Who and when, if ever, one may kill varies from culture to culture, definitions of truth vary greatly, and some groups permit far more freedom of sexual behavior than others; but killing and maiming at will are accepted in no culture; all groups manifest some concern over whether or not the statements of others can be trusted; and there are always sexual restrictions. Such similarities are significant as evidence for certain kinds of universal human concerns. Ethical similarities and differences among human groups are not entirely accidents of group preference.

Anthropologists and others have made so little headway with the question of ethical universals because of the great diversity of beliefs and practices from culture to culture. The problem of how ethical concepts might be related to a fundamental human nature shared by all human groups is obscured because every human's preferences and standards are formed by social experience before it is possible for subjects to answer an investigator's questions about them. Consequently, it seems virtually impossible to find out what kinds of customs and ethical standards provide the greatest fulfillment in the long run. If all humans could be fully experienced in all possible cultural alternatives, entirely familiar with all their consequences, and completely free to choose among those alternatives, their choices might teach us more about universal human tendencies than we now know. If people were really free to choose their standards of behavior without the distorting effects of socialization, we might find out whether they would choose the shifting marital standards of the nineteenth-century Crow over the more stable ways of their Cheyenne neighbors, and if so, how often. But humans are not free to make such objective, informed choices, and science has not devised an equivalent way to get behind the great cultural diversity. So we have no way of knowing from science whether the prevalence of intergroup combat or the tolerance of premarital intercourse in most cultures means that fighting and premarital sex are basically more fulfilling to people than their alternatives. Cultural diversity teaches us that the range and variety of human preferences are vast, but it teaches us little about whether some are basically more fulfilling than others. It seems reasonable to suppose that many would commit themselves to alternatives more congenial to basic human tendencies if their preferences were not already molded by the specific cultural situations into which they were born.

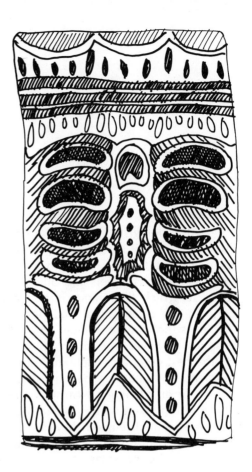

12

RELIGION

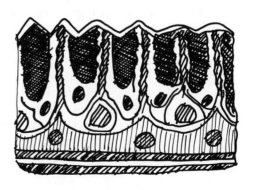

Anthropologists agree that religious customs are found in all known cultures. In many cultures religious beliefs and practices play a major role in integrating the lifeways into a functioning unity. It is true, of course, that the religious beliefs and practices of some cultures differ greatly from those to which the reader is accustomed, but all are alike in that they concern the supernatural and perform similar functions.

It is no simple matter to distinguish religious from nonreligious customs, however, and anthropologists are by no means in full agreement on the best criteria for defining religion. Some emphasize emotional commitment to something beyond one's self, whether it be a supernatural person or an ideological cause. Others have emphasized a sense of awe. The position taken here is different. It appears that most phenomena that have been called religious have to do with what is called the supernatural, and that it is most useful to limit the concept in that way.

It remains necessary to define the supernatural. The difference between the natural and the supernatural is an etic distinction that may be absent from the emic distinctions of a particular culture. Many groups lack a word for religion, and a number of societies include both natural and supernatural phenomena (as Euroamericans distinguish them) in the same category. The Nyoro, for example, make no distinction between setting fire to a man's house with a match and placing a magical medicine in the roof of a house so as to damage the resident. Both practices are sorcery (Beattie 1960:73). But Euroamericans apply the term supernatural to whatever cannot be confirmed as "real" by their logic and science. So they end up rather ethnocentrically applying their own distinctions, which makes the Nyoro's use of a magical medicine on his enemy's roof supernaturalistic, and the setting the roof afire a purely technological act.

This approach may be acceptable as long as we understand what we are doing and why. As noted on page 42, we cannot confine ourselves to emic distinctions. We require manageable categories by which we can compare the customs of different cultures, and it is natural to use categories that are meaningful to us. At the same time, if our goal is to understand specific cultures, we must remain aware that their categories and distinctions may not coincide with ours. The supernatural here is defined as anything that appears to Euroamericans to be unexplainable by the rationalistic, naturalistic assumptions that govern their logic and science, and any culture's religion is composed of its beliefs and practices regarding these supernaturalistic phenomena.

As an extension of this issue, there is evidence that some European and American beliefs and practices thought to be naturalistic are no more verifiable by reason and science than some of the so-called superstitions of nonliterate and peasant societies. As children, many Americans were taught that going into water too soon after a meal would cause abdominal cramps, and many have taught their own offspring to believe this. Few of us had much idea what the relationship between cramping and being in water might be, but we had faith in it. But now, we are told, scientific research shows no relationship between abdominal cramping and being in water too soon after eating. Apparently, it is the strenuous physical activity of swimming after a meal which is dangerous, rather than immersion in water. Psychologically, there seems to be no fundamental difference between this belief and the Nyoro's notion that putting a medicine in someone's roof can hurt him.

The converse of the foregoing point is that Western scientists are unable to demonstrate that all supernaturalistic beliefs of folk cultures are false. Euroamericans and others sometimes use logic to argue for the reality of a supernatural order, and they often interpret empirical phenomena as evidence of its existence. But the scientific method is unsuited for either providing or disproving the supernatural, which can be embraced only as a matter of what the believer considers to be reasonable faith. The issue for anthropology is not which beliefs are correct, but what are the nature and functions of the customs that involve belief in what Euroamericans call supernaturalistic phenomena.

RELIGIOUS BELIEFS

Europeans and Americans tend to regard religion as belief in personal supernatural entities, specifically deities, spirits, souls, ghosts, and the like. Such beliefs in supernatural persons have generally been referred to in anthropology as *animism*. The supernatural beings of animistic belief have the attributes of people: they are conscious; they have will and intention; and they experience the emotions that humans feel. Some have characterized nonliterate peoples as animists, but this is hardly appropriate, since animistic beliefs are part of every society's religion. Traditional biblical Christianity teaches that the one God is a spiritual person, and some Christians believe in a class of spiritual beings known as angels; an evil deity known as Satan; and an unknown number of evil spirits or demons. There are, of course, some religious systems which feature belief in a great number of spirits of various kinds.

Westerners make a distinction between the personal and the impersonal that is not always so sharply drawn in nonliterate and peasant cultures. But, in terms of this distinction, anthropologists have found that people around the world conceive of entities, power, states, and other qualities that do not fit into our category of personal supernaturalism. Some people see the universe as infused or permeated with a kind of mysterious potency, which they define as neither personal or impersonal; it is simply mysterious, powerful, or something of the kind. People may also think of mysterious or sacred potency as dwelling in, concentrated in, or attached to objects, places, persons, or actions. These kinds of beliefs or feelings were referred to by Marett as *animatism* (Marett 1914:14), and anthropologists have often used the Oceanian word *mana* for the impersonal potency itself.

The !Kung San include among their religious beliefs a mana-like concept of a kind of energy called *n/um* (Katz 1976:286). N/um originally came from the gods, but now men give n/um to other men. Those who have acquired n/um and know how to use it are "masters of n/um." It is considered good for as many as possible to have n/um, and perhaps half have acquired it. It is specially important for getting into a transcendent state called *!kia,* a dance experience. N/um is located in the pit of the stomach, and as a master of n/um becomes warm and sweaty from his energetic dancing, the n/um heats up and turns to vapor, rising up the spine until it reaches the base of the skull. At that time the dancer enters the !kia state. During !kia the !Kung cures, handles and walks on fire, enjoys x-ray vision, and sees over great distances. He becomes "more than himself"—able to contact the realm where the ghosts of dead ancestors live. If his n/um is strong enough, ghosts who are trying to carry away an ill person will be driven away and the sick one will live.

The Dugum Dani regard *wusa* as a rather dangerous power inherent in certain things of ritual significance (K. Heider 1970:136). There is wusa associated with a certain grove of araucaria trees and also with a specific tree near one of the residential compounds. Men come into contact with *wusa,* for example, when they handle a corpse or build a watchtower along the military frontier and must remove the potency from themselves by means of a feather ritual.

Americans do not regard belief in luck as part of their religion, but as a supernaturalistic concept it qualifies as a religious belief. Many Americans believe that some kind of mystical power indwells or is associated with certain acts, places, or persons. The number 13 is considered unlucky or dangerous by some, and some feel that a Bible has special power to protect against evil. College students may feel that they are likely to do better on examinations if they use a certain pen, and athletes have been known to believe that a rabbit's foot or some other object gives them special prowess.

Marett (1914) and others have defined animatism as belief in mana, contrasting it with animism, the belief in supernatural persons. But it is important to remain aware that these are Euroamerican distinctions not necessarily made or shared by others. Animistic and animatistic concepts blend and intergrade, or, more accurately, the people simply may fail to consider whether or not the powers or entities are personal. The *manitou* of the Fox and other Algonkian-speaking Indians of North America is sometimes treated as sheer extraordinary power and other times as a supernatural person. The Gitche Manitou or Great Spirit of the Fox was often described in quite nonpersonal terms, yet it was also referred to as one of the two original supernatural brothers. As a supernatural force manitou could be found in particular locations, such as in the heart of a very brave warrior. Animatistic concepts such as n/um, wusa, mana, luck, and manitou occur in a considerable variety of specific forms in different cultures.

The variety of supernatural entities is so great it is difficult to classify them. Describing a soul, for example, is no simple matter, since souls come in many natures. Some have definite personal qualities; others seem rather impersonal. Some are completely invisible, and others may not be. Some souls outlive the body and some do not. A *soul* is simply a non-material entity existing within and fundamental to the life of the body, and the concept is found in every culture. Functionally, people use the soul concept to account for illness, death, and dreams. Illness may be due to partial or temporary loss of a soul, and death may occur when the soul is completely and permanently separated from the body. Dreams are explained as the travels and experiences of the soul while one is asleep.

The Dani of New Guinea have two soul-type entities. One of these is the *edai-egen,* which is thought of as an internal organ but is also the seat of the personality (K. Heider 1970:226). When a Dani is physically and emotionally normal, his edai-egen is about the size of his fist and rests just below the base of the sternum, but during illness and mourning it shrinks and retreats toward the vertebral column. The other entity, the *akotakun,* may escape from the body during stress, and Heider found some evidence that it is the akotakun which becomes a ghost when a Dani dies. The Dani share the belief of many other groups in different parts of the world that one could lose his soul by being jolted too hard. When a person falls, they may shout "Your akotakun stay in place!"

Souls of the dead become *ghosts* according to many groups. Ghosts may take up residence in some abode of souls of the dead and live there in some kind of immaterial or semimaterial state similiar to life on earth or, sometimes the reverse of it. After a short period of wandering or of frequenting the grave or places its human owner frequented during life, a ghost may cease to exist entirely. There is a variety of customs concerning souls of the dead, including conversations with them and making offerings to them. Such a complex of customs has sometimes been referred to as the *cult of the dead.* In a cult of the dead the ghosts are not elevated to the status of gods and worshipped; there is simply a complex of relationships maintained with them. Both the Dani and the !Kung maintain relationships with the ghosts of the dead without worshiping them as deities. When a Dani dies, the ghost leaves the corpse and, a few days later goes to a ghost house in the woods, where the ghosts remain most of the time. Sometimes they come to the compounds, and at night a ghost may ambush a passerby who lacks a torch. Ghosts can be pleased or displeased like humans, they can hear requests and demands that people shout at them, and they can eat. During one part of a funeral ceremony the ghosts are invited to eat, and food is set before them at the ghost houses. Ghosts cause a lot of trouble, being the basic cause of sickness, death, and pig diseases. They influence the weather also, and they come in the clouds and rain. They also like to attend battles, and they may warn the people of an impending enemy attack and actually help them in battle. The Dani have a variety of customs for coping with the ghosts of the dead.

In other cultures some souls of the dead, particularly those of deceased kinsmen, may possess enough interest in and power over human affairs that the people regard them as deities. The religious complex associated with this view has been called *ancestor worship*. Ancestor worship has been found in China, in certain places in Southeast Asia, and in some Polynesian cultures, but it is especially common in parts of Africa.

The world's cultures manifest a great variety of other kinds of spirits which are not ghosts or disembodied souls. They come in a great diversity of forms and function in many ways, but all are alike in that they are modeled after the personal attributes of people. Many of these spirits roam the countryside rather than dwelling in something, though they may be present in greater numbers in some places than in others. Objects, particularly portable ones, in which spirit-persons dwell are sometimes called *fetishes*. Mountains, trees, waterfalls, mysterious-looking places, and other natural features also may be inhabited by one or more personal spirits, though the word fetish is not so commonly applied to them. A personal spirit may inhabit a human and still not be thought of as a soul. Spirit possession would be an example. Cultures differ in whether most personal spirits are good or bad. A number of religions are characterized by belief in an abundance of demons or evil spirits.

Many cultures include a kind of *guardian spirit concept,* whereby a person develops a special relationship with a spirit which confers power and knowledge of specific kinds and which acts as guide and protector, perhaps through the rest of one's life. The quest for a guardian spirit is a significant element in the religion of the Crow and many other North American Indian cultures. The Crow believed in a variety of diverse spirits, but the seeking of a revelation from a tutelary spirit was an especially important part of their religion. The importance of a vision to success in life was so important to the Crow that the young men sought a revelation without encouragement by their elders (Lowie 1935:239). In later life almost any major trouble or consuming desire would trigger a vision quest. Usually the seeker went alone to some remote place and tried to attract the attention or pity of the supernatural by fasting and self-torture. In addition to going largely naked in the cold night and doing without food and water, the seeker might chop off a finger joint or cut a piece of flesh from his body, exert himself in various ways, or pierce his breast or back in order to attach himself by a cord to something that he would drag or pull against. Finally, usually on the fourth night, some being would appear to him and grant him special knowledge, power, or good fortune. In addition, it was common for various kinds of kindly supernaturals to appear unsolicited to rescue people from disastrous situations.

The distinction between an ordinary personal spirit and a deity is sometimes difficult to make. It is, perhaps, useful to think of a god as a supernatural person of greater power than most spirits, and deities are usually associated with some kind of phenomenon or aspect of life. Rain gods, thunder gods, gods of the directions, fertility deities, and patron deities of craft groups are among the many kinds. In many cultures a god is commonly a local personage. A god may be good, bad, both, or neither. Religions that are characterized by a number of gods are commonly said to be *polytheistic*. Before the coming of Christianity, the Samoans of Manua island had at least one major deity as well as a number of local and family gods (Mead 1969:158). Tagaloa was the great creator god, though there also may have been other major deities, such as an earthquake god, a patron deity of housebuilders, and a patron of travelers. Ordinary Manuans worshipped and prayed to deities incarnate in a bird, fish, or plant, and sometimes to village deities. The main function of these minor deities seems to have been to warn of danger and death.

The familiar term *monotheism* is used for belief in one god only, though true monotheism is extremely rare. Christianity may be viewed as not truly monotheistic, since it incorporates belief in an evil deity, Satan. Religions that manifest belief in a deity of greater power than other deities and spirits are often said to have a *high god* or *supreme being*. Such deities are found in a number of nonliterate cultures, including hunting and gathering cultures. The !Kung of the Nyae Nyae region believe in a great sky god of the east, who lives at the place where the sun rises (Marshall 1962:223). The great god created himself, then wrought a lesser god of the east and wives for himself and the lesser god. He also created the earth, people, and all things. He praises himself with the various names he has given himself, and no one can command him. He is the cause of sickness and death, and he makes the rain thunder. He is deeply involved with the people and rewards or punishes them according to whether he is pleased by what they do. He is not concerned with sin and morality but punishes people for his own reasons. The people pray to the great god, and shamans get their power from him.

There are other supernatural beings that do not fit well into any of the categories discussed so far. These beings are much more material than most supernaturals and they may be quite visible, though they may be rather immaterial and invisible part of the time. The most distinctive thing about them, perhaps, is that they take various unnatural forms. They are commonly identified with certain places such as a pool, a glen, or a well, and they are often thought of as malevolent or, at least, tricksters. The

Nootka of British Columbia say that there are huge supernatural quartz crystals living in mountain caves, where they sway back and forth, making strange humming sounds. Brightly colored, headless, mallard-like beings; birds with human faces; and a mountain lion which walks backward and kills men with its long, sharp tail are among an almost infinite number of supernaturals of this type in Nootka culture (Drucker 1951:151).

RELIGIOUS PRACTICES

Prayer, sacrifices and offerings, and magic are three major ways of dealing with the supernatural. *Prayer* is conversation addressed to the supernatural, ordinarily to supernatural persons. Euroamericans generally associate prayer with supplication and praise, but any kind of verbal communication with a supernatural is included in prayer by many anthropologists. Personal spirits or gods who are stupid enough may be victims of deceit. One may lie to them and get away with it, or one may make a false promise to get the god or spirit to do something. Flattery, threats, and commands may also be used. Any verbal communication one may use with a fellow human may be used with a supernatural person, and this constitutes prayer. While the !Kung are fairly respectful in their prayers to the great god, they are less so with the spirits of the dead. They pray to them for sympathy and mercy, but they also express anger. During the curing ceremonies the shamans call the spirits obscene names. The Tikopia of the southern Pacific feel free in their prayers to exaggerate their poverty or misery, for gods can be deceived and made to feel ashamed at letting their dependents suffer from want (Firth 1967:299).

Dealing with the supernatural through offerings and sacrifices is also widespread. First fruits offerings, such as the first rice, fish, or game of the season, may be offered to the spirits or gods, or meals may be offered in search of a favor from the supernaturals. Tobacco is thought by many American Indians groups to be pleasing to the deities. Many groups suppose that the ghosts, spirits, or other supernaturals to which they make food offerings actually partake of the food, and many suggest that they abstract the essence of the food. The pre-Christian Miskito put out food for the ghost of the deceased at their funerals. The spirit of the dead person was believed to hover around the bed for several days after death, and it required feeding several times daily. Hot meals were placed on the bed and left until they became cold, which indicated that the spirit had finished partaking. The family then consumed the cold food (Helms 1971:199). Stock-raising groups often sacrifice their animals. The Nuer frequently sacrifice sheep, goats, and cattle (Evans-Pritchard 1940:-26). They sacrifice when a man is sick, when sin has been committed, when a wife is barren, when twins are born, at initiations, at marriages, at funerals, after homicides, when a ghost is troubling them, and on a great number of other occasions. In such cases, the Nuer are seeking the intervention in human affairs of their supreme god, Kwoth.

Figure 12–1   *Nuer sacrificing a goat. The Nuer frequently sacrifice sheep, goats, and cattle, seeking the intervention in human affairs of their supreme god, Kwoth.*

Many students of religion have contrasted prayer as a technique with magic. Sometimes magic and religion are defined as mutually exclusive phenomena, a usage rejected here because magic, as a supernaturalistic phenomenon, fits under religion as defined earlier. Magic differs from prayer and sacrifice in its mechanical nature. The key feature of magic is the practice of some specifically prescribed procedure, which is assumed to have a predictable result. The magician utters a verbal formula or performs an action, perhaps through the use of some supernaturally powerful substance or object called a *medicine;* if he has done these things properly and there is no interference, the result he seeks is assured. The power which insures the automatic result is viewed by some as inherent in the procedure itself or in the procedure and the medicine used, while others appear to regard the procedure as compelling a spirit person or other supernatural potency to act in a predictable way. If one who prays feels that he thereby coerces a god or spirit, his prayer actually amounts to no more than verbal magic, and it seems that what Euroamericans call prayer is sometimes highly magical in nature.

It is common to recognize two aspects of magic. Magic is *imitative* to the degree that procedure resembles the result one desires. Placing slivers or pins in an image of one's enemy to cause him to sicken and die is an example. The Upper Palaeolithic practice of painting realistic pictures of a bleeding animal, perhaps with an arrow through its heart, is thought to be a case of imitative hunting magic. Ritual sexual inter-course at the time crops are planted is also imitative magic, since a parallel between human fertility and seed fertility is involved. Imitation in magic is surely universal and varies infinitely in its specific forms. A Crow magician of the nineteenth century who wanted to draw buffalo toward the Crow camp placed a buffalo's skull with its nose toward the camp, and the next morning the hunters sighted and killed six animals. A day or so later, after they had taken enough, the magician turned the skull the other way, and no more game came.

A second major aspect of much magic is *contagion*. Magic is conta-gious to the degree that the magician works with something that has been or will be in contact with whatever is to be influenced. A hair from an enemy's head may be stamped upon, submerged under water, or burned in the supposition that its former owner may be damaged in this way. Magical acts for doing evil may be called *sorcery* or *black magic*.

Taboo sometimes seems to be a kind of negative magic, since one avoids certain consequences by refraining from some act. The Samoans made extensive use of the concept that sacred and defiling things are contagious (Mead 1969:117). For example, the remains of a high chief's food and his hair clippings and fingernail parings were sacred and, there-fore, dangerous. And his bed was so sacred that not even his wife could sleep on it. Anyone who came into contact with certain of the high chief's things, would develop swellings that only the touch of the high chief's food could remove. The Samoans had a number of taboos, and violating them would result automatically in a supernatural penalty.

Magic is part of the religious practice of some Americans, also, though some who practice it profess not to believe in the supernatural. American basketball coaches have been known to wear only certain garments during games, because they feel the team is more likely to win that way. Good luck charms are carried by some, and others use statuettes of Christ or a saint to ward off evil. Sorcery and witchcraft tend to be limited to certain remote rural groups in the United States, though the 1960s and 1970s have been marked by revival of such beliefs and practices in urban places.

Witchcraft as a supernaturalistic practice may be distinguished from sorcery. Contrary to sorcery, which is evil magic, witchcraft is performed as a kind of psychic act, often simply by means of the will. It is also common for witches to have *familiars*, which are supernatural entities used by the witch. Witches are often thought to appear in the form of an animal. Often the power of witchcraft is the supernatural power of the witch, though some witches are said to lack control of the supernatural power within them and are unable to avoid what they do. While witchcraft and sorcery are distinguishable from one another as etic categories, people known as witches often perform both witchcraft and magical acts, and an act of sorcery is often bolstered by the power of witchcraft.

The Nyoro distinguish black magic or sorcery from witchcraft. To the Nyoro sorcery is injuring people by secret use of harmful medicines and techniques (Beattie 1960:73). It includes practices such as taking bits of hair, nail clippings, and other parts of a person's body, putting them in an animal horn, and hiding the horn in the roof of the victim's house. As already noted, however, sorcery to the Nyoro includes harmful activities that Americans do not think of as supernaturalistic, such as setting someone's house on fire. With sorcery a poison or a learned technique is involved, but in witchcraft the damage comes in another way. The Nyoro acknowledge the existence of people who dig up and eat corpses, dance naked in the fields at night, and cause the death of anyone who sees them; and they also recognize the presence of witches in other societies. But while they distinguish witchcraft from sorcery, they are little concerned with the former among themselves, attributing virtually all illness and misfortune caused by humans to sorcerers (Beattie 1963:30.)

In some cultures witchcraft and sorcery provide major explanations of illness, and they also function to drain off frustration and consequent hostility. People can blame their troubles on witchcraft or sorcery rather than on one another; and in some groups there is much talk of witchcraft, even if no one intentionally practices it and few, if any, can identify any specific person as a witch. Witches, incidentally, may be either male or female.

Divination, the practice of ascertaining the unknown through supernatural means, is an important element in many religions, particularly in determining causes of illnesses. It is so important that part-time diviners are found in many societies. The variety of specific means of divination employed is great, but many of the techniques are magical in nature, and they ordinarily require equipment. The Nyoro diviners, for example, commonly use cowry shells, which are scattered on a goat skin to see how they fall. A rather different kind of divination is direct contact and communication with a personal spirit, who provides the desired information or, perhaps, possesses and speaks through the diviner.

RELIGIOUS PERSONNEL

Many of the religious techniques mentioned may be practiced by an ordinary person, but all groups exhibit some specialization. The commonest kind of religious personage, especially among hunting and gathering groups, is the *shaman*. Shaman is a Tungus word, from a major tribalistic group of Siberia, a region well known for its high development of shamanism. A shaman is a religious specialist with individual ability to communicate and deal with supernaturals who applies this ability primarily as an individual rather than as the representative of a group. This type of person is also known as a medicine man and witch doctor. The major function of shamanism is dealing with illness, both by divining its cause and by healing. Generally a shaman has spirit-helpers (familiars), or other supernatural power sources with which he deals in the application of his abilities. Shamanism is not far removed from witchcraft, and the shamans of a number of societies engage in witchcraft part of the time by using their supernatural power to bring illness or otherwise damage people. Some shamans employ magic and also use herbal preparations of sometimes actual pharmacological value. One of the most common healing techniques is sucking from the body the intrusive object or substance believed to have caused the sickness.

Shamans acquire their supernatural power by some direct personal religious experience: a vision, dream, or some such visitation. Often the power comes against the person's will, there may be a period of recurrent sickness, and the newly developing shaman struggles in resistance or to properly assimilate the new power. Often there is a period of training by another shaman. Shamans may wear special clothing of various kinds and use special equipment. As they heal they commonly put on a display of dealing with the spirits and getting rid of the sickness. Shamans may engage in violent struggle with their familiars, be possessed by them, and end up unconscious, exhausted by their successful efforts to utilize supernatural powers in behalf of the patient. Shamans may have or specialize in other abilities besides healing, such as divination, weather control, locating game animals, and so forth. Both male and female shamans are found.

Shamans in pre-Christian Miskito society would divine which kind of evil spirit had caused a disease and then expel the spirit from the sick person's body (Helms 1971:183). The Miskito shamans used tobacco or other narcotics to help work themselves into a trance, during which time they would be interacting with friendly spirits who would reveal the source of the illness and the proper cure. Curing techniques consisted of whistling over the ill person, blowing tobacco smoke over the body, and massaging and sucking on the afflicted body parts (Conzemius 1932:-124). The Miskito also consulted shamans for help in finding lost and stolen objects, curing bad luck, increasing courage, successful hunting, and so on. Most of the shamans were men, but some of the women were shamans. The Crow, Dani, !Kung, Nuer, Nyoro, and Samoans also have or have had shamans. There also are a small number of shamans in modern American society, healers who are believed to have special ability to draw on God's power or whom God has chosen to use in a special way to cure people's diseases.

The other major kind of religious personage is the *priest,* a ceremonialist who operates as a representative of the group and under its approval. Priests are found most commonly in larger societies with fairly elaborate cultures and organized religious cults having theological doctrines and standardized ceremonies. In small-scale societies with less elaborated cultures, priestly functions are usually performed as needed by a shaman, a headman, a family head, or any other person regarded as qualified. In some cultures there may be recognized priests who have no special religious function other than the conducting of ritual when needed. The Nuer have no religious cults, but the leopard-skin priest conducts sacrifices and other rituals in connection with the avoidance and settlement of blood feuds, to taking of oaths, and cleansing from the sin of incest (Evans-Pritchard 1956:298).

RELIGIOUS FUNCTIONS

During the last century and the early part of this century, many anthropologists were interested in the problem of the origin and evolution of religion. Edward B. Tylor, possibly the most renowned nineteenth-century anthropologist, felt that the soul concept was the earliest religious belief and that it formed the basis for other concepts, such as spirits, ancestor deities, and, eventually, monotheism (Tylor 1889:426). The notion of souls, he felt, came about as people tried to account for the difference between a living body and a dead one or between a sick person and a well person on the one hand and, on the other hand, the images in dreams. Their answer, he concluded, was to assume the existence of spiritual entities which dwell within the body during life, health, and consciousness but which are absent during death, sickness, and sleep. It has been noted already that the soul concept does, in fact, perform these functions. The theory was abandoned not because it was demonstrated to be false, but because there are other equally logical ways by which supernaturalistic concepts could have originated.

Other theorists propounded various explanations of the origin of religion, but anthropologists generally have given up efforts to determine what the earliest religious beliefs were like in favor of trying to understand the functions of religion. When these are understood, it is reasonable to suppose that they have something to do both with the origin and continued existence of supernaturalism in human culture.

Certainly, one of the major functions of religion is *explanation.* Psychological investigations demonstrate the propensity of humans to account for things, to make sense out of the circumstances of life. People all over the world have wondered how things got started, why people die rather than live forever, why people suffer from diseases and other troubles, and so on. Nonscientific cultures lack means of getting at natural explanations, and, given the human demand for explanations, they are left with supernaturalistic ones. A spring dries up because the spirit

Figure 12–2   *Dani examining a black and white robin chat. One of the major functions of religion is explanation, often embodied in the sacred stories known as myths. Death comes to the Dani because the bird won an argument with a snake over whether or not humans should renew their lives just as a snake renews his skin.*

who lives there is displeased at not being supplied with the desired offerings. The earth quakes because the gods are displeased with people's behavior. Mountains were formed as blobs of mud dropped from the feet of the creator as he plodded across the landscape. The severe pain in a man's chest is from a splinter of bone magically sent into his body by an enemy sorcerer. Great is the diversity of specific explanations produced by people's inventive minds. Many of them are embodied in the universally found sacred stories known as *myths.*

A second important function of religion is *reassurance.* "Man is born to trouble," said Eliphaz the Temanite (Job 5:7), and so it is. People are faced with sickness and death, hunger, cold, pain, itches, and many other uncomfortable physical sensations. Moreover, they worry about the possibility and probability of those things for themselves and those they love, and physical discomfort is translated thereby into psychological discomfort—anxiety and fear. Their friends, relatives, and strangers treat them badly. They fail to be friendly; they insult them and injure their egos; they threaten physical injury; they cause them to fail in the pursuit of their desires. Life would be too much to endure were it not for the divination that determines what is wrong, the magic or prayer that brings healing, the sorcery by which the enemy is vanquished without the danger or discomfort of direct confrontation. Thus, religious beliefs and practices provide the comfort and reassurance that comes from having some way to explain and cope with the troubles and uncertainties of living. Some wonder why "primitives" continue to believe in magical and other supernatural approaches when they so often fail. A large part of the answer appears to be the psychological comfort derived from having something to do which holds some promise of coping successfully with troubles.

A third major function of religion is *validation* of people's customs and values. Religious beliefs are important in all cultures as powerful support for the things people believe they should or should not do and as explanations for these customs. Female infanticide seems a horrible custom to most Euroamericans, but if one lives where it seems unlikely that there will be enough food to keep alive a newborn child and where it is believed that the spirit of a killed child will later be born into another body, taking the child's life may seem the right thing to do. Such practices may be validated, justified, or sanctioned by a religious belief.

Social integration, binding together the members of a society in a feeling of belonging and cooperation, is another important function of religion, especially in cultures where there is a common set of religious beliefs and practices for the whole group. In such societies the group's solidarity is enhanced by the sense of believing in the same things and participating in the same religious rituals. In Euroamerican societies, however, religion has often been socially disruptive rather than integrative because of the competition and conflict among religiously diverse groups.

Finally, *cultural integration* is an important function of religion in many cultures. A culture, viewed as a system of interdependent customs, may be given unity by the presence of various religious themes that indirectly link many of the customs. This linking together of the group's customs is conceptually different from social integration, which is the binding together of people. Bronislaw Malinowski, particularly, emphasized how religion may penetrate all aspects of a culture. He showed how magical rituals intruded into every phase of the life of the Trobriand Islanders of the South Pacific. This differs from the situation in many Western communities, where religion is a compartment seen as having only limited relevance to most aspects of everyday life.

There is little doubt that religion is much less important in American and other scientifically oriented cultures than in most other groups, and there seems to be a trend toward what has been called the abolition of religion. To the extent that this is so, it may be understood in light of the functions of religion just discussed, since some of these functions have been greatly reduced in importance by the success of science in providing natural explanations and more effective means of coping with hunger, disease, and other discomforts. A personal deity is no longer needed to explain many phenomena. Moreover, science has shown many specific supernaturalistic explanations to be in error, thereby reducing the confidence of people in such explanations and augmenting a growing faith that the unexplained will ultimately be explained by science. When Americans are threatened by disease, they feel considerable confidence that modern medicine may banish it or, at least, allow them to live their remaining days in some comfort. The suffering of hunger and cold or even insect bites is banished by a scientifically based technology. Humans still seem to be suffering quite a bit of psychological disturbance from their intractable fellow humans, but even now the developing psychological and social sciences are holding forth the promise of scientific resolution of interpersonal and intergroup conflict.

As the result of the cross-cultural approach, anthropologists strongly tend to see supernaturalistic beliefs and practices as human creations having no real referents. Such beliefs are held to exist only because they have functional value, and if other means can be found to perform those functions, religion might cease to exist. In fact, some feel, religion might be found dysfunctional. There is disagreement as to whether supernaturalism can be replaced successfully by nonsupernaturalism. Some people seem to have shed religiosity with little maladjustment, but many others experience difficulty. There is, in fact, an interesting way-station between supernaturalism and frank nonsupernaturalism which insists on the retention of Christian terminology and other symbols of the Christian religion, such as salvation, the sovereignty of God, Christ as the Lord of Life, and the like, to stand for essentially nonsupernaturalistic phenomena and concepts. The sovereignty of God, for example, may symbolize the significant fact that the total milieu of existence determines an individual's fate. This kind of position is held possibly because of the psychological disturbance of giving up words and concepts which have some functional value, even though they no longer are believed to refer to any supernatural reality.

Many writers doubt that people are ready to abandon supernaturalistic concepts completely. They see people as requiring something to which they can commit themselves, something they feel is bigger than humanity. They see those societies which abandon supernaturalism entirely as suffering from secularism and other damaging commitments. Anthony Wallace has suggested that secular ideologies may produce "unfortunate consequences for world peace and human welfare when directed toward people improperly perceived and toward organs of political action and cultural ideologies" (1956:277). He suggests, further, that the abolition of religion may well be accompanied by a "corresponding incidence and severity of transference neuroses, or human relationships will be increasingly contaminated by character disorders, neurotic acting out, and paranoid deification of political ideologies" (1956:278).

The proven functional value of religion accounts for its persistence as well as the recent revival of supernaturalistic elements such as witchcraft, astrology, belief in spirits, and supernaturalistic Christianity. The British anthropologist, Raymond Firth, views religious systems in terms of means for handling the fundamental problems of social organization: "for reducing uncertainty and anxiety, for increasing coherence in human relationships, for assigning meaning to human endeavor, for providing justification for moral obligation" (1951:250). He concludes that it is impossible for human society to exist without some kind of symbolic solutions that go beyond those based on empirical evidence. The range of workable symbolic solutions is great.

13

THE ARTS

All cultures include ideas and behaviors that provide aesthetic pleasure. Standards of beauty differ from culture to culture and from time to time, and anthropologists seldom concern themselves with whether or not there are universal standards of taste. But they do emphasize that all peoples engage in activities that provide them with satisfactions beyond practical usefulness.

Art is defined here as a process. It is the exercise of skill in the expression or communication of sentiment or value (Honigmann 1963: 219). This covers the sense of creativity or the aesthetic satisfaction obtained by the person exercising the skill. It also means that many kinds of activities may be considered art. Rituals, dancing, painting and drawing, carving, horseback riding, bull fighting, story telling, speech making, and a host of other human endeavors may be art to the degree that skill is exercised to express emotion. Many of these activities do not produce objects, but a material product is not necessary to have art. And perhaps artistic efforts of the same kind may be compared for the degree of skill exercised, though it would not be possible to say that activities involving a high degree of skill are better in any absolute sense than those requiring less skill. Evaluators of art would have to agree to this criterion for it to be used.

FOLKLORE

Folklore is a term commonly used to include the various stories told in a society, but it also includes such things as riddles, proverbs, and other verbal arts. It is conventional to divide stories into *myths,* which have to do with supernatural characters and events, and *legends,* which are concerned with secular and supposedly historical persons and episodes. Many stories, however, are difficult to distinguish this way, and often the difference is only a matter of emphasis. Perhaps most stories of nonliterate groups contain supernatural elements.

Major regions of the world can be distinguished by the kinds of folklore prevailing in each. In some areas, as in Polynesia, many myths are concerned with philosophical themes to a greater extent than in many other portions of the globe. In the aboriginal Americas there was relatively little in the way of riddles and proverbs, whereas they are important in the Old World. Some areas exhibit a relatively high incidence of complex creation stories, myths about families of gods, morality stories, or myths and tales about animal tricksters. Differences of these kinds are strong enough to enable scholars to classify the world into major folklore areas and to differentiate such regions into sub-areas.

In spite of these regional differences, many of the world's stories are widely found, and some are present in most major folklore regions. Flood stories are widely distributed, and so are obstacle-flight tales. The latter, which occur as episodes in longer stories, tell of someone being pursued by an ogre, with escape being accomplished by throwing down a series of objects such as a comb, a stone, or a bottle of oil. Each object magically becomes an obstacle which slows down the pursuer, eventually enabling the hero to escape. Folklore specialists believe that the widespread occurrence of the obstacle-flight tale resulted from borrowing rather than independent invention because of its continuous distribution over much of the world and because of the high frequency of the combination of three elements; a landscape barrier due to a magical stone, a thicket or forest due to a magical comb, and a body of water due to magical liquid or a mirror (Kroeber 1948:545).

Folklorists have studied extensively how story elements are combined and recombined as they are borrowed by different groups. Characters, incidents, and plots may vary independently from culture to culture, and even within the same culture to a degree. Stories seem to diffuse readily from society to society, as the obstacle-flight tale has, and their elements are inevitably reworked to reflect the content and interests of the story-teller's culture.

There are many functions of folklore, some being the same as those noted for religion and ritual. Myths are highly *explanatory,* and they *provide validation* for cultural behavior. Stories are also important in *maintaining group solidarity.* Another important function is *education.* Around the fire in the evenings or during long winters, children are told or overhear all kinds of stories which have a lesson to them, and the lesson may be stated explicitly before, during, or after the telling.

No less important is the sheer *enjoyment* of interesting, skillfully told stories, and from this point of view folklore is very much an art. The nineteenth-century Crow often listened to the stories of accomplished raconteurs on long winter evenings as people sat by the fire or were stretched out in readiness for sleep. Listeners were expected to say, "Yes!" after every few sentences, and when no one continued to respond the storyteller knew it was time to quit. Crow children often asked for stories, and in this way the tales were passed through the generations (Lowie 1935:105). Storytelling is also an important verbal skill among the Dani, though they relate recent events and experiences rather than myths and legends (K. Heider 1970:190). After a battle or when a man has returned from a long journey, he will hold forth at great length, dramatically varying his voice and using gestures for his attentive and responsive audience.

Apparently folklore also functions to *reduce tension and conflict.* Many stories incorporate accounts of characters who behave in ways that are culturally disapproved. Mythological gods violate standards of behavior by which humans must abide. Perhaps people derive psychological release from identifying with characters who express desires that real human beings must suppress. Tension may be reduced by the telling and hearing of stories in which those who exert burdensome authority and power or are otherwise the source of trouble get their comeuppance. In many stories release is provided by accounts of solutions to the problems of living which come far more readily than in real life.

The functions of folklore are similar in all cultures, and the tendency to separate Euroamerican stories and other compositions from those of nonliterate groups is misleading. Social scientists have shown that magazine stories, novels, and television soap operas perform the same functions as oral folklore. Just as !Kung or Crow storytellers add episodes and rework them as they tell their myths and legends, so American historians, biographers, novelists, and others add to and modify stories. Undoubtedly many a novel or short story about the nineteenth-century American West and many a movie or television production have functioned to validate the opinions of most Americans that the Indians were savages, and that our ancestors' battles with them, the policy of confining them to reserves, and present anti-Indian attitudes and actions are basically just. Such books and films also reinforce stereotypes of Indians as steely-eyed, silent except to say things like "ugh!" and "how!", unnaturally dignified, and unable to resist or handle liquor. In some cases the legend-making process has distorted the truth about Washington, Lincoln, and other historical figures. For decades Americans were brought up on stories of Lincoln's love for Ann Rutledge, only to discover that the tale was overdone at least, and possibly false. By now the story has been dropped from the schoolbooks, but its earlier appearance and acceptance by the American public may indicate that the love of a good story, the dramatic quality added to the life of an admired hero, the feeling of solidarity from common devotion to a public symbol, and other functions of narrative compositions are by no means limited to nonliterate and peasant groups.

MUSIC

Ethnomusicology is the term sometimes applied to the cross-cultural study of music. It is not a highly developed branch of ethnology, partly because scientific study of the structure of non-western music had to await the development of high-quality recording equipment. It is a significant area, however, and the rate of its development has increased. Now that excellent recordings of non-western music are readily available, the cross-cultural study of music is one of the most effective ways of elucidating the significance of cultural differences. Ethnomusicologists are interested in both the techniques and structure of music and its linkages to nonmusical cultural elements.

Structural and Technical Variability

As with other forms of art, our understanding of the music of other cultures is distorted by our cultural backgrounds: our reactions are inevitably ethnocentric. Hearing is thought ordinarily to be a purely physiological process, but it is a culturally conditioned psychological process as well. So, music from nonliterate cultures contains richness we do not hear because we have not been conditioned to hear it. One who attempts to reproduce a melody from an alien society inevitably alters it to fit familiar musical patterns. This is why recording equipment is essential to this kind of study.

The music of nonliterate peoples differs from Western music in that it seldom has more than one tone—it is not tonally polyphonic (Nettl 1956:77). This applies to both singing and instrumental music. Singers vocalize in unison, and instruments played in groups commonly play the same notes. A limited amount of harmony singing is found in a few widely scattered nonliterate cultures. People of cultures without harmony either do not hear the separate parts in Western music or they detect nothing but a jumble of confusing, unattractive noises. One investigator, convinced that the tribespeople he was studying should hear some of the wonders of Beethoven's music, played it for them on his phonograph. He reports that people stopped all they were doing and, after a moment of stunned silence, fled into the forest.

Another common characteristic of nonliterate music is the lack of emphasis on exact pitch. Euroamericans use precisely tuned instruments, and their musical training emphasizes the ability to recognize particular tones, with deviation being a source of distress. Our singing, of course, follows this instrumentally dominated standard. In most nonliterate groups singing is ordinarily not in a fixed key. Repetitions of a song will manifest relatively the same intervals between tones, but not absolutely.

There is nothing inevitable about the seven-tone scale. In fact, the most widely found scale is five-toned (pentatonic), not only among nonliterate peoples but among literate Oriental groups as well (Nettl 1956: 48). Less frequently found are scales of two, three, four, or six tones. However, scales also differ from one another in the range between the highest and lowest tones and in the intervals between adjacent tones. Accordingly, there are many kinds of scales in the world's music, though some are much more common than others.

Song melodies are distinguished in a variety of ways not explored here. Suffice it to say that melodies which either descend or move about equally in both directions are far more frequent than ascending melodies. It also has been noted that many groups sing with much more tension of the vocal cords than Euroamericans find acceptable. This may be accompanied by a good deal of ornamentation with trills, grace notes, and similar devices (Nettl 1956:57). There is no denying that many melodies of other cultures fail to please the Western ear. Yet, an understanding of a given composition's functions and meanings and its musical characteristics, along with repeated listening sessions, can result in greater appreciation of alien music. The listener becomes aware of the song's value in its cultural context and learns to hear musical qualities not detected at first.

Of course, the lack of tonal polyphony and exact tone intervals makes impossible the kind of tune manipulation and combinations of tunes so pleasing to Westerners, but music among other groups may achieve great richness through use of various rhythm combinations uncommon or absent in Euroamerican music. The music of nonliterates often emphasizes rhythm instead of tunes, and the rhythmic complexity of such music ranges from the very simple to combinations more intricate than anything in Western music. In several parts of the world—specifically in black Africa, portions of central Asia, and Melanesia—ethnomusicologists have found true rhythmic polyphony, that is, blending of parts having different stress patterns or metric units (Nettl 1956:68). The abandon which many find in so-called primitive dancing and music actually may seem uncontrolled only because the listeners are not culturally prepared to detect and appreciate the complex texture of rhythms. When !Kung, /Gwi, or other San men dance at the all-night healing performances, the women sit around the fire and sing the curing songs in falsetto voices while clapping their hands in counterpoint to the rhythm of their singing. The men may also sing as they dance, and the rattles on their legs and their feet thumping against the ground produce still other rhythms. In spite of the complexity and variability of the musical pattern, Thomas describes /Gwi healing rhythms as "always precise" (1958:131). They are the result of a lifetime of practice for perfection in the quality and timing of singing, dancing, and clapping. The healing ceremony amounts to a musical production made up of intricately interwoven elements, rather than the accidental hodgepodge that some culturally alien persons expect to hear.

Percussion instruments are more common than other kinds in nonliterate cultures. Many types of drums are found, some with membranes over one or both ends of a frame or cylindrical body, and others which lack membranes. Some drums are adjustable for tone variation. The Dahomeans of West Africa have drums which can "talk" by modification of the pitch to conform with the tonal patterns of sentences. As many as three tones can be sounded on some of them, depending on whether the head is struck on the rim or near the center and whether or not the heel of the hand is used against the head to change the pitch (Herskovits 1938:ii:319).

Xylophones and many kinds of rattles are found among nonliterates. Wind instruments include a diversity of flutes, flageolets, trumpets, and panpipes made from a variety of materials. The most common stringed instrument is the musical bow, which is plucked or tapped to produce such a low sound that it is often played for the sole enjoyment of the player. The Nyae Nyae !Kung commonly play on their hunting bows, whiling away the time as they are following game. To play the bow a !Kung loosens the tension, then may place the end of the bow in his mouth and strike the string with a piece of reed or a small stick or pluck it with his finger or wrist. By altering the opening of his mouth he produces a second tone in addition to the fundamental tone produced by the vibrating string itself (Marshall 1976:367). Another important !Kung instrument is the

Figure 13–1   *!Kung with a //gwashi. "Almost everyone plays the //gwashi—though only a few are highly skilled."*

//gwashi, a four or five-stringed instrument with a resonator made from a section of mangetti log. While men play the bow, almost everyone plays the //gwashi, though only a few are highly skilled. Most songs sung with the //gwashi have titles that reveal what experience or event the song commemorates. A number of the songs lack words. The Marshalls noted twenty-seven men's songs and fifteen women's songs in addition to women's ball game songs and other singing game songs (1976:375). The !Kung have other instruments besides these two, some of which they have acquired from whites or African blacks relatively recently.

There is a fair variety of instruments in nonliterate cultures, but they are not technologically of the sort that stimulates development of the tonally polyphonic music so valued by many Westerners. Nonliterate music, nevertheless, possesses a richness unexpected by the cultural alien, and as previously indicated, it is possible to be conditioned to detect and appreciate this richness.

Music in Culture

In view of the range of effects music has and the variety of uses to which it can be put, it is hardly surprising that it is one of the universal aspects of culture. Protest, communication, dancing, expression of love, insult, prayer, work, healing, hunting, divination and magic, story telling, mourning, political support, and education are only a few of the many uses of music (Merriam 1964:216). The Miskito Indians have a large body of love songs, which are sung at night by young men whose attentions have been thwarted by a girl's angry parents. They are sung to the accompaniment of a guitar, although a bambo flute was used in pre-Christian times (Helms 1971:86). !Kung San women and girls play ball games accompanied by singing, dancing, and clapping; and their running, throwing, and catching are governed by a strict rhythmic pattern and done with excellent timing. They draw on a repertory of ball game songs which is slow to change (Marshall 1976:324). The Nuer constantly sing and recite poetry to and about their cattle. The Dani sing lullabies to their babies, loud and boisterous songs at dances and girls' puberty ceremonies, dirges at funerals, and simple tunes while roaming the fields and woods (K. Heider 1970:191). Samoans sing on many kinds of occasions. Specially talented singers, for example, compose and sing songs of welcome, praise, ridicule, and the like for special times (Grattan 1948:116). Among the nineteenth-century Crow Indians a jilted lover might compose and sing a song ridiculing the offender; songs of derision were sung to shame people who transgressed the rules; praise songs were sung to honor returning warriors; and a successful seeker of a vision received a song from his guardian spirit (Lowie 1935:113, 243).

It seems that music has such a variety of uses because of its effectiveness in expressing sentiments and its impact on those who participate and hear it. Art was defined as the exercise of skill in expressing or communicating sentiment or value, and music fits the definition well. Music induces emotion and communicates feelings and information not easily expressed in speech and other nonmusical ways. Undoubtedly, music sometimes functions to increase tension, as when some old song reminds us of a long forgotten unpleasantness, but it frequently is an important way of draining off tension as well. It is also used to accompany other means of augmenting or reducing tensions, as in the songs used with war dances designed to build up aggressive feelings, or the dirges sung as a part of funeral rituals. Language and music are linked rather intimately, too, especially when songs are involved. This is most striking, perhaps, when language is tonal, since shifts from syllable to syllable make a difference in meaning.

Systematic research has been done in an attempt to test hypotheses about the relationships of song styles to subsistence patterns, governmental complexity, degree of class differentiation, severity of sexual restrictions, the relative positions of men and women, and degrees of social solidarity. Raspy singing, for example, appears to be associated with hunting as a subsistence mode, supposedly because hunting societies emphasize masculine assertiveness and assertive persons tend to sing in raspy voices (Lomax 1968:160). Such studies also suggest that rhythmic complexity tends to go with political complexity; highly stratified societies tend to embellish melodies more than egalitarian ones; tense-voiced singing is more common in societies with severe premarital sex proscriptions than in permissive societies; and egalitarian relationships between the sexes tend to go with cohesive, well-integrated singing. These and other hypotheses are highly suggestive and undoubtedly will be explored further in ethnomusicological research.

DANCING

Dancing has already been mentioned in connection with music and in other contexts. It may be considered an art form, an amusement, or a ritual activity. One or another of these purposes may be emphasized in a particular dance event, or all may be combined.

Dance forms and the arrangements governing dancing occasions are highly variable. Some involve vigorous physical movement and high excitement; others involve rather slight movement, perhaps only a swing of the body with little or no foot movement. There are extensive variations from culture to culture in how much of the body is involved, which parts are most active, whether the trunk is held as a single unit or twisted or undulated as though it consists of two or more parts, whether the transitions from one movement to another are fast or slow, jerky or smooth, and so forth. The variety of postures and movements possible for the human body is great.

Dancing arrangements vary from performances by a single person to those in which all join. Dancers may arrange themselves in circles, opposing lines, clumps, ranks, pairs, and many other ways. Sometimes only one sex dances at a time, but some societies have dances in which the opposite sexes not only perform at the same time but move in relation to one another and/or touch one another. Groups who prescribe separation of the sexes in dancing often find American ballroom dancing highly offensive. Ballroom dancing seems uniquely Euroamerican.

Dancing also varies in respect to its uses, symbolism, kinds of costumes and accessories used, and a number of other features. Actions in imitation of game animals are common in the dances of hunting groups, which serves to illustrate that artistic activities are linked to subsistence concerns.

Alan Lomax and his colleagues have developed systematic methods of describing the characteristics of dance movements and have explored the relationships between those movements and other cultural characteristics (1968:233). The notion underlying their research is that a dance type is an expression of the nature and needs of a group. A part of this is that the dance movements and their organization correspond with the postures and movements of subsistence work. The greatest hunters of the Netsilik Eskimo take turns drumming, singing, and dancing, while the women sit in a cluster at one side, chanting in accompaniment. The dance consists basically of vigorously and swiftly delivered diagonal downstrokes of the right arm as the performer strikes the lower edge of his drum with a short stick, followed by a quick upstroke to the drum's rim. The large, flat, single-headed drum is held in the left hand by a handle extending from its edge, and the force of the downstroke turns the drum, while the upstroke flips it back to its original position. The downstroke is accompanied by a slight bending of the knees. The trunk is held stiff, the feet are apart, and the rhythm is maintained with sustained vigor for a long time (Lomax 1968:226). This posture and the movements are fundamentally similar to those used by an Eskimo in hunting seal or fishing for salmon. He stands in place and, when it is time, he must deliver a powerful, lightning-quick diagonally-directed downstroke with the harpoon, a motion basically similar to that used in the dance. The movement is quickly reversed, also as in the dance. The dance, then, dramatizes the speed, strength, accuracy, and endurance for which Eskimo hunters are praised in songs and stories.

DRAMA

Westerners sometimes fail to see anything in nonliterate cultures akin to Western dramatic performances. This is partly because many cultures lack theatrical production as a specialty. The notion of having specialists who write plays which other specialists produce and perform is foreign to most cultures. In nonliterate cultures, perhaps most people participate in developing and staging a dramatic performance at least occasionally.

Drama is defined here as actional expression of beliefs, values, moods, fantasies, desires, or events and conditions that are remote from the dramatizers in time, place, or probability. Remoteness is a key concept here. Drama appears to be partly a result of a human desire to portray through actions things that seldom, no longer, or never exist just that way in ordinary life. Spirits and gods are not seen or heard, but they authorize humans to adorn themselves in costumes and masks and behave as gods behave. Highly valued historical or mythological events are depicted to remind people of their heritage and to reinforce their commitment to significant ideals. Circumstances people wish for or hope for, but do not realize in real life, are acted out to achieve vicarious satisfaction. Drama also communicates the impact or significance of an event for those who have not observed it.

Drama is so integrally related to other aspects of life that anthropologists only occasionally grant it separate treatment. Frequently dramatic activities are described in connection with religious ritual, for ritual is essentially dramatic and frequently religious. Dancing is also dramatic. Dramatic events commonly occur in everyday life, for example, the performance of a brief magical act during the building of a house or the gathering of plants. Often drama is unscheduled, involving only a limited use of props. The !Kung and other San tribes of South Africa accurately dramatize animal behavior, depicting things that they have experienced or heard of around their camps or on the hunting trail. Among the Khomani San, Doke observed a performance of a gemsbok hunt (1936: 456). The man playing the part of the antelope imitated its behavior in some detail: tossing his horns, biting at the grass, and so forth; and the yelping, biting, and running about of the dogs was faithfully depicted, too. Observers attest to the realism of such unscheduled San performances.

Yet, nonliterate peoples also stage dramatic performances as special occasions distinguished from the routine of daily life. Such occasions often involve the planned accumulation of supplies, costumes, and other paraphernalia, and there may be nonparticipating spectators. Such special dramatic events manifest structure just as surely as Western dramas. In a few Pacific island cultures voluntary associations specialize in dramatic and related forms of entertainment. They travel from community to community and are very popular. The ritual dramas of the Indians of the southwestern United States are well-known for their complexity, long duration, beauty, and dramatic impact. In the Hopi kachina observances which occur from about mid-December to mid-July, the men impersonate the kachina supernaturals by donning masks and costumes that represent the various kinds of kachinas and behaving as kachinas do. They depict the sleepy return of the first kachina of the season, the people's concern that the sun return to its highest position to bring warmth for the crops, episodes in their mythology, and many other matters of concern. These spectacles serve to maintain proper relationships with the supernaturals, thus ensuring certain benefits and keeping the universe in order. In addition, they provide aesthetic pleasure and the enjoyment of participation in a social event.

Among nonliterate cultures, then, dramatic occurrences vary in complexity and duration from the brief ritual or magical act to highly intricate pageants performed, in some cases, by specialists. It is the cultural alien's lack of familiarity with their drama that accounts for the failure to detect sequence, climax, or plot in nonliterate dramatic productions.

GRAPHIC AND PLASTIC ARTS

It is difficult for Westerners to divorce themselves from their own cultural values in understanding the art objects of other societies, and Western artists have sometimes misinterpreted "primitive art" for this reason. For example, they have often supposed that nonliterate artists are highly original, whereas they nearly always conform closely to culturally established standards. They also view technologically crude and, possibly, esthetically unappealing art objects as evidence of inferior ability, whereas the truth may be that the artist regards the quality of the work to be irrelevant to his purpose for it.

Anthropologists insist on a relativistic approach to art, which means that it can be properly understood only by discovering how it fits into the cultural context in which it was produced and has meaning. A notable example is one kind of dance mask used by the Yoruba of West Africa. Western art critics depicted it as a conventionalization or abstraction of the human face involving creative and skillful reworking of facial proportions to produce the abstract, distorted version. But in its cultural context it is used as an accurate depiction of a face. The modification of its features is actually related to the fact that it is worn on top of the head, not over the face. When properly worn, it provides a realistic impression of a human face. Lacking knowledge of its cultural context, however, Western artists customarily exhibit the mask in the vertical position and misinterpret it accordingly (Herskovits 1948:382). The specific functions of art forms may vary extensively between civilized and nonliterate cultures and from one nonliterate culture to another.

Anthropological objectives do not require aesthetic evaluation of the art of nonliterates, but such evaluations inevitably come as a reaction against misinterpretations. If only technological skill is considered, many examples of nonliterate art qualify as highly competent work, especially when the simple tools employed are considered. And while the question of universal standards of beauty is a difficult one, nonliterate groups produce many forms aesthetically pleasing to Westerners.

Many anthropologists admire art not only for its appearance, but mostly for the way it expresses and is functionally integrated with religion, mythology, and other cultural elements. One of the outstanding features of art in many nonliterate cultures is that it is part of everyday life. Yes, certain persons specialize in an art because of greater interest or ability, but there ordinarily are no professional artists who produce objects for a segment of society which specializes in the appreciation and evaluation of art. There is no significant distinction between professional art and popular art in nonliterate cultures. Pots, baskets, tipi covers, dishes, trays, and other everyday items are elaborated for aesthetic reasons and for the pleasure of the creator. Masks, totem poles, pottery figurines, useless but pleasing woodworking tools, carved wooden figures, and the like are produced to impersonate the gods and spirits in a ceremony, proclaim ownership of a chiefly title, provide a dwelling place for a spirit, and a variety of other nonaesthetic purposes. Dani men produce sacred red drawings on rock walls in connection with the initiation of young boys into one of their moieties. The drawings are made with a red clay that is imported from a neighboring area, and the initiates are painted during the ceremonies. This area of their life is so sacred to the Dani that they would not talk about it to the anthropologist, and Heider was unable to place this aspect of Dani art in its full cultural context (K. Heider 1970: 188). A few of the Dahomeans of West Africa carved calabashes, mainly as expressions of love for a woman. The designs on the calabashes stood for proverbs that indicated affection or passion (Herskovits 1938, i:346). The man would send a woman the calabash with a gift in it, and if she was responsive, she would return the calabash. The Dahomeans manifested unmistakable appreciation of the beauty of these carved calabashes. They also were accomplished in making appliquéd cloths, casting brass figures, wood carving, ivory carving, iron working, clay bas-relief work, and painting on the walls of sacred buildings. There were even specialists who produced for the royalty.

Art media differ considerably from culture to culture. Some groups, notably in parts of Africa, the southern Pacific, and British Columbia, excel in woodcarving. Various kinds of carving in the round may be highly developed, whereas painting and engraving may be neglected in the same society. To give pencil and paper to an artist who has never used them and to find fault for the failure to draw skillfully is cross-culturally naive. Any artist is competent only in familiar kinds of art activity. Among other kinds of nonliterate art are making three-dimensional pottery figures; painting and engraving the surfaces of pots, basketry materials, cloth, or hide; carving and engraving of bone and stone; netting, lace, and other cord work; feather work; metal casting; and bodily decoration. Which arts are developed in a culture depends on culturally defined interests and resources.

Just as in other cultures, the art of nonliterate peoples may be either highly abstract or highly realistic. In fact, the cave art of the Upper Palaeolithic is outstandingly realistic, possibly because the artist felt that accuracy would provide greater magical potency. The bronze heads pro-

Figure 13–2 *Shield belonging to Crow indian chief, Rotten Belly. "Art expresses and is functionally integrated with religion, mythology, and other cultural elements." Rotten Belly's shield was noted for the great war and prophetic powers associated with it.*

duced by the Yoruba of Ife, Nigeria, are both skillfully done and realistic in appearance (Adam 1963:112). But nonliterates also produce designs so conventionalized as to communicate little or nothing beyond geometric form to the cultural alien. In some cases the aesthetic pleasure of viewing the form is all that concerns the artist, but in other instances the form has additional meanings or functions for those familiar with them. The Kaingang of Brazil, for example, sometimes paint their bodies with dots, circles, or lines. These are meaningless to one unfamiliar with the culture, but for the Kaingang they provide magical protection from the souls of the dead (Henry 1941:175).

GAMES AND OTHER PASTIMES

Story telling, dancing and music, and production of art objects all have an element of play involved. Some anthropologists, in fact, have been impressed with the mammalian play impulse as the motivation for vast areas of human culture. Kroeber has suggested that without the trait of playfulness, our cultures would have many fewer aesthetic and intellectual developments (1948:29).

If the range and variety of aesthetic pursuits testifies to the power of human tendencies toward experimentation and play, so does the variety of games. Games requiring vigorous physical activity, which can be called *sports,* are found in all parts of the world of nonliterate and peasant cultures. In terms of the pleasure of participating in and observing skilled body control, this kind of game certainly includes an aesthetic element. Ball games of many kinds are widely found, and some are quite elaborate. A number of other athletic contests are held using equipment other than balls, such as the hoop and pole games of the American Indians and some other groups. In these games a shaft of some sort is thrown through a rolling hoop. The Crow Indians used darts some forty inches long and two types of hoops. One was a plain ring between nine and ten inches in diameter and wrapped with bark, while the other was a netted wheel about a foot across with a circular opening in the center. As one player rolled the hoop, another tried to throw the dart through it. Score was kept with small willow sticks as counters (Lowie 1935:101).

Racing is found in many forms. Some groups have long-distance footraces. Horse racing is found among the Plains Indians and among the Basseri and others of interior Asia. Horse races are an important activity among Basseri men at their wedding feasts (Barth 1961:140). Stilt races are staged in several places. Groups living near water may have swimming races, boat races, or diving contests. Other athletic contests include tree climbing, high jumping, broad jumping, and pulling or lifting. Contests in which opponents attempt to overcome one another physically are also common among nonliterate groups. Wrestling is virtually universal, but boxing is found only occasionally. A form of fencing also occurs in a few nonliterate groups, as do kicking bouts and several other forms of athletic combat. Even familiar types of contests vary culturally more than one might realize. Wrestling stances and holds are not the same for all groups, nor is boxing always limited to males. The tug-of-war is a fairly common kind of physical competition.

Contests and games involve varying degrees of physical strength and bodily control. Archery competition and throwing spears or other objects at targets require both dexterity and strength. Still others require much finger or arm control, such as the nearly universal cat's cradle, a string figure game, and the ring (or cup) and pin game so widely found in North America. In this game a stick or pin is used to flip a ring or perforated object into the air, and the player attempts to catch the object on the pin. Many other games emphasize intellectual ability rather than strength or dexterity. A number in the general nature of checkers and chess are found in all parts of the world.

Games of chance come in a seemingly endless variety, many of them being guessing games. Widespread in North America is the *hand game,* in which the player guesses which hand of an opponent contains an object. This was a notably popular game among the nineteenth-century Crow Indians. Sometimes there were only four or five players to a side, but two military societies played one another at times, with the members of each organization sitting in several rows on opposite sides of a large tipi. One player at a time represented each club, using marked bones, elk teeth, or, perhaps, shells as the objects hidden in the hand. One player concealed the bones in his hands, and at an appropriate moment the guesser would indicate by conventionalized motion which hand contained either an unmarked bone or one marked in a certain way. Among the Crow the guesser would strike his chest hard with one hand while extending the other hand to indicate which hand concealed the bone. Jeers greeted a wrong guess, and the guesser's team lost one of their stock of tally-sticks to their opponents. The game ended when three of them had been forfeited. During the game men behind their teams performed magic in their behalf, drums were beaten, songs were sung, and each player sought the help of his guardian spirit—pawing like a horse, flapping his arms in bird-fashion, hissing like a snake, and so on, depending on the nature of his guardian animal (Lowie 1935:98). In some of the California Indian tribes hand games would continue for more than a day without a break.

A variety of card games, dice games, and lotteries also occurs. These games are universally used for gambling, and the stakes may be high. The games are played in great earnest, and people have been known to gamble away their most valued possessions, including members of the immediate family.

Children's pastimes consist of many kinds of play, often educative in that they imitate adult activities. Just as small girls in American society may change doll diapers and play at ironing clothes, in some agricultural groups a girl may have her toy grinding stone. Dani boys have a war game in which they throw shafts of grass at one another, and small boys and girls may play "house." Toys for amusement alone are common, too. Dolls, noisemakers, tops, and the like, sometimes made by the children themselves, are found in all parts of the world. Beyond play with objects, children everywhere also enjoy a great variety of exuberant activities such as jumping games, swinging on trees, hide and seek, chasing rabbits, playing leapfrog, sliding, and rolling. Organized games for children are lacking or unimportant in many nonliterate communities.

Many games are related to supernaturalism and legal procedure. Some North American Indian groups use a ball full of seeds in one game. If the players manage to break the ball early in the game and the seeds are well scattered, the supernaturals are expected to send an early and abundant harvest. The Eskimos of the Hudson's Bay region would play the cat's cradle in the fall so as to catch the sun in its meshes and delay its disappearance (Boas 1907:151). Games are sometimes used to determine whether or not an accused person is guilty, for the supernaturals will see that the test indicates guilt or innocence.

14

LIFE-CYCLE
CUSTOMS

Biological factors can be among the most demanding in an ecosystem. Some, of course, produce more cultural responses than others, and among these are the physiological changes and states of the human life-cycle. Every culture includes customary responses to pregnancy, birth, infant helplessness, the biological vigor of young adulthood, sexual capacity, the decrepitude of old age, and death.

Instead of dividing culture into conventional aspects like those of the foregoing chapters, it is possible to use the individual life-cycle as a framework for describing and comparing cultures. While this chapter uses the life-cycle framework, its main concern is with direct cultural responses to the biological states of human life.

PREGNANCY AND BIRTH

Most peoples recognize that sexual intercourse may result in pregnancies and births, which indicates that biological realities provide a tendency for this cultural belief to occur. A few groups, however, have been reported to be ignorant of the father's role. Some Australian aborigines have the notion that a woman conceives as an ancestral soul enters her when she passes near the places where the ancient totem ancestors entered the ground, and one who wishes to avoid pregnancy should go wide of such places. Some anthropologists suggest that the Australians and others with similar views actually understand the necessity of intercourse but merely emphasize other explanations. This notion is supported by the belief of a number of groups that intercourse must be coupled with other circumstances to bring about pregnancy. The Hidatsa Indians, neighbors of the Crow, agreed that intercourse was necessary for a baby to develop, but a certain spirit also had to enter the mother. Spirits who were to become human beings lived in special hills, each believed to be an earth lodge where the spirits were cared for by an old man. A woman who wanted a child put toys at the feet of these hills, and men who wanted children fasted there. When a spirit baby wanted to be born, it would crawl across a ditch inside the lodge on an ash pole, and if it got across without falling into the ditch, it was born into the tribe before long. Some Hidatsa were able to remember when they lived in the "baby hills." In other groups, soul reincarnation, the moon, fertility deities, and consumption of juices are among the causes of conception (Ford 1945:35). Ford points out that the failure of many sexual unions to result in pregnancy is not ignored by nonliterate peoples, and it is a logical reaction to think that pregnancy occurs only when intercourse is combined with other factors. A number of groups believe that a single union is not enough for conception but that repeated intercourse is required. The Samoans of Manua believed that ten or fifteen unions were necessary (Mead 1969:87). And still others believe that intercourse is entirely unnecessary.

In spite of the nearly universal belief that intercourse and conception are related, nonliterate peoples do not have a scientific understanding of the biological processes of conception and fetal development. Apparently most believe that the germ of the fetus comes from the man only, and that he places it within the female. The people of the southern Pacific island of Tikopia, for example, feel that a woman's secretions have nothing to do with the origin of the fetus and that her body is only a place for the infant to develop (Firth 1936:479). Some groups believe that both male and female substances have a part. The !Kung and other San are said to believe that the man's semen unites with the mother's menstrual blood to form a child, and similar beliefs have been reported from many places.

The desire to avoid conception is found in a number of nonliterate cultures, and this is most commonly done by avoiding intercourse. Dani men observe a four to six-year period of sexual abstinence so that their wives will not have children too close together (K. Heider 1976:188). In many groups children are nursed for over two years, and intercourse is avoided so that lactation will not be interrupted by the arrival of another child. In addition to continence, magical means of contraception are fairly common, and some groups use physical techniques, such as withdrawal and interfemoral coitus.

When measures for avoiding conception fail or are not employed, abortion may be used, though many nonliterate groups abhor it. Both medicinal and mechanical means have been reported. A Samoan woman who wanted to end her pregnancy would submit to violent massage or chew kava leaves to stimulate abortion (Mead 1969:87).

For some couples, of course, the problem may not be avoiding conception but bringing it about. Barrenness commonly is a source of concern and shame, and a diversity of means of preventing or overcoming it have been developed. Usually, the husband is considered innocent, and a woman without offspring may be an object of pity, contempt, or derision, and sometimes her husband divorces her. To the Nuer a marriage is incomplete until a child has been born, and Nuer husbands have been known to send their wives back to their parents on grounds of childlessness (Evans-Pritchard 1951:92). Among the Crow the use of a special medicine bundle to cure barrenness has been reported (Wildschut 1960:142).

The physiological changes which come with pregnancy can hardly be ignored. Enlargement of the abdomen eventually becomes obvious, but other symptoms, most frequently the failure to menstruate, are ordinarily taken as first signs. Some groups reckon the date of birth by counting from the first missed menstrual period. Breast enlargement, nausea, laziness, and loss of appetite are among other pregnancy symptoms reported from some cultures (Ford 1945:43). The Samoans recognize cessation of menstruation, brownness and swelling of the breasts, fatigue, headaches, and nausea as signs of pregnancy (Mead 1969:87).

Cultures vary notably in responses to a fully accomplished pregnancy, but some kind of restriction is nearly universal during this time. Most often, certain foods thought to be harmful to the fetus are prohibited, and restrictions on intercourse are common. In Samoa a pregnant woman should not eat while walking around, or her child will be a runaway; and she should avoid hot food so the child will not be blistered (Mead 1969:88). In some societies there are proscriptions against heavy exertion during pregnancy, while in other groups the mother works until the time of delivery.

Although women in many societies may engage in normal physical activity until near birth, they nearly always receive assistance during delivery. Elderly women usually serve as midwives, with all others excluded. The husband may be present in only a few societies, and a priest or shaman will be on the scene only when supernatural aid is thought necessary. A !Kung San woman is assisted by her mother and others even though she goes into the open veld for the birth. The impression sometimes given in movies and elsewhere of the "primitive" woman giving birth by herself in the bush is not characteristic.

The most common position for childbirth is sitting, though kneeling is fairly frequent (Ford 1945:58). Less common are squatting and reclining. Usually the woman hangs onto something during childbirth or is supported by someone. Samoan women preferred to give birth while squatting on one of the short posts which stand between the house posts, but they also recognized kneeling and lying on the back as legitimate positions (Mead 1969:87). The infant was delivered over a specially prepared piece of bark cloth. Crow women knelt with legs wide apart and their elbows resting on a pillow while they hung on to two sticks that had been fixed in the ground at the head of the pillow (Lowie 1935:33).

The notion that childbirth is inevitably simple and easy for nonliterate women is false. There is a good deal of difference on this from group to group and person to person, just as there is in Western society. Solomon Island Siuai women, for example, find birth a painful experience, and mothers in their first delivery cry a great deal with considerable anguish (Oliver 1955:171.) Ford stresses that the possibility of a difficult and painful delivery is recognized in all societies (1945:62).

It is of interest to note that birth and its aftermath may also be difficult for the husband. In a few societies he takes to his bed during and after his wife's parturition and even imitates her labor. This custom is known as the *couvade* and appears to be of highest incidence among South American Indians. Among the Witoto of the Amazon region the mother returns to her garden work the day after a child's birth, but the father rests for a week or so in his hammock, receives visitors, and observes dietary restrictions (Murdock 1934:464). Traces of the couvade were found in pre-Christian Miskito culture. The father would refrain from hard work for the first few days after his wife had given birth, and he remained out of the bush. He also avoided salt, chili pepper and certain other foods (Conzemius 1932:151).

When the birth is accomplished, the umbilical cord is cut and disposed of, often in some magically significant fashion. The Samoans of Manua buried a girl's umbilical cord under a paper mulberry tree or a hala bush so as to ensure that she would be skillful in making bark cloth or plaiting mats (Mead 1969:89). All groups appear to exercise care in disposing of the afterbirth. Newborn infants are usually bathed immediately. Most peoples require mother and child to remain secluded for a time, thereby avoiding the spread of infection and giving opportunity for recovery. In some groups the recovery period lasts many weeks. Mothers of Tepoztlán, a modern Aztec town in Mexico, are expected to remain in bed thirty or forty days if possible (Lewis 1951:361). In most societies sexual intercourse is avoided for a period after birth.

If a newborn child is unwanted, infanticide may occur. This tends to be practiced by hunters or collectors whose subsistence systems are inadequate to support large families. !Kung women occasionally feel it necessary to kill an infant. This may be done if a birth follows another so closely that the baby would compete with an older sibling for the mother's milk, when the woman feels she is too old to produce enough milk, in cases of birth defects, and when twins are born (Howell 1976:-147). The Arunta of Australia, who also practice infanticide, believe that the child's soul returns to the place it came from and can be reborn later in the same or another woman (Spencer and Gillen 1927:39,221). It must be understood that nonliterate peoples ordinarily desire children, and that those who practice infanticide are not doing it out of cruelty or with lack of feeling.

CARE AND REARING OF CHILDREN

Infants manifest two major characteristics that all societies must respond to: they are unable to care for themselves physically, and they are culturally inexperienced. Consequently, all cultures must incorporate a large number of socially standardized ways of keeping children alive and healthy and providing them with experiences that will enable them to

Figure 14–1 *Basseri baby in its hammock. Infants are unable to care for themselves physically and are culturally inexperienced. The relatively long period of helplessness provides the child's elders with the chance to impose learning experiences.*

become full-fledged participants in the adult culture. The two characteristics are interrelated in that the relatively long period of helplessness, as contrasted with the condition in other mammals, provides the child's elders with the chance to impose the necessary learning experiences.

How a person is influenced and learns to participate in the society's customs is sometimes referred to as *enculturation* (Herskovits 1948:39). From the anthropological view, all people who have become able to practice their way of life are "cultured." While most enculturation goes on during the early years of life, it remains a lifelong process. In even the smallest culture there is always more to learn about one's lifeway.

It is important that the context of the enculturation experience be understood. It always involves interaction between individuals, with the result that the ideas and other esotraits of a culturally inexperienced person become similar to those of the more experienced members of the society. Picture a group having a set of multi-individual esotraits—that is, a culture. The individuals comprising the society regularly express their esotraits through utterances, actions, and the artifacts which some actions produce. Unless they make their ideas and unconscious esotraits objective in these ways, the neophyte can hardly know of their existence, since ideas do not move directly from the mind of one person to that of another.

A culturally experienced person who expresses an idea or other mental trace by an utterance or an action may be referred to as an *objectifier*. When anyone does this, it makes it possible for a child or anyone else lacking the esotrait in question to experience empirically its verbal, actional, or material manifestations. Culturally inexperienced persons may be called *respondents,* since they will react by ignoring the experience, by forming ideas unlike those of the objectifier, or by developing one closely similar to it. When the last reaction occurs and the trait to which people have reacted is multi-individual; the respondents have been enculturated in respect to the custom in question. This is what happens when a child learns how to tie a shoe, that the world is round, what to call a mother's sister, or any other cultural trait. *Enculturation* may be defined as the ongoing response of culturally inexperienced persons to esotrait objectifications, with the result that they develop personality traits similar to those of culturally experienced members of their society.

Not only the content of what is objectified but also the means of caring for and training children are standardized for a given community. This means that children in different families have similar experiences and logically may be expected to develop similar personalities. On the other hand, cultures differ from one another in what and how children learn. Some groups reward aggressive behavior, and some do not. Some encourage cleanliness, while others do not care. Some are permissive, and some are not. There are those who nurse infants on demand, and others who let them cry until feeding time. Some permit children great physical freedom; others restrict them. Some treat them consistently; others inconsistently. The culturally inexperienced may be treated in many different ways, and cultures may be expected to differ from one another in the types of personalities produced. The type of personality seen to prevail in a given culture has been referred to variously as the *modal personality, basic personality structure,* or, if the idea has validity at the national level, *national character.*

Nonliterate cultures are relatively lacking in the formal schooling, conducted particularly by specialists, that we refer to as *education.* It is fairly common for grandparents and other elders to take responsibility for a child's enculturation. Sometimes there are special periods of training, perhaps in isolation from the community, for one or both sexes at about the time they are initiated into adult society. Blacks of West Africa have arrangements of this sort which have been called "bush schools." Australian tribes, as well as other societies, give special instruction in supernaturalistic concepts and rituals to boys during their initiations. Nowhere, however, is education divorced from everyday life to the degree that it is in Western communities.

A major response of many anthropologists to the diversity of child-rearing customs has been the attempt to correlate them with certain adult personality traits and with the adult culture in general. This so-called *culture and personality* approach amounted to a kind of anthropological fad for a few years, but it suffered from the difficulty of substantiating supposed relationships between given kinds of childrearing practices and adult culture. Gorer's notion that the Great Russian custom of tightly swaddling infants to hold their legs straight and their arms tightly to their sides was a major cause of the alleged submissiveness to dictatorial government, pervasive guilt feelings, and enjoyment of orgiastic feasts and drinking bouts in Russia provoked a storm of controversy. It was pointed out that other groups, the Hopi of the American Southwest, for example, practice swaddling without manifesting such character traits (Barnouw 1963:128). Some anthropologists have rejected culture and personality studies, partly because of such difficulties; but many of the early problems have been corrected, and similar studies survive as an aspect of what is now called psychological anthropology (see page 8).

The appeal of the culture and personality approach is powerful, since it is easy to find childrearing customs that harmonize well with adult traits. The !Kung San are a peaceful people. Tensions arise among them, as in all groups, but they thoroughly enjoy one another's company and are considerably upset by circumstances that threaten to rend human relationships or cause physical violence. Though homicides do occur, !Kung bands do not war with one another or with other tribes. All this seems in harmony with the ways they treat their children. Infants are carried in soft leather slings, are in constant skin-to-skin contact with their mothers, and nurse at will. Children are treated gently and affectionately by all their elders. They are handled, kissed, danced with, and sung to (Marshall 1976:316). There seems little reason to question that there is a relationship between the way the children are raised and the peaceful, pleasant temperaments of !Kung adults, but in the last analysis the connection is inferred from the similarity of childhood and adult states rather than demonstrated scientifically. It also seems reasonable to suppose that the adult Nuer fight at the slightest excuse because they teach their little ones to settle their problems by fighting with one another (Evans-Pritchard 1940:151). And perhaps the lack of interest in eroticism among the Dugum Dani is connected with the absence of genital stimulation of small children. (Heider 1976:194). But in spite of the apparent agreements between childrearing and adult relationships, causal connections cannot be assumed without further proof. The Dani, like the !Kung, are very gentle with their infants, but unlike the !Kung they have engaged in both controlled ritual warfare and treacherous, bloody, nonritual battles (K. Heider 1970:118). Surely whether infants are handled gently or roughly, the nature of the weaning process, toilet training, training for or against aggression, and many other childrearing practices influence the adult personality and culture, but when a particular type of childrearing seems to yield one kind of adult character in one society and a different one in another

Figure 14–2 *Dani at battle. The Dani are very gentle with their infants, but unlike the !Kung they have engaged in both controlled ritual warfare and treacherous, bloody nonritual battles.*

society, we are given pause. The effects of infant experiences may be more easily undone by later experiences than some have supposed, and so many kinds of circumstances reinforce and cancel one another in personality formation that it is risky to causally relate specific childhood experiences with given adult traits.

Students of culture and personality, now more often called psychological anthropology, have turned away from impressionism to more careful formulation and testing of hypotheses. A well-known example is the hypothesis that initiation ceremonies for boys are apt to occur in cultures in which the mother and baby sleep together, separate from the father, for at least a year (Whiting et al., 1958:864). Cross-cultural testing of these and other hypotheses may be expected to reveal more about the effects of enculturation experiences on adult culture and personality than has been learned so far.

ADOLESCENCE AND ADULTHOOD

With the onset of puberty young people enter a period during which, in most cultures, they are expected to take on more adult roles. Often, shortly after puberty, they are fully recognized as adults and are expected to get married. Boys may be initiated into a pan-societal fraternity (see page 176) about this time. Other cultures may have little or nothing in the way of puberty observances. Barth mentions nothing of this sort for Basseri young people, though secret sweetheart relationships may be established (1961:139). A significant milestone in a Samoan boy's life, which proves his bravery and prepares him for adulthood, is circumcision. Basseri boys are circumcised at about two months of age, but a Samoan boy makes his own decision to have the operation when he is about nine or ten years of age (Holmes 1974:79). Accompanied by a friend, he goes to a native specialist or to a medical practitioner. Sometimes a group of boys will go through this ordeal together. At fourteen or fifteen Samoan boys take up membership in the society of untitled men. A Nuer boy is initiated into a newly forming age set by the making of four deep cuts across the forehead from ear to ear, which leaves lifetime scars. At that point he becomes a man; therefore, he no longer milks the cattle but enters a life of herding, garden cultivation, warring, duelling, dancing, and love making (Evans-Pritchard 1940:254).

Euroamerican societies contrast with many others in that adolescence is culturally prolonged beyond the onset of biological maturity, and the young person is kept in a dependent position. In the United States adolescence is thought to be a period of awkwardness, rebellion, conflict, and stress, but anthropological evidence indicates that many cultures exhibit little or none of this. Mead found this so when she studied Samoan life in 1927 and 1928 (1928:157), and in the 1950s and 1960s Lowell Holmes noted that "Samoan culture is characterized by a smooth and gradual coming of age process." (1974:79). Unlike American children, Samoan young people are never told that they are "too young" for a task.

Menstruation requires some kind of cultural response in all groups, and many cultures include ceremonies at this time. It may be a time for pride and celebration or an occasion of danger and consequent seclusion. At the first menstruation of a Valley Tonga girl of East Africa, her father would kill a goat and give a feast of celebration, and the girl wore a special costume (Reynolds 1968:206), but the traditional Nyoro of East Africa concealed the first menstruation from nonfamily. The girl was secluded and permitted only gruel, porridge, plantains, beer, and water, according to Roscoe (1923:263). The pre-Christian Miskito also had special puberty observances for girls, including seclusion in a small hut

(Conzemius 1932:148). Married women also were secluded in this way. Hunting societies around the world tend to regard menstrual fluid as dangerous to masculinity and offensive to animals, and they often isolate menstruating women in various ways throughout their lives. During a !Kung girl's first menstruation the men and boys must not look at her nor she at them for fear that the men will become highly visible to animals and will be unable to get close enough to them to shoot (Marshall 1965:265). Throughout their lives !Kung women must be careful not to touch hunting equipment; and hunters should neither talk about menstruation nor listen to talk about it, since it might make them lazy hunters.

Sexual reactions are culturally standardized to a high degree. Erotic arousal is a biological fact in all groups, but cultures vary in frequency of arousal and in what they define as having erotic significance. In American culture the exposed female bosom is erotically interpreted, whereas this is not so in many other cultures. Women's breasts are of no sexual significance to the !Kung, but the back and the buttocks are, and the women are careful to wear the kaross on the back and keep the buttocks covered with an apron (Marshall 1976:244).

Some societies are much preoccupied with sexual thoughts and the acquisition of sexual experience, while others are less preoccupied. Most anthropologists and other social scientists hold that the level of sexuality is naturally high in humans and that cultures which greatly restrict sexuality have curbed a basically strong drive. This coincides with a widespread belief among contemporary Americans that people are often helpless to resist their sexual urges and that those who fail to find adequate sexual outlets must suffer psychological constriction and stress. The opposing view is that cultural learning is significant in determining the level of sexuality. Heider argues that the Grand Valley Dani manifest a very low level of sexuality, thereby supporting the view that the degree of sexuality is relative to the culture. He notes that Grand Valley Dani men abstain from sexual intercourse with their wives for from four to six years after a child has been born; that most of them have no alternative sexual outlets; that the period of abstinence is supported neither by powerful explanations nor by strong sanctions; and that no one shows signs of stress or unhappiness during periods of abstinence (K. Heider 1976:188). By contrast, the sexuality level is much higher in Western Dani culture and among many other New Guinea groups.

Many other cultures permit and often encourage sexual activity on occasions when it is prohibited or discouraged by many Americans. Still, no culture is free of restrictions, which seems to reflect the fact that complete sexual freedom would seriously disrupt social relationships. Premarital sexual activity is permitted to some degree in many cultures. In one sample of 456 cultures for which information is available, about 45 percent permit premarital intercourse for females. A slightly higher percentage prohibit premarital sex relations, though in close to half of these societies the ideal is violated fairly frequently. Nineteenth-century Crow women were admired if they remained virgins until marriage, but departures from this ideal were not greatly condemned (Lowie 1935:47). But even in societies in which premarital intercourse is encouraged, there are restrictions. Nuer young people engage in considerable flirting and love making, but they must be careful not to have intercourse with someone in their own lineage or clan, or with any close relative. Moreover, Evans-Pritchard was told that when couples pair off alone in the high grass, a girl is likely to refuse intercourse unless she feels sure that the young man intends to marry her and has the cattle for the bride price (1951:53).

After marriage both husband and wife in most cultures are expected to confine their sexual activities to one another, though some groups expect fidelity of women only. In many societies marital fidelity is successfully maintained in most marriages, but in others adultery is common and may be a source of much trouble. At the same time some cultures have standardized provision for a married person to have sexual experience with someone other than the spouse. The custom by which Eskimo men who maintain special partnerships with one another may allow the partner sexual access to the wife is well known. And, while it is not common, the !Kung permit two men to agree to exchange wives temporarily, but only if the wives agree (Marshall 1976:279).

Cultures differ in the nature of sexual congress. In some places much foreplay occurs, whereas in others there is little. Postures considered normal in one culture are regarded as aberrant or abhorrent in another. Of the most commonly used positions, available evidence indicates that no one of them is preferred in more than a minority of the world's cultures (Kluckhohn 1949:97).

Adulthood in the fullest sense begins with marriage in most societies. This may follow soon after puberty or it may be delayed for some time. Frequently, the marriageability of a girl is advertised by a change of attire or hair style. In a number of societies marriages are arranged while one or both of the partners are still children, and girls are often married at a younger age than boys. !Kung girls may be betrothed and married to an older boy or a man while they are still small children, but their husbands do not have sexual congress with them until they have reached puberty. A !Kung male is not eligible to marry until he has killed a great antelope, a buffalo, or one of the other large animals hunted for meat. Then he is scarified by several vertical cuts on his face, arms, back and chest (Marshall 1976:270). Marriage generally occurs long after puberty in American society; in fact, the general tendency is to defer the age when one is considered an adult well beyond biological maturity. Being psychologically and biologically mature, yet treated as sub-adults, many American young people become resentful and actively rebel against their elders' control and object to the denial of full participation in adult culture. Not only is teenage marriage discouraged, but little is done to prepare young people for marriage, though it is recognized as a time of major adjustments.

DISEASE

Disease may strike at any point in the life-cycle. Infant mortality is especially high among nonliterate and peasant peoples, and fatal sickness is frequent enough during all phases to reduce the life expectancy to a level two or three decades lower than in some Western communities. Moreover, disease, as the word itself indicates, is uncomfortable. Such unpleasantness, regardless of one's age, requires cultural responses, and healing practices and explanations for sickness are found in all cultures.

Ideas about the causes of illness and its treatment fall under *ethnomedicine,* a category previously dealt with in connection with shamanism, knowledge, medical anthropology, and other topics. There are two main theories in the world's cultures about what is wrong in the body of an ill person. One is the notion that something alien has entered the body, such as an evil spirit, a bone sliver sent by a sorcerer, or viruses and bacteria. The other theory is the concept of soul loss. The intrusion of something alien or loss of the soul may result from a variety of specific actions and circumstances, such as witchcraft, violation of a taboo, poor diet, falling down, a fright, an encounter with a sprite, and so on. Some ailments, of course, occur without any indication of intrusion or soul loss. The nineteenth-century Crow thought sickness or some tangible object might get into a person's blood, and a Dani sorcerer may send a ghost into a victim's body in the form of a certain rat-like animal (K. Heider 1970:228), which then nibbles at the person's soul matter. The Dani also believe that one of the souls may be jarred loose from the body by a fall.

Curing methods must be suitable to the suspected cause, and they often center on extracting the alien object or spirit or recovering the soul. Shamans ordinarily specialize in divining the specific causes of illnesses and curing. If the condition is due to sorcery or witchcraft, it may be necessary to neutralize the attack by magical or other supernaturalistic counteraction. As noted in the section on knowledge, practical curing without resort to supernatural means is also found in many nonliterate groups.

OLD AGE AND DEATH

The age at which one is considered elderly differs from culture to culture. In some places people in their late thirties may be thought elderly, whereas some Western communities now tend to postpone such designation until age sixty-five or seventy. Retirement from an age class system, having grandchildren, loss of vitality, and passage of menopause are among the variety of criteria of old age used in various cultures.

In some societies old age is culturally defined as a time of cheerless

Figure 14–3 *Elderly Samoan. The Samoans are among those who greatly respect the aged. Old age is regarded as the best time of life.*

resignation or even despair. The aged are most secure, of course, in societies where they have high prestige. Respect for the elderly is sometimes high in slowly changing cultures, since it is of advantage to others to be able to draw on their great cultural experience. The Samoans are among those who greatly respect the aged (Holmes 1974:89). Traditionally it has been the elderly who have been regarded as being most accomplished in story telling, tattooing, bush medicine, massage, and midwifery, and the important office of advisor to the village council always goes to an elderly High Chief. The concept of retirement is foreign to the Samoans, and the elderly can work at anything they want to or do nothing, as they prefer. Old age, which begins at about age fifty, is regarded as the best time of life. Older people in Samoa are well integrated into the life of their society and feel themselves to be valuable participants in family and village affairs.

By contrast, the aged are not valued much in American society, since the main emphasis is on the beauty and vigor of youth and the pursuit of youthful goals without the nuisance of having to care for the aged. Americans either feel sorry for the elderly, find them repulsive, or make them the butt of caricature humor. Many deeply dread becoming old and cannot accept the limitations of advanced age with equanimity. In spite of this, a great deal of expense and effort is devoted to keeping Americans alive as long as possible. Some Americans devote themselves to promoting a more general understanding and amelioration of the difficulties of old age, and more and more of the elderly are objecting to being treated as second class citizens and are trying to promote greater respect for the aged and the utilization of their special talents.

Prestige for the aged may also be low among food gatherers, for the limited food supply may make anyone who cannot engage in foodgetting a serious burden to the family and community. In some cultures respect for the aged is enhanced by their control of inheritable wealth or by a belief that the ancestors exercise much influence over the living.

Death is a significant event in all communities. There is always the problem of separating the dead from the living, and the disturbing reminder that death will be the fate of each survivor. In addition, there is the psychological disturbance from the new vacancy in a network of valued interaction patterns. Accordingly, anthropologists have found that major functions of death rituals include the permanent separation of the dead person's ghost from the survivors and the reestablishment of social solidarity. The pre-Christian Miskito believed, as many other groups do, that the soul of the dead was reluctant to leave the survivors. They would call in a shaman to capture the lingering soul and take it to the burial ground (Helms 1971:199). The !Kung try to get a dead person's soul to return to the place where the person was born so that it will not hover around the grave for a long time. They break up the person's hut and scatter the household possessions, build a fire in front of the shattered hut, and plant a bent reed in the ground so that the hut's ruins, the fire, and the reed form a line pointing in the direction of the dead one's birthplace (Service 1978:105).

People commonly wash and clothe or wrap the corpse in preparation for disposal. It may be interred within a few hours, as in tropical Samoa, or after several days. The body may be buried, placed in a cave or tomb, left in the open, placed on a platform, tower, or in a tree, or cremated. If buried, it may be placed in a flexed position oriented in one of several ways, or arranged in a seated, squatting, or extended position. The nineteenth-century Crow disposed of their dead either on a scaffold resting on four forked posts, in the fork of a tree, or beneath a pile of rocks on a hilltop (Lowie 1935:67). The Dani cremate their dead on a specially built cremation pyre of large split logs. When the ashes have cooled a woman closely related to the deceased picks out the remaining fragments of bone, bundles them into a banana leaf, and hangs them on the wall of the compound cook house. The next day the ashes are deposited in a special low enclosure where the remains of everyone cremated in the compound are disposed of (K. Heider 1971:271). The Nuer bury a body several feet down, with the corpse on its right side on a strip of ox-hide, the legs flexed, and the arms over and under the head. A strip of ox-hide is also laid on top of the body (Evans-Pritchard 1956:145).

Some peoples retain part of the body for ceremonial or magical purposes, or all portions of the body may be exhumed and used for one of these purposes or secondarily interred. Mummification is known in only a few places. A number of peoples, including the pre-Christian Miskito, inter objects with the dead, either for use in the next world or because it may not be thought suitable for the living to use them.

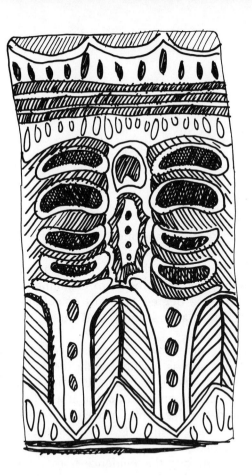

15

CULTURAL
STABILITY
AND CHANGE

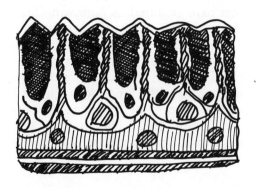

One of the most important subdivisions of cultural anthropology is *cultural dynamics,* the study of the processes and conditions of cultural stability and change. Anthropologists have found that all cultures are always in the process of changing and, also, that all cultures resist change to some degree. Students of cultural dynamics investigate the reasons for change and stability and study the consequences of various kinds of change.

Some have pictured so-called primitive cultures as completely stagnant and as having exactly the same ways of life they had hundreds and thousands of years ago. It still is common to encounter statements to this effect in nonanthropological articles and books, television documentaries, and the like. Anthropologists have not been able to confirm such a lack of change; in fact, they feel they have evidence of regular, unceasing change.

Among this evidence is the archaeological finding that objects made by various societies inevitably differ from one time level to the next. Second, historical accounts provide evidence of change. Third, in every society there are some cultural differences between generations, with the older generation expressing its displeasure over the tendency of the young to ignore some traditions and substitute new customs, and the younger generation regarding the old people as too conservative. Finally, in all parts of the world large areas are found where there is gradual variation from one culture to another. The cultures are different from one another, but they are too much alike to assume that independent invention accounts for the variability. The inescapable conclusion is that cultures have borrowed from one another, and the slight differences are due to changes that have occurred as borrowing took place and as the people gradually changed their ways from generation to generation (Herskovits 1948:481).

Whenever groups without agriculture or metal tools are discovered in some remote place they are almost inevitably presented to the fascinated public as long-unchanged survivors of man's primeval past, usually referred to as the Stone Age. The response to the recently found Tasaday, who live mostly by collecting wild plants and small stream life (MacLeish and Launois 1972), illustrates the tendency to assume lack of change in so-called primitive groups. The suggestion of some that the ancestors of

today's Tasaday (or even some of today's Tasaday) could have been agriculturalists has been rejected by one writer on the grounds that people
who know agriculture never forget or abandon it. Anthropologists, however, know that groups do abandon agriculture, the nineteenth-century
Crow and the Kaingang of Brazil being two examples. Anthropologists
generally agree that we can examine the cultures of groups like the San
tribes and Australian aboriginals for clues to the basic features of prehistoric hunting and collecting societies. But they also know that all
cultures change, that they do not change in one direction only, that all
of today's cultures are different in many ways from earlier times, and
that it is unsafe to conclude without sound and independent evidence
that a technologically simple group has always been that way.

ORIGINATION

This book stresses that cultural traits are sets of similar, learned
personality traits and that understanding change requires the investigation
of why individuals change. My argument is that if anthropologists can
determine what prompts individuals to respond as they do to opportunities
and pressures to change their ideas and behaviors, we will improve our
understanding of the conditions and processes of change.

Incidence of Origination among Nonliterates

To what extent do members of nonliterate societies originate customs
which then spread among the group's members? There are few data on
this, partly because scientific observers are so seldom present when
originations having obvious cultural potential occur, and partly because
few are oriented toward watching for such events. Everyone realizes that
all customs begin with some person, but few think it possible to detect
those beginnings. But even the fragments of cultural diversity described
in this book should teach us that there must have been a colossal amount
of origination throughout human history, and it is surely continuing. Concerning a culture he studied in the Solomon Islands of the southern
Pacific, Oliver asks, "How did Siuai culture get to be what it is?" (1955:
467). He goes on to say that we should not overlook the roles played
by individual Siuai in originating or actively spreading new cultural elements; moreover, the very fact that their culture is so different from
neighboring cultures implies inventiveness. Oliver has evidence for origination of the kind so seldom included in anthropological reports. One
Siuai, for example, is credited with discovering the idea that certain kinds
of demons can be attracted by whistling. Another invented a larger size

carrying-pouch for men. Oliver also feels that the increasing use of familiar spirits in Siuai magic is the work of a few inventive magicians and that the increasing emphasis on competitive feasting is due to the innovative activities of three or four persons. Special attention to this kind of occurrence might teach us much about the causes of cultural variability. Without question every culture has been different in some measure at the time an ethnographer studied it than it was a few years before.

The Origination Process

Inasmuch as cultural traits are multi-individual customs, it should be remembered that any trait is ultimately brought into being by a specific person. The process of bringing an esotrait (see page 47) into being, which may become a part of a culture, may be called *origination*. This is essentially a psychological process; the individual perceives a new relationship between two or more pre-existing ideas or portions of them, which are combined into an idea that is new to the innovator. H. G. Barnett (1953) has probed the nature of this process in depth. There seems to be good reason for viewing the process as basically the same in all situations, with only the content varying from one context to another. In all cases origination involves conscious or unconscious manipulation of mental configurations by someone. Such configurations can either be viewed as units or analyzed into their parts. What happens in origination is that people substitute part of one mental configuration for part of another one to create something psychologically new to them. This, Barnett suggests, is made possible by their analysis of configurations into their parts and identification of a part in a familiar configuration with one in another configuration (1953:188). The identification is possible because the originator experiences the elements of the analyzed configurations as similar to one another in some way. It is because the parts of the two configurations are experienced as similar that one can be substituted for another to form a new combination.

A simple example is the origination of the idea of a motor-powered bicycle. People in the United States were familiar with a configuration consisting of internal combustion engines in combination with four-wheeled vehicles. Anyone who thought of four-wheeled vehicles as similar to two-wheeled vehicles would be able to substitute two-wheeled for four-wheeled vehicles to arrive at the notion of a bicycle powered by an internal combustion engine.

Another example, an actual occurrence, is the innovation of the idea that socialism is atheistic. Let us say that an American who has in mind the notion that communism is atheistic learns that both socialists and Russian communists advocate government ownership of industry. This feature in common makes possible the identification of socialism with Russian communism and the substitution of socialism for communism in the configuration, "communism is atheistic," to form the new mental configuration, "socialism is atheistic."

Causes of Originations

There are various incentives for producing percepts and concepts experienced as qualitatively new (Barnett 1953:97–180). One of the most important is *devising and maintaining satisfying self-concepts.* People of all cultures constantly select and interpret things to conform with their notions of themselves and their relationships with the environment. Consciously and unconsciously, they devise ways of expressing their deepest needs and desires and avoiding or hiding whatever would undermine valued self-concepts. Perhaps the comment, "Some of my best friends are Negroes," has been an invention that helped some people reject the image of themselves as prejudiced against blacks. Among other incentives for origination are the sheer *enjoyment of creating,* the *desire to be recognized or admired* for creating something new, and *compensation for blocked goals.* People who have been prevented from reaching goals important to them may replace them with newly invented goals, may devise new ways of destroying or nullifying the barriers to accomplishing what they want, or, simply, may develop new means of reaching their goals.

Sometimes *accidental convergence of two or more desires* results in something new. One may be trying to satisfy one desire and accidentally come upon the solution for something else, or the satisfaction of one desire may conflict with another in such a way as to result in a compromise origination. In other cases originations occur as people engage in *random tension-releasing* activities. Doodling, fiddling with objects, and the like sometimes produce results that people recognize as new and valuable. Many an inventor has come up with a new idea while aimlessly manipulating things. Finally, people often invent *to increase or decrease the amount of something they already have.*

SOCIAL ACCEPTANCE AND CROSS-CULTURAL DIFFUSION

An origination is not part of a culture, in the view of most anthropologists, until it is multi-individual. People other than the originator must accept the new custom. No doubt most originations fail to spread to others. They remain personal and unique, or they are abandoned by their inventor. And many which do spread are not accepted by enough people to become of much cultural significance. Anthropologists have seldom focused on what happens to inventions, but the issues are similar to those affecting responses to customs from alien cultures. In both cases, someone must accept or reject the custom of another person.

When a culture is being modified by the diffusion of customs from culturally different societies, anthropologists refer to the situation as *acculturation*. Acculturation consists of all that happens to a particular culture as the result of contact between its carriers and those of other cultures. The term *diffusion* is usually applied to the study of particular traits or complexes of traits as they spread from culture to culture.

In their study of how and why customs spread from one society to another anthropologists have tended to emphasize the effects of Western cultures on technologically similar ones. Some of the evolutionary anthropologists of the last century and early part of this century were interested in how cultures at supposedly inferior levels on the evolutionary scale could be changed so as to move toward the top rung of the ladder of cultural evolution. And later on, Malinowski and other advocates of functionalism (see page 51) recommended an understanding of the functions of the customs of Africans and other nonliterate groups as valuable to colonial powers in changing those customs (Bastide 1973:11, 16). In recent years there has been more interest in how nonliterate and peasant cultures have changed industrial and urban cultures, but studies of the effects of dominant cultures upon subordinate or less developed cultures still prevail.

Figure 15–1 *Nyoro King signing a 1955 agreement with the British to relinquish monarchical powers. Anthropologists have tended to emphasize the effects of Western cultures on technologically simpler ones.*

In regard to both social acceptance and the diffusion which occurs in acculturation, it is important to remember the two kinds of people involved. There are at least one *objectifier* and one or more *respondents,* just as in enculturation (see page 259). The issue is why a respondent accepts or rejects a custom objectified by someone else and, also, how people reinterpret customs they accept. In a sense these are psychological problems, but they are also cultural and, therefore, anthropological, because the reactions of respondents are determined in great measure by the multi-individual notions they share with other members of their society.

If an idea or other esotrait can be objectified only by utterances and/or actions, the objectifier and respondent must be close enough to see or hear each other. But if objectification involves an artifact, including written and electronic items, the two need not be aware of each other's existences or even exist on the same time level. An interesting case in point is the restoration of pottery making to the Hopi Indian villages of First Mesa in Arizona. For some reason the Hopi gave up this important craft after the first century of Spanish rule. Then, near the end of the seventeenth century, a group of Tewa Indians fled Spanish oppression in the Rio Grande Valley and established their new village on First Mesa next to the Hopi villages of Sichomovi and Walpi; and it was a Tewa woman, Nampeyo, who revived the art. The objectifiers were pre-Spanish Hopi, for Nampeyo was able to study the pots they had made and the designs on them as the result of archaeological work at the nearby ruins of Sikyatki. She succeeded in producing pottery similar to that of the prehistoric Hopi, and she became an objectifier for Hopi and Tewa respondents on First Mesa (Dozier 1966:29).

PREREQUISITES FOR ORIGINATION AND RESPONSE

The ideas and experiences that people respond to as they change come from the unique circumstances of their lives, the inventory of customs in their culture, and the customs of culturally alien persons. It is important to remember that the responses cannot occur unless there is something to respond to, and culturally this means one's own and other cultures.

Other conditions being equal, change rates should be higher for a culture with a high volume of customs than for a less complex culture. The large number of traits provides people more to think about and to respond to. Negatively stated, this means that people will not acquire the bits and pieces of knowledge necessary to origination and acceptance unless they have sources. In European cultures the concepts and information necessary to invent Gothic cathedrals were present, but one would not expect to find Gothic cathedrals standing in the desert territory of an Australian tribe (Goldenweiser 1970:473). Australian aboriginal cultures simply lack the numerous prerequisites to develop cathedrals. Since they have fewer cultural resources to draw upon, it is hardly surprising that change is slow in small-scale cultures.

Contact with alien cultures provides a major source of ideas for many societies. Those in isolated areas, such as the San tribes of the Kalahari desert, have had limited opportunities until recently for contact with groups greatly different from them. This seems to be one reason why their cultures have changed more slowly than some others. By contrast, the world's most complex civilizations originated in areas where many groups of a wide variety of cultural backgrounds came into contact, stimulating a ferment of change. This happened around the eastern end of the Mediterranean Sea, in the river valleys of India and Pakistan, and also in Middle America and the adjacent portions of South America. No such concatenation of cultures occurred in sub-Saharan Africa, which may be one reason that no black society developed a complex, literate civilization.

The fundamental reason culture contact increases change rates is that originators have the ideas of other cultures available as well as their own, increasing the possibility of new combinations many times. Contact with alien ideas also challenges people to rethink or defend their own ideas, values, and behaviors. Much of the seminal thought of ancient Greece seems to have been stimulated by just such challenges. Plato, for example, reacted against what he felt were fallacious teachings of aliens moving into the area. Much of his thought seems to have resulted from attempts to discredit foreign ideas, and in the process he seems to have originated new mental configurations which incorporated parts of culturally alien thoughtways.

It is not enough for ideas to be available, either from one's own culture or others. Since individuals, rather than societies or cultures, make the changes, new ideas must be objectified in some fashion and become lodged in the minds of potential originators and respondents. Applying the concept to origination, Barnett has noted that it is impossible for people to come up with new ideas unless they have, concentrated in their minds, the necessary components (1953:41). Studies have shown that inventors are people with a wide range of knowledge; they do not pluck their ideas from the blue.

Commonly, more than one member of a society has acquired the same or similar ideas. This is especially so if many opportunities for sharing ideas are provided by the culture, and it has often resulted in *simultaneous inventions*. Charles Darwin and Alfred Wallace independently originated the idea of natural selection at about the same time. Wallace deferred to Darwin, so it is Darwin's name we know so well. Alexander Bell got to the patent office only a few hours before Gray, or we might be using "Gray Telephones." An eminent anthropologist has compiled an impressive list of such simultaneous inventions (Kroeber 1948:341). They are accounted for by the concentration of the necessary building blocks in the minds of more than one person. Moreover, the individuals involved in simultaneous inventions share similar cultural goals and interests, with the result that more than one person is thinking about the same problems at the same time.

In regard to acceptance and rejection of alien customs, people who have not observed an objectification of a particular custom are in no position to respond. It is not realistic to suppose, as some have, that failure of one society to adopt something from another culture means that the custom in question has been rejected. Parsons noted that the Zapotec Indian women of Mitla, Mexico were, at the time of her field work from 1929–1933, probably unaware that Mexican women gave birth in a reclining position. They had had no opportunity to observe this area of Mexican life, even though Zapotec culture could be said to be in contact with Mexican culture (Parsons 1936:512). In order to assess the possibilities for change in a culture, it is necessary to learn whether or not people have had the opportunity to acquire the ideas necessary for responses to occur.

FACTORS AFFECTING RESPONSES TO CHANGE POSSIBILITIES *

Assuming that people under study have observed actions, utterances, or artifacts which objectify percepts and concepts in the minds of an objectifier or objectifiers and, also, that these experiences have stimulated percepts and concepts in the minds of a respondent or respondents which are similar to those in the minds of objectifiers, the problem is to determine why a respondent accepts or rejects the new ideas. Space prohibits exhaustive treatment of this issue, but some of the crucial factors reviewed by anthropologists will be noted.

In many instances a fundamental issue is the respondent's judgment of the *efficiency* of the novelty in accomplishing whatever is understood to be its use. The ancestors of the present-day Miskito Indians understood well that one of the uses of guns is to kill people, and they found them to be so efficient that they used them with great effect to establish their dominance over the unarmed peoples of the interior (Helms 1971: 15). But the Cheyenne and other Plains Indians did not find the early muzzle-loaders to be very efficient for killing buffalo; so they continued to use the bow and arrow until more effective weapons became available (Hoebel 1978:70).

Many customs are accepted or rejected for reasons other than their efficiency, and an inefficient custom may be adopted on other grounds. Many people have accepted customs on the grounds that they would likely or certainly enable them to realize some goal other than the custom's alleged purpose. Around the world, some have accepted Christianity, not

* Many of the main concepts contained in this and the following section have been adapted from Barnett 1953, especially chapters 4–6 and parts of chapters 10, 11, and 13.

to be saved from hell and separation from God, but because they felt that becoming a Christian would bring them various goods and experiences they desired. As the Samoan chiefs deliberated concerning whether or not to accept Christianity, one of the most common reasons advanced for a favorable response was that they would acquire material possessions like those of the white people (Holmes 1974:60). In other cases, respondents have decided that a new custom would aid them in competition or conflict with a rival. It was the combination of efficiency and advantage in conflict that prompted Miskito acceptance of firearms. This principle that acceptance may occur as a way of realizing something other than the novelty's immediate purpose may be called *instrumentality*. It will be seen as an aspect of several of the factors yet to be mentioned.

Many customs or complexes of customs are accepted *to gain relief from physical, mental, or emotional stress.* People often are open to alternatives that promise relief from unpleasant circumstances or from some aspect of their lifeway that they find burdensome. One of the most widespread sources of stress has been the dominance of some groups over others. In countless instances, aboriginal societies have been exploited and oppressed. War and natural disasters have also brought stress in many places, precipitating major change responses. Anything that is perceived as threatening security may result in change. The launching of the Russian Sputnik in 1957 was perceived as such a great threat that it stimulated a flurry of inventive effort in the American space program as well as a reevaluation of our entire system of formal education.

People often seek relief from feelings of deprivation. In many cases aboriginal societies have acquired desires for goods, services, and experiences enjoyed by a dominant society but either unavailable to the native peoples or denied them. Responses to this kind of deprivation have been of major scope in many places, resulting in social or religious movements to bring about the desired changes. These are explored further in the discussion of consequences of change.

Several influences on responses to change opportunities have to do with one's relationships with other people, subsumed here under the heading of *social pressures*. For one, some changes are advocated and others not, and the very fact of advocacy may make a difference in the response. Many people accept something or pretend to under the pressure of the advocate, though under some conditions advocacy may provoke stronger resistance in the respondent. Often the personality of the advocate or objectifier is a factor, and many people have found themselves accepting something they were uninterested in simply because of the force of a pleasant or persuasive personal manner. Sometimes people accept changes because they are recommended by a relative or friend. Anthropologists have sometimes found that a sequence of acceptances of some customs can be traced from relative to relative. Prestige may also be a factor in one way or another. People who hope to enhance their prestige before others may accept a new custom advocated or practiced by someone who already has high prestige, or they may seek the recognition and admiration that they expect to come with the acceptance of something new or significant. In many instances social pressure may come in the form of majority affiliation. Some people go along with a change because so many others are. As Barnett suggests, majorities are intimidating (1953:328). If respondents are subordinate to someone who advocates change, they often submit to authority accordingly. If someone has the power to impose a penalty on the respondent, either for accepting or failing to accept a change, that may prove to be the deciding factor.

In connection with social pressures for or against change possibilities, the question of whether people feel free to explore and to decide for themselves whether to change is significant. Whole societies and individuals as well may differ in the *amount of freedom allowed for inquiry, creativity, or experimentation* with alien ideas. Totalitarian political units, professional societies, religious groups, and tightly knit small-scale societies are among those which sometimes suppress or limit independent thought in areas where new ideas might undermine conventional standards. This has been true to some extent within medicine as an aspect of American culture. Some types of research and innovation are encouraged, but physicians who pursue some avenues of novelty do so at the risk of their colleagueship and professional reputations. According to Margaret Mead, there is only one area of traditional Samoan culture in which individual variation is encouraged: the dance. In other areas of life the emphasis is on careful conformity to Samoan ways. The result of Samoan modes of enculturation is that the "precocious, the combative, the ambitious are muted, nagged into dullness, until . . . the slowest and steadiest man has gained self-confidence, the gayest and most brilliant has been steadied into reliability" (Mead 1961:311).

During periods of social and political disorganization authoritarian controls may break down, and emphasis may be shifted to the resourcefulness and initiative necessary for readjustment and restoration.

Another factor in change decisions is the question of *mastery*. If a custom is hard for respondents to learn, they may well reject it. In the course of my fieldwork in a Zapotec town of Mexico I contributed to the decision of one man to buy a box camera. He was very interested in using the device to take pictures of people. But when I asked him about it on a return trip a couple of years later, he told me he had gotten rid of it because it was too hard to operate.

Changes cannot occur or be maintained unless the respondents have the necessary *resources*, whether they are social, mental (knowledge), monetary, or material. Many a custom that people desired has been rejected or dropped following initial acceptance because it cost too much money, because supportive social institutions necessary to its adoption and maintainence were lacking, because the necessary knowledge for the custom's performance was absent, or because supplies of various kinds needed for the custom's practice were not available. Presumably, one of the main reasons Miskito seldom if ever tour the United States is for lack of money. A Tarascan Indian of Mexico failed to continue development of a new device for firing pottery kilns because his community lacked the social arrangements for assisting inventors (Foster 1967b:254). And San tribes in Botswana have been unable to continue to use the wells that were drilled for them because they have no source of replacement parts for the pumps. No change can be adopted and sustained if the necessary resources are lacking, a fact that many trying to help deprived groups have failed to take sufficiently into account.

Novel customs are often rejected because of *undesired consequences*. A community of Spanish-speaking farmers in New Mexico initially accepted the idea of raising hybrid corn in place of traditional Indian corn, but this required that they also accept working with tortilla dough of a different consistency or texture than what they were accustomed to—and their tortillas tasted different! Growing hybrid corn was certainly effective for its alleged purpose, the increased yields, but the people were unwilling to endure the different dough consistency and the new taste. After a short trial they returned to raising the low-yielding Indian corn.

The foregoing example also illustrates one of the most fundamental issues in change decisions: *compatability*. Compatability refers to the new custom's agreement or harmony with other elements of the respondent's lifeway. If a proposed trait cannot coexist with present items in the lifeway, items which the people are unwilling or unable to modify or drop, it is likely to be rejected. The Spanish-Americans were unwilling to give up the traditional taste and texture of tortillas.

An impressive example of the compatability issue comes from Indian Guatemala. When anthropologist Ruben Reina first studied Chinautla, a Pokoman-speaking community of Maya Indians near Guatemala City, he concluded that the impact of the city would change Chinautla culture greatly within a few years (1966:xiv). When he returned three years later he found that the community was resisting urban influences stiffly and was being very selective about what they accepted from Guatemalan national culture. They were rejecting much that they found out of harmony with important values that they refused to abandon. In the world view of Chinautla, men are charcoal makers and maize farmers, and women are housekeepers and makers of utilitarian pots. Charcoal making and maize production are firmly linked with their concept of ideal manhood, while production of practical pots and traditional women's activities symbolize ideal womanhood. No other occupational activities carry these meaning (see page 57). During his study in Chinautla Reina found that a young man had turned to the raising of vegetables by methods he had learned while working for a Chinese gardener in Guatemala City. Also, a young woman had taken up the production of artistic animal pottery figurines (Reina 1963:24). There was little difficulty until the young man and his family made arrangements for him to marry the young woman. At that point the adults of Chinautla were confronted with a momentous change possibility. They would have to accept as part of their community life the presence and participation of married adults practicing nontraditional occupations. They would have to abandon the position that the traditional activities were the only proper and acceptable occupations for Chinautlecos and grant that Chinese gardening and pottery figurine production were also compatible with their values. This they refused to do. Rumors about the fitness of the young man to be the husband of the young woman began to be repeated to the man's family, and questions about the woman were also raised. It became apparent to the couple and to their families that they would not be acceptable members of their community if they married and continued their deviant occupations. They did not marry, and, eventually, both of them abandoned their occupations and turned to traditional ways. Their new economic life-styles had been judged incompatible with important ideals in the community culture.

It should be understood that compatibility does not in itself insure change. Rather change cannot occur unless the people find the custom under consideration compatible with those cultural ways of thinking, feeling, and acting that they value and plan to continue. The foregoing example is negative. Had the people been willing to accept the nontraditional occupations, the issue of compatibility would not have arisen and, possibly, no one would have commented on it.

It is also true, however, that compatibility can be positive rather than simply neutral. Helms notes that there were many points of similarity between Moravian Christianity and Miskito Indian values (1971:214). For example, the Miskito emphasized showing respect for relatives, and the Moravians stressed the doctrine of Christian brotherhood and spiritual unity among "brothers" and "sisters" in Christ. Both groups also manifested strong concern for individual welfare. Helms credits much of the success of Moravian missions among the Miskito to this kind of compatibility.

CONSEQUENCES OF CHANGE

The foregoing discussion of change determinants has inevitably included references to consequences of change, but several common results of change are worth special emphasis. These are reinterpretation, syncretism, drift, and functional repercussion.

Reinterpretation

As customs pass from objectifier to respondent they are always at least slightly reworked. When people observe other's behavior they never

Figure 15–2 *Moravian church building in Asang, Nicaragua. There were many points of similarity between Moravian Christianity and Miskito Indian values.*

apprehend precisely what is in the objectifier's mind, and they do not duplicate the behavior exactly when they imitate it. People are unaware of much of this reinterpretation, but it also may be quite intentional and/or obvious, with results that may be both interesting and significant. Cross-cultural reinterpretation of borrowed customs results in large part from the fact that the respondent is refitting the trait to a new cultural context. Especially if the acceptor is unfamiliar with the context in the objectifier's lifeway, he or she may reinterpret a trait in ways that surprise or amuse those who are familiar with it. For instance, American personnel installed flush toilets for the use of a local population in the southern Pacific. Americans would naturally assume that anyone should know what flush toilets are for and use them accordingly, but the islanders used them to wash their feet.

Syncretism

Reinterpretation on a large scale results in cultural syncretism, the formation of cultural complexes which are blends of elements taken from different cultures. Instead of substituting Christianity in its entirety for their pre-Christian religion, the Samoans blended the two sets of beliefs and, among other things, retained many of their minor deities as "devils" in the new Christian theology (Holmes 1974:59). It is also common for people to attach unaccustomed meanings and functions (see page 57) to new forms to produce a new synthesis. The religions of many contemporary Indians of Latin America consist of the Christian saints, God, Christ, the Holy Spirit, the Cross, and other Christian forms linked to pre-Columbian functions and meanings. Though knowing from the works of other anthropologists that I would find this sort of thing among the Zapotec, I was, nevertheless, startled to learn that St. Peter was the god of rain.

Cultural Drift

In a given culture changes of certain kinds often accumulate in a definite direction over an extended time. Often the modifications are either unnoticed or only dimly sensed. They may be detected as significant only as people look back over the years and realize that a change of considerable magnitude has occurred. The changes take place as the proportion of a society's members who practice certain customs increases or decreases and as people perform the customs more frequently than before. Such gradual, directional change results from the presence of shared incentives or goals which affect people's daily choices. Often unwittingly, people choose variations that conform to their shared goals instead of those which do not, giving direction to the course of change.

The late Melville Herskovits interpreted the trend toward going without ties as an example of drift in American culture, and observation of male dress since he commented on the matter over thirty years ago seems to bear him out. Herskovits felt that the shared goal which would account for the drift toward "necktielessness" was a well-established interest in comfort and informality in male dress (1948:582).

Functional Repercussions

It is worth repeating that one of the most significant of all perspectives on the human condition is that the customs that make up any lifeway are interdependent. This is what makes the question of compatibility so important as a determinant of change responses. The principle is so elementary as to strike people as obvious, but its very obviousness may contribute to the abundantly documented fact that reformers and other change-makers often overlook it. People say that they understand that the parts of any lifeway are interrelated, then they behave as though they do not understand. Spicer thinks that Americans act this way because they are trained and educated to specialize narrowly (1952:16). Consequently, they tend to forget that any cultural or ecological system is a unit comprised of linked elements. If a changed custom has many strong links to other customs, either directly or through a chain of traits, a single modification may greatly alter an entire lifeway. The ancestors of the Crow were formerly one with the horticultural Hidatsa, but they resumed a nomadic way of life as the result of the introduction of horses. The acceptance of horse riding made it profitable for the Crow to hunt bison as a major subsistence mode and sparked a virtually endless chain of cultural adaptations, bringing the Crow and other Plains peoples into a lifeway rather greatly different from those of other North American tribes. It is the lifeway white Americans now associate with Indians, but it is atypical and did not exist before the Indians received horses from the Spanish of the American Southwest.

Sometimes the adoption of a single tool or kind of tool has had a chain of effects of considerable cultural significance. The coming of iron adzes, axes, and knives enabled the woodworking of the Northwest Coast Indians to flourish to a degree not possible before. It appears that the large totem poles thought to be so characteristic of the Northwest Coast were not carved until after contacts with Euroamericans, and elaborate masks, carved and strung so that the jaws opened and closed, were also a post-contact development.

Among the Western Dani the coming of Christian missionaries and the availability of Western goods provoked a series of correlated changes, though they had little impact on the Dugum and other Grand Valley Dani. The Western Dani burned their weapons and stopped their warring with one another, stopped greasing their long hair and cut it shorter, dropped their kinship terms, permitted men and women to mingle at public gatherings, began to speak to their in-laws, came to believe that their skins would turn white like those of the Europeans, built new kinds of houses, adopted the belief that they would become immortal if they became Christians, and so forth (O'Brien and Ploeg 1964:285). Many of the new customs, and the elimination of old ones, were not suggested or intended by the missionaries. They stemmed from the kinds of linkages that existed between the missionaries' message as the Dani understood it and other elements of Dani culture.

Revitalization Movements

Around the globe small-scale cultures have undergone extensive acculturation as the result of long continued contact with often dominant and technologically complex civilizations. Often the people are less satisfied with the new way of life than they were with the old, sometimes because of oppression and discrimination and sometimes because they have been unable to acquire goods and life experiences that they have come to desire. When people become dissatisfied with their lot and seek relief, their efforts often take the form of a *revitalization movement,* which has been defined as "a deliberate, organized, conscious effort by members of a society to construct a more satisfying culture " (Wallace 1956:265). Such movements may manifest nativistic or acquisitive features or both. Anthropologists have referred to those dominated by the notion of maintaining or returning to aboriginal ways as *nativistic movements*. One of the best examples of revivalistic nativisim is the Ghost Dance religion, which swept through western American tribes during the last decades of the nineteenth century. Many tribes had reached an acute stage of frustration and despair as the result of the exterminative wars against them and the attempts to civilize the tribes and confine them to reservations. The major prophet of the Ghost Dance predicted exclusion of the whites and called for a return to ceremonial aspects of the old way of life. The widespread acceptance of his doctrines testifies to the appeal of his program.

A nativistic movement of a milder sort has developed among the !Kung and other San who have taken up farm work in the Ghanzi district of western Botswana (Guenther 1976:129). They long for relief from hunger and from the cruelty of their employers, the Africans, the police, and jail. They talk about the old ways with nostalgia and pride and look on their hunting and gathering past as a golden age. Comparatively speaking, this is realistic, since anthropological study has documented the relatively secure and easygoing hunting and gathering life still existing as recently as the 1960s. As an expression of their nativistic orientation, the San of Ghanzi grant great prestige, glamor, and wealth to a religious specialist known as the trance-dancer, whose performances symbolize for them their cultural identity. They are also organizing to demand that the government set aside land for them, permit them to have their own headman, and allow those who want to to return to the hunting and gathering life.

Acquisitive movements may occur when a subordinate group wants more of certain things that only the dominant group can provide. In many parts of the world, so-called *cargo cults* have sprung up, calling for goods and services for which people have acquired tastes as the result of contact. When not enough of what they want is available, or when a previous source of goods dries up, a feeling of deprivation may set in. The reason this type of reaction is called a cargo cult is that a common element of such movements in New Guinea and other Melanesian places is a prediction that a ship will arrive bearing the desired goods. Of course, disillusionment may set in when none arrives, and a state of considerable disorganization may follow. Frequently, a society becomes receptive to new ideas or even a whole new lifeway because of intolerable situations of this kind. One reason the Manus of Admiralty Island welcomed the reform proposals of a man named Paliau was that they had just failed in a cargo cult movement. As the cult spread quickly from village to village the people spoke in tongues, threw their possessions into the ocean, and awaited for the arrival of planes, ships, bulldozers, and the like, which were to revamp their existence. In this state of deprivation the people were more open to Paliau's recommendations to move their old homes on stilts in the lagoon to the land and to abandon their old ceremonial and economic institutions in favor of Western ways (Mead 1964:209).

DIRECTED CHANGE AND APPLIED ANTHROPOLOGY

The principles of cultural dynamics are especially relevant to practical human affairs, because we live in a world that is changing more than ever before, and interaction between culturally different groups is the order of the day. Rapid modes of long distance travel and communication bring culturally different people into contact, increase peoples' awareness of one another's special interests and problems, and force us to work out ways of living and working with culturally different societies with a minimum of friction, violence, and destruction. Some think that Americans of the mid and late seventies have become less concerned than before with understanding and relating to culturally different people in our own and other nations. If this is so, it is a less than realistic development in the light of the increasing need to understand and work effectively with various kinds of people. The situation is complicated by the view of many policy makers and executives that only common sense

Figure 15–3 *San examining Land Rover. We live in a changing world more than ever before, and interaction between culturally different groups is the order of the day. We are forced to work out ways of living and working with culturally different societies.*

is needed to solve human problems and, also, the tendency of Americans to neglect effective planning to cope with cultural dislocations and threats until things reach emergency proportions (Arensberg and Niehoff 1971:230).

Cultural anthropology is especially relevant to modern life because of its comparative, cross-cultural approach and its insights into how cultures work. Culturally different people are interacting with one another, not only across national boundaries, but also within modern nations that include significant class, occupational, ethnic, or tribal differences. The solution of international problems requires that national leaders appreciate and understand how cultural differences affect their efforts; and citizens who select, support, and oppose their governmental leaders can do so intelligently only if they too understand how culture affects human behavior.

In addition there are more people and groups of people than ever before who specialize in helping others achieve their goals and ameliorate their afflictions. If they are to be successful, they, too, must understand cultural processes and the factors governing cross-cultural contacts.

The principles of cultural anthropology may be applied either by professional anthropologists in the employ of public or private agencies or by operational people such as public health workers, medical personnel, diplomats, missionaries, social workers, Peace Corps workers, county agents, and housing authority officials. The work of H. G. Barnett, who was Staff Anthropologist from 1951 to 1953 for the United States Trust Territory of the Pacific Islands, provides an example of professional applied anthropology. His responsibility was to organize and conduct field research and maintain professional relations with specialists wishing to do research in the territory. There also was an anthropologist assigned to each of the five districts of the Trust Territory (Barnett 1956:86). Margaret Kiefer's position as a disaster consultant with Intertect is another example of professional applied anthropology (see page 13).

Applied positions are much less common than academic jobs and tend to last no more than a few years, so most applications of cultural dynamics to human affairs rest in the hands of operational people with training in cultural anthropology. Some have a bachelor's or master's degree, while others have taken special courses or programs. The work of anthropologist James Downs illustrates the application of anthropology through training of operational people. Early in his career he taught a class of student nurses at a university hospital, and since then he has taught anthropology to teachers in the Bureau of Indian Affairs, police officers, and Peace Corps workers (1975:ix).

A number of the principles of change are commonly violated by people in the "helping professions" and by other agents of cultural change. Many change agents are hampered by attitudes of racism and ethnocentrism, causing them to behave toward people in patronizing or other ways which hinder efforts to help them. Frequently they mis-understand the nature of alien customs because they are trying to interpret them through the screen of their own culture rather than by discerning their nature from the perspective of the cultures of which they are part. Often they fail to locate the proper social units and leaders they must work through if they are to work effectively with a group to help solve their problems. And, as noted before, change agents often behave as though they do not realize that a culture is a system of interdependent parts, thereby neglecting to understand social, political, and economic problems in their larger contexts and failing to anticipate and prepare to cope with resource deficiencies, incompatibilities, functional repercussions, revitalization movements, goal-undermining reinterpretations, and the like.

Failure to act on the implications of the functional nature of cultures is well illustrated by the recent comments of T. Graydon Upton to the *Christian Science Monitor* (February 27, 1979). In reference to the Iranian revolution, Upton noted that professionals have long been aware of the inevitability of social and political reactions to intensive accelerated development of the kind that has characterized Iran during recent decades. The nature of these reactions, he points out, requires the analysis of specialists in social, cultural, and religious factors. He further suggests that if several years ago the U.S. government had commissioned a competent research agency to make a forecast of Iranian political developments, including not only economic and political analysts, but a competent social anthropologist, the current developments could have been anticipated and the United States prepared to follow a different course of action. The point is that the conceptual and research tools for better understanding human problems are available, but they are either not used or are used ineptly. One source of concern is that too few administrators, policy makers, and government officials are aware of the value of cultural and cross-cultural perspectives; accordingly, they fail to enlist the expertise of cultural scientists in understanding complex human issues.

When Americans attempt to assist the starving people of an African country to develop a reliable food supply, or when representatives of an American corporation try to develop a market for some product in another country, it is obvious that they are reaching across cultural boundaries and that cross-cultural perspectives are relevant. But Anglo-Americans who work with Hispanic Americans to help solve their educational problems, city officials who work with ghetto blacks on housing and job matters, and American Indian organizations seeking justice before the law from white Americans are just as surely reaching across cultural boundaries. Misunderstanding of cultural differences and how cultures work is surely one of the major reasons for the friction and failure that so often result from such efforts.

Anthropologists learn about human nature by studying human characteristics and customs in every possible time and place, seeking to understand customs and complexes of customs by discovering how they function and have meaning within the cultures and ecosystems within which they operate. Since this approach to understanding human behavior does not come naturally and easily to most humans, anthropology has an important message to communicate and a valuable role to play in the understanding and solution of human problems.

APPENDIX A
STUDYING
CULTURAL WAYS

Many introductory texts include chapter summaries and review questions, but my conviction is that it is most desirable for beginning college students and other adults to possess the ability to recognize the main points of academic writings and discern how those points relate to one another. Since many students have not been taught this skill, and since it can be learned quickly, I have provided instructions in this appendix on how to analyze a writing for its emphasized ideas.

A legitimate way to learn from reading is to absorb the concepts and data that come easily to us because our pre-existing concepts and frames of reference prepare us for them. We learn much in this way, but we may fail to receive important messages from writers if we limit our learning to this mode. Though many textbooks may have summaries and review questions, and instructors may tell students what to learn from their books, the most valuable scholarly works lack these aids. In our complex society the well-informed person must develop the ability to recognize what writers are emphasizing—what they are trying to put across to their readers.

Anyone who wishes to find out what an author is trying to communicate can do so by successfully pursuing two goals. One is to discover what problems (questions) are being discussed; the other is to find out what the author's answers to those questions are. In addition, if you desire to confine your learning to the emphasized points, a third goal—distinguishing the strongly emphasized points from incidental, tangential, and other minor concepts and data—becomes important. Within the scope of a course, for example, the instructor can choose to test the students mainly on the most strongly emphasized points, and students who pay special attention to them can be confident of performing well. This is possible because the students, as they decide what is important enough to learn, use the same clues to importance as the instructor uses when deciding what questions to ask. The preparatory task, then, is to learn how to identify problems and their answers and to distinguish those which are emphasized from those which are not.

Basic to accomplishing these three goals is the analysis of how the writer has structured a written selection. To analyze the presentation structure, answer several simple questions.

1. What is the central idea or problem of each paragraph?
2. How do the paragraphs relate to one another?
3. What problem (question) is stated or implied by a paragraph, a block of paragraphs, a section of a selection, or the entire chapter or article?
4. What is the author's answer to the problem?
5. Does the writer announce that he or she views something as being important?
6. Does the author use devices—such as numbers, section headings, italics or bold print—to emphasize points and reveal the structure?
7. Are there any points to which the writer devotes more space than other points?
8. Are there any summary statements?
9. Are there ideas that are repeated, perhaps several times?

Written selections often appear to students to be unintegrated jumbles of facts and ideas, but consciously keeping questions such as the foregoing in mind as one selects what to learn from a reading can help greatly.

Many students can figure out how to answer these questions, but those who want help can consult an instructor or a more experienced student or read a book on studying written material such as some of the booklets in the Essential Skills Series by Walter Pauk. *Getting the Main Point: Separating the Wheat from the Chaff* and *Perceiving Structures: How Are the Ideas Organized?* are among the most relevant of these helpful works.

For those who would like some guidance keyed to this text, here is a brief analysis of the structure of Chapter 1.

First, by looking at the main headings in the table of contents you learn that the chapter deals with the uniqueness of anthropology and anthropolgy's status in the changing occupational scene. Accordingly, you can commit yourself initially to two study goals: to find out how the author thinks anthropology is unique and what the relationship is between anthropology and the current occupational situation. Then, under the heading THE UNIQUENESS OF ANTROPOLOGY you find these subheadings: Physical Anthropology, Cultural Anthropology, and Some Newer Anthropological Specialties. You can establish three more study objectives from these headings. You want to find answers to three problems: (1) What is physical anthropology? (2) What is cultural anthropology? and (3) What newer anthropological specialities are discussed?

With these objectives in mind, you can tackle the task of discovering the nature of anthropology by reading the chapter. As you read strive to understand how each sentence is given meaning by the immediately previous statements. Then, at the end of each paragraph, you should be able to pause and mentally summarize the main thrust of the paragraph. In this case, the point has been made that anthropologists study many kinds of things about humankind because of their ideal of trying to understand human nature by drawing together and interrelating information on every facet of the human condition from every possible kind of human group. Do not overlook the presence of a couple of indicators of emphasis in this paragraph. One is "The most important characteristic of anthropology is . . . ," and the other is the italicization of the term "holistic ideal." Accordingly, you should set yourself the goal of learning what the author thinks is the most important characteristic of anthropology and what the term "holistic ideal" means to him. In this case, the answer to both problems is the same, and both answers concern the main idea of the paragraph.

As you proceed with the next paragraph, notice that it builds on the first, since it mentions the diversity of anthropology and reiterates the holistic ideal concept. When you finish the paragraph, you can see that the major problem is why and how anthropologists try to keep their diverse field unified, and in the process of answering this question, you'll find that anthropology is defined in terms of two orientations. From this and the preceding paragraph, then, you should learn how anthropologists approach the study of human nature, why they approach it that way, a definition of anthropology, and the meaning of the concepts of biocultural orientation and comparative orientation.

The final paragraph continues the theme by mentioning three ways that anthropologists try to keep their field from fragmenting. When you have completed the three introductory paragraphs, you should have a sense of the unity of the introductory section as having answered the problems, "How do anthropologists approach the study of human nature?", "What is the field like in relation to this approach?" and "How does the definition of anthropology reflect the approach?"

When you move to the next section note that the question of how anthropology is unique is answered in a general way in the first sentence. Also note that the section is related to the previous one in that it elaborates at length on the biocultural and comparative aspects of anthropology. Along the way several problems are brought up and answered. The problem of the first paragraph is how anthropologists use the biocultural approach and why. The next paragraph continues that same problem, so it is a continuation of the first. The answer to the first problem is that anthropologists try to consider both genetically determined and socially learned elements of human nature, avoiding exclusively biological or entirely cultural explanations, since, for one thing, this helps avoid the error of giving too much credit to biological factors. This error is illustrated by reference to the notion that children should look like their parents, that blacks have unique inherited abilities, and the current tendency of some scholars to explain too much biologically. The third paragraph of the section is tied to the previous two paragraphs in that it considers the other possible consequence of failing to use the biocultural approach. The problem is whether or not it is possible to overlook biological influences, giving too much credit to cultural factors. The answer is yes, and an illustration is given.

The first three paragraphs of this section hang together in that they stress the biocultural aspect of anthropology. The fourth paragraph turns again to the comparative aspect. The problem posed in the paragraph is how anthropologists apply the comparative orientation to avoid the erroneous notion that American and European traits are universal or natural, and two examples are given.

The final paragraph sets the stage for the first subdivision under the uniqueness of anthropology. The challenge is to see how the biocultural approach is reflected in the division of anthropology into subareas, and the answer is that physical anthropology deals mainly with genetically inherited aspects of human nature while cultural anthropology is concerned with socially acquired aspects. In addition, the question of how the comparative approach is applied in both physical and cultural anthropology is dealt with. So the last part of the paragraph is a repetition and elaboration of points made earlier.

The foregoing comments illustrate how written material can be studied thoughtfully so that the student identifies problems under discussion, finds the answers to the problems, and detects the development of major concepts and how those concepts are built up from paragraph to paragraph and section to section. Instead of facing rote learning of a jumble of unrelated pieces, the student can see how ideas relate to one another, with each idea making sense in terms of the larger context. By applying this approach to the rest of the chapter and the book, you can identify the things that are important to learn. When people apply this approach, rather than relying on review questions and lists of things to learn, they develop the ability to handle the many scholarly works whose authors assume that their readers have the intelligence and skill to recognize the main concepts that they are trying to communicate.

For the rest of Chapter 1, I will outline the major problems.

Under physical anthropology, the first problem is, "What two lines of investigation pursued during the decades before anthropology existed eventually became major concerns of twentieth-century physical anthropology?" They are biological evolution and the physical characteristics of non-Europeans. Note that the definition of physical anthropology is reinforced by the notation that both areas are concerned mainly with inherited biological features.

The next paragraphs present a general problem, "What are the subdivisions of physical anthropology, and how are they defined?" They are the fields indicated by their italicized names. For each of these the question to be answered is, "What is the problem and/or subject matter of this speciality?" Under comparative human biology, another problem is dealt with briefly: "What is the physical anthropologist's attitude toward the race concept, and why?" The answer is that there is so much overlapping of physical characteristics that anthropologists have largely given up trying to put people into racial categories, and some have rejected the race concept.

The paragraph on human genetics explores the problem of why that has become significant in anthropology and how it is used. A similar question is dealt with in the paragraph on comparative primatology.

Under the next section, the cross-cultural approach is introduced and defined, and the problem of what two forms this orientation took in the days before anthropology became a single field is discussed. Therefore, the reader should learn that amateur archaeology and interest in the lifeways of so-called primitives became the basis for the two main branches of modern cultural anthropology: prehistoric archaeology and ethnology. The question is raised as to why both of these belong under cultural anthropology, and the answer reiterates the fact that cultural anthropology has to do with socially learned traits rather than with biological factors.

The next paragraph deals with the problem, "How is ethnology defined?" You know that the answer should be learned, because ethnology was said to be one of the two main branches of cultural anthropology and, also, because this book is about cultural anthropology. The general theme of the paragraph is how archaeology and ethnology manifest the cross-cultural approach. On page 7 further emphasis to the importance of knowing what ethnology means is given by the statement that this book is on ethnology. This is followed by the generalization that ethnology can be divided into specialties in different ways, with an indication of the first way it can be divided. This implies that an additional way or ways will be indicated, and a skimming of the next few paragraphs confirms it. This reveals a general problem for study, "In what ways can ethnology be divided into specialties?" The twofold answer is (1) by aspects of culture which ethnologists choose to focus on, and (2) according to problems or sets of problems on the nature of cultures. Other problems are, "What specialties result from the first way of dividing ethnology?" and "What is social anthropology, and how does it fit into ethnology?"

From the paragraphs on the subdivision of ethnology according to problems on the nature of cultures you can recognize a series of questions concerning what the various specialties are, what problems they study, and what they are trying to accomplish.

Note that linguistic anthropology, discussed on page 9, is not listed as one of the specialties according to problems on the nature of cultures but is explicitly indicated to have a separate status as a third major area of cultural anthropology in addition to archaeology and ethnology. The problem implied by this is, "What are the three subdivisions of cultural anthropology?"

Following the paragraph on linguistic anthropology it is noted that the entire field may be divided into four major divisions or specialties, and the problem is what they are. The final paragraph on cultural anthropology is a repetition and summary of key ideas in the section on the uniqueness of anthropology.

The general problem of the final section is, "What newer specialties have emerged as anthropology has grown and changed according to its biocultural and comparative emphases?" The ones discussed are medical anthropology, nutritional anthropology, urban anthropology, and educational anthropology, and a major study objective should be to develop one's understanding of what each is about. Several subproblems introduced in the course of the discussion should be identified and answered. For example, a major problem under urban anthropology is, "How did this field which formerly showed little concern with urban life come to include urban anthropology as one of its major specialties?" The answer is that remote communities traditionally studied by anthropologists became subject to urban industrial societies and many moved to urban locations, and, as they did, anthropologists continued to study them. The section ends with an italicized statement on how the unique nature of anthropology has led to the newer kinds of specialties.

The main problem of the final section is, "How are anthropologists reacting to the changing occupational situation in the United States?" A subproblem is what about the occupational situation causes these reactions. Another is what three anthropological careers illustrate these reactions and, also, what the examples illustrate about anthropology and anthropologists. As in other places, the importance and interrelationships of the answers to the last problem are indicated by an enumerated listing.

Beginning on page 14 the question of the kind and amount of training needed to apply anthropological perspectives in one's career is briefly explored. The last paragraph in the chapter builds on this subject by raising the problem of whether anthropology is no more than an interesting subject to study. The question is answered by reiterating what has been emphasized in much of the chapter—that anthropological study and the field's unique perspectives are relevant to daily life.

This review may indicate to some that this approach expects too much of the student. Two responses seem in order. One is that in many conventionally taught university courses students make their way mainly by mastering their lecture notes and completing assigned projects. Relatively speaking, the reading assignments commonly are slighted. Since few students get into the reading deeply, even those who neglect it may do well in a course as compared with the class as a whole. The result is that educators are, perhaps unwittingly, teaching students to learn mainly by listening to lectures and giving them little opportunity or encouragement to develop the ability to handle journal articles and books. Yet these will be major sources of continuing education after the students leave the lecture halls. In the light of this, the possibility of teaching courses by modes which encourage students to learn how to identify problems and answers in written material might be in order.

My second response is that, by this method, there remain many things in the material that one need not learn. The task, again, is to identify and learn *emphasized* concepts and information. Much tangential and supportive material will be run through the student's mind as a means of absorbing the main notions, but no special learning effort need be applied to the minor points. The main messages are our concern. Moreover, the student who is familiar with the technique of sorting main ideas from minor points saves time as compared with the wastefulness of repeated readings, detailed outlining, and other study approaches which may miss the main emphases.

Here are some things in the first chapter that need not be learned because they are not emphasized.

Anthropologists have studied Navajos in Los Angeles.
The author of *The Naked Ape* is Desmond Morris.
Bronislaw Malinowski studied the Trobriand Islanders.
Zinjanthropus is among the many noted fossil forms studied by
  human palaentologists.

Lorises are primates.

Manuel Hidalgo used a banner with the image of Our Lady of Guadalupe on it.

James Fitting was once chairman of the department of anthropology at Case Western Reserve University

Aymará women sometimes kick one another's stoves apart when they quarrel.

These and many other minor points are in the chapter only to assist the student in understanding more important notions. Yet, some students try to learn these kinds of things and miss some of the main thrusts.

For the busy student there are also what may be called things of "second level importance." These items are more important than the kinds of things just listed, but they are not emphasized nearly as much as the major ideas. In studying you should always be sure to learn *all* of the ideas of top-level importance, and if there is time you may go on to learn as many of the lesser concepts as possible. It doesn't work well to spend most of the time on lesser points and miss the main ones.

For illustration, here are some of the "second level" points of the chapter:

Races are sometimes defined as populations sufficiently isolated from others that there is little or no exchange of genes among them.

The study of cultural ecology draws anthropology into interdisciplinary endeavors.

Medical anthropology falls under both physical and cultural anthropology.

Urban anthropologists are proposing that cities be studied holistically.

Any of these could be emphasized, and are, in some anthropology books, but in this chapter of this book they are not among the most strongly emphasized ideas. Instructors normally should test students largely on the top-level points, only to a limited extent on second-level concepts, and not at all on the most minor points.

Some students, for whatever reason, already have the ability to discern emphasized concepts in written material. The foregoing remarks are for the many that twenty years of teaching have taught me have not developed these capacities.

APPENDIX B
SOURCES OF NINE
CULTURES

An ethnographic summary for each culture, if available, is indicated for the benefit of those who would like to read them in connection with *Cultural Ways* for a more balanced view of the culture. Study questions for integrating these readings with *Cultural Ways* may be found in the Instructor's Manual.

!KUNG SAN

Ethnographic Summary

"The !Kung Bushmen of the Kalahari Desert." Pages 91–110 in *Profiles in Ethnology*, 3rd ed., Elman R. Service.

Other Works

Kalahari Hunter-Gatherers: Studies of the Kung San and Their Neighbors, Richard B. Lee and Irven DeVore, eds.
The !Kung of Nyae Nyae, Lorna Marshall

BASSERI

Nomads of South Persia: The Basseri Tribe of the Khamseh Confederacy, Frederik Barth.

CROW

Ethnographic Summary

"The Crows of the Western Plains." Pages 264–290 in *Our Primitive Contemporaries*, George Peter Murdock.

Other Works

The Crow Indians, Robert H. Lowie
The Material Culture of the Crow Indians, Robert H. Lowie.
Social Life of the Crow Indians, Robert H. Lowie.
Societies of the Crow, Hidatsa and Mandan Indians, Robert H. Lowie.

DANI

Ethnographic Summary

Gardens of War: Life and Death in the New Guinea Stone Age, Robert Gardner and Karl G. Heider.

Other Works

The Dugum Dani: A Papuan Culture in the Highlands of West New Guinea, Karl G. Heider
Grand Valley Dani: Peaceful Warriors, Karl G. Heider

MISKITO

Ethnographic Summary

The Health and Customs of the Miskito Indians of Northern Nicaragua: Interrelationships in a Medical Program, Michael Pijoan, pages 10–26.

Other Works

Asang: Adaptations to Culture Contact in a Miskito Community, Mary W. Helms
Ethnographical Survey of the Miskito and Sumu Indians of Honduras and Nicaragua, Edward Conzemius

NUER

Ethnographic Summary

"The Nuer of the Upper Nile River." Pages 157–175 in Profiles in Ethnology, 3rd ed., Elman R. Service

Other Works

> *Kinship and Marriage Among the Nuer,* E. E. Evans-Pritchard.
> *The Nuer,* E. E. Evans-Pritchard.
> *Nuer Religion,* E. E. Evans-Pritchard.

NYORO

> *The Bakitara or Banyoro: The First Part of the Report of The Mackie Ethnological Expedition to Central Africa,* John Roscoe
> *Bunyoro: An African Kingdom,* John Beattie
> *The Nyoro State,* John Beattie

SAMOANS

> "The Samoans." Pages 282–312, in *Cooperation and Competition among Primitive Peoples,* Margaret Mead

Other Works

> *Coming of Age in Samoa,* Margaret Mead
> *Samoan Village,* Lowell Holmes
> *Social Organization of Manua,* Margaret Mead

UNITED STATES
Ethnographic Summary

> "American Cultural Values" (Chapter 9) in *Introducing Social Change: A Manual for Community Development,* 2nd ed., Conrad M. Arensberg and Arthur H. Niehoff

Other Works

> *The Cultural Experience: Ethnography in Complex Society,* James P. Spradley and David W. McCurdy
> *The Nacirema: Readings on American Culture,* James P. Spradley and Michael R. Rynkiewich

APPENDIX C
BOOKS FOR
FURTHER READING

The following highly selective sample may prove useful to those who wish to consult full-length works on cultural anthropology and its major specialties. Complete citations can be found in the bibliography.

ANTHROPOLOGY

Bidney, David, 1967. *Theoretical Anthropology,* 2nd ed. A commentary on various modes of anthropological thought.

Dubbs, Patrick J. and Daniel D. Whitney, 1980. Cultural Contexts: An Introduction to the Anthropological Perspective. An introduction incorporating problems and field exercises.

Eames, Edward and Judith Granich Goode, 1977. *Anthropology of the City: An Introduction to Urban Anthropology*. An overview.

Fried, Morton H., 1972. *The Study of Anthropology*. A look at anthropology as an occupation.

Harris, Marvin, 1968. *The Rise of Anthropological Theory*. A comprehensive review and critique of anthropological approaches from the discipline's beginnings to the present.

Hays, Hoffman R., 1964. *From Ape to Angel*. Summarizes the contributions of many anthropologists to the development of the field.

Kessler, Evelyn S., 1974. *Anthropology: The Humanizing Process*. A broad overview of the four major areas of anthropology. Directed toward beginning students.

Langness, L. L., 1974. *The Study of Culture*. A good brief survey of the contributions of major theorists and schools of thought in cultural anthropology.

Leaf, Murry J. et al, 1974. *Frontiers of Anthropology: An Introduction to Anthropological Thinking*. Several anthropologists introduce current developments in all major areas of the discipline, basing their presentations on their own research.

Roberts, Joan I. and Sherrie K. Akinsanya. *Educational Patterns and Cultural Configurations: The Anthropology of Education*. Studies in educational anthropology.

Spindler, George D. and Louise Spindler, eds. Case studies in Cultural

Anthropology. A growing number of brief paperback ethnographies on cultures from all parts of the world. Over ninety were available in 1979.

Tax, Sol and Leslie Freeman, 1976. *Horizons of Anthropology,* 2nd ed. Young anthropologists indicate significant developments in various specialties.

CULTURE

Freilich, Morris, ed., 1972. *The Meaning of Culture: A Reader in Cultural Anthropology.* A collection of statements on the nature of culture by leading anthropologists, including a final synthesis by the author.

Kroeber, Alfred L. and Clyde Kluckhohn, eds., 1952. *Culture: A Critical Review of Concepts and Definitions.* The most comprehensive examination of how anthropologists have defined and used the culture concept.

FIELD METHODS

Beattie, John, 1965. *Understanding an African Kingdom: Bunyoro.* Beattie's account of his field work among the Nyoro.

Chagnon, Napoleon, 1974. *Studying the Yanomamo.* Chagnon's account of his field study of the Yanomamo.

Edgerton, Robert B. and L. L. Langness, 1974. *Methods and Styles in the Study of Culture.* A survey of how anthropologists collect and process cultural data.

Freilich, Morris, ed., 1977. *Marginal Natives: Anthropologists in the Field.* Ethnographers report on their methods and experiences.

Pelto, Pertti, 1978. *Anthropological Research: The Structure of Inquiry.* A text for the training of ethnographers and research methodologists.

Spindler, George D. *Being an Anthropologist: Fieldwork in Eleven Cultures.*

Williams, Thomas Rhys, 1967. *Field Methods in the Study of Culture.* A brief, systematic treatment of the major phases and problems of ethnographic work.

LANGUAGE IN CULTURE

Burling, Robbins, 1970. *Man's Many Voices: Language in its Cultural Context.* Emphasizes language in relation to other aspects of culture.

Gleason, Henry A., Jr., 1961. *An Introduction to Descriptive Linguistics,* rev. ed. Sound and well-balanced introduction to the structure of languages, and not too difficult.

Hymes, Dell, ed., 1964. *Language in Culture and Society*. A comprehensive treatment of ethnolinguistic problems. A book of readings integrated by the author.

TECHNOLOGY

Sayce, R. U., 1933. *Primitive Arts and Crafts*. A review of the technology of nonliterate groups.

Spier, Robert F. G., 1970. *From the Hand of Man: Primitive and Preindustrial Technologies*. A brief description of the main nonindustrial manufacturing techniques.

ECONOMIC ORGANIZATION

Dalton, George, ed., 1976. *Tribal and Peasant Economies: Readings in Economic Anthropology*.

Herskovits, Melville J., 1952. *Economic Anthropology*. A good general work on the economic life of nonliterate groups.

LeClair, Edward E., Jr., and Harold K. Schneider, eds., 1968. *Economic Anthropology: Readings in Theory and Analysis*.

Nash, Manning, 1966. *Primitive and Peasant Economic Systems*. A brief review of economic anthropology.

SOCIAL ORGANIZATION

Bohannan, Paul, 1963. *Social Organization*. A perceptive statement of the range and variety of social arrangements.

Bohannan, Paul and John Middleton, eds., 1968. *Kinship and Social Organization*. A collection of readings.

Cohen, Ronald and John Middleton, eds., 1967. *Comparative Political Systems: Studies in the Politics of Pre-Industrial Societies*.

Eisenstadt, S. N., ed., 1971. *Political Sociology*. A large collection of cross-cultural readings, including a chapter on nonliterate political organization.

Fox, Robin, 1967. *Kinship and Marriage: An Anthropological Perspective*. A brief, highly readable treatment.

Hoebel, E. Adamson, 1968. *The Law of Primitive Man: A Study in Comparative Legal Dynamics*. Defines law and its functions and indicates the range and variety of nonliterate legal customs.

Keesing, Roger, 1975. *Kinship and Social Structure*. A brief treatment incorporating case materials from a number of cultures.

Kessler, Evelyn, 1976. *Women: An Anthropological View*.

Murdock, George P., 1949. *Social Structure*. An important, detailed analysis of kinship arrangements.

Pospisil, Leopold, 1978. *The Ethnology of Law: A Comparative Theory*. Sets forth a cross-cultural theory of law.

Schusky, Ernest L., 1972. *Manual of Kinship Analysis,* 2nd ed. Brief and effective explication of basic principles of kinship.

Swartz, Marc J. et al., eds., 1966. *Political Anthropology*. A collection of readings.

RITUAL

Moore, Sally Falk and Barbara G. Meyerhoff, eds., 1978. *Secular Ritual.* The nature and functions of nonreligious ritual in various cultures.

Turner, Victor, 1974. *Dramas, Fields, and Metaphors: Symbolic Action in Human Society*. One of several books by Turner on the symbolic functions of ritual in human society.

RELIGION

Howells, William W., 1948. *The Heathens: Primitive Man and His Religions*. An easy-to-read account of the range and variety of nonliterate religious beliefs and practices.

Lessa, William A. and Evon Z. Vogt, eds., 1979. *Reader in Comparative Religion: An Anthropological Approach,* 4th ed.

Middleton, John, ed., 1976a. *Gods and Rituals: Readings in Religious Beliefs and Practices*.

Middleton, John, ed., 1976b. *Magic, Witchcraft and Curing*. A collection of readings.

Norbeck, Edward, 1974. *Religion in Human Life*. A good general statement on religion as an aspect of culture.

IDEOLOGY

Diamond, Stanley, ed., 1964. *Primitive Views of the World*. A collection of readings.

Edel, May and Abraham Edel, 1970. *Anthropology and Ethics: The Quest for Moral Understanding*. Analyzes the range and variety of ethical principles and explores their implications.

Forde, C. Daryll, ed., 1954. *African Worlds: Studies in the Cosmological and Social Values of African Peoples*. Presents the world views of nine African groups.

Radin, Paul, 1955. *Primitive Man as Philosopher*, rev. ed. A sound presentation of the modes and content of nonliterate thought.

THE ARTS

Adam, Leonhard, 1963. *Primitive Art*. One of the best general introductions.

Dundes, Alan, ed., 1965. *The Study of Folklore*. A collection of readings.

Lomax, Alan, 1978. *Folk Song Style and Culture*. Relates music styles and dancing modes to other aspects of culture.

Merriam, Alan P., 1964. *The Anthropology of Music*. Explores the problems and findings of ethnomusicology. Emphasizes linkages between music and other aspects of culture.

Nettl, Bruno, 1956. *Music in Primitive Culture*. Explores the range and variety of musical forms.

Royce, Anya Peterson, 1977. *The Anthropology of the Dance*. Explores the place of the dance within the context of culture.

Smith, Marian W., ed., 1957. *The Artist in Tribal Society*. A symposium on the functions of art within cultures.

Thompson, Stith, 1946. *The Folk Tale*. Explores the range and variety of folktales and approaches to their study.

THE LIFE-CYCLE (THE INDIVIDUAL IN CULTURE)

Barnouw, Victor, 1979. *Culture and Personality*, 3rd ed. A general review.

Ford, Clellan S., 1945. *A Comparative Study of Human Reproduction*. Explores the range and variety of customs concerning menstruation, coitus, conception, pregnancy, childbirth, and infanthood.

Hunt, Robert C., ed., 1976. *Personalities and Cultures: Readings in Psychological Anthropology*.

Landy, David, 1977. *Culture, Disease, and Healing: Studies in Medical Anthropology*. An integrated collection of many of the most important studies in medical anthropology.

Spindler, George D., ed., 1979. *The Making of Psychological Anthropology*. An up-to-date overview of the development and major contributions to the study of individuals in culture.

CULTURAL DYNAMICS

Arensberg, Conrad M. and Arthur H. Niehoff, 1964. *Introducing Social Change: A Manual for Americans Overseas*.

Barnett, H. G., 1953. *Innovation: The Basis of Cultural Change.* Detailed analysis of the processes by which cultures change.

Bee, Robert L., 1974. *Patterns and Processes: An Introduction to Anthropological Strategies for the Study of Sociocultural Change.* A survey of the various approaches to change study which have been and are used by anthropologists.

Clifton, James A., ed., 1970. *Applied Anthropology: Readings in the Uses of the Science of Man.*

Foster, George M., 1973. *Traditional Societies and Technological Change.* Explores the barriers and stimuli to change as well as approaches to planned change.

Herskovits, Melville, 1964. *Cultural Dynamics.* A general view.

Spicer, Edward H., ed., 1952. *Human Problems in Technological Change.* Case studies on introduced change with analysis in terms of basic principles of change.

Woods, Clyde M., 1975. *Culture Change.* A very brief sketch of the principles of change and their practical applications.

BIBLIOGRAPHY

Adam, Leonard, 1963. *Primitive Art,* rev. ed. Harmondsworth, Middlesex: Penguin Books. Ltd.

Adam, Leonard, 1947. "Virilocal and Uxorilocal." *American Anthropologist* 49 (4), part 1:678.

Apodaca, Anacleto, 1952. "Corn and Custom: The Introduction of Hybrid Corn to Spanish American Farmers in New Mexico." In *Human Problems in Technological Change: A Casebook,* edited by Edward H. Spicer. New York: Russell Sage Foundation.

Arensberg, Conrad M. and Arthur H. Niehoff, 1971. *Introducing Social Change: A Manual for Americans Overseas,* 2nd ed. Chicago: Aldine-Atherton Press, Inc.

Barnett, Homer G., 1956. *Anthropology in Administration.* Evanston, Ill.: Row, Peterson and Company.

Barnett, Homer G., 1953. *Innovation: The Basis of Cultural Change.* New York: McGraw-Hill Book Company.

Barnouw, Victor, 1979. *Culture and Personality,* 3rd ed. Homewood, Ill.: The Dorsey Press.

Barnouw, Victor, 1963. *Culture and Personality.* Homewood, Ill.: The Dorsey Press.

Barth, Fredrik, 1961. *Nomads of South Persia.* Boston: Little, Brown and Company.

Bascom, William R., 1955. "Urbanization among the Yoruba." *American Journal of Sociology* 60(5): 446–454.

Bastide, Roger, 1973. *Applied Anthropology,* translated by Alice L. Norton. New York: Harper & Row, Inc.

Beattie, John, 1971. *The Nyoro State.* London: Oxford University Press.

Beattie, John, 1965. *Understanding an African Kingdom: Bunyoro.* New York: Holt, Rinehart and Winston.

Beattie, John, 1963. "Sorcery on Bunyoro." In *Witchcraft and Sorcery in East Africa,* edited by John Middleton and E. H. Winter. London: Routledge & Kegan Paul.

Beattie, John, 1960. *Bunyoro: An African Kingdom.* New York: Holt, Rinehart and Winston.

Beattie, John, 1959. "Rituals of Nyoro Kinship." *Africa: Journal of the International African Institute* 29(2): 134–145.

Beattie, John, 1957. "Nyoro Kinship." *Africa: Journal of the International African Institute* 27(4): 317–339.

Bee, Robert L., 1974. *Patterns and Processes: An Introduction to Anthropological Strategies for the Study of Sociocultural Change.* New York: Macmillan and Company.

Benedict, Ruth, 1946. *The Chrysanthemum and the Sword.* Boston: Houghton Mifflin Company.

Benedict, Ruth, 1934. *Patterns of Culture*. New York: Houghton Mifflin Company.

Berlin, Brent, Dennis E. Breedlove, and Peter H. Raven, 1974. *Principles of Tzeltal Plant Classification: An Introduction to the Botanical Ethnography of a Mayan-speaking Community of Highland Chiapas*. New York: Academic Press, Inc.

Bernard, H. Russell and Willis E. Sibley, 1975. *Anthropology and Jobs: A Guide for Undergraduates*. Washington, D.C.: American Anthropological Association.

Bidney, David, 1967. *Theoretical Anthropology*, 2nd ed. New York: Columbia University Press.

Boas, Franz, 1907. *The Eskimo of Baffin Land and Hudson Bay*. Bulletin of the American Museum of Natural History, no. 15. Washington, D.C.: Government Printing Office.

Bohannan, Paul, 1963. *Social Anthropology*. New York: Holt, Rinehart and Winston.

Bolton, Ralph, 1973. "Aggression and Hypoglycemia Among the Qolla: A Study in Psychobiological Anthropology." *Ethnology: An International Journal of Cultural and Social Anthropology* 12(3): 227–257.

Bowers, Alfred W., 1965. *Hidatsa Social and Ceremonial Organization*. Smithsonian Institution, Bureau of American Ethnology, Bulletin 194. Washington, D.C.: U.S. Government Printing Office.

Braidwood, Robert J., 1967. *Prehistoric Men*, 7th ed. Glenview, Ill.: Scott, Foresman and Company.

Bromley, H. Myron, 1961. *The Phonology of Lower Grand Valley Dani: A Comparative Structural Study of Skewed Phonemic Patterns*. Verhandelingen van Het Koninklijk Instituut voor Tall-, Land-, en Volkenkunde, Deel 34. 'S-Gravenhage—Martinus Nijhoff.

Brues, Alice, 1959. "The Spearman and the Archer." *American Anthropologist* 61(3): 458–469.

Buck, P. H. (Te Rangi Hiroa), 1930. *Samoan Material Culture*. Bernice P. Bishop Museum Bulletin 75. Honolulu: Bernice P. Bishop Museum.

Burleson, Noel-David, 1978. "Profile of an Anthropologist." *Anthropology Newsletter*. Washington, D.C.: American Anthropological Association.

Burling, Robbins, 1970. *Man's Many Voices: Language in Its Cultural Context*. New York: Holt, Rinehart and Winston.

Burling, Robbins, 1962. "Maximization Theories and the Study of Economic Anthropology." *American Anthropologist* 64(4): 802–821.

Chagnon, Napoleon A., 1977. *Yanomamo: The Fierce People*, 2nd ed. New York: Holt, Rinehart and Winston.

Chagnon, Napoleon A., 1974. *Studying the Yanomamo: Studies in Anthropological Method*. New York: Holt, Rinehart and Winston.

Chapple, Elliot D. and Carleton S. Coon, 1942. *Principles of Anthropology*. New York: Henry Holt and Company.

Clark, J. Desmond, 1970. *The Prehistory of Africa.* London: Thames and Hudson, Ltd.

Clifton, James A., ed., 1970. *Applied Anthropology: Readings in the Uses of the Science of Man.* Boston: Houghton Mifflin Company.

Clinard, Marshall B., 1962. "The Public Drinking House and Society." In *Society, Culture, and Drinking Patterns,* edited by David J. Pittman and Charles R. Snyder. Carbondale and Edwardsville: Southern Illinois University Press.

Cohen, Ronald and John Middleton, eds., 1967. *Comparative Political Systems: Studies in the Politics of Pre-Industrial Societies.* Garden City, N.Y.: Natural History Press.

Coleman, Richard P. and Bernice L. Neugarten, 1971. *Social Status in the City.* San Francisco: Jossey-Bass, Inc.

Colton, Harold S., 1959. *Hopi Kachina Dolls: With a Key to Their Indentification.* Albuquerque: University of New Mexico Press.

Conklin, Harold C., 1955. "Hanunoo Color Categories." *Southwestern Journal of Anthropology* 11(4).: 339–344.

Conzemius, Eduard, 1932. *Ethnographical Survey of the Miskito and Sumu Indians of Honduras and Nicaragua.* Smithsonian Institution, Bureau of American Ethnology, Bulletin 106. Washington, D.C.: U.S. Government Printing Office.

Dalton, George, 1965. "Primitive Money." *American Anthropologist* 67(1): 44–65.

Dalton, George, 1961. "Economic Theory and Primitive Society." *American Anthropologist* 63(1): 1–23.

Diamond, Stanley, ed., 1964. *Primitive Views of the World.* New York: Columbia University Press.

Doke, C. M., 1936. "Games, Plays and Dances of the Khomani Bushmen." *Bantu Studies* 10(4): 461–471.

Downs, James F., 1975. *Cultures in Crisis,* 2nd ed. Beverly Hills: Glencoe Press, Inc.

Dozier, Edward P., 1966. *Hano: A Tewa Indian Community in Arizona.* New York: Holt, Rinehart and Winston.

Driver, Harold E., 1969. *Indians of North America,* 2nd ed. Chicago: University of Chicago Press.

Drucker, Philip, 1965. *Cultures of the North Pacific Coast.* San Francisco: Chandler Publishing Co.

Drucker, Philip, 1951. *The Northern and Central Nootkan Tribes.* Smithsonian Institution, Bureau of American Ethnology, Bulletin 144. Washington, D.C.: U.S. Government Printing Office.

Dubbs, Patrick J. and Daniel G. Whitney, 1980. *Cultural Contexts: An Introduction to the Anthropological Perspective.* Boston: Allyn and Bacon, Inc.

Duncan, Otis Dudley, 1961. "From Social System to Ecosystem." *Sociological Inquiry* 31(2): 140–149.

Dundes, Alan, ed., 1965. *The Study of Folklore*. Englewood Cliffs, N.J.: Prentice-Hall, Inc.

Eames, Edwin and Judith Granich Goode, eds., 1977. *Anthropology of the City*. Englewood Cliffs, N.J.: Prentice-Hall, Inc.

Edel, May, and Abraham Edel, 1970. *Anthropology and Ethics: The Quest for Moral Understanding*. New Brunswick, N.J.: Transaction Books, Inc.

Edgerton, Robert B. and L. L. Langness, 1974. *Methods and Styles in the Study of Culture*. San Francisco: Chandler and Sharp Publishers, Inc.

Eisenstadt, S. N., ed., 1971. *Political Sociology*. New York: Basic Books, Inc.

Ember, Carol R., 1977. "Cross-Cultural Cognitive Studies." In *Annual Review of Anthropology*, edited by Bernard J. Siegel et al. Palo Alto, Cal.: Annual Review, Inc.

Ember, Melvin, 1959. "The Nonunilinear Descent Groups of Samoa." *American Anthropologist* 61(4): 573–583.

Evans-Pritchard, E. E., 1956. *Nuer Religion*. London: Oxford University Press.

Evans-Pritchard, E. E., 1951. *Kinship and Marriage among the Nuer*. London: Oxford University Press.

Evans-Pritchard, E. E., 1940. *The Nuer*. London: Oxford University Press.

Fenton, William N., 1941. *Iroquois Suicide*. Smithsonian Institution, Bureau of American Ethnology, Bulletin 128. Washington, D.C.: U.S. Government Printing Office, pp. 79–137.

Firth, Raymond, 1967. *Tikopia Ritual and Belief,* 2nd ed. London: George Allen and Unwin, Ltd.

Firth, Raymond, 1951. *Elements of Social Organization*. London: Watts and Co.

Firth, Raymond, 1936. *We, The Tikopia*. London: George Allen and Unwin, Ltd.

Fischer, John L. with the assistance of Ann M. Fischer, 1957. *The Eastern Carolines*. New Haven, Conn.: Human Relations Area Files Press.

Fishman, Joshua A., ed., 1968. *Readings in the Sociology of Language*. The Hague, The Netherlands: Mouton and Company.

Fitting, James E., 1978. "Profiles of Anthropologists at Work." *Anthropology Newsletter 19(1):* 24.

Fitzgerald, Thomas K., ed., 1976. *Nutrition and Anthropology in Action*. Amsterdam: Van Gorcum, Assen.

Ford, Clellan S., 1945. *A Comparative Study of Human Reproduction*. Yale University Publications in Anthropology, no. 32. New Haven: Yale University Press.

Forde, C. Daryll, ed., 1954. *African Worlds: Studies in the Cosmological Ideas and Social Values of African Peoples*. London: Oxford University Press.

Foster, George M., 1973. *Traditional Societies and Technological Change,* 2nd ed. New York: Harper & Row.

Foster, George M., 1967a. "Introduction: What Is a Peasant?" In *Peasant Society: A Reader,* by Jack M. Potter, May N. Diaz, and George M. Foster, eds. Boston: Little, Brown and Company.

Foster, George M., 1967b. *Tzintzuntzan: Mexican Peasants in a Changing World.* Boston: Little, Brown and Company.

Foster, George M. and Robert V. Kemper, 1974. "Introduction: A Perspective on Anthropological Field Work in Cities." In *Anthropologists in Cities,* edited by George M. Foster and Robert V. Kemper. Boston: Little, Brown and Company.

Fox, Robin, 1967. *Kinship and Marriage: An Anthropological Perspective.* Baltimore: Penguin Books, Inc.

Frake, Charles O., 1964. "A Structural Description of Subanun 'Religious Behavior!' " In *Explorations in Cultural Anthropology,* edited by Ward Goodenough. New York: McGraw-Hill.

Frake, Charles O., 1961. "The Diagnosis of Disease among the Subanun of Mindanao." *American Anthropologist* 63(1): 113–132.

Fried, Morton H., 1972. *The Study of Anthropology.* New York: Thomas Y. Crowell Company.

Friedl, John and Noel J. Chrisman, 1975. "Continuity and Adaptation as Themes in Urban Anthropology." In *City Ways: A Selective Reader in Urban Anthropology,* edited by John Friedl and Noel J. Chrisman. New York: Thomas Y. Crowell Company.

Freilich, Morris, ed., 1977. *Marginal Natives: Anthropologists in the Field.* Cambridge, Mass.: Schemkman Publishing Company, Inc.

Freilich, Morris, ed., 1972. *The Meaning of Culture: A Reader in Cultural Anthropology.* Lexington, Mass.: Xerox College Publishing.

Gardner, Robert and Karl G. Heider, 1968. *Gardens of War: Life and Death in the New Guinea Stone Age.* New York: Random House, Inc.

Gleason, Henry A., Jr., 1961. *An Introduction to Descriptive Linguistics,* rev. ed. New York: Holt, Rinehart and Winston.

Gluckman, Max, 1955. *Custom and Conflict in Africa.* Glencoe, Ill.: The Free Press.

Goldenweiser, Alexander, 1970 (orig. 1937). *Anthropology: An Introduction to Primitive Culture.* New York: Johnson Reprint Corporation.

Goodenough, Ward H., 1965. "Yankee Kinship Terminology: A Problem in Componential Analysis." *American Anthropologist* 67(5), pt. 2: 259–287.

Gould, Richard A., 1970. "Journey to Pulykara." *Natural History* 79(6): 56–67.

Grattan, F. J. H., 1948. *An Introduction to Samoan Custom.* Apia: Samoa Printing and Publishing Company.

Gregory, T. E., 1933. "Money." *Encyclopedia of the Social Sciences,* Vol. 10, edited by Edwin R. A. Seligman. New York: Macmillan.

Guenther, Mathias G., 1976. "From Hunters to Squatters: Social and Cultural Change among the Farm San of Ghanzi, Botswana." In *Kalahari Hunter-Gatherers: Studies of the !Kung San and Their Neighbors,* edited by Richard B. Lee and Irven DeVore. Cambridge, Mass.: Harvard University Press.

Haas, Mary R., 1964. "Men's and Women's Speech in Koasati." In *Language in Culture and Society: A Reader in Linguistics and Anthropology,* edited by Dell Hymes. New York: Harper & Row.

Haley, Alex, 1976. *Roots.* Garden City, N.Y.: Doubleday.

Hanson, F. Allan, 1970. *Rapan Lifeways.* Boston: Little, Brown and Company.

Harris, Jack S., 1940. "The White Knife Shoshoni of Nevada." In *Acculturation in Seven American Indian Tribes,* edited by Ralph Linton. Reprint. Gloucester, Mass.: Peter Smith, 1963.

Harris, Marvin, 1979. *Cultural Materialism: The Struggle for a Science of Culture.* New York: Random House.

Harris, Marvin, 1978. "Author's reply." (Letters) *Human Nature* 1(5): 10.

Harris, Marvin, 1974a. *Cows, Pigs, Wars, and Witches: The Riddles of Culture.* New York: Random House.

Harris, Marvin, 1974b. "Why a Perfect Knowledge of All the Rules One Must Know to Act Like a Native Cannot Lead to the Knowledge of How Natives Act." *Journal of Anthropological Research* 30(4): 242–251.

Harris, Marvin, 1968. *The Rise of Anthropological Theory: A History of Theories of Culture.* New York: Thomas Y. Crowell Company.

Hart, C. W. M. and Arnold R. Pilling, 1969. *The Tiwi of North Australia.* New York: Holt, Rinehart and Winston.

Hays, Hoffman R., 1964. *From Ape to Angel.* New York: G. P. Putnam's Sons, Publishers.

Heider, Eleanor Rosch, 1972. "Probabilities, Sampling, and Ethnographic Method: The Case of Dani Color Names." *Man* 7(3): 448–466.

Heider, Karl G., 1979. *Grand Valley Dani: Peaceful Warriors.* New York: Holt, Rinehart and Winston.

Heider, Karl G., 1976. "Dani Sexuality. A Low Energy System." *Man* (N.S.) 11(2): 188–201.

Heider, Karl G., 1975. "Social Intensification and Cultural Stress as Determining Factors in the Innovation and Conservatism of Two Dani Cultures." *Oceania* 46(1): 53–67.

Heider, Karl G., 1970. *The Dugum Dani: A Papuan Culture in the Highlands of West New Guinea.* Viking Fund Publications in Anthropology, no. 49. New York: Wenner-Gren Foundation for Anthropological Research, Inc.

Helms, Mary W., 1971. *Asang: Adaptations to Culture Contact in a Miskito Community.* Gainesville: University of Florida Press.

Henry, Jules, 1963. *Culture Against Man.* New York: Random House.

Henry, Jules 1941. *Jungle People: A Kaingang Tribe of the Highlands of Brazil* (reprint). New York: Random House, 1964.

Herskovits, Melville J., 1964. *Cultural Dynamics.* New York: Alfred A. Knopf.

Herskovits, Melville J., 1952. *Economic Anthropolgy*. New York: Alfred A. Knopf.

Herskovits, Melville J., 1948. *Man and His Works: The Science of Cultural Anthropology*. New York: Alfred A. Knopf.

Herskovits, Melville J., 1938. *Dahomey: An Ancient West African Kingdom*. 2 vols. (reprint) Evanston: Northwestern University Press, 1967.

Hoebel, E. Adamson, 1978. *The Cheyennes: Indians of the Great Plains*, 2nd ed. New York: Holt, Rinehart and Winston.

Hoebel, E. Adamson, 1968. *The Law of Primitive Man: A Study in Comparative Legal Dynamics*. Paterson, N.J.: Atheneum Publishers, Inc.

Hoffman, W. J., 1891. "The Midewiwin or 'Grand Medicine Society' of the Ojibwa." In *Seventh Annual Report of the Bureau of American Ethnology to the Secretary of the Smithsonian Institution, 1885–1886*. Washington, D.C.: U.S. Government Printing Office.

Holmes, Lowell, 1974. *Samoan Village*. New York: Holt, Rinehart and Winston.

Honigmann, John J., 1970. "Field Work in Two Northern Canadian Communities." In *Marginal Natives: Anthropologists at Work*, edited by Morris Freilich. New York: Harper & Row.

Honigmann, John J., 1963. *Understanding Culture*. New York: Harper & Row.

Honigmann, John J., 1959. *The World of Man*. New York: Harper & Row.

Howell, Nancy, 1976. "The Population of the Dobe Area !Kung." In *Kalahari Hunter-Gatherers: Studies of the !Kung San and Their Neighbors*, edited by Richard B. Lee and Irven DeVore. Cambridge, Mass.: Harvard University Press.

Howells, William W., 1948. *The Heathens: Primitive Man and His Religions*. Garden City, N.Y.: Doubleday.

Hunn, Eugene S., 1977. *Tzeltal Folk Zoology: The Classification of Discontinuities in Nature*. New York: Academic Press, Inc.

Hunt, Robert C., ed., 1976. *Personalities and Cultures: Readings in Psychological Anthropology*. Austin: University of Texas Press.

Hymes, Dell, ed., 1964. *Language in Culture and Society*. Harper & Row.

Hymes, Dell, 1962. "The Ethnography of Speaking." In *Anthropology and Human Behavior*, edited by Thomas Gladwin and William C. Sturtevant. Washington, D.C.: Anthropological Society of Washington.

Jensen, Arthur R., 1969. "How Much Can We Boost IQ and Scholastic Achievement?" In *Environment, Heredity and Intelligence*. Harvard Educational Review Reprint Series no. 2. Cambridge, Mass.: Harvard University Press.

Kang, Gay Elizabeth, 1976. "Conflicting Loyalties Theory: A Cross-Cultural Test." *Ethnology: An International Journal of Cultural and Social Anthropology* 15(2).: 201–210.

Kaplan, Bert, 1961. "Cross-Cultural Use of Projective Techniques." In *Psychological Anthropology*, edited by F. L. K. Hsu. Homewood, Ill.: Dorsey Press.

Katz, Richard, 1976. "Education for Transcendence: !Kia-Healing with the Kalahari !Kung." In *Kalahari Hunter-Gatherers: Studies of the !Kung San and Their Neighbors,* edited by Richard B. Lee and Irven DeVore. Cambridge, Mass.: Harvard University Press.

Keesing, Felix, 1941. *The South Seas in the Modern World.* New York: The John Day Company.

Keesing, Roger, 1975. *Kinship and Social Structure.* New York: Holt, Rinehart and Winston.

Kessler, Evelyn S., 1976. *Women: An Anthropological View.* New York: Holt, Rinehart and Winston.

Kessler, Evelyn S., 1974. *Anthropology: The Humanizing Process.* Boston: Allyn and Bacon, Inc.

Kiefer, Margaret M., 1978. "Profiles of Anthropologists at Work." *Anthropology Newsletter* 19(6): 15.

Kluckhohn Clyde, 1949. *Mirror for Man.* New York: McGraw-Hill.

Krader, Lawrence, 1968. *Formation of the State.* Englewood Cliffs, N.J.: Prentice-Hall, Inc.

Kroeber, Alfred L., 1948. *Anthropology.* New York: Harcourt, Brace and Company.

Kroeber, Alfred L. and Clyde Kluckhohn, eds., 1952. *Cultures: A Critical Review of Concepts and Definitions.* New York: Alfred A. Knopf.

Lagacé, Robert O., ed., 1977. *Sixty Cultures: A Guide to the HRAF Probability Sample Files,* Part A. New Haven, Conn.: Human Relations Area Files, Inc.

Landy, David, ed., 1977. *Culture, Disease, and Healing: Studies in Medical Anthropology.* New York: Macmillan.

Langness, L. L., 1974. *The Study of Culture.* San Francisco: Chandler and Sharp Publishers, Inc.

Layard, John, 1942. *Stone Men of Malekula.* London: Chatto and Windus.

Leach, E. R., 1954. "Primitive Time-Reckoning." In *A History of Technology,* Vol. 1, edited by Charles Singer et al. London: Oxford University Press.

Leaf, Murray J. et al., 1974. *Frontiers of Anthropology: An Introduction to Anthropological Thinking.* New York: Van Nostrand-Reinhold.

LeClair, Edward E., Jr. and Harold K. Schneider, eds., 1968. *Economic Anthropology: Readings in Theory and Analysis.* New York: Holt, Rinehart and Winston.

Lee, Richard B., 1972. "The !Kung Bushmen of Botswana." In *Hunters and Gatherers Today: A Socioeconomic Study of Eleven Such Cultures in the Twentieth Century,* edited by M. G. Bicchieri. New York: Holt, Rinehart and Winston.

Lee, Richard B., 1968. "What Hunters Do for a Living, or How to Make Out on Scarce Resources." In *Man the Hunter,* edited by Richard B. Lee and Irven DeVore. Chicago: Aldine Publishing Company.

Lee, Richard B. and Irven DeVore, eds., 1976. *Kalahari Hunter-Gatherers:*

Studies of the !Kung San and Their Neighbors. Cambridge, Mass.: Harvard University Press.

Lehmann, Winifred P., 1976. *Descriptive Linguistics: An Introduction.* New York: Random House, Inc.

Lessa, William A. and Evon Z. Vogt, Eds., 1979. *Reader in Comparative Religion: An Anthropological Approach,* 4th ed. New York: Harper & Row.

Levi-Strauss, Claude, 1969. *The Elementary Structures of Kinship.* Revised Edition. Translated from the French by James Harle Bell, John Richard von Sturmer, and Rodney Needham, editor. Boston: Beacon Press.

Levi-Strauss, Claude, 1956. "The Family." In *Man, Culture and Society,* edited by Harry L. Shapiro. New York: Oxford University Press.

Lewis, Oscar, 1951. *Life in a Mexican Village.* Urbana: University of Illinois Press.

Linton, Ralph, 1952. "Universal Ethical Principles: An Anthropological View." In *Moral Principles of Action,* edited by Ruth Nanda Anshen. New York: Harper and Brothers, Publishers.

Linton, Ralph, 1936. *The Study of Man.* New York: Appleton-Century-Crofts, Inc.

Litchfield, Edward H., 1956. "Notes on a General Theory of Administration." *Administrative Science Quarterly* 1(1): 3–29.

Logan, Michael H., 1973. "Humoral Medicine in Guatemala and Peasant Acceptance of Modern Medicine." *Human Organization: Journal of the Society for Applied Anthropology* 32(4): 385–395.

Lomax, Alan, 1968. *Folk Song Style and Culture.* Washington, D.C.: American Association for the Advancement of Science.

Lowie, Robert H., 1959. *Robert H. Lowie, Ethnologist: A Personal Record.* Berkeley and Los Angeles: University of California Press.

Lowie, Robert H., 1935. *The Crow Indians.* New York: Rinehart and Company.

Lowie, Robert H., 1913. *The Material Culture of the Crow Indians,* Anthropological Papers of the American Museum of Natural History, 21, part 3. New York: American Museum of Natural History.

Lowie, Robert H., 1913. *Societies of the Crow, Hidatsa and Mandan Indians.* Anthropological Papers of the American Museum of Natural History 11, part 3. New York: American Museum of Natural History.

Lowie, Robert H., 1912. *Social Life of the Crow Indians.* Anthropological Papers of the American Museum of Natural History 9, part 2. New York: American Museum of Natural History.

MacLeish, Kenneth and John Launois, 1972. "Stone Age Cavemen of Mindanao." *National Geographic* 142(2): 219ff.

Malinowski, Bronislaw, 1944. *A Scientific Theory of Culture and Other Essays.* Chapel Hill: University of North Carolina Press.

Malinowski, Bronislaw, 1937. *Sex and Repression in Savage Society.* New York: Harcourt, Brace and Company, Inc.

Malinowski, Bronislaw, 1929. *Argonauts of the Western Pacific* (reprint). New York: E. P. Dutton and Co., 1961.

Mandelbaum, David G., 1956. "Social Groupings." In *Man, Culture and Society*, edited by Harry L. Shapiro. New York: Oxford University Press.

Marett, R. R., 1914. *The Threshold of Religion*. New York: Macmillan.

Marsh, Gordon and William S. Laughlin, 1956. "Human Anatomical Knowledge Among the Aleutian Islanders." *Southwestern Journal of Anthropology* 12(1): 38–78.

Marshall, Lorna, 1976. *The !Kung of Nyae Nyae*. Cambridge, Mass.: Harvard University Press.

Marshall, Lorna, 1965. The !Kung Bushmen of the Kalahari Desert." In *Peoples of Africa*, edited by James L. Gibbs, Jr. New York: Holt, Rinehart and Winston.

Marshall, Lorna, 1962. "!Kung Bushman Religious Beliefs." *Africa: Journal of the International African Institute* 32(3): 221–252.

Mead, Margaret, 1978. *Culture and Commitment: The New Relationships Between the Generations in the 1970s*. Garden City, N.Y.: Anchor Press/Doubleday.

Mead, Margaret, 1969. *Social Organization of Manu'a*, 2nd ed. Bernice P. Bishop Museum Bulletin 76. Honolulu: Bernice P. Bishop Museum.

Mead, Margaret, 1964. *Continuities in Cultural Evolution*. New Haven, Conn.: Yale University Press.

Mead, Margaret, 1961. *Cooperation and Competition Among Primitive Peoples*, rev. pbk ed. Boston: Beacon Press.

Mead, Margaret, 1940. *The Mountain Arapesh*. Vol. 2: *Arts and Supernaturalism*. Anthropological Papers of the American Museum of Natural History, 37, part 3. New York: American Museum of Natural History.

Mead, Margaret, 1928. *Coming of Age in Samoa*. New York: William Morrow and Company.

Merriam, Alan P., 1964. *The Anthropology of Music*. Evanston, Ill.: Northwestern University Press.

Metzger, Duane, and Gerald E. Williams, 1966. "Some Procedures and Results in the Study of Native Categories: Tzeltal 'Firewood'." *American Anthropologist* 68(2): 389–407.

Middleton, John, ed., 1976a *Gods and Rituals: Readings in Religious Beliefs and Practices*. Austin: University of Texas Press.

Middleton, John, ed., 1976b. *Magic, Witchcraft and Curing*. Austin: University of Texas Press.

Montagu, Ashley, 1963. *Race, Science and Humanity*. Princeton: D. Van Nostrand Company.

Moore, Sally Falk and Barbara G. Meyeroff, eds., 1978. *Secular Ritual*. Atlantic Highlands, N.J.: Humanities Press, Inc.

Morris, Desmond, 1967. *The Naked Ape*. New York: Dell Publishing Company.

Murdock, George P., 1971. *Outline of Cultural Materials*. New Haven, Conn.: Human Relations Area Files, Inc.

Murdock, George P., 1967. "Ethnographic Atlas: A Summary." *Ethnology: An International Journal of Cultural and Social Anthropology* 6(2): 109–236.

Murdock, George P., 1949. *Social Structure*. New York: Macmillan.

Murdock, George P., 1934. *Our Primitive Contemporaries*. New York: Macmillan.

Murdock, George P. and Douglas White, 1969. "Standard Cross-Cultural Sample." *Ethnology: An International Journal of Cultural and Social Anthropology* 8(4): 329–369.

Nadel, S. F., 1947. *The Nuba: An Anthropological Study of the Hill Tribes in Kordofan*. London: Oxford University Press.

Nadel, S. F., 1942. *A Black Byzantium: Kingdom of Nupe in Nigeria*. London: Oxford University Press.

Naroll, Raul and Frada Naroll, 1973. *Main Currents in Cultural Anthropology*. New York: Appleton-Century-Crofts.

Nash, Manning, 1966. *Primitive and Peasant Economic Systems*. San Fransisco: Chandler Publishing Company.

Nettl, Bruno, 1956. *Music in Primitive Culture*. Cambridge, Mass.: Harvard University Press.

Nida, Eugene A., 1957. *Learning a Foreign Language,* rev. ed. New York: Friendship Press.

Nida, Eugene A., 1954. *Customs and Cultures*. New York: Harper & Row.

Norbeck, Edward, 1974. *Religion in Human Life*. New York: Holt, Rinehart and Winston.

Numelin, Ragnar, 1950. *The Beginnings of Diplomacy*. London: Oxford University Press.

O'Brien, Denise and Anton Ploeg, 1964. "Acculturation Movements Among the Western Dani." *American Anthropologist* 66(4) pt. 2: 281–292.

Odum, Howard T., 1971. *Environment, Power and Society. New York:* John Wiley and Sons.

Oliver, Douglas, 1955. *A Solomon Island Society*. Boston: Beacon Press.

Opler, Morris Edward, 1945. "Themes as Dynamic Forces in Culture." *American Journal of Sociology* 51(3): 198–206.

Parsons, Elsie Clews, 1936. *Mitla: Town of the Souls*. Chicago: University of Chicago Press.

Pelto, Pertti, 1978. *Anthropological Research: The Structure of Inquiry,* 2nd ed. New York: Cambridge University Press.

Perchonock, Norma and Oswald Werner, 1969. "Navaho Systems of Classification: Some Implications for Ethnoscience." *Ethnology: An International Journal of Cultural and Social Anthropology* 8(3): 229–242.

Petrullo, Vincenzo, 1939. *The Yaruruos of the Campanaro River, Venezuela*. Anthropological Papers, no. 11, Smithsonian Institution, Bureau of American Ethnology, Bulletin 123. Washington, D.C.: U.S. Government Printing Office.

Pierce, Joe E., 1954. "Crow vs. Hidatsa in Dialect Distance and in Glotto-chronology." *International Journal of American Linguistics* 20(2): 134–136.

Pijoan, Michel, 1946. *The Health and Customs of the Miskito Indians of Northern Nicaragua: Interrelationships in a Medical Program.* Mexico, D.F.: Instituto Indigenista Interamericano.

Pike, Kenneth L., 1954. *Language in Relation to a Unified Theory of Human Behavior,* Part I. Glendale, Cal.: Summer Institute of Linguistics.

Polanyi, Karl, 1944. *The Great Transformation: The Political and Economic Origins of Our Time.* New York: Rinehart and Company.

Pospisil, Leopold, 1978. *The Ethnology of Law: A Comparative Theory.* Second Edition. New York: Harper & Row.

Pospisil, Leopold, 1965. "A Formal Analysis of Substantive Law: Kapauku Papuan Laws of Land Tenure." *American Anthropologist* 67(5). pt. 2: 186–214.

Pospisil, Leopold, 1963a. *Kapauku Papuan Economy.* Yale University Publications in Anthropology, no. 67. New Haven, Conn.: Yale University Press.

Pospisil, Leopold, 1963b. *The Kapauku Papuans of West New Guinea.* New York: Holt, Rinehart and Winston.

Prins, A. H. J., 1953. *East African Age-Class Systems.* Groningen, The Netherlands: J. B. Wolters.

Radcliffe-Brown, A. R., 1952. *Structure and Function in Primitive Society: Essays and Addresses.* Glencoe, Ill.: The Free Press.

Radcliffe-Brown, A. R., 1932. *The Andaman Islanders. New York:* Crowell-Collier, 1964 reprint.

Radin, Paul, 1955. *Primitive Man as Philosopher, rev. ed.* New York: Dover Publications, Inc.

Reina, Ruben E., 1966. *The Law of the Saints: A Pokomam Pueblo and its Community Culture.* Indianapolis: Bobbs-Merrill.

Reina, Ruben E., 1963. "The Potter and the Farmer." *Expedition* 5(4): 18–30.

Reynolds, Barrie, 1968. *The Material Culture of the Peoples of the Gwembe Valley.* New York: Frederick A. Praeger, Inc.

Roberts, Joan I. and Sherrie K. Akinsanya, eds., 1976. *Educational Patterns and Cultural Configurations: The Anthropology of Education.* New York: David McKay, Inc.

Roscoe, John, 1923. *The Bakitara or Banyoro: The First Part of the Report of the Mackie Ethnological Expedition to Central Africa.* Cambridge: Cambridge University Press.

Royce, Anya Peterson, 1977. *The Anthropology of the Dance.* Bloomington: Indiana University Press.

Sahlins, Marshall D., 1968. *Tribesmen.* Englewood Cliffs, N.J.: Prentice-Hall, Inc.

Sahlins, Marshall D. and Elman R. Service, eds., 1960. *Evolution and Culture.* Ann Arbor: University of Michigan Press.

Sayce, R. U., 1933. *Primitive Arts and Crafts* (reprint). New York: Biblo and Tannen, Inc., 1963.

Schaeffer, Francis, 1971. *Pollution and the Death of Man: A Christian View of Ecology*. Wheaton, Ill.: Tyndale House Publishers.

Schmidt, Peter and Donald H. Avery, 1978. "Complex Iron Smelting and Prehistoric Culture in Tanzania." *Science* 201(4361): 1085–1089.

Schusky, Ernest L., 1972. *Manual of Kinship Analysis*, 2nd ed. New York: Holt, Rinehart and Winston.

Service, Elman R., 1978. *Profiles in Ethnology*, 3rd ed. New York: Harper & Row.

Service, Elman R., 1958. *A Profile of Primitive Culture*. New York: Harper & Row.

Smith, Marian, ed., 1957. *Symposium on the Artist in Tribal Society* (reprint). New York: Free Press of Glencoe, 1961.

Smith, Raymond T., 1956. *The Negro Family in British Guiana: Family Structure and Social Status in the Villages*. London: Routledge and Kegan Paul, Ltd.

Spencer, Sir Baldwin, and F. J. Gillen, 1927. *The Arunta: A Study of a Stone Age People*. 2 vols. London: Macmillan and Company, Ltd.

Spicer, Edward H., ed., 1952. *Human Problems in Technological Change*. New York: Russell Sage Foundation.

Spier, Leslie, 1928. *Havasupai Ethnography*. Anthropological Papers of the American Museum of Natural History, no. 29, part 3. New York: American Museum of Natural History.

Spier, Robert F. G., 1970. *From the Hand of Man: Primitive and Preindustrial Technologies*. Boston: Houghton Mifflin Company.

Spindler, George D., 1978. *The Making of Psychological Anthropology*. Berkeley and Los Angeles: University of California Press.

Spindler, George D., ed., 1970. *Being an Anthropologist: Fieldwork in Eleven Cultures*. New York: Holt, Rinehart and Winston.

Spott, Robert and A. L. Kroeber, 1943. *Yurok Narratives*. University of California Publications in American Archaeology and Ethnology, no. 35. Berkeley: University of California Press.

Spradley, James P., 1970. *You Owe Yourself a Drunk*. Boston: Little, Brown, and Company.

Spradley, James P. and David W. McCurdy, eds., 1972. *The Cultural Experience: Ethnography in a Complex Society*. Chicago: Science Research Associates, Inc.

Spradley, James P. and Michael A. Rynkiewich, eds., 1975. *The Nacirema: Readings on American Culture*. Boston: Little, Brown and Company.

Stair, John B., 1897. *Old Samoa: or Flotsam and Jetsam from the Pacific Ocean*. London: The Religious Tract Society. New Haven, Conn.: Human Relations Area Files, reprinted 1956.

Steward, Julian H., 1955. *Theory of Culture Change. Urbana*: University of Illinois Press.

Sumner, William Graham, 1906. *Folkways*. Boston: Ginn and Company.

Swadesh, Morris, 1964. "Linguistics as an Instrument of Prehistory." In *Language in Culture and Society,* edited by Dell Hymes. New York: Harper & Row.

Swartz, Marc J. et al., eds., 1966. *Political Anthropology.* Chicago: Aldine Publishing Company.

Tax, Sol and Leslie Freeman, eds., 1976. *Horizons of Anthropology,* 2nd ed. Chicago: Aldine Publishing Company.

Taylor, Robert B., 1966. "Conservative Factors in the Changing Culture of a Zapotec Town." *Human Organization* 25(2): 116–121.

Taylor, Robert B., 1960. *Teotitlán del Valle: A Typical Mesoamerican Community.* Ann Arbor: University Microfilms, Inc.

Thomas, Elizabeth Marshall, 1958. *The Harmless People.* New York: Alfred A. Knopf, Inc.

Thompson, Stith, 1946. *The Folk Tale.* New York: Dryden Press.

Titiev, Mischa, 1944. *Old Oraibi.* Papers of the Peabody Museum of American Archaeology and Ethnology. Harvard University, 22, no. 1. Cambridge, Massachusetts: Peabody Museum.

Tobias, Philip V., 1970. "Brain-size, Grey Matter and Race—Fact or Fiction?" *American Journal of Physical Anthropology* 32(1): 3–26.

Turner ,Victor, 1974. *Dramas, Fields, and Metaphors: Symbolic Action in Human Society.* Ithaca, New York: Cornell University Press.

Turney-High, Harry H., 1968. *Man and System: Foundations for the Study of Human Relations.* New York: Appleton-Century-Crofts.

Tyler, Stephen A., ed., 1969. "Introduction." In *Cognitive Anthropology,* edited by Stephen A. Tyler. New York: Holt, Rinehart and Winston.

Tylor, Edward B., 1889. *Primitive Culture,* Vol. I. New York: Henry Holt and Company.

Voegelin, C. F., and F. M. Voegelin, 1977. *Classification and Index of the World's Languages.* New York: Elsevier North-Holland, Inc.

Wallace, Anthony F. C., 1956. "Revitalization Movements: Some Theoretical Considerations for Their Comparative Study." *American Anthropologist* 58(2): 264–281.

Warner, William Lloyd, 1953. *American Life: Dream and Reality.* Chicago: University of Chicago Press.

Whiting, John W. M., R. Kluckhohn, and A. Anthony, 1958. "The Function of Male Initiation Ceremonies at Puberty." In *Readings in Social Psychology,* edited by E. Macoby et al. New York: Holt, Rinehart and Winston.

Whorf, B. J., 1956. "Science and Linguistics." In *Language, Thought, and Reality,* edited by John B. Carroll. Cambridge, Mass.: The M.I.T. Press.

Whorf, B. L., 1941. "The Relation of Habitual Thought and Behavior to Language." In *Language, Culture, and Personality.* Menasha, Wis.: Sapir Memorial Publication Fund.

Wildschut, William, 1960. *Crow Indian Medicine Bundles,* edited by John C. Ewers. New York: Museum of the American Indian, Heye Foundation.

Williams, Thomas Rhys, 1967. *Field Methods in the Study of Culture.* New York: Holt, Rinehart and Winston.

Williams, Thomas Rhys, 1965. *The Dusun: A North Borneo Society.* New York: Holt, Rinehart and Winston.

Wilson, Monica, 1959. *Communal Rituals of the Nyakyusa.* New York: Oxford University Press.

Wissler, Clark, 1923. *Man and Culture. New York:* Thomas Y. Crowell Company.

Wolf, Eric, 1966. *Peasants.* Englewood Cliffs, N.J.: Prentice-Hall Inc.

Woods, Clyde M., 1975. *Culture Change.* Dubuque, Iowa: William C. Brown and Company.

Yellen, John E., 1976. "Settlement Patterns of the !Kung: An Archaeological Perspective." In *Kalahari Hunter-Gatherers: Studies of the !Kung San and Their Neighbors,* edited by Richard B. Lee and Irven DeVore. Cambridge, Mass.: Harvard University Press.

Yellen, John E. and Richard B. Lee, 1976. "The Dobe-/Du/da Environment: Background to a Hunting and Gathering Way of Life." In *Kalahari Hunter-Gatherers: Studies of the !Kung San and Their Neighbors,* edited by Richard B. Lee and Irven DeVore. Cambridge, Mass.: Harvard University Press.

INDEX AND GLOSSARY

on Dahomean culture, 242, 283
on technological ingenuity, 92
Hidalgo, Manuel, 8
Hidatsa of the Northern Plains:
    age sets, 179, 187
    government, 187
    language, 85
High gods, 225
Historical linguistics, 78
History, cultural, 55
Hoe, 105
Hoebel, E.:
    on Cheyenne culture, 215, 277
    definition of law, 191
    on origins of laws, 193
Hoffman, W., on Ojibwa Grand Medicine Society, 178
Holistic approach 12
Holistic ideal of anthropology, 2
Holmes, L., on Samoan culture, 54, 56, 88, 103, 109, 117, 119, 120, 122, 125, 132, 139, 156, 178, 188, 262, 266, 278, 283
Honduras. See Miskito
Honigmann, J.:
    definition of art, 238
    definition of logic, 195
    definition of technology, 92
    ethnographic work among Kaska Indians, 67
Hopi of Arizona:
    kachinas, 38, 39, 247
    language, 86
    pan-societal association, 176
    pottery revival, 275
    village locations, 35
Horn artifacts, 95
Horse racing, 251
Horticulture, 104–105, 110
Hot-cold concept, 11
Houses, 29–30, 100, 182 (see also Dwellings)
Howell, N., on !Kung infanticide, 257
Human palaeontology, 5
Human Relations Area Files, 74
Hunn, E., on animal taxonomies, 41
Hunting, 20, 102–103, 109–110
    and menstruation, 263
Hunting and gathering, 93, 109–110
Hymes, D., on ethnography of speaking, 87
Ideality:
    in culture, 61
    in field work, 68
Ideology, 208–218
Illiteracy: Inability to read or write the writing of one's culture, 25
Illness, 223, 229 (see also Disease)
Imitative magic, 228
Implicitness in culture, 60
Inheritance:
    property, 123
    social class, 180
    wife, 141
Incest taboo, 135, 217
Indians of Middle America, cultures of. See Aztecs; Maya; Miskito; Mixtec; Pokomám; Sumu; Tarascans; Zapotec
Indians of North America, cultures. See Apache; Arikara; Cheyenne; Crow; Havasupai; Hidatsa; Hopi; Kaska; Koasati; Kwakiutl; Iroquoís; Lipan; Mandan; Navajo; Nootka; Ojibwa; Pomo; Shoshoni; Tewa; Yurok
Indians of South America. See Aymará; Kaingang; Witoto; Yanomamö; Yaruro
Inequality, 215

Infant helplessness, 257
Infant mortality, 265
Infanticide, 233, 257
Infixation: Insertion of a morpheme within another morpheme to modify its meaning, 83
Informants. See Interviewing
Initiation, 88, 176, 178, 199, 202, 259, 261, 262
Institutions, 56
Instrumentality, and change acceptance, 278
Instruments, musical, 242–243
Intelligence, 32–34
Interest, 123–124
Interviewing, 64, 67–69
Inventors, 276
Iran, 228 (see also Basseri)
Iron working, 32, 98
Iroquois of North America, use of suicide, 195
Iroquois kinship terminology: Use of reference terms which lump parallel cousins under the same term or set of terms as brothers and sisters but use other terms for cross cousins, 164–165
Irrigation, 105, 181
Isolation, and cultural variability, 36
Jensen, A., on intelligence testing, 33–34
Jobs:
    in applied anthropology, 13, 14, 287
    for bachelor's degree holders, 14
    for professional anthropologists, 13, 14, 287
Joint family: A social unit composed of the families of siblings or cousins, 144
Joint ownership: Ownership by a family, clan, or other group smaller than the community or tribe, 122
Joking relationship, 151, 203–204
Kachinas, 38, 247
Kaingang of South America:
    abandonment of agriculture, 271
    body painting, 250
    ethnographic study of, 215
    wedding, 138
    world view, 215
Kalahari Research Group, 73
Kalahari Desert, 116
Kang, G., on feuding and divided group loyalties, 75
Kansas City, Missouri, social classes, 180–181
Kapauku of New Guinea. See Ekagi
Kaplan, B., on projective testing, 71
Kaska of western Canada, ethnography among, 67
Katz, R., on !Kung religion, 222
Kayak, 101
Kemper, R., on studying peasant cultures, 12
Kenyan blacks, brain anatomy and intelligence of, 34
Khomani San of southern Africa, 247
Kiefer, M.:
    on what anthropologists do, 10
    on her anthropological career, 13
Kindred: A category of kin related to a person through both males and females in ascending and descending generations and collateral lines, 148–151
King, Nyoro, 183, 188, 198
Kinship (see also Kinship terms; Lineage; Clan; Sib; Unilineal descent; Ambilineal descent; Bilateral descent)
    fictive, 172–173
    in nonliterate communities, 23, 176
    varieties, 134–164

Phoneme: A set of alternative sounds, the phonetic differences among which make no difference in meaning to the speakers of a given language, 80, 82, 83

Phonemics: The analysis of speech in order to identify the phonemes of a language, 79

Phonemic alphabet: An alphabet with a symbol for each phoneme in a particular language, 84

Phonetics: The study of how humans produce speech sounds and the field identification of the phones present in a particular language, 79

Phonetic alphabet: A set of symbols, one for each of the phones a linguist can distinguish in a people's speech., 79

Phonology: The phonetic and phonemic characteristics of language, 79-82,

Phratry: One of three or more social components of a community or tribe, made up of two or more clans, 163

Physical anthropology: The study of the biological characteristics of human groups in different times and places, 5-6, 9, 11

Pierce, J., on glottochronology, 85

Pig feast, Dani, 88

Pigs, 107

Pike, K., on emic and etic approaches, 40, 79

Pilling, A., on Tiwi marriage, 145

Pipes, tobacco, 93

Pit ovens, 107-108

Plastic arts, 248-250

Play, and culture, 250

Ploeg, A., on Western Dani cultural change, 284

Plow, 105

Pokomám Maya of Guatemala, rejection of ocupational change by, 280

Polanyi, K., on non-Western economic systems, 114, 128

Police, 178, 191

Political anthropology, 7

Political organization, 26-29, 52, 184-189

Polyandrous family, 144

Polyandry: The concurrent marriage of one woman to two or more men, 145-146

Polygamy: Marriage involving multiple spouses, specifically polyandry, polygyny, or group marriage, 144

Polygynous family, 146

Polygyny: The concurrent marriage of one man to two or more women, 132, 145-146

Polytheism, 225

Population and culture, 36

Pospisil, L.:
  on Ekagi culture, 124, 129, 211
  definition of law, 191
  on land tenure taxonomies, 41

Potlatch: A Northwest Coast Indian ceremony involving ritual display of privileges and titles and distribution of goods among the guests for the purpose of validating and enhancing the host's privileges and prestige, 131

Pottery, 97, 275

Practical anthropology, 286-289

Prayer, 201-202, 226-227

Prefixation, 83

Pregnancy signs, 256

Pregnancy taboos, 256

Premarital sexual behavior, 263-264

Prestige:
  and age, 266-267

in change, 278-279
and wealth, 132

Prestige consumption, 131

Prices, 114, 124

Priest: A person who, as a representative or official of a religious group, performs ceremonies and other religious duties, 231

Primates, social behavior of, 6

Primatology, comparative, 6

Primitive culture:
  concept of, 22, 24
  level of sociocultural integration in, 26-27

Primitive thought, 208-209

Primogeniture: Inheritance of property by the oldest son, 123

Prins, A., on Galla age sets, 179

Production, 93-98, 115-118

Projective testing, 71

Property, 43, 120-123, 162

Proverbs, 239

Psycholinguistics, 85

Psychological anthropology, 8, 261

Puberty, 199, 262 (*see also* Initiation)

Pueblo Indians, 53, 119 (*see also* Hopi; Tewa)

Pulykara of Australia, foodgetting, 116

Purchase society, 25

Pygmies, 14-15

Race, 5, 31-32 (*see also* Biology and Culture)

Radcliffe-Brown, A.:
  on Andaman Islander fire making, 98
  on functionalism, 51

Rafts, 101

Ramage: A kinship group each of whose members can trace their relationship with a common ancestor through one person, male or female, in each generation, 153

Rank, 179-181

Rapa of the South Pacific, 213

Raven, P., on plant taxonomies, 41

Reasoning, primitive, 208-209

Reciprocity:
  economic, 114, 124-128
  in social control, 194

Recreation, 251-252

Redistribution, economic, 80, 88, 114, 124, 128-129, 130

Reina, R., on Pokomám Maya conservatism, 280-281

Reindeer, 101, 106

Reinterpretation in change, 281

Relativism:
  in art, 238, 248
  cultural (*see* Cultural relativism)
  ethical and moral, 43-44, 216-218

Religion, 52, 53, 108, 198, 220-235

Religious beliefs, 221-226

Religious functions, 231-235

Religious personnel, 229-231

Religious practices, 226-229

Research. *See* Ethnography

Residence:
  rules, 142-143
  and descent, 160

Respect relationships, 55

Respondent: One who observes the results of someone's objectification of ideas or other mental traces and reacts postively or negatively to the observation, as in acculturation and enculturation contexts, 259, 275

Restricted kindred: All of a person's relatives who function in relation to the individual in question, 150

Travois: A transportation device consisting of two poles, each of which are tied to the sides of an animal with the ends dragging behind on the ground, 101

Tribal level of sociocultural integration, 27

Tribal road of the Basseri, 122

Tribe: A group of culturally similar communities within a given territory whose members think of themselves as belonging to the same cultural unit, 183–184

Trobriand Islanders of Melanesia:
  magic, 233
  oedipal relationship between father and son, 4

Tswana of southern Africa, 126

Tumpline: A head, chest, or shoulder band for carrying burdens on the back, 101

Tungus of Siberia, shamanism, 230

Turner, V.:
  on ritual liminality, 202
  on symbolism in the Mexican revolution, 8

Turney-High, H., on U. S. war, 190

Tyler, S., on ethnoscience, 41

Tylor, E., on evolution of religion, 231

Uganda. *See* Nyoro

Ultimogeniture: Inheritance of property by the youngest son, 123

Unilineal descent: Tracing one's ancestry through one person in each generation when that person is the same sex in all generations, 152–153, 156–170 (*see also* Matrilineal descent; Patrilineal descent)

Unilineal descent group: A kinship group whose members believe themselves to have descended from a common ancestor through forebears of one sex only, 156–170 (*see also* Clan; Lineage; Phratry)

Universal: A custom practiced by all normal adult members of a particular society, 59

Upton, T., on understanding the Iranian revolution, 288

Urban anthropology, 11, 12

Usufruct: A system of land tenure whereby ownership is in the hands of a tribe, community, or kinship group, with individual members and/or families holding specific units of land as long as they use them properly, 121

Uxorilocal residence, 143

Values, 114, 129–130, 216–218

Village, 182

Virilocal residence, 143

Vision quest, 224

Vocabulary, 85, 89–90, 198

Voegelin, C. and Voegelin, F., on language families, 85

Wages, 117

Wallace, A. W., origination of natural selection, 276

Wallace, A.F.C.:
  on abolition of religion, 234–235
  on revitalization movements, 285

War, 60, 128, 172, 181, 189–191, 260

Warner, W., on Memorial Day ritual, 201

Wealth, 132

Weaning, 260

Weapons, 102

Weather concepts, 211

Weaving, 96–97

Weddings, 125, 138

Weights, 213

Werner, O.:
  on eliciting techniques, 74
  on food taxonomies, 41

White, D., on sampling the world's cultures, 74

White Knife Shoshoni, 121

White, Leslie, evolutionism of, 26

Whiting, J., on sleeping arrangements and intiation ceremonies, 261

Whorf, B., on language and behavior, 86

Wickerwork, 96

Wife exhange, 264

Williams, G., on firewood taxonomies, 41

Wilson, M., on Nyakyusa age villages, 179

Wissler, C., on universal cultural pattern, 29

Witchcraft: Doing evil by utilizing one's own power or drawing on the power of a spirit or other familiar, 228–229

Witoto of South America, couvade, 257

Wolf, E., on nonliterate economics, 23

Women:
  associations of, 176, 177
  and barrenness, 255
  Basseri, 119
  and divorce, 141
  Dani, 119
  as Dinka captives, 172
  and division of labor, 118–119
  and ethnography, 67
  descent through, 156
  Hidatsa age sets, 178–179
  suicide among Iroquois, 195
  as Maori envoys, 190
  menstruation of, 262–263
  Mexican, 277
  Pokomám ideal of, 280
  and property, 123
  and slave marriage, 181
  specialties of, 59
  virginity of, 264
  as war captives, 172
  as witches, 229
  Zapotec, 277

Wood working, 94, 249, 284

Words, 83

Work, 54, 115–118

World view, 214–216

Wrestling, 251

Writing, 22, 32 (*see also* Alphabet)

Yam displays, 131

Yanomamö of South America:
  brother-sister exchange, 139
  headman, 24

Yaruro of South America, philosophy of, 214

Years, 212

Yellen, J.:
  on !Kung band territories, 121
  on !Kung seasons, 212

Yoruba of Africa:
  bronze heads, 250
  cities, 23, 183
  dance masks, 248

Yurok of California, social control, 195–196

Zapotec of Mexico:
  camera rejection, 279
  contact with Mexicans, 277
  rain sign, 211
  regional specialization, 120

Zoological knowledge, 209, 213 (*see also* Ethnozoology)